BELIEVER'S BAPTISM

OTHER BOOKS IN THIS SERIES:

James M. Hamilton, Jr. *God's Indwelling Presence: The Holy Spirit in the Old and New Testaments*

NAC STUDIES IN BIBLE & THEOLOGY

BELIEVER'S BAPTISM

SIGN OF THE
NEW COVENANT IN CHRIST

EDITED BY

THOMAS R. SCHREINER
& SHAWN D. WRIGHT

SERIES EDITOR: E. RAY CLENDENEN

ACADEMIC

NASHVILLE, TENNESSEE

Believer's Baptism
by Thomas R. Schreiner and Shawn D. Wright

Copyright © 2006 B&H Publishing Group
All rights reserved.

ISBN 10: 0-8054-3249-3
ISBN 13: 978-0-8054-3249-7

Dewey Decimal Classification: 243.161
Subject Heading: DOCTRINE \ BAPTIST

Printed in the United States of America
1 2 3 4 5 6 7 8 • 10 09 08 07 06
LB

Dedication

To Diane and Gretchen,
Our dear wives who daily live out the reality of the gospel before us,
our children, and our church.

"An excellent wife is the crown of her husband" (Prov 12:4)

TABLE OF CONTENTS

LIST OF ABBREVIATIONS

AB	Anchor Bible
ABD	*Anchor Bible Dictionary*
ANF	*The Ante-Nicene Fathers*
ASR	*Austin Seminary Review*
AThR	*Anglican Theological Review*
BA	*Biblical Archeologist*
BBR	*Bulletin for Biblical Research*
BDAG	Bauer, W., F. W. Danker, W. F. Arndt, and F. W. Gingrich. *Greek-English Lexicon of the New Testament and Other Early Christian Literature.* 3rd ed.
BDB	Brown, F., S. R. Driver, and C. A. Briggs. *A Hebrew and English Lexicon of the Old Testament*
BECNT	*Baker Exegetical Commentary on the New Testament*
Bib	*Biblica*
BJRL	*Bulletin of the John Rylands University Library*
BSac	*Bibliotheca Sacra*
BTB	*Biblical Theology Bulletin*
CBQ	*Catholic Biblical Quarterly*
CBQMS	Catholic Biblical Quarterly Monograph Series
CH	*Church History*
CRINT	Compendia rerum iudaicarum ad Novum Testamentum
CTM	*Concordia Theological Monthly*
CTR	*Criswell Theological Review*
DBI	*Dictionary of Biblical Imagery*
DJG	*Dictionary of Jesus and the Gospels*
DOTP	*Dictionary of the Old Testament Pentateuch*
DPL	*Dictionary of Paul and His Letters*
EBC	*The Expositor's Bible Commentary*
Eng.	English Translation
EvQ	*Evangelical Quarterly*
ExAud	*Ex auditu*
ExpTim	*Expository Times*

GOTR	*Greek Orthodox Theological Review*
GTJ	*Grace Theological Journal*
HeyJ	*Heythrop Journal*
HTR	*Harvard Theological Review*
ICC	International Critical Commentary
IDB	G. A. Buttrick, ed., *Interpreter's Dictionary of the Bible*
Int	*Interpretation*
ISBE	*International Standard Bible Encyclopedia*
IVPNTC	IVP New Testament Commentary Series
JBL	*Journal of Biblical Literature*
JETS	*Journal of the Evangelical Theological Society*
JR	*Journal of Religion*
JSNT	*Journal for the Study of the New Testament*
JSNTSup	Journal for the Study of the New Testament: Supplement Series
JSS	*Journal of Semitic Studies*
JTS	*Journal of Theological Studies*
LCL	Loeb Classical Library
LQ	*Lutheran Quarterly*
LSJ	H. G. Liddell, R. Scott, H. S. Jones, *A Greek-English Lexicon.* 9th ed. with revised supplement
MM	Moulton, J. H., and G. Milligan. *The Vocabulary of the Greek Testament*
MT	Masoretic Text
NA^{27}	*Novum Testamentum Graece*, Nestle-Aland, 27th ed.
NAC	New American Commentary
NCE	*New Catholic Encyclopedia.* Ed. W. J. McDonald et al. 15 vols. McGraw-Hill, 1967–79
NDBT	*New Dictionary of Biblical Theology*
Neot	*Neotestamentica*
NICNT	New International Commentary on the New Testament
NIDNTT	*New International Dictionary of New Testament Theology*
NIDOTTE	*New International Dictionary of Old Testament Theology and Exegesis*
NIGTC	New International Greek Testament Commentary

NIVAC	NIV Application Commentary
NovT	*Novum Testamentum*
NovTSup	Supplements to Novum Testamentum
NPNF[1]	A Select Library of the Nicene and Post-Nicene Fathers of the Christian Church, Series 1
NPNF[2]	A Select Library of the Nicene and Post-Nicene Fathers of the Christian Church, Series 2
NTApoc	*New Testament Apocrypha*
NTS	*New Testament Studies*
OTL	Old Testament Library
OTP	*Old Testament Pseudepigrapha*
PNTC	Pillar New Testament Commentaries
RefR	*Reformed Review*
ResQ	*Restoration Quarterly*
RevExp	*Review and Expositor*
RevQ	*Revue de Qumran*
RTR	*Reformed Theological Review*
SBJT	*The Southern Baptist Journal of Theology*
SBLDS	Society of Biblical Literature Dissertation Series
SBET	*Scottish Bulletin of Evangelical Theology*
SBT[2]	Studies in Biblical Theology, Second Series
SBTS	Sources for Biblical and Theological Study
SCJ	*The Sixteenth Century Journal*
SJT	*Scottish Journal of Theology*
SNTA	Studiorum Novi Testamenti Auxilia
SNTSMS	Society for New Testament Studies Monograph Series
SP	Sacra Pagina
StPatr	*Studia patristica*
SwJT	*Southwestern Journal of Theology*
TDNT	*G. Kittel and G. Friedrich, eds., Theological Dictionary of the New Testament*
TDOT	*Theological Dictionary of the Old Testament*
Them	*Themelios*
ThTo	*Theology Today*
TJ	*Trinity Journal*

TJT	*Toronto Journal of Theology*
TOTC	Tyndale Old Testament Commentaries
TynBul	*Tyndale Bulletin*
UBS[4]	*The Greek New Testament*, United Bible Societies, 4th ed.
VE	*Vox evangelica*
WBC	Word Biblical Commentary
WUNT	Wissenschaftliche Untersuchungen zum Neuen Testament
ZAW	*Zeitschrift für die alttestamentliche Wissenschaft*
ZNW	*Zeitschrift für die neutestamentliche Wissenschaft und die Kunde der älteren Kirche*
ZTK	*Zeitschrift für Theologie und Kirche*

SERIES PREFACE

We live in an exciting era of evangelical scholarship. Many fine educational institutions committed to the inerrancy of Scripture are training men and women to serve Christ in the church and to advance the gospel in the world. Many church leaders and professors are skillfully and fearlessly applying God's Word to critical issues, asking new questions and developing new tools to answer those questions from Scripture. They are producing valuable new resources to thoroughly equip current and future generations of Christ's servants.

The Bible is an amazing source of truth and an amazing tool when wielded by God's Spirit for God's glory and our good. It is a bottomless well of living water, a treasure house of endless proportions. Like an ancient tell, exciting discoveries can be made on the surface, but even more exciting are those to be found by digging. The books in this series, *NAC Studies in Bible and Theology,* often take a biblical difficulty as their point of entry, remembering B. F. Westcott's point that "unless all past experience is worthless, the difficulties of the Bible are the most fruitful guides to its divine depths."

This new series is to be a medium through which the work of evangelical scholars can effectively reach the church. It will include detailed exegetical-theological studies of key pericopes such as the Sermon on the Mount and also fresh examinations of topics in biblical theology and systematic theology. It is intended to supplement the *New American Commentary,* whose exegetical and theological discussions so many have found helpful. These resources are aimed primarily at church leaders and those who are preparing for such leadership. We trust that individual Christians will find them to be an encouragement to greater progress and joy in the faith. More important, our prayer is that they will help the church proclaim Christ more accurately and effectively and that they will bring praise and glory to our great God.

It is a tremendous privilege to be partners in God's grace with the fine scholars writing for this new series as well as with those who will be helped by it. When Christ returns, may He find us "standing firm in one spirit, with one mind, working side by side for the faith of the gospel" (Phil 1:27, HCSB).

E. Ray Clendenen
B&H Publishing Group

AUTHOR PREFACE

We are grateful to Broadman and Holman for their enthusiastic support of a book on believer's baptism. Unfortunately we live in an age where many Christians think that clarity on baptism is unimportant. Some even feel a bit embarrassed and abashed about staking out a position on baptism, thinking that such an issue should be relegated to the past. As editors we are convinced that we should proclaim the whole counsel of God accurately and that the truth God has revealed is profitable for the church of Jesus Christ and for living in a way that pleases God.

This book would have been impossible without the authors who have taken time from their busy schedules to contribute to the work. We are deeply grateful for their labors and the excellent essays they have produced. We also want to express our thanks to Ray Clendenen, the series editor, for his expert assistance every step along the way and for his unfailing encouragement to us as we worked on this project. And thanks should also be extended to The Southern Baptist Theological Seminary where both of us teach. What a joy it is to work in an institution that believes in scholarship, and where we are reminded that scholarship serves the church of Jesus Christ. We dedicate this book to our wives, Diane and Gretchen. Their godliness, support, and love has meant more to us than words can express. Finally, we pray that what is contained in these pages will edify the church and bring glory to God through Jesus Christ our Lord.

Thomas R. Schreiner
Shawn D. Wright

FOREWORD

by Timothy George[*]

On February 19, 1812, Adoniram and Ann Judson, a couple of newlyweds, bade a tearful farewell to their family and friends and boarded the *Caravan*, a three-mast brig in Salem harbor, and began the long ocean voyage from Massachusetts to India. Convinced that God had called them to spend their lives in missionary service, the Judsons devoted themselves to prayer and intensive Bible study during their four months at sea. Judson had studied the Greek New Testament at Andover Seminary, and he poured over the meaning of the word *baptizō*. As he and Ann studied the meaning of baptism in the NT, they both became convinced that this sacred rite was intended for believers only. Both of them had been baptized as infants and brought up in godly Congregationalist families, but when they reached India they made contact with the renowned Baptist missionary William Carey and requested baptism in keeping with their newfound convictions. On September 6, 1812, they were immersed at Calcutta in the baptistry of Carey's Lal Bazar Chapel by William Ward.[1]

Their friend Luther Rice, who had followed the Judsons to India on another ship, also became unsettled in his own views about baptism. After further study and prayer, he too was baptized as a believer on November 1, 1812. In his diary for that day he wrote, "Was this day baptized in the name of the Holy Trinity. The Lord grant that I may ever find his name to be a strong tower to which I may continually resort and find safety."[2]

The "conversion" of the Judsons and Rice to a new understanding and practice of baptism became the catalyst for the rise of the

[*] Timothy George received his Th.D. from Harvard University and is Dean and Professor of Divinity at Beeson Divinity School in Birmingham, Alabama. He is also an executive editor of *Christianity Today*.

[1] Excerpts from "The Reformed Doctrine of Believers' Baptism," published originally in *Interpretation* 47 (1993): 242–54. Revised and reprinted as "Believer's Baptism: More than American Individualism." *Modern Reformation* 6 (1997): 41–47.

[2] O. K. Armstrong and M. M. Armstrong, *The Indomitable Baptists* (Garden City, New York: Doubleday & Company, Inc. 1967), 116.

modern missionary movement among Baptists in America. But their
experience was not unique. Ever since the Reformation, a steady
stream of evangelical Christians had come to this same conclusion,
and often by the same route—a careful reading of the NT with the
intent of finding therein what John Owen (who was not a Baptist)
called "the old glorious, beautiful face of Christianity."[3] Carey himself, while still working as a journeyman shoemaker in England,
had come to the same place and he was baptized as a believer in the
River Nene in 1783. Likewise, many "new light" Congregationalists
who had been converted under the preaching of George Whitefield
left that connection to become "new light" Baptists when they found
no evidence of infant baptism in the apostolic church. When told
of this development, Whitefield famously quipped that he was glad
to hear about the fervent faith of his followers but regretted that so
many of his chickens had become ducks!

The essays in this volume raise anew the much-debated questions about baptism that have often proved divisive among sincere
Christians in the past. It is certainly possible to put too much emphasis, or the wrong emphasis, on the external act of water baptism.
The traditional Baptist protest against sacramentalism makes precisely that point. And the same criticism, from a different direction,
can be leveled against certain practitioners of "baptistic" baptism
as well. For example, in the sixteenth century Michael Servetus rejected infant baptism and insisted that a literal following of the NT
would require baptism by immersion at age thirty, the age of Jesus
when he was baptized in the Jordan. But Servetus' views on baptism did not prevent him from denying the doctrine of the Holy
Trinity. Even today, it is not impossible to find certain Baptists who
are adamant about maintaining "Baptist distinctives" but who are
not so sure Jesus was born of a virgin, really walked on water, or
rose bodily from the dead.

It is well to keep such deviations in mind, but the greater concern for most Baptists today is of a different sort. Baptism is too often down-played as an optional add-on to the Christian life. It is too

---

[3] John Owen, *A Vindication of the Animadversions on Fiat Lux* (London: Printed for Ph. Ste-
phens and G. Sawbridge 1664), 207.

frequently administered in a casual or sloppy manner, without careful teaching of its biblical basis and theological meaning. Whenever baptism is covered in the religious press, the point of interest is usually baptismal statistics rather than baptismal substance. By becoming safely routinized as part of the ecclesiastical landscape, baptism is apt to lose its basic NT meaning as the decisive transition from an old way of life to a new way of life, as an act of radical obedience in which a specific renunciation is made and a specific promise is given.

The recovery of a robust doctrine of believers' baptism can serve as an antidote to the theological minimalism and atomistic individualism that prevail in many Baptist churches in our culture. Baptism is not only the solemn profession of a redeemed sinner, our "appeal to God for a clear conscience," as the NT puts it (1 Peter 3:21); it is also a sacred and serious act of incorporation into the visible community of faith. Such an understanding of baptism calls for the reform of our baptismal practice at several critical points.

First, baptism should be restored to its rightful place as a central liturgical act of Christian worship. Too often it is tagged on to the beginning or end of the service as an appendage to the "main event." Many early Baptists, both in England and America, practiced the laying on of hands following baptism. This consecration or setting apart recalls the baptismal rites of the early church in which confirmation, enacted through anointing with oil or the laying on of hands, was seen as an integral part of baptism itself and not as a separate sacrament.

Along with prayer and the reading of Scripture, the baptismal liturgy should include the personal confession of the one being baptized, preferably spoken from the baptismal waters, as well as the renewal of baptismal vows by the participating congregation. The tradition of an outdoor ceremony performed in a creek, river, or lake has much to commend it. The trauma of death and resurrection, which baptism symbolizes, is hardly conveyed when things are too neat and convenient. Such is the case with a new-fangled baptistry in which the minister does not even enter the water but, standing behind a plastic shield, simply reaches over and submerges the baptismal candidate who is seated on a reclining chair!

Secondly, baptism should be related directly to the discipline and covenantal commitments of the congregation. The role of catechesis in the process of baptismal preparation is also crucial if we are to avoid trivializing the meaning of baptism. As James F. White has pointed out, "No system is immune from indiscriminate baptism."[4] As Baptists have evolved from small sectarian beginnings to what might be called the catholic phase of our history, both the covenantal and disciplinary features of our church life have become marginal to our identity. We have reacted against the harshness and legalism that has sometimes characterized this dimension of our tradition. Still, the faith we confess in baptism requires us to deal with these issues. What standards of holiness ought to distinguish a man or woman of God? What are the ethical implications of our corporate decisions? Can we recover a structure of accountability in our congregational life without relapsing into narrow judgmentalism?

Finally, believers' baptism must be practiced alongside a proper theology of children. While there is no hereditary right to salvation or church membership inherent in the circumstances of one's birth, children of believing parents do stand in a special providential relationship to the people and promises of God. John Tombes, a seventeenth-century Baptist, spoke of the privileged status of such children who are "born in the bosom of the church, of godly parents, who by prayers, instruction, example, will undoubtedly educate them in the true faith of Christ."[5]

Jesus took a special interest in children, received them into his arms, and blessed them. He did not baptize them. It is right that the children of Christian parents be set aside in a service of infant consecration in which the parents, along with the congregation, pledge to bring up these children in the nurture and admonition of the Lord. We should always be sensitive to the evidences of God's grace in their tender years and encourage their early interest in prayer, the reading of Holy Scripture, and the life of the church. However, because biological childhood can never be transformed into spiri-

---

[4] J. F. White, *Sacraments as God's Self-Giving* (Nashville: Abingdon Press 1983), 46.
[5] *Examen of the Sermon of Mr. Stephen Marshall About Infant Baptism* (London, 1645), 33, quoted in D. Kingdon, *Children of Abraham: A Reformed Baptist View of Baptism, the Covenant, and Children* (Haywards Heath, Sussex: Carey Publications 1973), 99.

tual childhood, we do not say to our children, "Be a good Christian child," but rather, "Repent and believe the gospel." The spiritual awakening and discernment of children, even within the same family, do not proceed at a uniform pace. Thus, Christian parents and ministers of the church must be ever vigilant in the nurture and counsel they offer.

Several years ago, Michael Green, a prominent evangelical Anglican, wrote a book about baptism entitled *The Waters that Divide*. Must baptism ever remain a source of controversy and contention among equally sincere, Bible-believing Christians? Many of us yearn for the unity of Jesus' followers for which our Lord himself prayed. But unity in love must also be unity in truth, else it is not genuine unity at all. The historic Baptist witness to believers' baptism is grounded on such a commitment to unity in truth. This witness to believers' baptism is important, not because Baptists have nothing to learn from other Christians who hold different views, nor because one denominational label should be given precedence over another, but precisely because of that to which believers' baptism itself visibly and eloquently points—the self-giving of the triune God himself in the life, death, and resurrection of Jesus Christ, the benefits of which are freely bestowed by grace alone on all who truly repent and believe.

This divine self-giving is celebrated in a baptismal hymn written by Robert T. Daniel:

> Lord, in humble, sweet submission,
> Here we meet to follow thee;
> Trusting in thy great salvation,
> Which alone can make us free.
> Nought have we to claim as merit;
> All duties we can do
> Can no crown of life inherit:
> All the praise to thee is due.
> Yet we come in Christian duty,
> Down beneath the wave to go;
> O the bliss! The heavenly beauty!
> Christ the Lord was buried so.[6]

[6] Robert T. Daniel, (1832), Hymn 823 in *The Service of Song for Baptist Churches*, New York: Sheldon and Company (1971), 331.

Introduction

Some within the Christian confession claim that baptism should be classified as a minor issue. Such a sentiment is misdirected, for baptism is regularly connected in scripture with belief and salvation. Baptism, as this book will demonstrate, is the initiation rite into the Christian church. Those who label it as minor are imposing their own categories onto the Scriptures instead of listening to the Scriptures.

Timothy George reminds us that those who practiced believer's baptism during the Reformation risked "persecution and martyrdom," and hence did not view baptism as a minor matter.[1] We are not claiming, of course, that a right understanding of baptism is necessary for salvation. Still, to say that a right understanding of baptism is unnecessary for salvation does not lead logically or biblically to the conclusion that baptism is inconsequential. In saying the above, we do not wish to engage in a polemical debate which ratchets up the temperature to a fever pitch. Our hope is that this book will defend believer's baptism with a charitable and irenic spirit. We realize that other evangelical believers disagree with us, but we hope to persuade many that the course we chart fits with the scriptural witness.

Baptism is important precisely because it is tied to the gospel, to the saving work that Christ accomplished in his death and resurrection. We do not think baptizing infants is merely a minor mistake, even though we rejoice in the evangelical credentials of many with whom we disagree.[2] Paul Jewett captures the importance of believer's baptism in saying, "*To baptize infants apart from faith threatens the evangelical foundations of evangelicalism.*"[3] This is an awesome statement that stands up under scrutiny, for in Scripture baptism is

---

[1] T. George, "The Reformed Doctrine of Believers' Baptism," *Int* 47 (1993): 242.

[2] Interestingly, Douglas Wilson claims that nothing less will do than showing that infant baptism is required in the Scriptures (*To a Thousand Generations—Infant Baptism: Covenant Mercy for the People of God* [Moscow, Idaho: Canon Press, 1996, 9]). We claim that the arguments contained in this book demonstrate that infant baptism is not only not required but is a clear violation of what the Scriptures teach.

[3] P. K. Jewett, *Infant Baptism and the Covenant of Grace* (Grand Rapids: Eerdmans, 1978), 162 (emphasis his).

regularly linked with admission into the people of God—the church of Jesus Christ. The fundamental teaching of the gospel is that human beings can be right with God only through faith in Jesus Christ (Rom 5:1). Infant baptism compromises that teaching by counting infants as members of the church, either via sacramental theology, the alleged faith of the infant, presumptive regeneration, the faith of sponsors, or covenant theology. Sacramental theology clearly compromises the gospel since it teaches that infants enter God's kingdom by virtue of the sacramental action.[4] Believer's baptism accords with the gospel because it teaches that the objective work of God in salvation necessarily leads to the subjective response of faith. God's work in Christ is not suspended on nothing, with no answering response of faith. The objective work of God in Christ secures a believing response in his people, so that the sign of the new covenant is only applied to those who give evidence by belief of membership in that covenant.

When churches practice infant baptism or allow into membership those who were baptized as infants, they have sundered the biblical connection between baptism and faith. Those who are baptized as infants, upon reading the NT, may think they belong to God by virtue of their infant baptism since baptism is invariably linked with belonging to the church of Jesus Christ in the NT.[5] We believe that baptism should be reserved for believers because it preserves the testimony of the gospel by showing that only those who have repented and believed belong to the church. Only those who have

---

[4] Stanley K. Fowler (a Baptist) argues in his book that baptism is more than a symbol and should be understood sacramentally (*More Than a Symbol: The British Baptist Recovery of Sacramentalism*, Studies in Baptist History and Thought 2 [Carlisle: Paternoster, 2002]). Fowler rightly argues that baptism is more than a symbol, but the use of the word "sacramental" is unfortunate since it is liable to a number of different interpretations. Fowler's own use of the word may fit with what is argued in this book since he claims that those who are unbaptized but believers may still be saved. It seems, however, that Fowler's book suffers from lack of clarity in using the word "sacramental," and the vagueness of his language makes it difficult to determine precisely what he means.

[5] Venema objects that this is not the position of covenantal paedobaptists, and laments that they are often misunderstood. See C. P. Venema, "Covenant Theology and Baptism," in *The Case for Covenantal Infant Baptism*, ed. G. Strawbridge (Phillipsburg, NJ: P & R, 2003), 228–29. But the point made here is not that covenantal paedobaptists claim that infants are saved by virtue of being baptized. Rather, we are arguing that such a mistake easily creeps in since baptism is connected in the NT with saving faith and induction into the church of Jesus Christ.

exercised faith are justified. Hence, only those who have trusted in Christ should be baptized. Restricting baptism to believers only, therefore, preserves the pure witness of the gospel.

In addition, believer's baptism also demonstrates that the church is a new covenant community—all those within it know the Lord (Heb 8:11). The church of Jesus Christ is not a mixed community of believers and unbelievers. It consists of those who have confessed Jesus Christ as Savior and Lord. Paedobaptists often say that Baptists do not escape from the charge of a mixed community since some of those who claim to be converted do not truly belong to the people of God.[6] It is true, of course, that some of those who claim to believe are subsequently revealed to be inauthentic (e.g., 1 John 2:19). Nevertheless, a profound difference still exists between Baptists and paedobaptists, for Baptists do not allow anyone into the church without trying to discern whether the person is truly saved, whereas paedobaptists knowingly include some who do not believe into the covenant community.[7]

Another objection raised by paedobaptists relates to the warning passages. It is common knowledge that Hebrews (e.g., Heb 2:1–4; 3:7–4:13; 5:11–6:8; 10:26–31; 12:25–29) has a number of warning passages, and indeed severe warnings exist throughout the NT. One recent book on paedobaptism indicates that the warning passages played an important role in the authors adopting a paedobaptist position, and the argument from the warning passages is regularly adduced in the book to support infant baptism.[8] According to this reading, not all those in the new covenant community truly know the Lord. Such a reading of Hebrews faces severe problems exegetically, for now (if this position is followed) some who have the law

---

[6] So, Venema, "Covenant Theology and Baptism," 227.

[7] Many Baptist churches, of course, do not evaluate carefully whether people believe before joining the church. But such a reality shows the weakness of many Baptist churches and their failure to do what their Baptist ancestors preached and proclaimed.

[8] This argument is often made in Strawbridge, *The Case for Covenantal Infant Baptism*. All of the essays noted here make this point and come from this volume. Strawbridge notes in the introduction that the texts on apostasy were a turning point for him (4). See also J. D. Niell, "The Newness of the New Covenant," 133, 153 n 37; R. L. Pratt Jr., "Infant Baptism in the New Covenant," 169–70, 173–74; R. Booth, "Covenant Transition," 198–99; G. Strawbridge, "The Polemics of Anabaptism from the Reformation Onward," 280–83. The same argument from apostasy is advanced by Wilson, *To a Thousand Generations*, 81–96.

written on their heart and who have received forgiveness of sins
(Heb 10:16–18) are not truly forgiven. Paedobaptists who defend
this view drive a wedge between those who are elect and those who
are forgiven of their sins. Apparently not all of the latter enjoy the
former! Now one can even be a partaker of the Holy Spirit (Heb
6:4), and not belong to the elect. Perhaps we will be pardoned if we
argue that such paedobaptists would be more consistent if they argued that those who are saved can lose their salvation. Perhaps some
of their theological offspring will come to such a conclusion.

We can only refer here to another book that we believe handles
the warning passages in a way that avoids these errors.[9] On this
view, the warnings are the means God uses to preserve his own, and
the warnings are always effective in the lives of the elect. Arminians,
naturally, view such a conclusion with suspicion. But such a view
of the warnings should not trouble any Calvinist, for Calvinists insist that one must repent and believe to be saved, and that we must
preach the necessity of repentance and belief. At the same time,
Calvinists are convinced that God will fulfill the condition to believe
in the lives of the elect. In the same way, the warning passages are
nothing other than a call to believe until the last day, and God uses
those very warnings to stoke the fires of faith in his own. Hence,
there is no exegetical warrant for diminishing what Hebrews means
when it says that all those in the new covenant know the Lord (Heb
8:11).[10] This is not merely an external knowing in Hebrews, but

---

[9] T. R. Schreiner and A. Caneday, *The Race Set Before Us: A Biblical Theology of Perseverance and Assurance* (Downers Grove: InterVarsity, 2001). The difference between Wilson's view
and our own surfaces when Wilson claims that the warnings are not directly addressed to true
saints, but he adds to this the thought that believers should "regularly examine their own hearts
in the light of such warnings" (*To a Thousand Generations*, 85). Such a view fails to understand
the function of the warnings and also makes them unnecessarily complicated, for believers are
required, according to Wilson's view, to engage in the strange practice of applying to themselves
warnings written to others.

[10] Pratt argues that Baptists fail to see that the new covenant is not fulfilled completely until
the Lord returns. Currently, the new covenant is inaugurated but not consummated. Hence,
some in the new covenant community are not truly believers ("Infant Baptism," 156–74). This
is an intriguing argument, but it misapplies the categories of inaugurated and consummated.
We agree that the new covenant is inaugurated and not yet consummated. But such a truth does
not mean that some of those who know the Lord, have the law written on their heart, and are
forgiven of their sins may not be truly believers. The not-yet element of the eschatology of Hebrews means that those who are now partakers of the Holy Spirit (Heb 6:4) are not yet perfected,

represents the law truly written on the heart by the Spirit of God, so that there is no need to resort to the idea that some of those with the law written on the heart are not truly saved.[11]

The baptistic view, in other words, preserves the purity of the church and emphasizes (or at least should emphasize) that those who are living in unrepentant and significant sin should be disciplined. Paedobaptist churches face a problem here, for they may uphold such a standard for adult believers, but they have also admitted into membership children who are not believers, and these children will not be disciplined for failing to believe. Hence, a mixed membership has been deliberately introduced into the church.

Moreover, paedobaptists face a problem with the Lord's Supper that Baptists do not encounter. The Lord's Supper is reserved for believers who have been baptized, but many paedobaptists do not allow children to partake of the Lord's table until the children have expressed personal faith. But such a divide between baptism and the Lord's Supper cannot be sustained from the NT, for it is clear that those baptized participated in communion. Baptism has been waived as the initiation rite for believers by paedobaptists, and hence some kind of initiation (like confirmation) is substituted before people take of the Lord's Supper. Now a new ritual (confirmation), which is not located in the NT witness, is introduced so that the Lord's Supper is reserved for believers. Baptists insist that such an expedient is unnecessary if the biblical requirement of believer's baptism is maintained. Some paedobaptists have recently responded to this inconsistency and claimed that infants and young children who are baptized may eat and drink at the Lord's table. Such consistency is to be saluted, but an even greater problem exists on this scheme. For now unbelievers are taking of the Lord's Supper, and clearly they are

but they will truly be perfected on the last day. The point of the not-yet in Hebrews is not to cast doubt on whether believers will be saved on the last day. Rather, the not-yet urges God's people to continue to believe until the last day with the firm assurance that God will complete what he has started (Heb 6:13–20).

[11] The argument of Hebrews is amazingly truncated when its newness is limited to the abolishing of the ceremonial law (Niell, "Newness of New Covenant," 142–46), and knowing the Lord is interpreted to mean that new covenant believers know the Lord without the mediation of the Levitical priesthood (148–53).

not discerning the body, and hence are eating and drinking in an unworthy manner (1 Cor 11:27–34).

At the outset, we need to be clear about what baptismal position the contributors to this volume are advocating, as well as what baptismal theology primarily they are opposing. The authors are promoting "credobaptism," that is, the doctrine that Christian baptism should be reserved for believers (from the Latin for "believe,") in the Lord Jesus Christ. The "belief" required of those seeking baptism is more than mere intellectual assent to some doctrinal truths. Rather, as the Protestant reformers spelled out in helpful detail, belief encompasses a person's intellect and affections and leads one to entrust himself to Christ. We agree with the 1689 Baptist *Second London Confession* which says that "the principle acts of saving faith have immediate relation to Christ, accepting, receiving, and resting upon him alone for justification, sanctification, and eternal life."[12] Attentive readers, however, will note that there are some differences among the contributors on a few minor issues of baptismal theology (e.g., how to interpret a particular text) and practice (e.g., the wisdom of baptizing young people who profess faith in Christ). These are issues that credobaptists need to discuss in order more faithfully to understand and implement God's truth in our churches, so we do not want to pretend that these disagreements do not exist. But we want to stress that these are in-house debates. These points of dispute are important, but the contributors to this volume agree on the doctrine of credobaptism.

The book is written to correct a certain form of infant baptist theology, as a perusal of the footnotes will show. There are as many types of "paedobaptists" (i.e., those who baptize infants) as there are Baptists, so we need to clarify whose theology we are addressing. Many paedobaptists around the world believe in a sacerdotal baptismal theology, which asserts that the baptism of the infant (apart from any faith on the infant's part) cleanses him of original sin. This theory of "baptismal regeneration" is sometimes denoted by the words *ex opere operato* throughout this volume. This phrase (literally, "by the work performed") is the belief that baptism is ef-

---

[12] *Second London Confession* 14.2, in W. L. Lumpkin, *Baptist Confessions of Faith* (Valley Forge, PA: Judson Press, 1969), 269.

fective through the operation of the rite of baptism itself. It conveys God's grace to the recipient unless he or she "places a spiritual impediment *(obex)* in the way of grace."[13] However, this is not the paedobaptist theology that we are primarily answering in this volume.[14] Our desire, rather, is to respond to evangelical paedobaptists, primarily in the Reformed tradition, who baptize infants not because they believe that baptism regenerates the child but because they believe that baptism brings the child into the covenant community where he or she will have the blessing of hearing the gospel preached as they grow up as members of the church. Certainly there are variations among our paedobaptist brethren, and we shall note some of them in the following pages. The view of paedobaptism affirmed by the Reformed tradition is fraught with an inconsistency: as evangelicals they believe salvation is by faith in Christ alone, but as paedobaptists they give the sign of that faith (baptism) to those who have not exercised faith (infants). It is primarily this theology we are trying to correct in this book.

In this book we begin with Scripture, arguing from the NT Scriptures that believer's baptism is the clear teaching of the NT. Andreas Köstenberger prosecutes this case in the Gospels, Robert Stein in Acts, and Thomas Schreiner in the epistles. Stephen Wellum, then, considers the whole matter biblically and theologically in a crucial chapter. What is the relationship between the covenants? Most evangelicals who defend infant baptism defend their practice from their understanding of the covenants and the relationship between circumcision and baptism. Wellum demonstrates that the theological connection that paedobaptists draw between the covenants cannot be sustained biblically. They rightly see continuity between the old covenant and the new, but they fail to note the significant elements of discontinuity. Wellum unpacks the Bible's teaching on the covenants, showing that it requires believer's baptism. These four chapters of careful biblical exegesis and theology demonstrate that paedobaptism is untenable biblically.

---

[13] See R. A. Muller, *Dictionary of Latin and Greek Theological Terms: Drawn Principally from Protestant Scholastic Theology* (Grand Rapids: Baker, 1985), 108.

[14] Hence, when we refer to the *ex opera operato* view of baptism in this work, we are not in these instances criticizing the Reformed view of paedobaptism.

In the next section of the book we consider the historical and theological challenge to believer's baptism. Here we consider the witness of history and interact with those who have preceded us. We must state at the outset that the Scriptures are the norm, and the practice of the church throughout history is not decisive. Still, any serious defense of believer's baptism must consider the witness of history. Steve McKinion surveys the first centuries of the church, a period that has been much considered in baptism debates. He demonstrates that the evidence shows that paedobaptism arose late and for various practical and theological reasons. Jonathan Rainbow demonstrates that the defense of infant baptism proposed by Ulrich Zwingli, one of the founders of the Reformed tradition in the sixteenth century, was truly a novelty. For the first time in history, baptism was severed from faith and regeneration. The view that the Reformed take for granted as historic, represented in Zwingli's day a break with previous tradition. Shawn Wright interacts carefully with some of the most influential proponents of infant baptism— John Calvin, John Murray, and Pierre Marcel—and shows their biblical and internal inconsistencies. A fascinating and creative defense of infant baptism has been proposed by Meredith Kline. The fertile mind of Kline has fascinated scholars and students, but Duane Garrett demonstrates that Kline's arguments are more creative than biblical. The connections he draws to support infant baptism are insupportable when carefully examined, and the substance of his argument, therefore, collapses. Ardel Caneday unpacks the baptismal thinking of Alexander Campbell. Campbell's theology—difficult to understand, eccentric at points, and very wrong at others—is different from some of the Campbellite thinking that followed him.

In the final chapter Mark Dever considers the practical application of believer's baptism for churches today. What we have written in this book is not merely a theoretical exercise. We believe that the biblical theology of baptism has profound implications for our churches. Dever considers a host of practical questions that pastors wrestle with: from who should do the baptizing to when a person should be baptized. He also sets forth why it is important for the life of the church for baptism to be reserved for believers. Baptism is not an idle question, for it speaks to the nature of the church as the community of believers.

Our hope is that readers will be challenged and encouraged by what is written in this book. For those who disagree, we only ask that our arguments would be countered with the Scriptures. For those who agree, we pray that what is advocated here will be implemented, by God's grace, ever more faithfully in our churches.

BAPTISM IN THE GOSPELS

Andreas J. Köstenberger[*]

T he purpose of the present chapter is to investigate the material on baptism in the four canonical Gospels. This will
take on the form of a narrative analysis of the Gospels of
Mark, Matthew, Luke, and John. In this way the Gospels themselves
will be allowed to determine the parameters for our discussion of
baptism, in particular the activity of John the Baptist, Jesus' baptism
by him, and the literal and figurative baptisms administered, or undergone, by Jesus and his followers. As a brief prolegomenon, it will
be helpful to look first at Jewish proselyte baptism, which, together
with Jewish ritual washings and immersion practices, forms an important backdrop to our discussion of the material on baptism in the
Gospels. The essay concludes with several important implications
for our understanding of baptism today.

Proselyte Baptism

It is difficult to know when the Jews began to practice proselyte
baptism as an initiation rite for Gentile converts to Judaism, so we
cannot assume it was a precursor of John's and Christian baptism.[1]

[*] Andreas J. Köstenberger received his Ph.D. from Trinity Evangelical Divinity School, and is
Professor of New Testament and Director of Ph.D. Studies at Southeastern Baptist Theological
Seminary in Wake Forest, North Carolina.

[1] See S. McKnight, *A Light among the Gentiles: Jewish Missionary Activity in the Second Temple
Period* (Minneapolis: Fortress, 1991), 82–85, followed by D. Dockery, "Baptism," *DJG*, eds. J. B.
Green and S. McKnight (Downers Grove: InterVarsity, 1992), 56; against G. R. Beasley-Murray,
Baptism in the New Testament (Grand Rapids: Eerdmans, 1962), 18–31; and A. Oepke, "*baptō,
baptizō*," *TDNT* 1:535, who contends that "it is hardly conceivable that the Jewish ritual should
be adopted at a time when baptism had become an established religious practice in Christianity"
(similarly, H. H. Rowley, "Jewish Proselyte Baptism and the Baptism of John," in *From Moses to
Qumran* [New York: Association Press, 1963], 211–12). On the possible antecedents of Chris-
tian baptism, see also G. R. Osborne, "Baptism," *Baker Encyclopedia of the Bible*, ed. W. A. Elwell
(Grand Rapids: Baker, 1988), 1:257–58; J. Delorme, "The Practice of Baptism in Judaism at the
Beginning of the Christian Era," in *Baptism in the New Testament: A Symposium*, trans. D. Askew
(Baltimore: Helicon, 1964 [1956]), 25–60; and the essays by B. Chilton, "John the Baptist: His
Immersion and His Death," and C. A. Evans, "The Baptism of John in a Typological Context," in
Dimensions of Baptism: Biblical and Theological Studies, ed. S. E. Porter and A. R. Cross, JSNTSup
234 (London/New York: Sheffield Academic Press, 2002), 25–44 and 45–71.

It appears that the import of this practice was both purificatory—Gentiles were generally considered to be ritually unclean and in need of purification—and initiatory. Also, proselyte baptism conveyed the notion of a conversion to a new kind of life, which involved the proselyte's acceptance of the "yoke of the Torah."[2] Hence, the initiation represented a commitment, as well as bestowing certain benefits.

Unlike Jewish proselyte baptism of Gentile converts to Judaism, however, John baptized Jews, not Gentiles.[3] Most likely, John's baptism and Jewish proselyte baptism both harken back to Jewish ritual cleansing and bathing practices.[4] This is supported by mishnaic passages such as *m. Pesah.* 8:8 ("If a man became a proselyte on the day before Passover he may immerse himself and consume his Passover-offering in the evening") that discuss proselyte baptism in the context of Levitical cleansing in preparation for the Passover. At Qumran, too, we find ritual washings in the context of repentance and the community's preparation for entering the eschatological community (1QS 3:4–9; 6:14–23; see 4:18–22).[5] Unlike John's baptism, however, these rites were repeated and self-administered.

It may be concluded, therefore, that the early Church's practice of baptism cannot be adequately explained by, or accounted for, by appealing to proselyte baptism as a precedent. Apart from the question of whether or not proselyte baptism predates Christian baptism (which is far from certain), there are important theological distinctions in the way in which baptism was conceived that makes a link

[2] D. Daube, *The New Testament and Rabbinic Judaism* (repr. New York: Arno, 1973), 106–13; E. R. Hardy, "Jewish and Christian Baptism: Some Notes and Queries," in *A Tribute to Arthur Vööbus*, ed. R. H. Fischer (Chicago: Lutheran School of Theology, 1977), 317; G. F. Moore, *Judaism* (Cambridge: Harvard Univ., 1962), 3:334. Note also the Talmud's reference to a baptized proselyte as a newborn child (b. Yebam. 22a). While conversion in Judaism was marked by circumcision, baptism prepared the new convert to offer a sacrifice as the initial act of worship (Dockery, "Baptism," 56).

[3] See Dockery, "Baptism," 56; Witherington, "John the Baptist," DJG 386. Witherington concludes that John considered heredity as an inadequate safeguard from God's coming wrath and that Israel, like the Gentiles, was lost, unless people repented and received God's forgiveness.

[4] See Lev 11–17; Num 19:11–22; see the use of *baptizō* for Jewish ritual washing in Mark 7:4; Luke 11:38; see Matt 15:2; John 3:25; Heb 6:2; Sir 34:25 LXX; Jud 12:7 LXX. See McKnight, *Light among the Gentiles*, 82–85.

[5] See L. F. Badia, *The Qumran Baptism and John the Baptist's Baptism* (Lanham, MD: Univ. Press of America, 1980); Dockery, "Baptism," 56–57. See also B. E. Thiering, "Inner and Outer Cleansing at Qumran as a Background to New Testament Baptism," *NTS* 26 (1980): 266–77.

between these two kinds of baptism tenuous at best and illegitimate at worst.

Baptism in the Gospel of Mark[6]

A significant number of all occurrences of the *bapt-* word group in Mark's Gospel are found in Mark 1:4–9.[7] Mark's conflated quotation of Mal 3:1 and Isa 40:3 identifies John the Baptist as God's messenger sent to "prepare the way for the Lord." Mark 1:4 immediately adds that, in keeping with these prophetic passages, "John came baptizing in the wilderness and preaching a baptism of repentance for the forgiveness of sins"[8] (see Acts 19:4).

The references to repentance and the forgiveness of sins make clear that John's baptism is to be understood not merely in terms of ritual purification and religious observance but as essentially *moral* and *ethical*. This, in turn, is set within a prophetic-apocalyptic eschatological framework which contrasts the impending divine judgment with the coming of the Messiah.

In its original context, Isa 40:1–9 calls God's people to prepare Yahweh's way in the wilderness.[9] While not explicitly stated, the

---

[6] Markan priority (i.e. the notion that Mark wrote his Gospel prior to the other canonical Gospels, including the other so-called Synoptic Gospels, Matthew and Luke) is tentatively assumed in the presentation of this essay, but little in the argument rests on this assumption.

[7] For an investigation of the historicity of Jesus' baptism by John, see R. L. Webb, "Jesus' Baptism: Its Historicity and Implications," posted at www.ibresearch.com, who concludes that "the baptism of Jesus by John is historically very probable or even virtually certain." See also id., "John the Baptist and His Relationship to Jesus," in *Studying the Historical Jesus: Evaluations of the State of Current Research*, ed. B. Chilton and C. A. Evans (Leiden: Brill, 1994), 179–229.

[8] Scripture quotations are from the HCSB.

[9] For a full-fledged analysis of the use of Isa 40:3 in John 1:23 see A. J. Köstenberger, "John," in *Commentary on the Use of the Old Testament in the New* (ed. D. A. Carson and G. Beale; Grand Rapids: Baker, forthcoming). Compare the use of Isa 40:3 in the DSS (1QS 8:14; 4Q176 frag. 1–2 cols. 6–7; 4Q259 3:4–5), on which see J. H. Charlesworth, "Intertextuality: Isaiah 40:3 and the Serek Ha-Yahad," in *The Quest for Context and Meaning. Studies in Biblical Intertextuality in Honor of James A. Sanders*, ed. C. A. Evans and S. Talmon, Biblical Interpretation Series 28 (Leiden: Brill, 1997), 197–224; G. J. Brooke, "Isaiah 40:3 and the Wilderness Community," in *New Qumran Texts and Studies,* ed. G. J. Brooke with F. G. Martínez, Studies on the Texts of the Desert of Judah 15 (Leiden: Brill, 1994), 117–32; S. Metso, "The Use of Old Testament Quotations in the Qumran Community Rule," in *Qumran between the Old and the New Testaments,* ed. F. H. Cryer and T. L. Thompson, JSOTSup 290 (Sheffield: Sheffield Academic Press, 1998), 217–31; and J. C. VanderKam, "The Judean Desert and the Community of the Dead Sea Scrolls," in *Antikes Judentum und Frühes Christentum,* ed. B. Kollmann, W. Reinbold and A. Steudel, BZNW 97 (Berlin/New York: de Gruyter, 1999), 159–71.

probable manner in which this is to be done is by way of repentance. If Yahweh is to return, his people must prepare the way by repenting of their sins that caused them to be led into exile (see Matt 3:8). As Isa 40:1–2 makes clear, God's ultimate purpose for his people is not judgment but salvation. In its original Isaianic context, exodus typology is interwoven with the figure of the coming Servant of the Lord (see esp. Isa 52:13–53:12). The Messiah and his redemption will bring about a new exodus in which God's glory will be revealed.

John's message meets with a large response, and many come from Jerusalem and the Judean countryside to confess their sins and be baptized in the Jordan River. Dressed in the manner of the OT prophet Elijah, John points people to one after him who is more powerful than he and the thongs of whose sandals he is not worthy to untie, one who will baptize, not with water, but with the Holy Spirit (1:8; see Joel 2:28–29; Isa 32:15; 44:3).[10] Then Jesus comes from Nazareth in Galilee and is baptized by John, with attesting signs of God's approval (1:9). As Jesus is baptized with water by John and the Spirit descends on him (1:10), so he will in turn baptize others with the Holy Spirit in the future. Jesus' baptism is the occasion of a major Trinitarian manifestation, with the Father voicing approval and the Spirit descending on Jesus the Son (1:10–11). It seems that Jesus' baptism signifies his identification with sinful Israel and points to the cross.[11]

[10] On Spirit baptism, with special reference to Pentecostalism, see J. D. G. Dunn, *Baptism in the Holy Spirit*, SBT 2/15 (London: SCM, 1970). The Holy Spirit is mentioned elsewhere in Mark only in 3:29 (no forgiveness for blasphemy against the Holy Spirit); 12:36 (David in Ps 110:1 speaking by the Holy Spirit); and 13:11 (the Holy Spirit will speak on believers' behalf in times of persecution). Chilton, "John the Baptist," 25–44, against Webb, *John the Baptizer*, and the vast majority of commentators, denies that John was a prophet, seeing him as a purifier in a Jewish cultic tradition. Chilton holds that the Baptist was killed when Jesus was only a young man (in AD 21), which would render the Gospel account of Jesus' baptism by John unhistorical (against L. Hartman, "Baptism," *ABD* 1:584, who affirms, "That Jesus was baptized by John is historically certain"). C. Evans, "Baptism of John," 45–71, says there is no need to choose between the alternatives presented by Webb and Chilton: the Baptist was both a prophet and a purifier, similar to the Essenes. Chilton's cavalier dismissal of the reliability of the Gospel accounts of John the Baptist cannot be excused, however, nor can it be denied that Jesus' words in Matt 11:13–14 clearly imply that John was a prophet: "For all the prophets and the Law prophesied until John. And if you are willing to accept it, John himself is Elijah who was to come." What was Elijah if not a prophet?

[11] See J. A. Gibbs, "Israel Standing with Israel: The Baptism of Jesus in Matthew's Gospel (Matt. 3:13–17)," *CBQ* 64 (2002): 511–26. The theme of Jesus' identification with Israel is not as explicit in Mark as in Matthew, but it is probably implied.

In essence, then, Mark shows that John's baptism fulfills OT prophecy and prepares people for Jesus' ministry. His baptism in the wilderness of the Jordan has salvation-historical significance, invoking the exodus motif in continuity with passages in Isaiah.[12] The Baptist is presented as a prophet like Elijah, preaching a message of repentance for the forgiveness of sins.[13] In light of the reality and certainty of God's judgment, John called for conversion—a reorientation of one's life, a return to God, and a restoration of one's relationship with him—whereby people's confession of sins resulted in divine forgiveness. As the one who administered baptism, John mediated this forgiveness in a way similar to the priest who performed sacrifices within the context of the OT sacrificial system (e.g., Lev 5:5–10).[14] Also, John's baptism had a purifying function, in keeping with OT and Second Temple notions that immersions were concerned with cleansing from uncleanness.[15]

John's baptism with water is contrasted with baptism with the Holy Spirit, which will be administered by one "more powerful" than he. This characterizes the relationship between John and Jesus both in terms of continuity (both baptize) and discontinuity (literal vs. metaphorical reference to baptism, Jesus mightier). Against the backdrop of references to God's judgment, John's baptism, as well as Jesus' later "baptism," doubtless has an *eschatological* dimension. It marks baptism as an initiatory rite into the "true Israel," the believing remnant. Hence many of John's disciples later became disciples of Jesus (see John 1:35–37), though doubtless there were those who were baptized by John but who did not accept Jesus as Messiah. In contrast to Jewish ritual washings, which were self-administered, John baptized others, which may have given rise to the designation, John "the Baptizer" (see Mark 6:14,24).

[12] See R. L. Webb, *John the Baptizer and Prophet*, JSNTSup 62 (Sheffield: Sheffield Academic Press, 1991), 181–83, 360–66; Hartman, "Baptism," *ABD* 1:584.

[13] On John's prophetic role, see Webb, *John the Baptizer and Prophet* and id., "Jesus' Baptism," 14–17.

[14] As Webb, "Jesus' Baptism," 12, notes, this parallel is all the more striking as the NT indicates that John came from a priestly family (see Luke 1:5,23).

[15] Webb, "Jesus' Baptism," 12 and 29 n 62 (with further bibliographic references). References in Jewish intertestamental literature are helpful in that they show the way in which OT injunctions were applied in the centuries surrounding the coming of Christ.

We can now survey references to baptism in the rest of Mark's Gospel. Mark 6:14,24–25 mentions rumors that Jesus was John the Baptist raised from the dead, which results in a flashback to the Baptist's beheading (see Josephus, *Ant.* 18.5.2).[16] In 7:4, the words *baptizō* and *baptismos* are used in the evangelist's explanatory reference to Jewish ceremonial washings (Matt 15:2 has *niptō*, "wash"; also Luke 11:38). In Mark 8:28, Jesus' disciples state that some think Jesus is John the Baptist (see Mark 6:14; Matt 16:14). Mark 9:13 recounts Jesus' assertion that, in John the Baptist, Elijah has come (see Matt 17:10–13).

Mark 10:38–39 features six occurrences of the *bapt-* word group. Here Jesus speaks of a future "baptism" which he must undergo, namely, the crucifixion. In response to a question by John and James, the sons of Zebedee (a question stemming from their mother, see Matt 20:20–21), asking Jesus for the places on his right and left in the coming kingdom, Jesus asks whether they can drink the "cup" he will drink or be baptized with the "baptism" with which he will be baptized. This seems to be a reference to the painful destiny and physical distress experienced by Jesus, and later by his followers by virtue of their association with him (see Mark 8:34–38), issuing in his crucifixion.[17]

The final reference involving baptism in Mark,[18] which may be designed to provide closure to the theme of baptism in this Gospel by corresponding to the first mention of baptism in 1:4–9, is found in 11:29, where Jesus challenges his opponents to identify the authority behind John's baptism, whether divine or human. The Jews' response reveals people's respect for John as a true prophet of God.[19]

The references to baptism in Mark's Gospel present themselves therefore as follows:

[16] On John's life and death, see Webb, "Jesus' Baptism," 17–18.

[17] Dockery, "Baptism," 58.

[18] The reference to baptism in 16:16 is considered to be part of the "longer ending of Mark" which many scholars consider to have been added subsequent to the original publication of the Gospel and will therefore not be considered here. See D. M. Doriani, "Matthew 28:18–20 and the Institution of Baptism," in *The Case for Covenantal Infant Baptism*, ed. G. Strawbridge (Phillipsburg, NJ: Presbyterian & Reformed, 2003), 30, 43–48.

[19] On Chilton's curious denial that John the Baptist was a prophet, see note 8 above.

(1) 1:4–9: John the Baptist's baptism of repentance and his baptism of Jesus

(2) 6:14,24–25: Rumor that Jesus is the Baptist raised from the dead; John's beheading

(3) 7:13: Elijah has come in the person of John the Baptist

(4) 8:28: Some say Jesus is John the Baptist (see 6:14)

(5) 10:38–39: Jesus' reference to a future "baptism" he must undergo (his crucifixion)

(6) 11:30: Jesus' challenge to the Jews to identify the source of John's baptism

The presentation of baptism in Mark's Gospel can be shown to proceed against the backdrop of the following salvation-historical pattern: (1) John's baptism, in conjunction with his preaching of repentance and the forgiveness of sins, fulfills OT prophecy in preparing the way for the Messiah (1:4–8); (2) Jesus is baptized by John and attested as God's Son by the Father and the Spirit (1:9); (3) John is martyred (6:24–25); (4) Jesus speaks of the "baptism" of his crucifixion (10:38–39); and (5) Jesus will baptize with the Holy Spirit (1:9). Hence the Gospel begins with Jesus' literal, water baptism by John and concludes with Jesus' metaphorical "baptism" at the cross, with the Spirit baptism still in the future. Jesus is the one greater than John: the Baptist's ministry is concluded, while Jesus is the future Baptizer; the Baptist is a true prophet of God (11:30–33), while Jesus is the true Messiah and Son of God (1:1,11; 9:7; 15:39). The underlying symbolism of the Baptist's baptism is that of cleansing from sin and of spiritual renewal. Mark does little to flesh out the meaning of the future baptism with the Holy Spirit, although baptism with the Holy Spirit seems presupposed in the eschatological reference to the Holy Spirit aiding persecuted believers in the future (13:11).

Baptism in the Gospel of Matthew

About half of the references to the *bapt-* word group in Matthew occur in the account of the beginnings of John the Baptist's ministry in Matt 3:1–16. In addition to John's call for repentance, the

Matthean account makes specific reference to John's preaching of the nearness of the "kingdom of heaven" (Matt 3:2). While restructured (e.g., in Matthew the Isa 40:3 quote follows John's message rather than preceding it as in Mark's account), John's Elijah-like appearance and people's response are recorded in terms virtually identical with Mark.

In a major addition to Mark, Matthew in 3:7–10 recounts Jesus' denunciation of the Jews' ethnic presumption upon their Abrahamic descent, threatening God's imminent judgment.[20] As does Mark, Matthew includes John's reference to one more powerful than he who will baptize with the Holy Spirit, though Matthew (see Luke 3:16) also adds the phrase "and fire" (Matt 3:11). In keeping with both the preceding and subsequent contexts, "fire" here probably serves as an emblem of God's judgment (see Matt 5:22; 7:19; 13:40,42,50; 18:8–9; 25:41), which is conveyed by strongly apocalyptic language (see Matt 3:10,12, neither of which are found in Mark; see Dan 7:10; Rev 20:10).[21] Jesus' reference to his future "baptism" in the context of

[20] This is part of a tradition Matthew shares with Luke (see Luke 3:7–9).

[21] See Isa 4:4, which speaks of a "washing away" of filth from Jerusalem by a "spirit of judgment and a spirit of fire" (cited in Dockery, "Baptism," 55); and Mal 3:2–3, which speaks of the day of the Lord's coming as that of "a refiner's fire" for the purpose of purification resulting in offerings presented to the Lord in righteousness. See also the Qumran references cited in the introduction above. I. H. Marshall, "The meaning of the verb 'to baptize,' " EQ 45 (1973): 130–40, citing Dunn, Baptism in the Holy Spirit, esp. 8–10, notes several apocalyptic passages where fire and water imagery is merged (Dan 7:10; Rev 19:20; 20:10,14; 21:8; 4 Esdr 13:10–11; Sib Or 2.196–205; 1QH 3:29–32), in the context of judgment. He also points out that Spirit and water are related in the Dead Sea Scrolls (1QS 3:7–9; 4:20–21; 1QH 7:6–7; 17:26) and elsewhere (including John's Gospel: 7:38–39; see also Acts 2:33; 10:45), conceiving of the Spirit in liquid terms. In light of this apocalyptic background and the Spirit-water symbolism, Marshall concludes that the mode of NT baptism may be affusion rather than immersion, the emphasis being on the result of drenching and outpouring from above rather than on the mode of immersion in a stream or baptistry. However, Marshall fails to note that baptizō, as an intensive form of baptō, which clearly means "to dip," most likely also refers to immersion. He also fails to note passages in the LXX where baptizō indisputably conveys the notion of immersion (e.g., Naaman's "dipping himself" seven times in the Jordan, 2 Kgs 5:14: ebaptisanto) and does not consider the references to Jesus' "coming up out of the water" in Matt 3:16 par. Mark 1:10, which also strongly suggest immersion (see also Barn. 11:11; see Did. 7). In the updated version of his article, "The Meaning of the Verb 'Baptize,'" in Dimensions of Baptism, 8–24, Marshall adds (20 n 36) interaction with Webb, John the Baptizer, 179–81, who notes that baptism was performed in a river and that Jesus came up out of it but Marshall contends, in a case of special pleading, that "granted that the candidate went into the water, does the verb require that there was a total immersion rather than a total wetting by affusion?" Curiously, he cites J. Nolland, Luke 1–9:20, WBC (Dallas: Word, 1989), 142, for support, even though Nolland, by Marshall's own acknowledgment, believes the mode of John's baptism

"fire" in Luke 12:50 (see Luke 12:49) suggests that before baptizing others in this way, he must first undergo the "baptism" himself.[22]

In his narrative of Jesus' baptism by John, Matthew includes the account of John's initial objection and Jesus' encouragement that he proceed "to fulfill all righteousness" (Matt 3:15), a major Matthean theme especially in Jesus' Sermon on the Mount (Matt 5:6,10,20; 6:1,33; 21:32).[23] This is another way of saying that God's plan of salvation and of sending the Messiah included Jesus' baptism by the one who was sent to prepare the way for him. While the Messiah does not share with others baptized by John the need for repentance and the forgiveness of sins, he voluntarily subjects himself to this rite as part of his identification with humanity and of his role as Savior of humankind.

The next major pericope involving a reference to John the Baptist (not included in Mark) is found in Matt 11:1–19. From prison, and upon hearing what the Messiah is doing, the Baptist sends disciples to Jesus asking him whether or not he is "the one who was to come" (Matt 11:2–3). Jesus responds indirectly, intimating by his use of Isaianic messianic language that he did indeed perform the works of, and thus was, the Messiah (see Isa 35:4–6; 61:1). Jesus then uses the occasion to instruct the crowd about John's significance as a prophet, calling him "more than a prophet" (Matt 11:9). Citing Mal 3:1 (and hence providing the second part of Mark's double quotation in Mark 1:2–3; the first part is found in Matt 3:3), Jesus affirms that John is the greatest of all OT prophets, "for all the Prophets and the Law prophesied until John" (Matt 11:13). In addition, he is "the Elijah who was to come" (Matt 11:14; see Mark 9:13; see also Matt 3:4 and esp. 17:11–13).

Whether with John or with Jesus, people always find something to criticize; yet both fulfilled their ministries in keeping with the

---

was probably immersion. See also the critique of Marshall's view by C. Bennema, "Spirit-Baptism in the Fourth Gospel: A Messianic Reading of John 1,33," *Bib* 84 (2003): 37–38.

[22] See J. D. G. Dunn, "The Birth of a Metaphor—Baptized in Spirit," *ExpTim* 89 (1978): 134–38, 173–75, and the discussion of Luke 12:50 below.

[23] See B. Przybylski, *Righteousness in Matthew and His World of Thought*, SNTSMS 41 (Cambridge: Cambridge Univ. Press, 1980). Hartman, "Baptism," *ABD* 1:585, suggests that Jesus' baptism served as a model for believers, citing Matt 5:9,20,45; 28:19–20.

wisdom and predetermined plan of God (Matt 11:10–19). Jesus defends the Baptist and aligns his ministry with his. While both face opposition, they both pursue and fulfill God's redemptive mission and purpose. In this mission, John's baptism of repentance has an important part, yet it does so within the larger context of his mission of pointing to Jesus as the Messiah and Son of God, and as part of his preparation of the way for him. Once Jesus' messianic mission has begun to unfold, the Baptist's mission is close to being accomplished, and his baptism likewise has now fulfilled its temporary salvation-historical purpose and has become all but obsolete.

The account of the Baptist's death in Matt 14:1–12 parallels Mark 6:14–29 fairly closely, though it is less detailed than the Markan passage. The present account complements the just-discussed pericope, Matt 11:1–19, where Jesus, in response to the imprisoned John's apparent doubts regarding Jesus' messianic mission, elaborates on John's significance in light of people's misunderstanding and opposition. Now the Baptist's courageous preaching of righteousness (see Matt 14:4) issues in his beheading by Herod Antipas.

The Baptist's demise is thus part of the "misunderstanding" and "rejection" themes which encompass people's responses to both the Baptist's and Jesus' ministries. This is further underscored by Jesus' disciples' comment in Matt 16:14 that some think Jesus is John the Baptist (presumably raised from the dead; see Matt 14:1; see Mark 6:14) and is made even more clear by Jesus' clarification that "Elijah has already come, and they didn't recognize him. On the contrary, they did whatever they pleased to him. In the same way the Son of Man is going to suffer at their hands." (Matt 17:12). The teachers of the Law insisted that Elijah had to come first (presumably on the basis of passages such as Mal 3:1–2), so that the time had not yet come for the Messiah to make his appearance. Jesus here makes clear that Elijah had already come in the person of John the Baptist. Hence, the Jews' rejection of God's plan, both with regard to the roles of the Baptist and of Jesus, was groundless.

Remarkably, and for no obvious reason, both references to Jesus' future "baptism" in Mark 10:38–39 are not included in the parallel account in Matt 20:22–23. Matthew's account of the leaders' challenge of Jesus' authority and his counter-challenge with regard to the source of John the Baptist's authority in Matt 27:23–27, on the other hand, closely parallels Mark 11:27–33 (see also Luke 20:1–8). Again, Jesus stands in solidarity with John and links his mission to that of the Baptist with regard to their joint divine source of authority and purpose.

The final reference to baptism in Matthew is in the "Great Commission" passage in Matt 28:18–20:

> All authority in heaven and on earth has been given to me. Therefore go and make disciples of all nations, *baptizing them in the name of the Father and of the Son and of the Holy Spirit*, and teaching them to obey everything I have commanded you. And surely I am with you always, to the very end of the age.[24]

The passage is intricately interwoven with the Gospel as a whole,[25] which strongly supports the notion that the evangelist wrote the account of the "Great Commission" himself rather than taking it over as a whole from another source.[26]

Some significance is often attributed to the genre of this section. Rather than dealing with this issue in terms of competing, mutually exclusive options, we may detect elements of enthronement, covenant renewal, and commissioning.[27] In an echo of Dan 7:14, Jesus is portrayed as the exalted eschatological ruler of the world's

[24] Regarding the plethora of treatments of this passage, see the detailed bibliography in D. A. Hagner, *Matthew 14–28*, WBC (Dallas: Word, 1995), 878–80; and C. S. Keener, *A Commentary on the Gospel of Matthew* (Grand Rapids: Eerdmans, 1999), 715–21; also G. Bornkamm, G. Barth, and H. Joachim Held, *Tradition and Interpretation in Matthew* (London: SCM, 1963), 131–37.

[25] See O. S. Brooks, "Matthew xxviii 16–20 and the Design of the First Gospel," *JSNT* 10 (1981): 2–18; D. P. Scaer, "The Relation of Matthew 28:16–20 to the Rest of the Gospel," *CTQ* 55 (1991): 245–66.

[26] See J. D. Kingsbury, "The Composition and Christology of Matt 28:16–20," *JBL* 93 (1974): 573–74; A. Schlatter, *Der Evangelist Matthäus* (Stuttgart: Calwer, 1948), 801: "the ending of the first Gospel [is] . . . written by Mt."; G. D. Kilpatrick, *The Origins of the Gospel According to St Matthew* (Oxford: Clarendon, 1946), 48–49; and D. J. Bosch, *Transforming Mission: Paradigm Shifts in Theology of Mission*, American Society of Missiology Series 16 (Maryknoll, NY: Orbis, 1991), 57, who calls this the "most Matthean" pericope in the entire Gospel. See also J. La-Grand, *The Earliest Christian Mission to 'All Nations' in the Light of Matthew's Gospel* (Grand Rapids: Eerdmans, 1999), 235–47, whose chapter on the "Great Commission" is given almost entirely to a discussion and defense of the passage's authenticity.

[27] See P. T. O'Brien, "The Great Commission of Matthew 28:18–20: A Missionary Mandate or Not?" *RTR* 35 (1976): 66–71.

kingdoms (enthronement);[28] by assuring the disciples of his continuing presence, Jesus reaffirms his covenant with them (covenant renewal); and, reminiscent of OT commissioning narratives, Jesus issues to his followers his final charge (commissioning).[29] In the end, it is not any particular genre, or even a combination of these, that accurately describes Matthew's final pericope. The evangelist rather brings his own Gospel to his own intended conclusion.[30]

The commission is predicated upon the giving of "all authority . . . in heaven and on earth" to Jesus by the Father (Matt 28:18; an instance of the "divine passive").[31] Jesus' authority is comprehensive ("all"). In context, it may be inferred that the authority given to Jesus pertains to his mission, to be carried out through the disciples as his emissaries, on the basis of his word. The image in mind here may be that of a victorious military general who assures his followers of his unlimited authority.[32]

On this basis, Jesus' disciples are to "go . . . and make disciples." The aorist participle "go" *(poreuthentes)* modifies the aorist impera-

---

[28] This is suggested by O. Michel, "The Conclusion of Matthew's Gospel: A Contribution to the History of the Easter Message," in G. Stanton, ed., *The Interpretation of Matthew*, IRT 3 (Philadelphia: Fortress, 1983), 36 and adopted, among others, by Bornkamm, Barth and Held, *Tradition and Interpretation in Matthew*, 133–34. T. L. Donaldson, *Jesus on the Mountain: A Study in Matthean Typology*, JSNTSS 8 (Sheffield: JSOT, 1985), 181–88 contends that many important features of Dan 7:13–14 are missing in Matt 28:16–20: the coming on the clouds of heaven, the terms *basileia, doxa,* and the term "Son of Man" itself. He prefers to view the mountain setting, the terms *edothē, exousia,* and "Son" Christology as pointers to a background of a Zion eschatology.

[29] Note, however, that this commissioning is given to a group rather than to individuals as in OT narratives.

[30] See D. J. Bosch, "The Structure of Mission: An Exposition of Matthew 28:16–20," in W. R. Shenk, ed., *Exploring Church Growth* (Grand Rapids: Eerdmans, 1983), 222: "we have here a pericope which is *sui generis* and eludes the labels of form criticism."

[31] A. McNicol, "Discipleship as Mission: A Missing Dimension in Contemporary Discussion on Matthew 28:18–20," *Christian Studies* 10 (1989): 37, plausibly suggests that Matt 28:18–20, the last unit in Matthew, echoes 2 Chr 36:22–23, the last unit in the Hebrew Bible. LaGrand, *Earliest Christian Mission*, 238, referring to K. Barth, "An Exegetical Study of Matthew 28:16–20," in Gerald H. Anderson, ed., *The Theology of the Christian Mission* (Nashville/New York: Abingdon, 1961), 56, considers Matt 28:18b "the decisive fulfillment of 10.23."

[32] See P. Borgen, *Early Christianity and Hellenistic Judaism* (Edinburgh: T. & T. Clark, 1996), 59–60. Also K. L. Sparks, "Gospel as Conquest: Mosaic Typology in Matthew 28:16–20," *CBQ* 68 (2006): 651–63, who notes the contrast between Moses and Joshua, who upon entering the Promised Land were instructed to *conquer by killing* the Canaanites, and Jesus, whose vision was that of *converting* the Canaanites (Matt 15:21–28), and in fact all the nations (including believing Jews).

tive "make disciples" *(mathēteusate)*[33] as an auxiliary reinforcing the action of the main verb.[34] Jesus' followers must "go" in order to "make disciples." "All the nations" includes Israel.[35] The two present participles "baptizing" (*baptizontes*) and "teaching" (*didaskontes*) specify the manner in which disciples are to be made.[36] In both cases, further qualifiers are given. Baptism is to be administered in (*eis*, lit. "into") the name (singular) of the Father, the Son, and the Holy Spirit, one of the most explicit Trinitarian formulas in the entire NT.[37]

In light of the fact that the early church is shown to have baptized in the name of Jesus Christ (*Iēsou Christou*; Acts 2:38; 10:48) or "the Lord Jesus" (*kuriou Iēsou*; Acts 8:16; 19:5) and Paul refers merely to baptism in the name of Christ (*Christon [Iēsoun]*; Gal 3:27; Rom 6:3), the question arises whether this formulation reflects later baptismal practice. If Matthew was written prior to AD 70, however, there is hardly enough time for a Trinitarian practice of baptism to evolve if this was not already taught by Jesus himself as Matthew's Gospel indicates. It appears more likely that the early church felt no contradiction between Jesus' command to baptize in the name of the Father, the Son, and the Holy Spirit and its practice of baptizing in the name of Jesus, since the latter implied the former.

Regarding teaching, the disciples are enjoined to teach others "to observe everything I have commanded you" (Matt 28:20a; see Deut 4:1; 6:1). This charge indicates that mission entails the nurturing of

[33] The term occurs elsewhere only in 13:52; 27:57; and Acts 14:21.

[34] See 2:8; 9:13; 10:7; 11:4; 17:27; 28:7; see also 2:13,20; 5:24; 6:6; 9:6,18; 10:12; 21:2; 22:13. See Donaldson, *Jesus on the Mountain*, 184; O'Brien, "Great Commission," 72–73. Note that the present construction (preceding participle + imperative) occurs seventeen times in Matthew, only once in Mark, twenty-nine times in Luke/Acts, four times each in the Pauline and Petrine corpus, and once each in Hebrews and Jude; it does not occur at all in the Johannine writings. The occurrence of the construction in Mark 16:15 suggests assimilation to Matt 28:19. See C. Rogers, "The Great Commission," *BibSac* 130 (1973): 258–67.

[35] See 24:9,14; 25:32; see 21:43. The phrase "all the nations" (*panta ta ethnē*) also appears in Gen 18:18 LXX and 22:18 LXX (see Gen 12:3 LXX).

[36] Doriani, "Matthew 28:18–20," 36–37, distinguishes between three options of taking the participles, modal (manner), means, and imperatival, though by his own acknowledgment "there is some truth in each of these views" (p. 37), so that it is probably better to view manner/means and imperative jointly as implications inherent in the participial forms.

[37] On the use of the preposition *eis* with reference to baptism in the NT, see R. E. Averbeck, "The Focus of Baptism in the New Testament," *GTJ* 2/2 (Fall 1981): 267–68.

converts into the full obedience of faith, not merely the initial proclamation of the gospel. This was perhaps most admirably carried
out by the apostle Paul, whose ambition it was to "present everyone
mature in Christ" (Col 1:28). Finally, as the church disciples the
nations, it is assured of its risen Lord's continued spiritual presence
until his bodily return: "And remember, I am with you always, to
the end of the age." (Matt 28:20b; see Deut 31:6).

Jesus' command to his followers to make disciples of all nations
and to baptize and teach them clearly presupposes that the recipients of baptism and teaching are of sufficient age and maturity that
they can consciously choose to be baptized and be instructed in the
principles of the Christian faith. Even advocates of infant baptism
such as Daniel Doriani acknowledge that "doubtless, the conversion
of adults is on Jesus' mind in 28:18–20."[38] Doriani proceeds to assert, however, that "combined with the faith of an adult convert, or
with the faith of parents in the case of an infant, baptism both signifies and mediates a relationship with Jesus."[39] In fact, Doriani claims
that not only is there nothing in Matthew that "excludes children
from discipleship and baptism," but in fact "baptism is a valuable
means for discipling children," since "God in his grace can regenerate a child from the earliest age, even in conjunction with baptism
itself" (!), and "wise parents tell their children about their baptism,
perhaps on the occasion of an infant baptism in the church."[40]

Doriani's view is problematic for several reasons, however. First,
his assertion that baptism mediates a relationship with Jesus "combined . . . with the faith of parents in the case of an infant" is without basis in the text of Matt 28:18–20. Rather, it is clear that potential converts must respond, by way of repentance and faith in
Christ, *personally*, not "combined" with the faith of another person.
Infants are unable to repent or exercise personal faith in Christ in
any meaningful sense and should therefore not be the subject of
baptism judged by Jesus' "Great Commission."

[38] Doriani, "Matthew 28:18–20," 41.
[39] Ibid.
[40] Ibid.

For this reason also, second, Doriani's assertion that "God in his grace can regenerate a child from the earliest age, even in conjunction with baptism itself," is precarious at several levels. Since regeneration occurs upon personal repentance and faith in Christ (e.g., John 1:12–13; 3:3–8; Tit 3:5), and since, as has just been stated, infants are incapable of exercising personal repentance and faith, how can "a child from the earliest age" be regenerated? Judging by the teaching of Scripture, this seems to be impossible. Moreover, to speak, as Doriani does, of regeneration "even in conjunction with baptism itself" seems to point to baptismal regeneration, which clearly runs counter to biblical teaching (though a critique of this notion is beyond the scope of the present essay).

Third, to present baptism as a "valuable means for discipling children" also runs counter to the Matthean "Great Commission" passage, where baptism is presented as a corollary of Christian discipleship, not a teaching tool for children in hindsight looking back at their baptism as infants. This is clearly a revisionist view of Christian baptism that does not flow from textual exegesis but imports a rationale that is foreign to the text itself. It would seem to be more appropriate to wait until a person is able to exercise personal repentance and faith and then to instruct him or her about the meaning of baptism and subsequently to baptize them.

Finally, regarding Doriani's point that nothing in Matthew "excludes children from discipleship and baptism" (an argument from silence), it may be responded that there is equally nothing in Matthew that suggests that infants ought to be baptized or are capable of conversion. Moreover, a big part of the problem of Doriani's argument is that he fails clearly to distinguish between infants and older children. Jesus' invitation for children to come to him (Matt 19:13–15 pars.), for instance, clearly implies that these children were old enough to walk and on some level able to respond to him.[41] Even so, there is no mention of baptism in that passage, so that it seems questionable to use this reference to support the notion of infant baptism. While a ten year-old child, for example, may be capable of

---

[41] In the Lukan parallel the children are brought to Jesus, but see the note below as to why such does not establish the case for infant baptism.

responding to the gospel by way of repentance and faith, and hence
could legitimately request baptism, this would seem to be precluded
in the case of a six month-old infant. For these reasons we conclude,
against Doriani, that an argument for infant baptism cannot be sustained from the Matthean "Great Commission" passage.[42]

In comparison with Mark, Matthew's references to baptism and
the Baptist, then, are as follows:

Mk 1:4–9: John's baptism, b. of Jesus	Mt 3:1–16: John's baptism, b. of Jesus
—	Mt 11:11–12: John's greatness
Mk 6:14,24–25: John's beheading	Mt 14:1–8: John's beheading
Mk 8:28: Jesus = John the Baptist?	Mt 16:14: Jesus = John the B?
Mk 9:13: Elijah has come	Mt 17:13: The Baptist is Elijah
Mk 10:38–39: Jesus' future "baptism"	[Mt 20:22–23: "baptism" not included]
Mk 11:30: Source of John's baptism	Mt 21:25: Source of John's baptism
—	Mt 28:16–20: "Great Commission"

The above chart indicates that Matthew includes all of Mark's passages, with the partial exception of the reference to Jesus' future
"baptism" in Mark 10:38–39 (see Matt 20:22–23). In addition,
Matthew contains two additional important references, Jesus' teaching regarding John's greatness (Matt 11:11–12; also in Luke) and the
"Great Commission" (Matt 28:16–20; see Luke 24:44). These are
significant additions indeed, providing more material on John the
Baptist's role within the larger context of salvation history and the
risen Lord's command for his followers to disciple the nations, bap-

[42] Douglas Wilson claims that infants should be baptized because they are members of
Christ's kingdom (Matt 19:14; Mark 10:14; Luke 18:15–16). See *To a Thousand Generations—Infant Baptism: Covenant Mercy for the People of God* (Moscow, Idaho: Canon Press, 1996), 16–17.
The argument here is remarkably weak. First, it should be noted that the text says nothing about
baptism. Second, if we were to follow Wilson's argument then all infants should be baptized,
not only the children of believers. Wilson smuggles in from his own theology the idea that Jesus
speaks here only of the children of believers. But this is not what the text says. Jesus says that
the kingdom belongs to children in general, not merely children of believers. Third, Wilson
misinterprets what Jesus teaches here. Jesus does not say that children are members of the kingdom here. Carson rightly says Jesus encourages the children to come to him "not because the
kingdom of heaven belongs to them, but because the kingdom of heaven belongs to those like
them (so also Mark and Luke, stressing childlike faith)." See D. A. Carson, "Matthew," *EBC*, ed.
F. E. Gaebelein (Grand Rapids: Zondervan, 1984), 8:420.

tizing them in the name of the Father, Son, and Spirit, and teaching them to obey all of Jesus' commands.

Baptism in the Gospel of Luke

As in the other Synoptic Gospels, the account of John the Baptist's ministry and of his baptism of Jesus is a foundational passage in Luke (3:1–22). As in Matthew, Luke identifies John's baptism as a "baptism of repentance for the forgiveness of sins" (Luke 3:3) and recounts the Baptist's denunciation of people's presumption upon their Abrahamic descent (Luke 3:7–9). In addition to Matthew, Luke provides examples of what repentance meant in practical terms for the crowds, tax-collectors, and soldiers baptized by John (Luke 3:10–14). Also in addition to Matthew, Luke explicitly acknowledges that many were wondering if John could be the Messiah (Luke 3:15). In response, Luke recounts the Baptist's message in terms identical to Matthew (Luke 3:16–18; see Acts 1:5).[43]

As does Matthew (11:2–19), Luke also records the inquiry of John's disciples concerning whether or not Jesus was the Messiah (7:18–35). Overall, Luke's and Matthew's accounts resemble each other very closely, except for one additional parenthetical statement made by Luke in vv. 29–30: "And when all the people, including the tax collectors, heard this, they acknowledged God's way of righteousness, because they had been baptized with John's baptism. But since the Pharisees and experts in the law had not been baptized by him, they rejected the plan of God for themselves." By this statement Luke connects the present with the earlier account of tax-collectors being baptized by John the Baptist in Luke 3:12–14 (see above), contrasting their openness to the ways of God with the obduracy of Israel's religious leaders. Once again, this underscores the connection between the ministries of John the Baptist and Jesus.

---

[43] R. J. Erickson, "The Jailing of John and the Baptism of Jesus: Luke 3:19–21," *JETS* 36 (1993): 455–66, claims that Luke's reference to the Baptist's imprisonment in 3:19–20 even prior to Jesus' baptism by John (see Mark 1:14) is evidence of Luke's "antibaptistic polemic" (466). More likely, however, the order "represents a literary preference to present John and then focus on Jesus" (D. L. Bock, *Luke*, BECNT [Grand Rapids: Baker, 1996], 1:327).

Tax-collectors' receptivity to Jesus' ministry and the Jewish leaders' opposition to it thus find precursors in the identical attitudes of these groups toward the ministry of John the Baptist.

As do the other Synoptists, Luke records Jesus' disciples' acknowledgment that some regarded Jesus as (the raised) John the Baptist (Luke 9:19; cp. Matt 16:14; Mark 8:28). Luke also notes a Pharisee's surprise when he sees that Jesus did not "wash" *(baptizō)* before the meal (Luke 11:38; cp. Matt 15:2; Mark 7:5).

As does Mark (though not Matthew), although in a different context (Mark 10:38–39; see Matt 20:22–23), Luke records Jesus speaking about a future "baptism" he must undergo (Luke 12:50), indicating that Jesus may have spoken of this subject repeatedly. Again the context is judgment: Jesus has come "to bring fire on the earth," and has come, not to bring peace on earth, but division (Luke 12:49,51; cp. Matt 10:34,36). This suggests that the "baptism" includes the persecution issuing in Jesus' crucifixion interpreted as part of an eschatological tribulation.[44] As Bock states, Jesus "faces a period of being uniquely inundated with God's judgment" (Ps 18:4,16; 42:7; 69:1–2; Isa 8:7–8; 30:27–28; Jonah 2:3–6), and only subsequent to this "baptism" can God's plan and the coming of the Spirit's judging work of fire proceed.[45]

The sole reference involving the use of *baptō* in Luke's Gospel speaks of Lazarus "dipping" the tip of his finger in water in the parable of the Rich Man and Lazarus (Luke 16:24). The final reference to baptism in Luke is found in the context of Jesus' familiar challenge for his opponents to identify the authority behind John's baptism (Luke 20:4; see Mark 11:30; Matt 21:25).

The following chart provides a comparison between Luke's treatment of baptism and John the Baptist's ministry and the treatments in Mark and Matthew:

---

[44] Dockery, "Baptism," 58. It is also possible, as W. F. Flemington, "Baptism," *IDB* 1:349, suggests, that a parallelism is intended between Jesus' first baptism (by John), which inaugurated his ministry in Palestine, and Jesus' "baptism" by crucifixion, which "inaugurated a wider ministry, unfettered by the limitations of the earthly mission." This would be similar in import to Jesus' reference to his disciples' "greater works" in John 14:12.

[45] See Bock, *Luke*, 2:1193–94, with reference to Creed, Plummer, and Oepke.

Mk 1:4–9/Mt 3:1–16: John's b., b. of Jesus	Lk 3:1–22: John's b., b. of Jesus
— /Mt 11:11–12: John's greatness	Luke 7:18–35: John's greatness
Mk 6:14–25/Mt 14:1–8: John's beheading	— (cp. Lk 3:19–20)
Mk 8:28/Mt 16:14: Jesus = John the Baptist?	Lk 9:19: Jesus = John the Baptist?
Mk 9:13/Mt 17:13: The Baptist is Elijah	—
Mk 10:38–39 (cp. Mt 20:22–23): Jesus' "b."	cp. Luke 12:50: Jesus' future "b."
Mk 11:30/Mt 21:25: Source of John's b.	Lk 20:24: Source of John's b.
— /Mt 28:16–20: "Great Commission"	— (cp. Lk 24:44)

Overall, Luke's treatment is comparable and quite similar to that of the other Synoptic writers. On the one hand, Luke does not include the account (quite extensive especially in Mark) of John's beheading or the identification of the Baptist with Elijah (Mark 9:13/Matt 17:13). He also does not have anything comparable to the statement in Matthew's "Great Commission" passage involving baptism (though see Luke 24:44). On the other hand, Luke has an equivalent statement to Mark 10:38–39 speaking of Jesus' future "baptism" (Luke 12:50).[46] Also, Luke, like Matthew (11:11–12), includes Jesus' discussion of the Baptist's greatness (Luke 7:18–35). Luke appears to be less interested in the Baptist's fate subsequent to his imprisonment and seems to have no special interest in baptism, marking out Matt 28:16–20 as a truly exceptional passage on baptism in the Synoptic corpus.

Baptism in the Gospel of John

John uniformly uses the term *baptizō* with reference to baptism.[47] His usage is limited to three pericopes.[48] The first, similar to the

---

[46] The reference to baptism is absent in the Matthean parallel in Matt 20:22–23.

[47] John does not use the nouns *baptisma/mos* or *baptistēs*. There are also two references to *baptō* ("dip") in John 13:26.

[48] Against Hartman, "Baptism," *ABD* 1:592; H. Mueller, "Baptism (in the Bible)," *NCE* 2:56; and many Church Fathers, the reference to being born of water and spirit in John 3:5 most likely does not refer to baptism, which would not have been a meaningful subject for Jesus to discuss with Nicodemus. See A. J. Köstenberger, *John* (BECNT; Grand Rapids: Baker, 2004), 123, n 26. For a survey, see J. E. Morgan-Wynne, "References to Baptism in the Fourth Gospel," in *Baptism, the New Testament and the Church*, ed. S. E. Porter and A. R. Cross, JSNTSup 171 (Sheffield: Sheffield Academic Press, 1999), 116–35, esp. 116–21; also the essay in the same volume by J. R. Michaels, "Baptism and Conversion in John: A Particular Baptist Reading," 136–56.

Synoptics, concerns the Baptist's ministry of baptism (John 1:25–33). In this passage, the Pharisees challenge John to explain why he baptized if he was not the Messiah, or Elijah, or the Prophet (John 1:25). This seems to imply that for a recognized end-time figure such as the three personages just mentioned, it would have been considered legitimate, if not expected, to engage in a ministry of baptism. The objection in the Baptist's case was that they did not see him as a figure clearly related to OT expectation.

In John 1:26,33, John acknowledges that he baptized with water but that Jesus would baptize with the Holy Spirit. This is similar to the Synoptics, except that John's Gospel does not include the reference to baptism by "fire" (Matt 3:11; Luke 3:16). John's Gospel explicitly states that the reason for John's baptism was that the Messiah "might be revealed to Israel" (John 1:31). Hence John's baptism was not an end in itself but had a Christological orientation. Likewise, repentance or works in keeping with it were not the ultimate goal, but rather people's preparation for the Messiah. More explicitly than the Synoptics, John draws a connection between the Spirit descending on Jesus at his baptism and Jesus' future baptizing of others with the same Spirit (John 1:32–34).[49]

The second reference to baptism in John's Gospel intriguingly speaks of an overlapping period prior to John's imprisonment (John 3:24) in which both the Baptist and Jesus (or rather, Jesus' disciples; John 4:2) were engaged in ministries involving baptism.[50] John 3:23

---

[49] Bennema, "Spirit-Baptism in the Fourth Gospel," 35–60, esp. 39, contends that the focus of John 1:33 is not on the Spirit as a future gift bestowed by Jesus on others but on the Spirit as the means by which the Messiah will act toward Israel by way of "cleansing through revelation" (p. 53). However, this is rendered unlikely by the Synoptic parallels (and Acts 1–2) and the acknowledgment in John's Gospel that the giving of the Spirit had to await the period subsequent to Jesus' exaltation (John 7:39; see 20:22). The same critique also applies to A. W. D. Hui, "John the Baptist and Spirit-Baptism," *EQ* 71 (1999): 99–115, who claims that "John did not expect [that] the Coming One would bestow the Holy Spirit upon his followers."

[50] Webb, "Jesus' Baptism," 21–22, with reference to Murphy-O'Connor and R. E. Brown, suggests that Jesus, subsequent to his baptism by John, "probably remained with him for some time in the role of disciple" and later, "in alignment and participation with John and his movement, . . . also engaged in a baptizing ministry near John. Although he was still a disciple of John, Jesus perhaps should be viewed at this point as John's right-hand man or protégé." Indeed, Mark 1:14 reports that Jesus' Galilean ministry commenced once John was put in prison. The public's difficulty in sorting out the relationship between John and Jesus (e.g., Matt 16:14; Mark 6:14), too, may point in this direction. On the other hand, according to John 3:22 and

places Jesus and his disciples in the Judean countryside, administering baptism, subsequent to Jesus' attendance of the Passover in Jerusalem. John, too, was baptizing at Aenon near Salim (John 3:23). In light of the absence of references to baptism later on in any of the Gospels, it appears that the baptizing activity of Jesus and his disciples is limited to the early stages of Jesus' ministry. This marks off John's baptism as operating within the framework of OT expectations of righteousness in contrast to the early Church, which administered baptism in obedience to Jesus' command as a rite of initiation into the new messianic community.[51]

Upon hearing of Jesus' baptizing activity, John's disciples were concerned about Jesus' success and approached the Baptist (John 3:26). From their question, it is apparent that Jesus already had a large following. The Baptist, in a probable allusion to Mal 3:2, acknowledged that he was not the Messiah, but that he was "sent ahead" of him, and that his attitude was like that of the friend of the bridegroom, who shared in the latter's joy (John 3:27–29): "He must increase, but I must decrease." (John 3:30). As John 4:1–2 makes clear, this had in fact begun to take place. The reference to Jesus "making and baptizing more disciples" than John reflects the pattern described in the Matthean "Great Commission," indicating that baptism signaled the conversion and commitment to a new kind of lifestyle and discipleship.

The final reference to the Baptist in John's Gospel finds Jesus returning to the place where John had been baptizing in the early days. Many came to Jesus there, saying that while John never performed any signs, all that he said about Jesus was true (10:40–41). This is in keeping with the fourth evangelist's consistent portrait of the Baptist first and foremost as a witness to Jesus, whose testimony was both true and of

4:1, Jesus engaged in a separate and distinct ministry, including baptism, already prior to John's imprisonment (see 3:24), and there is little indication in these texts that Jesus served as John's "right-hand man or protégé." Apparently he had begun his own ministry after his baptism by John, with John continuing his own ministry until his imprisonment.

[51] See Dockery, "Baptism," 57. It is unclear whether the Eleven, or other followers of Jesus during his earthly ministry, were (re)baptized subsequent to the pouring out of the Spirit at Pentecost, though this may be suggested by John 19:1–7. Clearly, water baptism, as a sign of repentance, was mandated for the recipients of Peter's Pentecost message, which closely links water and Spirit baptism (Acts 2:38).

an abiding nature. Jesus' actual baptism by John, while presupposed, is not actually narrated in John's Gospel. This places John's baptism within a larger messianic framework and marks it as temporary and subservient to the Baptist's larger role as a witness to Jesus.

The references to baptism in John's Gospel indicate that, as in many other respects, the fourth evangelist charts his own course. Apart from the overlap between John 1:25–33 and the Synoptic parallels, John does not include any of the other pericopes involving the Baptist or baptism found in the Synoptics. At the same time, he provides the interesting supplement concerning the overlapping time period of John's and Jesus' baptizing ministries. Though he does feature a final commissioning (John 20:21–23), John does not include baptism in it, as in the Matthean "Great Commission."

Summary and Implications

Relatively few passages in the Gospels mention baptism. Most of these relate to the baptism of John the Baptist, which fulfilled an important, albeit transitional purpose and serve to clarify the role of the Baptist and his baptism with respect to Jesus. The purpose of John's baptism was to prepare the way for the Messiah, Jesus, by calling people to repentance and urging them to perform works in keeping with it in anticipation of the coming of God's kingdom in and through the Messiah.

John's Gospel also speaks of a baptism administered by Jesus (or rather, his disciples) at a time when John, too, still was active in his ministry. There is very little direct evidence available to assess the significance of this baptism in relation to the baptism performed by John the Baptist on the one hand, or to the baptism mandated in the Matthean "Great Commission" passage on the other. Apparently, this baptism belonged to the transitional period between the Baptist's and Jesus' ministries. Reference is also made to a future time when Jesus will baptize with the Holy Spirit (and "fire"), pointing to the outpouring of the Spirit at Pentecost by the exalted Jesus (Acts 2:3; see John 14:26; 15:26; Acts 1:5).[52]

---

[52] See Averbeck, "Focus of Baptism in the New Testament," 289.

The study of the references to baptism in the Gospels yields the following major implications for the Christian understanding of baptism. First, the rite of baptism is *designed for believers who have repented of their sin and have put their faith in God and in his Christ.* Believer's baptism is presupposed by both John's baptism and the Matthean "Great Commission" passage. This does not mean that fairly young people, say, at the age of seven or eight, should be barred from receiving believer's baptism if they have genuinely understood the implications of Christ's death on their behalf and have repented of their sin and placed their faith in Jesus Christ.[53] However, the Gospels provide no evidence or support for the baptism of infants, nor does the principle of believer's baptism enunciated in the Gospels allow for such a practice.[54] In fact, if (as is sometimes alleged) Jews were predisposed to baptize infants owing to the parallel with circumcision, it is remarkable—in fact, striking—that there is no mention of infant baptism anywhere in Jesus' teaching recorded in the Gospels.

Second, baptism is *an essential part of Christian discipleship.* This is clear from the Matthean "Great Commission" passage, where disciple-making is said to consist of baptizing converts and of teaching them to obey the commands of Jesus (see also John 4:1).[55] An obedient church will take to heart the risen Christ's command to engage in mission and evangelistic preaching, seeking to engender conversions that ensue in baptism, instruction, and Christian growth. On an individual level, those who have placed their faith in Jesus Christ and have repented of their sin must be baptized as part of their Christian discipleship. While there may be a period of instruction preceding baptism, no undue obstacle should be placed in the path of a person who is genuinely converted and desirous of baptism.

Third, the *mode* of John's and Jesus' baptism was most likely that of *immersion.*[56] This is suggested by the root meaning of the word

---

[53] Though not all would agree; space constraints prohibit a full discussion of the issue here.

[54] See A. T. Robertson, "Baptism: Baptist View," *ISBE* 1:417.

[55] See Dockery, "Baptism," 58, who cites Matt 28:19 and John 3:22–24.

[56] See Webb, "Jesus' Baptism," 11, 28 n 46; Beasley-Murray, "Baptism," *NIDNTT* 1:144; A. T. Robertson, "Baptism: Baptist View," *ISBE* 1:416.

baptō, "to dip" (e.g., Josh 3:15 LXX; Ruth 2:14 LXX), of which *baptizō*, "to baptize," is an intensive or frequentative form. It is also indicated by the LXX usage of *baptizō* with reference to immersion (see 2 Kgs 5:14). Another piece of supporting evidence is the statement that Jesus "came up immediately from the water" subsequent to his baptism (Matt 3:16 par. Mark 1:10, *euthus anebē/anabainōn apo/ek tou hudatos*). While there are differences of view as to the way in which baptism by immersion ought to be stipulated in church polity, evidence from the Gospels suggests that this was in fact the NT and early church's mode of baptism.

Fourth, theologically, *water baptism presupposes spiritual regeneration* as a prevenient and primary work of God in and through the person of the Holy Spirit. This follows plainly from the Baptist's announcement that the Messiah would baptize people in the Spirit. Thus repentance from sin and faith in Christ, accompanied by regeneration, are logically and chronologically prior to water baptism. This, in turn, puts water baptism in proper perspective. There is no warrant in the Gospels for the notion of baptismal regeneration.[57] There is also no support for viewing baptism as a sacrament, a sacred rite which mediates some sort of special grace to the recipient of baptism by virtue of the intrinsic efficacy of the rite (*ex opere operato*).[58]

---

[57] Robertson, "Baptism: Baptist View," *ISBE* 1:416–17

[58] Against B. Neunheuser, "Baptism," *Sacramentum Mundi: An Encyclopedia of Theology*, ed. K. Rahner et al. (New York: Herder & Herder, 1968), 1:136–44, who cites Tertullian: "Felix sacramentum aquae nostrae."

BAPTISM IN LUKE-ACTS

Robert H. Stein[*]

Within the NT the verb "to baptize" (*baptizō*) and the noun "baptism" (*baptisma*) are found ninety-six times. Almost half of these instances are found in Luke-Acts:[1] *baptizō* (ten times in Luke [Luke 3:7,12,16(2),21(2); 7:29,30; 11:38; 12:50]; twenty-one times in Acts [Acts 1:5(2); 2:38,41; 8:12,13,16,36,38; 9:18; 10:47,48; 11:16(2); 16:15,33; 18:8; 19:3,4,5; 22:16]) and *baptisma* (four times in Luke [Luke 3:3; 7:29; 12:50; 20:4]; six times in Acts [Acts 1:22; 10:37; 13:24; 18:25; 19:3,4]). The name "Baptist" (*baptistēs* is associated with John, the forerunner of Jesus, twelve times in the NT and three of these occur in Luke (7:20,33; 9:19). In the vast majority of instances the verb and noun refer to the act of baptism in water and/or the initiation rite associated with this act, whether with respect to John the Baptist (Luke 3:3,7,12,16a,21[2]; 7:29[2],30; 20:4; Acts 1:5a,22; 10:37; 11:16b; 13:24; 18:25; 19:3–4) or Christian baptism (Luke 3:16b; Acts 1:5b; 2:38,41; 8:12–13,16,36,38; 9:18; 10:47–48; 11:16c; 16:15,33; 18:8; 19:5; 22:16). In one instance (Luke 11:38), the verb is used with respect to the "washing"[2] of one's hands before eating, and in another (Luke 12:50) it is used as a metaphor for an immersion into suffering and death.[3] Some have argued that the references to "the baptism of the Holy Spirit (Matt 3:11; Mark 1:8; Luke 3:16; John 1:33; Acts 1:5, 11:16; and 1 Cor 12:13 are purely metaphorical in nature and do not refer to the conversion-initiatory rite of water baptism in Jesus' name.[4] It is incorrect, however, to understand this expression as

---

[*] Robert H. Stein received his Ph.D. from Princeton Theological Seminary, and is Senior Professor of New Testament Interpretation at The Southern Baptist Theological Seminary in Louisville, Kentucky.

[1] Luke was the author of both Luke and Acts, and baptism plays a central role, especially in Acts, it seems advisable to include a separate chapter on baptism in Luke-Acts.

[2] All quotations from Scripture come from the English Standard Version.

[3] G. R. Beasley-Murray, *Jesus and the Kingdom of God* (Grand Rapids: Eerdmans, 1986), 247–52.

[4] See J. D. G. Dunn, *Baptism in the Holy Spirit*, SBTSS 15 (London: SCM Press, 1970), 109–13, 127–31, 139–46, and "'Baptized' as Metaphor," in *Baptism, the New Testament and the Church*, ed. S. E. Porter and A. R. Cross, JSNTSup 171 (Sheffield: Sheffield Academic Press, 1999), 294–310.

contrasting the water baptism of John the Baptist that was associated
with repentance and the forgiveness of sins with a purely spiritual
"baptism of the Holy Spirit." These two baptisms are not an example
of antithetical parallelism but rather of step parallelism in which the
second baptism is an advancement on and fulfillment of the first.[5]
They are not portrayed in Luke-Acts (Luke 3:16; Acts 1:5; 11:16) as
standing in opposition to one another but in apposition.[6] Christian
baptism is not exclusive, but inclusive, with respect to the baptism
of John; the former is not only a baptism of repentance with water,
but a baptism of repentance with water and the Holy Spirit as well.[7]
Christian baptism and the baptism of John both involve immersion
in water, repentance, and the promise of forgiveness of sins, but, in
addition, Christian baptism involves the gift of the Spirit (2:38),[8]
i.e., the "baptism of the Spirit."

Luke's concern in Acts involves not so much explaining the meaning of baptism (contrast Rom 6:1–11) as describing the practice of
baptism in the early church. In so doing he shows how it is intimately
associated with the conversion-initiation experience of becoming a
Christian. When he refers to Christian baptism in Acts (and in his
Gospel as well), he describes the experience of baptism as it is related
to the process of becoming a Christian. In addition, Luke illustrates
how in that process repentance, faith, confession of Jesus as Christ
and Lord, baptism, and receiving the Spirit are interrelated and are all
integral parts of the experience of becoming a Christian.[9]

Baptism And Becoming A Christian

Within Luke-Acts baptism is an initiatory rite intimately associated with conversion to Christianity. This is seen by its association
with other aspects involved in becoming a Christian.

[5] A. R. Cross, "Spirit- and Water-Baptism in 1 Corinthians 12:13," in *Dimensions of Baptism*, ed. S. E. Porter and A. R. Cross, JSNTSup 234 (Sheffield: Sheffield Academic Press, 2002), 131.

[6] J. B. Green, "From 'John's Baptism' to 'Baptism in the Name of the Lord Jesus': The Signifi-cance of Baptism in Luke-Acts," in *Baptism, the New Testament and the Church*, ed. S. E. Porter and A. R. Cross, JSNTSup 171 (Sheffield: Sheffield Academic Press, 1999), 168.

[7] See K. McDonnell and G. T. Montague, *Christian Initiation and Baptism in the Holy Spirit: Evidence from the First Eight Centuries* (Collegeville: The Liturgical Press, 1991), 27.

[8] Unless designated all references come from Acts.

[9] See below section four, "The Multifaceted Nature of the Conversion Experience in Acts."

The Association of Repentance and Baptism

One of the important components of the human response to becoming a Christian involves "repentance." In this respect Christian
baptism follows the baptism of John the Baptist. John's proclamation "Repent, for the kingdom of heaven is at hand" (Matt 3:1) gives
to his practice of baptism its description as a "baptism of repentance" (Mark 1:4; Luke 3:3; Acts 13:24; 19:4) or a "repentance-baptism." The message of repentance was likewise an integral part of
Jesus' message (Matt 4:17; Mark 1:15), "Repent, for the kingdom of
heaven/God is at hand") and that of the early church. To the question raised by Peter's sermon on the day of Pentecost "What shall
we do?" (2:37), Peter replies, "*Repent* and *be baptized* every one of
you in the name of Jesus Christ for the forgiveness of your sins, and
you will receive the gift of the Holy Spirit" (2:38).[10] Another time repentance and baptism are intimately associated is in 11:15–18. Here,
after Peter informs the Jerusalem church of his being sent to preach
the gospel to a Roman centurion named Cornelius (11:4–14) and
how the gift of the Spirit had come upon Cornelius and his household, so that he consequently baptized them,[11] the Jerusalem church
concludes "Then to the Gentiles also God has granted *repentance*
that leads to life" (11:18).[12]

To these can also be added the reference to the "disciples" in
Ephesus who had experienced John's baptism of *repentance* (19:4a)
and upon hearing the gospel message (19:4b) *were baptized* into
the Christian faith and received the gift of the Spirit (19:5–6).
There is much confusion as to the nature of the Ephesian "disci-

[10] No great weight should be put on the fact that the dual command in 2:38 involves a second person plural imperative ("You repent") and a third person singular imperative ("each one
of you be baptized"). The latter simply seeks to underscore emphatically the command to each
one addressed. Examples of the use of a second person plural imperative and a third person
singular imperative side by side can be found in Exod 16:29; Josh 6:10; 2 Kgs 10:19; Zech 7:10;
1 Macc 10:63 in the LXX and in *Did.* 15:3. See C. D. Osburn, "The Third Person Imperative in
Acts 2:38," *Restoration Quarterly* 26 (1983): 81–84.
   Italics added in Scripture references by the author for emphasis throughout the chapter.
[11] Paul's report to the Jerusalem church in 11:4–18 is a shorter summary of the incident
recorded in 10:1–48, but Luke expects his readers to remember the earlier account of the conversion of Cornelius (see especially 10:47–48) as they read 11:1–18.
[12] The call to repentance as a requirement for becoming a Christian is also found in 3:19;
5:31 (where it is associated with the forgiveness of sins as in 2:38); 17:30; 20:21; 26:20.

ples." Elsewhere in Acts the term "disciples" (19:1) always refers to Christians, and "believe" (19:2) ordinarily refers to Christian faith. However, in the other instances in Acts the noun "disciples" is always preceded by the article "the," and this suggests that these "disciples" in Ephesus were not part of "*the* disciples." Paul's reference to their need to believe in Jesus (19:4) and their lack of knowledge concerning the Holy Spirit (19:2) also suggest this. It is, however, their lack of the *sine qua non* of the Christian experience—the Holy Spirit—that clearly indicates that they were not Christians, for the litmus test that determines if a person is truly a Christian in Acts is the reception of the Spirit (19:2; 10:47; 11:17–18; also Rom 8:9–10; Gal 3:2). Luke's recording that Paul baptized these disciples "in the name of the Lord Jesus" (19:5) upon their hearing about Jesus (19:4) clearly indicates that he did not consider them Christians before.[13] It should be noted that in this account the need of repentance (whether preached by John the Baptist or the Christian church) along with Christian baptism is assumed as necessary and inseparable in the experience of conversion to the Christian faith.

The Association of *Faith* and *Baptism*

Examples in Acts abound in which Christian baptism and personal faith are intimately associated.

8:12–13 But when they *believed* Philip as he preached good news about the kingdom of God and the name of Jesus Christ, they *were baptized*, both men and women. Even Simon himself *believed*, and after *being baptized* he continued with Philip.

10:43–48a "To him all the prophets bear witness that everyone who *believes* in him receives forgiveness of sins through his name." While Peter was still saying these things, the Holy Spirit fell on all who heard the word. And the believers from among the circumcised who had come with Peter were amazed, because the gift of the Holy Spirit was poured out even on the Gentiles. For they were hearing them speaking in tongues and extolling God. Then Peter declared, "Can anyone withhold water for *baptizing* these people, who have received the Holy Spirit just as we have?" And he commanded them to *be baptized* in the name of Jesus Christ.

16:31–34 And they said, "*Believe* in the Lord Jesus, and you will be saved, you and your household." And they spoke the word of the Lord to him and

---

[13] See Dunn, *Baptism in the Holy Spirit*, 83–89.

to all who were in his house. And he took them the same hour of the night and washed their wounds; and he *was baptized* at once, he and all his family . . . And he rejoiced along with his entire household that he had *believed* in God.

18:8 Crispus, the ruler of the synagogue, *believed* in the Lord, together with his entire household. And many of the Corinthians hearing Paul *believed* and *were baptized.*

19:4–5 And Paul said, "John baptized with the baptism of repentance, telling the people to *believe* in the one who was to come after him, that is, Jesus." On hearing this, they *were baptized* in the name of the Lord Jesus

In the story of Philip and the Ethiopian eunuch it is clear that faith is assumed to be present when people are baptized:

> Then Philip opened his mouth, and beginning with this Scripture he told him the good news about Jesus. And as they were going along the road they came to some water, and the eunuch said, "See, here is water! What prevents me from being baptized?"[14] And he commanded the chariot to stop, and they both went down into the water, Philip and the eunuch, and he *baptized* him. And when they came up out of the water, the Spirit of the Lord carried Philip away, and the eunuch saw him no more, and went on his way rejoicing (8:35–36,38–39).

Although faith is not specifically mentioned, Luke clearly expects his readers to assume that the eunuch's hearing of the gospel message and his request to be baptized implies that he believed in Jesus (8:35–36). His subsequent "rejoicing" (8:39) further supports this.[15] Still another example of the tie between faith and baptism can be found in the conversion of Lydia. There we read that the Lord "opened her heart[16] to pay attention to what was said by Paul" (16:14) "and she was *baptized* (16:15a). After this Lydia responds, "If you have judged me to be *faithful* to the Lord" (16:15c).[17]

---

[14] The words "'If you believe with all you heart, you may.' And he replied, 'I believe that Jesus Christ is the Son of God'" are not found in the best Greek manuscripts (P[45, 74] ℵ A B C P Ψ) and should not be read. This scribal addition, however, does reveal that in the early church faith was viewed as a prerequisite for baptism.

[15] See Gal 3:26–27 and Col 2:12 where faith and baptism are intimately associated. Also Eph 5:26 where the "washing of water" probably refers to Christian baptism and "with the word" assumes the hearing of the word in faith.

[16] Note the relationship of the heart to saving in faith in Rom 10:9 ("if you confess with your mouth that Jesus is Lord and believe in your heart") and 10:10 ("For with the heart one believes").

[17] Note how other translations render this verse: "If you consider me a believer in the Lord" (HCSB, TNIV, and NAB and "Now that you have accepted me as a believer in the Lord" (REB).

Peter's command on the day of Pentecost to "Repent and be baptized" (2:38) assumes faith on the part of the individual for several
reasons. For one, repentance believes something, i.e., that repentance will bring about a change in one's condition. It has faith that
a repentance-faith will enable one to receive the forgiveness of sins
(2:38) and enter the kingdom of heaven/God (Matt 3:2; Mark 1:15).
Second, when one is baptized "in/into the name of Jesus/Lord Jesus/
Jesus Christ" (2:38; 8:16; 10:48; 19:5; see 1 Cor 1:13, 15), this assumes one knows something about Jesus Christ and believes something about him. In 3:16 the expression "his name," an abbreviation
for "the name of Jesus/Lord Jesus/Jesus Christ," is associated with
faith ("faith in his name"). This is essentially a synonym for "faith
in our Lord Jesus Christ" in 20:21. One should also note that "calling on his name" (22:16) and "everyone who calls on the name of
the Lord will be saved" (Rom 10:13; cp. Acts 2:21) are associated
with believing in Jesus (see Rom 10:9–10). Third, baptism is described in Acts as preceded by: the proclamation of the gospel (8:12;
see 22:14–16); receiving or welcoming the word (2:41; 8:4 and 14);
listening to all that God has commanded (10:33–43); having one's
heart opened (16:14); being faithful (16:15); etc. These all assume
the presence of faith. Thus, even if only repentance is mentioned
with respect to baptism in 2:38, faith is assumed, for "repentance"
refers to "repentance-faith."

On the other hand, in the story of the conversion of the Philippian
jailor, upon asking what he must do to be saved (16:30), Paul states,
"Believe in the Lord Jesus, and you will be saved, you and your
household" (16:31). We then read that the jailor and his whole family believed (see 16:34) and were baptized. Here repentance is not
mentioned, yet, due to previous references to the requirement of
repentance for baptism, Luke expects his readers to assume that repentance was also part of this act of faith, for faith refers to "faith-
repentance." This intimate association of repentance and faith is
also found in 20:20–21, where Paul tells the Ephesian elders, "I did
not shrink from declaring to you anything that was profitable, and
teaching you in public and from house to house, testifying both to

Jews and to Greeks of *repentance* toward God and of *faith* in our Lord Jesus Christ."[18]

The Association Of Repentance, Faith, Baptism, And The Gift Of The Spirit

In this section we shall seek to demonstrate that repentance, faith, baptism, and the reception of the Spirit are integrally related components in the conversion-initiatory rite of water baptism. This will be shown by the fact that repentance, faith, and baptism are all portrayed in Acts as resulting in the reception of the Holy Spirit. In the next section the integral relationship of repentance, faith, and baptism will be shown by the fact that each results in the forgiveness of sins, one of the blessings associated with conversion to Christianity.

The Association of *Repentance* and *the Gift of the Spirit*

The clearest references to repentance being associated with the gift of the Spirit are found in 2:38, 10:47–48, and 11:16–18. In Acts 2:37 upon hearing Peter's sermon in 2:14–36, the hearers are "cut to the heart" and ask Peter, "Brothers, what shall we do?" The aim that they have in mind is not explicitly stated in their request but is provided in Peter's reply: "*Repent* and *be baptized* every one of you in the name of Jesus Christ for *the forgiveness of your sins*, and you will receive *the gift of the Holy Spirit*." They are seeking two divine benefits: the forgiveness of sins and the gift of the Spirit (2:38). Two necessary human responses are mentioned for receiving these two divine benefits: repentance and baptism. The connection between repentance and receiving the gift of the Spirit is clear.

The second reference requires that we read the two accounts of Cornelius' conversion (10:1–48 and 11:1–18) together. Luke expects his readers to interpret the conclusion of the Jerusalem church that God has granted "repentance" to the Gentiles that leads to life

---

[18] See 11:21, where faith and "turning to the Lord," a synonym for repenting, are associated together. Also Mark 1:15 where repentance and faith are again closely associated, and it is difficult to think of the former without assuming the latter. They are inseparable, like two sides of the same coin.

(11:18) in light of God having given the gift of the Spirit to the Gentiles in 10:44–48. Because the Spirit came upon Cornelius and his family, Peter had baptized them and stayed in their home, the home of a non-kosher Gentile. When Peter returned to Jerusalem, certain conservative Jewish believers criticized him for staying and eating in a Gentile home (11:3). To stay in the home of an uncircumcised Gentile and to share in table fellowship involving non-kosher food and utensils was unthinkable to these Jewish Christians. Consequently, Peter told how God had led him to the home of Cornelius (11:4–14; see 10:9–24), where he preached the gospel message (11:15a; see 10:25–43). He told how, as he preached, the Spirit came upon Cornelius and his household (11:15–17b; see 10:44–46), so that he baptized them (11:17c; see 10:47–48). Upon hearing that the Spirit had come upon believing Gentiles, the Jerusalem church concluded that, since God had given his Spirit to the Gentile Cornelius and his house, God had accepted them, i.e., he had granted "repentance that leads to life" (11:18) to Gentiles as well as Jews. As a result of Cornelius having received the Spirit, the church now realized that Gentiles did not have to be circumcised and become Jews in order to become Christians. Contrary to the view of the more conservative Jewish believers, that Gentiles also needed to be circumcised and keep the Mosaic law to be saved (15:1, 5), all that was necessary was that they repent-believe-be baptized.

The Association of *Faith* and *the Gift of the Spirit*

In other instances, faith is associated with receiving the gift of the Spirit, but repentance is not necessarily mentioned. This is seen most clearly in the question Paul asked the "disciples" in Ephesus, "Did you receive *the Holy Spirit* when you *believed*" (19:2)? In 5:32 as well, it is those who obey God, i.e., those who "believe" (see Rom 10:16; Heb 3:18–19), that are given the Holy Spirit. In the conversion of Cornelius it is upon hearing the gospel message and being told, "everyone who *believes* in him receives forgiveness of sins through his name" (10:43), he receives *the gift of the Spirit* (10:44–46) and is baptized (10:47–48). Nothing is mentioned about his having repented at this point. When, however, the story of his conversion is retold by Peter to the church in Jerusalem (11:4–17), upon hearing that Cornelius and his family had received the gift of the Spirit, just like the Jewish Christians did at Pentecost when they believed (11:17), they conclude, "Then to the Gentiles also God has granted repentance that leads to life" (11:18c). Thus just as in 5:31 where Peter declares that in Christ God has "give(n) repentance to Israel and forgiveness of sins," so in 11:18 the Jerusalem church now concludes that "to the Gentiles also God has granted repentance that leads to life." The close association of faith and repentance in Acts is also seen in Acts 20:21 where Paul testifies to both Jews and Greeks "of repentance toward God and of faith in our Lord Jesus Christ."[19] Still another example of this close association is found in 13:24 where Paul states in the synagogue in Pisidian Antioch that John's baptism of repentance and proclamation of the coming of the Messiah finds fulfillment in the forgiveness of sins that comes through faith in Jesus (13:38).[20]

In describing the reception of the gift of the Spirit, Luke at times singles out only one component of the conversion process. In such instances, however, other components not explicitly mentioned are nevertheless assumed to be included. In 3:19, 17:30, and 26:20 repentance is mentioned as a necessary human response in the conversion experience but faith is not. In 17:30, however, it is clear that faith is assumed, for in 17:34 we read that the command to repent results in some men joining them and "believing," and 26:20 is a summary of God's commission to Paul in 26:18 that he should go to the Gentiles so that they may "turn from darkness to light and from the power of Satan to God [i.e., they should repent], that they may receive the forgiveness of sins and a place among those who are sanctified by faith in me." Similarly, in 2:38 "faith" is not mentioned as a requirement for receiving the Spirit; yet it is assumed. The assumption that faith is a necessary part of the human response that includes repentance (as well as confession and baptism) in becoming a Christian is evident if one adds to Peter's words in Acts 2:38 the

[19] See the classic summary of Jesus' message in Mark 1:15, "Repent and believe in the Gospel."

[20] See Gal 3:2 and Eph 1:13, where hearing the word of truth ("in faith" being assumed) leads to being sealed with [the gift of] the promised Holy Spirit.

following words found in italics, "Repent, and be baptized every one of you in the name of Jesus Christ for the forgiveness of your sins [*but you do not have to believe*], and you will receive the gift of the Holy Spirit." Such an addition would clearly be absurd. If one is baptized "in the name of Jesus/the Lord Jesus/Jesus Christ" (2:38; 8:16; 10:48; 19:5; see also the synonymous "into Christ Jesus" [Rom 6:3; Gal 3:27]), this assumes faith in Jesus, for in baptism one is "calling on his name" (22:16). The expression "into the name of Jesus/the Lord Jesus/Jesus Christ" serves to distinguish Christian baptism from other baptisms or similar rites such as: the baptism of John the Baptist; Jewish proselyte baptism; the lustrations of Qumran; etc.[21] Christian baptism is associated with faith in a person. It involves believing in Jesus Christ (see 16:31 and 33). As to the variety of the names and titles for Jesus in the expression, "Luke, when writing Acts, hardly thought that there was any difference in the meaning of the different formulae."[22] When either faith or repentance is mentioned as a requirement for receiving the gift of the Holy Spirit, the other is assumed, as 5:31–32 indicates, "God exalted him at his right hand as Leader and Savior, to give repentance to Israel and forgiveness of sins. And we are witnesses to these things, and so is the Holy Spirit, whom God has given to those who obey him [i.e., believe]."

The Association of *Baptism* and *The Gift of the Spirit*

We have already seen with regard to the conversion of Cornelius (10:44–48) that baptism and the gift of the Spirit are intimately related. In this instance, the gift of the Spirit preceded baptism and was the justification for Peter having baptized Cornelius. This is also seen in the second account of Cornelius's conversion where Peter's "not stand[ing] in God's way" (11:17) refers back to the earlier statement in 10:47. "Can anyone withhold water for baptizing these people, who have received the Holy Spirit just as we have?" Because of their having received the Spirit, Peter did not "stand in God's way"

---

[21] L. Hartman, "'Into the Name of Jesus': A Suggestion concerning the Earliest Meaning of the Phrase," *NTS* 20 (1974): 440; A. J. Hultgren, "Baptism in the New Testament: Origins, Formulas, and Metaphors," *Word & World* 14 (1994): 9–10.

[22] L. Hartman, *'Into the Name of the Lord Jesus': Baptism in the Early Church*, Studies of the New Testament and Its World (Edinburgh: T & T Clark, 1997), 37.

and forbid their being baptized (11:17). It should be observed that it is the gift of the Spirit that legitimizes the experience of baptism, not *vice versa*. It is the reception of this gift that permits (and requires) Cornelius to be baptized. Another example of this is found in the account of Paul's conversion, where Paul is filled with the Holy Spirit (9:17) and then baptized (9:18). We can also compare with this the parallel account in 22:13–15 where Paul comes to faith, is chosen to be a witness for God (implying the reception of the Holy Spirit, see 1:8), and is then baptized (22:16). This appears to have been the normal pattern in these three instances. On the other hand, at times baptism is said to precede the reception of the Spirit. Compare the order in 2:38, "Repent and be baptized . . . and you will receive the gift of the Holy Spirit," and in 19:5–6, "On hearing this, they were baptized in the name of the Lord Jesus. And when Paul had laid his hands on them, the Holy Spirit came on them."

In Acts 8, however, we encounter something of an aberration that follows neither pattern.[23] Here the Samaritan Christians believe and are baptized (8:12) but do not receive the gift of the Spirit until some time later (8:14–17).[24] At other times the association of baptism and the reception of the Spirit are so integral that they are spoken of

[23] Luke's wording in 8:16, "for he [the Holy Spirit] had not yet fallen on any of them, but they had only [*oudepō*] been baptized in the name of the Lord Jesus," suggests the atypical nature of the Samaritans not having received the Spirit when they believed (8:12–14) and were baptized (8:12–13).

[24] The unusual nature of the Samaritan Christians' reception of the Spirit is acknowledged by all, for it fits neither Roman Catholic, Protestant paedobaptist, Baptist, nor Charismatic theologies very well. Some suggest that there was a major defect in the Samaritans' faith, of which Simon (8:18–24) was an example, and they were not truly Christians until after they received the Holy Spirit (8:14–17). So Dunn, *Baptism in the Holy Spirit*, 55–72, esp. 63–68. The strongest argument in favor of this view is that the Spirit is the single most identifying feature of being a Christian, and they lacked the Spirit. However, whereas this explanation is valid with respect to the Ephesian "disciples" in Acts 19, the fact that they were not subsequently baptized by Peter and John, whereas the Ephesian "disciples" were, indicates that Luke understood the Samaritan Christians as true Christians, who had believed in Jesus and been baptized in his name (8:12, 16). "Nothing indicates that Simon's (or the Samaritans') belief and baptism were in any way deficient" (A. A. Das, "Acts 8: Water, Baptism, and the Spirit," *Concordia Journal* 19 [1993]: 116). A different explanation is that since Philip's mission was not an authorized mission under the commission of the Apostles, the Spirit was withheld in order to maintain the unity of the church. Against this interpretation is the fact that in the next chapter in Acts, Luke tells of the reception of the Spirit by Paul (9:17–18) through a non-apostle, Ananias, who was not commissioned by the Apostles! Probably the least unsatisfactory explanation is that the Spirit was uniquely withheld from the Samaritan Christians in order to assist in the reconciliation into one

as being inseparable in time (see "the washing of regeneration and renewal of the Holy Spirit" [Tit 3:5] and "baptism in the Spirit" [Matt 3:11; Mark 1:8; Luke 3:16; John 1:33; Acts 1:5; 11:16; 1 Cor 12:13]).[25] At times, however, baptism is mentioned and the gift of the Spirit is not, as in 8:36–39; 16:14–15,31–34; and 18:8. Nevertheless, Luke expects his readers to assume in these abbreviated accounts that those baptized had received the Spirit. This is clear from 2:41 where three thousand of Peter's audience at Pentecost are baptized and no mention is made of their receiving the Spirit; yet Luke clearly expects his readers to assume this took place in light of Peter's message in 2:38, "Repent and be baptized every one of you in the name of Jesus Christ for the forgiveness of sins, and you will receive the gift of the Holy Spirit." It would be absurd to suppose that Luke wanted his readers to think that the three thousand repented and were baptized and, despite the promise of 2:38, did not receive the Spirit, but still became part of the believing community (2:41–42). As Beasley-Murray says, "Whatever the relationship between baptism and the gift of the Spirit elsewhere in Acts, there appears to be no doubt as to the intention of Acts 2:38; the penitent believer baptized in the name of Jesus Christ may expect to receive at once

body (Eph 4:6) of these bitter enemies. So G. R. Beasley-Murray, *Baptism in the New Testament* (Grand Rapids: Eerdmans, 1973), 117–18.

[25] Dunn, *Baptism in the Holy Spirit*, 227, argues that the verb "baptize" (*baptizein, baptizasthai*) "means either to baptize literally (in water) or to baptize metaphorically (in Spirit into Christ, in suffering into death), but it never embraces both meanings simultaneously" (also pp. 4, 129–30). However, the tie between baptism in water and the reception of the Spirit both in time and in the experience of conversion into the Christian faith, along with their combination in the expression "the baptism of the Holy Spirit," make it impossible to interpret this expression as a waterless metaphor (see Cross, "Spirit- and Water-Baptism," 126–37). In addition such metaphors as: "wash away your sins" (22:16); "the washing of water with the word" (Eph 5:26); "the washing of regeneration and renewal of the Holy Spirit" (Tit 3:5); "our hearts sprinkled clean from an evil conscience and our bodies washed with pure water" (Heb 10:22); and "you were washed, you were sanctified, you were justified in the name of the Lord Jesus Christ and by the Spirit of our God" (1 Cor 6:11), etc., when taken at face value, all suggest that the experience of regeneration by the Holy Spirit takes place at conversion when people repent, believe, confess Christ, and are baptized. Such terminology as "wash," "washing," "sprinkled," and "washed" would have recalled water-baptism and the reception of the Spirit. The intimate tie between water-baptism and the reception of the Spirit would also have led Christians to interpret the metaphor "baptism of the Holy Spirit" in light of their experience of water-baptism and reception of the Spirit at conversion. For additional arguments, see Beasley-Murray, *Baptism in the New Testament*, 169.

the Holy Spirit, even as he is assured of the immediate forgiveness of his sins."[26]

The association of baptism with the gift of the Spirit, while closely connected, is not portrayed as involving an automatic causal relationship. This is evident in those instances where the Spirit was received first and served as the basis for the ensuing baptism, as in the case of Cornelius and Paul. This is also true in the unusual case of the Samaritans who did not receive the Spirit until some time after their baptism. On the other hand, 2:38 and 19:5–6 portray the coming of the Spirit as closely following baptism. What is clear is that, except in the unusual instance of the Samaritan Christians in Acts 8, the gift of the Spirit and baptism occurred together and were both part of becoming a Christian. To this must be added that this was preceded by repentance toward God and faith in Jesus Christ, as well as confessing Christ or "calling on his name" (see 22:16; Rom 10:9).

The Association of Repentance, Faith, and Baptism and the Forgiveness of Sins

The interconnectedness of repentance, faith, and baptism in Acts can also be observed as each of these components of conversion are portrayed as leading to the forgiveness of sins. Because of their intimate relationship with one another, each of these components can be referred to as bringing about one of the benefits of salvation—the forgiveness of sins.

Repentance and the Forgiveness of Sins

Several examples can be found in Acts of repentance resulting in the forgiveness of sins. Preaching in the temple, Peter proclaims, "*Repent* therefore, and turn again, *that your sins may be blotted out*" (3:19). When called before the Sanhedrin (5:27), Peter in his defense states concerning Jesus, "God exalted him at his right hand as Leader and Savior, to give *repentance* to Israel and *forgiveness of sins*" (5:31). Similarly, Paul in his defense before Herod Agrippa II, states that God called him to go to his own people and the Gentiles

---

[26] Beasley-Murray, *Baptism in the New Testament*, 108; also 273.

"to open their eyes, so that they may *turn from*[27] darkness to light and from the power of Satan to God, that they may receive *forgiveness of sins* and a place among those who are sanctified by faith in me" (26:18; see also v. 20). To these can be added Jesus' departing commission to the disciples in Luke 24:47, "*repentance* for [*eis*] *forgiveness* of sins would be proclaimed in His name to all the nations, beginning at Jerusalem" (HCSB; see also Luke 3:3; 5:32; 15:7,10; 17:3–4).[28] One can also compare 8:22 where Peter tells Simon the Magician, "*Repent*, therefore, of this wickedness of yours, and pray to the Lord that, if possible, the intent of your heart *may be forgiven you.*"

Faith and the Forgiveness of Sins

As with repentance, so faith in Jesus Christ is also described in Acts as bringing about the forgiveness of sins. In Peter's sermon to Cornelius he states concerning Jesus, "To him all the prophets bear witness that everyone who *believes* in him receives *forgiveness of sins* through his name" (10:43). Likewise Paul in his preaching in the synagogue in Pisidian Antioch declares, "Let it be known to you therefore, brothers, that through this man *forgiveness of sins* is proclaimed to you, and by him everyone who *believes* is freed from everything from which you could not be freed by the law of Moses" (13:38–39). And before Herod Agrippa II Paul also declares that God sent him "to open their eyes, so that they may turn from darkness to light and from the power of Satan to God, that they may receive *forgiveness of sins* and a place among those who are sanctified *by faith* in me" (26:18). In 15:8–9 we have still another example, although a different expression is used. There Peter recalls that at the conversion of Cornelius, "God, who knows the heart, bore witness to them, by giving them the Holy Spirit just as he did to us, and he made no distinction between us and them, having *cleansed their*

[27] The verb "to turn from" (*epistrepsai*) is a synonym for "to repent" (*metanoeō*) as their parallel use in 3:19 ("Repent [*metanoēsate*] therefore, and turn again" [*epistrepsate*]) indicates.

[28] Some would include 2:38 as another example where repentance is portrayed as bringing about the forgiveness of sins, but see below the discussion on this verse in "Baptism and the Forgiveness of Sins."

hearts by *faith*" (see 8:22). Thus, like repentance, faith is also portrayed in Acts as bringing about the forgiveness of sins.

Baptism and the Forgiveness of Sins

In Acts the forgiveness of sins is also associated with being baptized. Peter's instructions to those seeking forgiveness of sins is "Repent and *be baptized* every one of you in the name of Jesus Christ *for the forgiveness of your sins*, and you will receive the gift of the Holy Spirit" (2:38). Although some have sought to interpret the expression "*for [eis] the forgiveness of your sins*" as "in the hope of forgiveness" or "because of your forgiveness," it is best to interpret the expression as indicating the purpose of repentance-baptism. The Greek preposition *eis, "for,"* often denotes purpose. This usage is found in the expressions, "[in order] that [*eis*] your sins may be blotted out" in 3:19, and "God has granted repentance [with the purpose of, *eis*] life" in 11:18. Compare also Matt 26:28 where the cup at the Last Supper is described as "my blood of the covenant, which is poured out for many for [*eis*] the forgiveness of sins." Here the purpose of the sacrificial death of Jesus is described as "for" (*eis*) the forgiveness of sins.[29]

A number of scholars have argued that the expression "*for the forgiveness of sins*" should be understood as modifying only the verb "repent."[30] Yet the separation of the verbs "Repent" and "be baptized" into two independent actions views these commands from the perspective of later church practice rather than the understanding of their interrelatedness in Acts, where they are intimately associated in time and effect. For those who asked the question "Brothers, what

[29] See Beasley-Murray, *Baptism in the New Testament*, 102–103. Other suggested examples of the use of "for" (*eis*) indicating the purpose of an action are: Rom 5:18 where Paul writes, "Therefore, as one trespass led to condemnation for all men, so one act of righteousness leads to [*eis*] justification and life for all men" and Rom 10:10 "for with the heart a person believes, resulting in [*eis*] righteousness" (NASB). These may, however, be better examples of the use of "for" (*eis*) to denote result. Whether "for" (*eis*) in Acts 2:38 refers to the result or purpose of baptism, however, is of little consequence to the argument, for they both would indicate that an intimate relationship exists between baptism, the forgiveness of sins, and the gift of the Spirit.

[30] See L. B. McIntyre, Jr., "Baptism and Forgiveness in Acts 2:38," *BSac* 153 (1996): 53–62, and J. D. G. Dunn, "Baptism and the Unity of the Church in the New Testament," in *Baptism & the Unity of the Church*, ed. M. Root and R. Saarinen (Grand Rapids: Eerdmans, 1998), 85–86.

shall we do?" (2:37), Peter's reply associates baptism with forgiveness. One cannot choose to repent and not be baptized or *vice versa*
and receive the forgiveness of sins. They are inseparable. The verb
"to repent" describes what is involved in baptism as the expression,
"baptism of repentance" (Luke 3:3; see Mark 1:4), indicates. The
forgiveness of sins promised in 2:38 comes through a repentance-
baptism. If Luke really wanted to demonstrate that the forgiveness
of sins was associated with repentance only, he could have said,
"Repent for the forgiveness of sins and in addition be baptized in
the name of Jesus Christ," but he does not. If anything the wording
of Peter's command associates forgiveness with baptism even more
closely than with repentance, for the expression "*for the forgiveness
of sins*" is separated from the verb "repent" by "and be baptized each
one of you in the name of Jesus Christ" (nine words in the Greek
text). Although it is true that word order is far more fluid in Greek
than in the English language, it is not entirely irrelevant.[31] The desire to refute a mechanistic understanding of baptism that leads to
the error of baptismal regeneration need not cause us to divide and
separate in time and intent these two components of the conversion
experience that are intimately associated by Luke and the NT.

The account of the conversion of Cornelius (his receiving the gift
of the Spirit [10:44–46] and his being baptized [10:47–48]) is pref-
aced by the statement that every one who believes in Jesus receives
forgiveness of sins (10:43). Thus forgiveness of sins is a result of
believing in Jesus, and the further consequence is that Cornelius received the gift of the Spirit and was baptized. Similarly, in Paul's address before his Jewish compatriots in the temple in Acts 22, he explains how he met the Lord Jesus on the road to Damascus and how

---

[31] The closest example that I have found of two imperatives placed side by side as in 2:38 is
Mark 1:15, "Repent and believe in the gospel." Here the end expression "in the gospel" clearly
defines the nearest imperative, "believe." In 3:19, however, the two imperatives "Repent therefore, and turn again" are essentially synonymous and the following "for" (*eis*) purpose clause
"that your sins may be blotted out," probably describes the single act of repentance-turning. If
one must attribute the purpose clause to only one of the two imperatives, however, it is probably best related to the nearest imperative "turn again." This is to be favored because the same
two verbs "repent and turn" are found in 26:20 and there the following prepositional phrase
("to God") describes the nearest verb, "turn to God," far better than "repent to God" (see Luke
1:16; Acts 9:35; 11:21; 14:15; 15:19; 26:18). Still, it is better in 3:19 to see one action described
by the two verbs.

later, when the Lord's servant, Ananias, came to heal his blindness, he told Paul, "And now why do you wait? Rise and *be baptized* and *wash away your sins*, calling on his name" (22:16). Here "washing away one's sins," i.e., the forgiveness of sins, is intimately associated with baptism, and the expression, "wash away your sins," suggests that there is not just a temporal but a causal relationship between baptism and the forgiveness of sins. A "repentance-faith-baptism" results in the forgiveness of sins. Luke, who in his Gospel describes John the Baptist as "proclaiming a *baptism* of repentance *for the forgiveness of sin*" (3:3), ties baptism and the forgiveness of sins intimately together. This fits well with what Paul says in Eph. 5:26, which is most simply interpreted, that Jesus gave himself for the church "having cleansed her [a reference to the forgiveness of sins] by the washing of water [a reference to baptism] with the word."

The interconnectedness of repentance, faith, and baptism is witnessed to by the fact that they all lead to the forgiveness of sins. It would certainly be wrong to think that Luke believed these were three separate ways of receiving forgiveness: the "repentance" way, the "faith" way, and the "baptism" way. On the contrary, he understood them as all part of the experience of becoming a Christian. This is even more evident on the occasions where these components are paired together in Acts as bringing about the forgiveness of sins. In 2:38 repentance and baptism are placed side by side ("repent and be baptized") as resulting in the forgiveness of sins, and in 26:18 repentance and faith ("turn from darkness to light . . . by faith in me") are associated together as the necessary response(s) for receiving the forgiveness of sins ("that they may receive forgiveness of sins"). Compare also 5:31–32 where repentance and the forgiveness of sins are mentioned together in 5:31 and the gift of the Holy Spirit and obedience/faith are mentioned together in 5:32. For Luke "repentance" is an example of synecdoche[32] in which "repentance" refers to "repentance-faith-baptism." Similarly, "faith"[33] refers to

---

[32] See A. R. Cross, "Spirit- and Water-Baptism," 138–42.

[33] Note how in 4:4; 9:42; 13:12; 14:1; 17:12,34 the verb "believe" is used to describe becoming a Christian and no mention is made of either repentance, confessing Christ, baptism, or receiving the Spirit. In these examples "believe" serves as an example of synecdoche and is a shorthand expression for "believed-repented-confessed Christ-received the Spirit-were baptized."

"faith-repentance-baptism" and "baptism" refers to "baptism-repen-tance-faith," i.e., a baptism preceded by repentance and faith.[34] Thus one can refer to becoming a Christian as "the day they repented," "the day they believed," "the day they were baptized," "the day they confessed Christ,"[35] and "the day they received the Spirit," or to use Johannine terminology "the day they were born again." All these are interrelated and integral components in the experience of conversion in becoming a Christian, and all take place in Acts on the same day. The case of the Samaritan Christians in Acts 8:4–24 is the lone exception.

The Multifaceted Nature
of the Conversion Experience in Acts

From what we have seen in Acts with respect to becoming a Christian, we can come to the following conclusion:

> In the experience of becoming a Christian, five integrally related components took place at the same time, usually on the same day: repentance, faith, confession, receiving the gift of the Holy Spirit, and baptism.[36]

The interrelatedness of these five components is shown by their appearance together in various accounts in Acts. The best-known is the account of the coming of the Spirit upon the disciples at Pentecost (2:1–13), Peter's explanatory sermon (2:14–36), and the response of the crowd (2:37–42). As with Jesus' opening address in Nazareth (Luke 4:16–30), Acts 2:14–37 serves as a paradigm for the rest of the book. Peter explains how the Spirit's coming and manifestation in the behavior of the disciples is the fulfillment of the long-awaited promise of the Spirit in Joel 2:28–32 and how Jesus' death, resurrec-

---

[34] Hartman, '*Into the Name of the Lord Jesus,*' 145, points out that, "we should . . . —in fairness to Luke—beware of isolating the different elements of the initiation from each other. They form a unity, and baptism is the gathering, visible, effective sign around which the others can be grouped. Acts 22:16 renders it a 'sacramental' function, but it should not be regarded in isolation from the other elements."

[35] The confession that Jesus is Christ and Lord (22:16; cp. Rom 10:9) is not emphasized to the same extent as the other components, but it is always present by the fact that a person is baptized "in/into the name of Jesus/Lord/Jesus Christ (2:38; 8:16; 10:48; 19:5). See Beasley-Murray, *Baptism in the New Testament,* 100–104.

[36] For support of this thesis with respect to the teaching of the NT as a whole, see R. H. Stein, "Baptism and Becoming a Christian in the New Testament," *SBJT* 2 (1998): 6–17.

tion, and exaltation demonstrate that he is Lord (2:25,34–36) and Christ (2:31,36). The people respond, "Brothers, what shall we do? (2:37). The question is an abbreviation for "What shall we do to be saved?" (see 16:30), as is clear in 2:21 ("And it shall come to pass that everyone who calls upon the name of the Lord shall be saved"), 2:40 ("Save yourselves from this crooked generation"), and Luke's editorial comment in 2:47 ("And the Lord added to their number day by day those who were being saved"). This is also evident in that the "forgiveness of your sins" in 2:38 is a synonym for being "saved" (see 2:40,47; see 10:43 and 11:14; Luke 1:77). Peter's reply lists three of the components involved in becoming a Christian: repentance, baptism, and the gift of the Spirit. These are all seen as occurring on the same day: "So those who received his [Peter's] word were baptized, and there were added *that day* about three thousand souls" (2:41). Whereas faith is not explicitly mentioned in the account, it is clearly assumed in the response to the sermon. Similarly, even if confession is not explicitly mentioned, the baptism in the name of Jesus Christ of those who repented (2:38) served as a confession of faith in Jesus as Lord and Christ.

In the account of the conversion of Cornelius four of these components are present. Faith is mentioned in 10:43 ("that everyone who believes in him receives forgiveness of sins through his name"); the Spirit's coming upon Cornelius and his household is mentioned in 10:44–46 ("While Peter was still saying these things, the Holy Spirit fell on all who heard the word"); the baptism of Cornelius and his household is referred to in 10:47–48 ("And he commanded them to be baptized in the name of Jesus Christ"); and repentance is mentioned in 11:18 in the conclusion of the Jerusalem church concerning what had taken place: "Then to the Gentiles also God has granted repentance that leads to life." All these components are portrayed as having taken place on the same day and as intimately involved in Cornelius' conversion to Christianity.

Lastly, in the account of the Ephesian "disciples" once again these same four components are mentioned together. They are presumed to have repented (19:3–4), and upon believing (19:4) and being baptized (19:5), they received the gift of the Spirit (19:2, 6). It should be noted that in the account of the conversion of the Philippian jailor, the importance of keeping baptism intimately associated in time with faith is clearly emphasized. Even though his conversion took place at night he was baptized "at once" (16:33)!

It seems clear in light of these three accounts and the interrelated nature of these five components in Acts that becoming a Christian was not simply a matter of repenting, or believing, or confessing Jesus as Lord and Christ, or being baptized, or receiving the Spirit.[37] It involved all of these and took place normally on the same day. Today baptism is regularly separated in time from these other components, whether in infant baptism (in which there is no evidence of the other components) or in believer's baptism that is usually delayed (and thus separated in time from the other components). These practices make it mandatory that we arrive at our understanding of what it meant to become a Christian from the examples Luke provides in Acts.

Within Acts, the experience of becoming a Christian involves a "trinitarian" partnership between God, his church, and the individual believer. Without entering the debate as to whether there is an irresistible grace or an enabling, prevenient grace, God clearly is the Giver of the Spirit. This is not something the believer or the church does. The relationship between the reception of the Spirit and baptism in Acts is an intimate one. It is, however, primarily a temporal relationship rather than a simple, causal *ex opere operato* one.[38] We see this in the example of the Samaritan Christians, who received Christian baptism in the name of the Lord Jesus (8:16; see also 8:12) but did not receive the Spirit. They subsequently received the Spirit through the apostles Peter and John by the laying on of hands (8:17), but their baptism was not then repeated (contrast 19:1–7). Thus Christian baptism did not serve as an automatic rite through which one received the Spirit. Cornelius and his household (10:44–48) received the Spirit (10:44–46) before their baptism

---

[37] These "different elements of entrance into the church belong together: hearing of Jesus, accepting this message - belief, baptism, gift of the Spirit, all forming a unit with several aspects" (Hartman, 'Into the Name of the Lord Jesus,' 139).

[38] *Ex opere operato* means that baptism (or any other sacramental action) saves by virtue of the action itself being performed.

(10:47–48). In their case the gift of the Spirit served as justification for their baptism, not *vice versa*. This is evident from the fact that the Jerusalem church did not assume that Peter's baptism of Cornelius and his household automatically bestowed the gift of the Spirit and added one to the church. The act of baptism did not obligate God to give his Spirit.

The intimate tie between the reception of the Spirit and baptism in Acts is due to both their close temporal relation and that both were essential components, along with faith, repentance, and confession, in becoming a Christian. Similarly, Paul received his commissioning (9:15–16; see 22:14–15), his filling with the Spirit, and his sight (9:17–18a) before he was baptized (9:18b). The experience of Christian believers through the centuries helps to shed light on this. Among Baptists, the general experience of believers involves receiving the Spirit before baptism. Likewise, among groups that do not practice any baptismal rite at all, the Spirit nevertheless is present among those who repent, believe, and confess Christ. On the other hand, paedobaptists baptize considerably before any visible manifestation or sense of the Spirit's presence. The first practice described is much closer to what we find in the Book of Acts.[39]

Along with God's prevenient work of conviction and his sovereign giving of his Spirit, the church is also intimately involved in the process of one's becoming a Christian in Acts because it baptizes the believer. Neither Jewish proselyte baptism, whose date is much debated, nor the baptism of John were autobaptisms (see *b. Yebam.* 47ab; Matt 3:6,13–14; etc.; see also John 4:2). Since Christian baptism is also not an autobaptism (note the use of the passive voice in Acts 2:38,41; 8:12–13,16,36,38; etc.), there must be a third party in the conversion process,[40] that is, the church. Luke points this

[39] Although much of paedobaptist teaching argues that infants receive the Spirit at baptism *ex opere operato*, the claim that baptized infants have received the Spirit stands in sharp contrast to the description in Acts of those who received the gift of the Spirit. With respect to infant baptism, Dunn, *Baptism in the Holy Spirit*, 228, is correct when he says that baptism in water "is not a channel of grace, and neither the gift of the Spirit nor any of the spiritual blessings which he brings may be inferred from or ascribed to it."

[40] In a recent article "Did Paul Baptize Himself? A Problem of the Greek Voice System," in *Dimensions of Baptism: Biblical and Theological Studies*, ed. S. E. Porter and A. R. Cross, JSNTSup 234 (Sheffield: Sheffield Academic Press, 2002), 91–109, Porter has argued that the use of the

out in 2:41 where being "added" to the church involves faith and baptism: "So those who received his word were baptized, and there were added that day about three thousand souls." This reinforces the corporate nature of the church as the body of Christ into which a person is baptized and helps prevent the extreme individualism frequently found in some forms of western Christianity.

Finally, the individual is also involved in the process of becoming a Christian. The individual is called upon to repent and believe. In various places he is also described as "calling on Jesus' name" (22:16) or "confessing Christ as Lord" (see Rom 10:9).

Thus becoming a Christian in Acts is a "trinitarian" affair in which the individual, the church, and God are all intimately involved. Yet the only clear, definitive evidence as to whether a person is a true believer is, "Did you receive the Holy Spirit when you believed?" (19:2). Questions concerning whether one has repented, believed, and confessed Christ are inconclusive, for a person's repentance-faith-confession may have been insincere or flawed. Similarly, the question of whether one has been baptized is inconclusive, for the church could have baptized someone in error, perhaps not recognizing the insincerity of the individual's repentance-faith-confession. It is the gift of the Spirit that is the conclusive, undeniable proof that a person is a Christian, for God, who gives the Spirit, does not err. Thus it is the gift of the Spirit that serves as the infallible seal of approval that the individual is a child of God (see Rom 8:9,14–17; Gal 4:6; 1 John 3:24b; etc.).[41]

Three places in Acts mention the "laying on of hands" in the experience of receiving the Spirit. The first involves the coming of the Spirit upon the Samaritan Christians in 8:17. The second is the con-

---

middle voice in the command of Ananias to Paul in Acts 22:16 ("Rise and be baptized [*baptisai*] and wash away your sins, calling on his name.") should be taken seriously. Yet this single reference must be interpreted in the light of the fact that all the other instances of the verb "baptize" in Acts are passive, and the fact that Paul "was baptized" [the passive *ebaptisthē*] by Ananias according to 9:18. Consequently, Porter acknowledges that Paul did not personally baptize himself ("it appears that Ananias was probably the one who baptized Paul") but that Ananias in 22:16 told Paul "to be involved in the baptismal process . . . '[to] get up, experience baptism and wash away [his] sins'" (108–9). Porter's first conclusion is far more certain in the mind of the present author than his second.

[41] Dunn, *Baptism in the Holy Spirit*, 91–96, esp. 91–93.

version of Paul in 9:17, and the third is 19:6, in the story involving the Ephesian "disciples." The laying of hands on Paul by Ananias (9:17) is primarily for the purpose of Paul receiving his sight as indicated in 9:12, where God tells Ananias that he should "lay his hands on [Paul] so that he might regain his sight." It is associated secondarily with his becoming filled with the Spirit in 9:17, where Ananias tells Paul, "Brother Saul, the Lord Jesus who appeared to you on the road by which you came has sent me so that you may regain your sight and be filled with the Holy Spirit." The two other references involve the two most confusing and unusual accounts of conversion to Christianity found in all of Acts. They scarcely provide normative examples of what usually took place in the repentance-faith-confession-baptism-receiving the Spirit experience of conversion in the early church. They are both "highly exceptional events."[42] Elsewhere the laying on of hands was for healing (9:12; 28:8; see Mark 6:5; 7:32–37; 8:22–26; etc.), blessing (Gen 48:14–16; Mark 10:13,16), or divine commissioning for a sacred task (6:6; 13:3). It is doubtful, however, that the laying on of hands was an integral part of conversion-baptism in the early church.[43] It is probably best to interpret these three texts as reporting what happened on these three occasions rather than as describing what is normative.

The Analogy Of Marriage

The analogy of marriage, used in various places in the NT with respect to the Christian faith (see Matt 22:1–14; 25:1–13; Rom 7:1–6; Eph 5:22–33; Rev 19:7–9; 21:1–27; 22:17), provides a helpful comparison for understanding what is involved in becoming a Christian according to the Book of Acts. Becoming married involves a number of components that are intimately interrelated and belong together. These usually include: the saying of vows; the giving and receiving of rings; the pronouncement of marriage by the minister; the signing of the marriage license by the minister and witnesses; and the sexual consummation. If asked "Which component actually resulted in becoming married?" how should one answer this ques-

---

[42] Beasley-Murray, *Baptism in the New Testament*, 123.
[43] McDonnell and Montague, *Christian Initiation and Baptism*, 39.

tion? Was it when you said your vows? Was it when you gave and received a ring? Was it when the minister pronounced you husband and wife? Was it when the marriage license was filled in and signed by the minister and witnesses? Was it when the sexual consumma- tion of the marriage took place? The answer is that all of these were involved in becoming married. One cannot isolate them from one another. In the normal experience of marriage[44] all of these are in- volved, and all of them take place together, that is, on the same day. It was not a single component that changed two single individuals into a married couple. It was all of the above. In a similar way, one does not become a Christian in Acts at the minute of faith, or the in- stant of repentance, or the time of confession, or the moment of bap- tism, or the point in time when God gave his Spirit. These were not separated in time as in the present day but occurred together, that is, on the same day, and thus "the need to pinpoint exactly when con- version took place and also to identify the normative sequence for the constituent elements of conversion-initiation are obviated."[45]

The Mode Of Baptism In Acts

At first glance it appears that Acts is not very helpful in describ- ing the form of baptism practiced in the early church. That water is involved is clear from the Eunuch's question to Philip in 8:36, "See, here is water! What prevents me from being baptized?"[46] as well as the reference to their going down into the water (8:38), and the statement that after Philip baptized him they came up out of the water (8:39; Mark 1:10/Matt 3:16). Whether this involved sprin- kling with water, the pouring of water, or immersion in water is not specified in Acts. As Hartman argues, this is probably because "baptism is taken for granted and apparently writers need not in-

[44] The example refers to a "normal" marriage experience, as traditionally understood and envisioned. How "normal" this may be today can be debated, but in the idealization of becom- ing married these elements are generally understood to be involved and take place on the same day.

[45] Cross, "Spirit- and Water-Baptism," 133.

[46] The eunuch's question in 8:36 assumes that the command to be baptized was an integral part of Philip's gospel message in 8:35, just as it was in Peter's Pentecost message (2:38), An- anias' message to Paul (9:17–19; 22:13–16), Peter's message to Cornelius (10:47–48), Paul's message to the Philippian jailor (16:31–32), and to Crispus (18:8).

struct their readers about it."[47] (One need only observe how, when Roman Catholics, Lutherans, or Presbyterians discuss baptism, the mode of sprinkling is assumed and generally not stated, even as when Baptists discuss baptism, the mode of immersion is assumed and generally not stated.) Luke does provide clues, however, that suggest we may assume immersion.

The first set of clues comes from the Gospel of Luke. When the Evangelist wrote Acts he built on the reality that his readers had already read his first work, the Gospel of Luke: "In the first book, O Theophilus, I have dealt with all that Jesus began to do and teach, until the day when he was taken up, after he had given commands through the Holy Spirit to the apostles who he had chosen" (1:1–2). Acts 1:2–5, in fact, recalls Luke 24:44–53. Luke assumes that Theophilus will interpret the references to baptism in Acts in light of his own experience of baptism and what Luke has already said about baptism in his Gospel. Unfortunately Theophilus's experience is not available to readers today, but the latter is. The comparison of the baptism of John the Baptist and Christian baptism is made several times in Acts (1:5; 11:16; 19:3–5). When the difference between them is described, it is not a difference in the mode of baptism that is pointed out but rather that John's baptism is associated with repentance and the forgiveness of sins whereas Christian baptism is associated with the gift of the Spirit. Yet Christian baptism is not seen as the antithesis of John's baptism, for both proclaim "a baptism of repentance for the forgiveness of sins" (cp. Luke 3:3 and Acts 2:38), but rather as its fulfillment. John's baptism was preparatory and looked forward to its fulfillment in Christian baptism, which involved the gift of the Spirit. It helped prepare for this by the initiatory rite of baptism in water, with the demand for repentance in light of the arrival of the kingdom of God and coming of the Spirit (Luke 24:49; Acts 1:4–5,8; 2:1ff.). In John 3:22, Jesus is described as having his disciples baptize during his ministry with a baptism of repentance like that of John the Baptist. In fact, John 4:1

---

[47] Hartman, *'Into the Name of the Lord Jesus,'* 3. See how Paul assumes that his teaching on baptism is common knowledge even in churches he did not personally establish or visit: "Do you not know that all of us who have been baptized into Christ Jesus were baptized into his death (Rom 6:3; see also Col 2:12)?"

states that Jesus' disciples baptized more people than John. When John's baptism and Christian baptism are compared to one another in Luke-Acts, only one difference is mentioned. Both are associated with the coming of the Holy Spirit, but John's baptism could only look forward to this, whereas Christian baptism indicates its fulfillment. The fact that this is the only difference mentioned suggests that the form of baptism practiced by both were the same. Thus what we can know about the form of John's baptism can help us understand the form of Christian baptism in Acts.

From the description of John's baptism in the Gospels it seems reasonably clear that this involved immersion. The description of this taking place "in the river Jordan" (Mark 1:5/Matt 3:6) and that Jesus after his baptism "came up out of the water" (Mark 1:10/Matt 3:16) all suggest immersion. The description of John baptizing at Aenon near Salim "because water was plentiful there" (John 3:23) also implies immersion, for one does not need a plentiful supply of water for the mode of sprinkling. The explanation of this as involving affusion or pouring of water while standing in the Jordan at Aenon is also unconvincing. In a recent attempt that seeks to argue for the legitimacy of affusion, Howard Marshall admits that immersion was the general rule but seeks to argue that affusion was also practiced.[48] It should be noted, however, that very few groups that practice the mode of sprinkling or affusion do so while the person being baptized is standing waist deep in water![49]

It should also be noted that Acts is not as silent concerning the mode of baptism as is often thought. In the baptism of the Ethiopian eunuch, "See, here is water!" (8:36) would be an unusual comment unless being baptized involved immersion. One needs only a small cup of water to baptize by sprinkling, and that much water the eunuch would certainly have had with him as he traveled by chariot

---

[48] I. H. Marshall, "The Meaning of the Verb 'Baptize,'" in *Dimensions of Baptism: Biblical and Theological Studies*, ed. S. E. Porter and A. R. Cross, JSNTSup 234 (Sheffield: Sheffield Academic Press, 2002), 23.

[49] Most groups that argue for a mode of sprinkling or pouring cannot practice this mode while the candidate is standing in water, because they use this form of baptism on infants, who cannot stand by themselves in water. Thus the practice of paedobaptism compounds an unlikely mode of baptism (sprinkling or pouring) with an unlikely candidate for baptism (one who cannot repent, believe, or confess Christ).

(8:27–28) in the desert (8:26). That Luke has immersion in mind is further supported by the comment that Philip and the Ethiopian eunuch "went down into the water" (8:38) and after baptism "came up out of the water" (8:39).[50] Immersion may also be implied as the mode of baptism in the account of the Philippian jailor. In the story in Acts there are a number of changes in scene that are stated and implied in the account. In 16:25–29 the scene is the jail. In 16:30–33a the scene changes from the jail to the house of the jailor where Paul and Silas tell him the gospel message (16:32), of which 16:31 is a summary. Upon tending to the wounds of Paul and Silas, the jailor and his household are immediately baptized (16:33b). This does not take place in the house of the jailor, for in 16:34 we read that after his baptism the jailor "brought them [Paul and Silas] up into his house." Although, as usual, the exact location of the baptism is not described (see 2:41; 8:12–13; 9:18; 10:47–48; 16:15; 18:8; 19:5; 22:16), it is outside the house. Does Luke intend his readers to understand this in light of the story of the Ethiopian eunuch as taking place in sufficient water that one goes down and comes up after baptism (8:38–39)? Does he expect Theophilus to read both accounts in light of the traditions of the baptizing ministry of John the Baptist in the Jordan River and of Jesus' coming up out of the water (Luke 1:4; see Mark 1:9–10)? In no instance in Acts is it said that water is brought to baptize the believer; the impression is that the one being baptized goes to the water (see 8:38–39; 22:16; see also 16:13,15).

Household Baptisms In Acts

Within Acts there are several instances in which households are described as being baptized. The one in which this is described in most detail involves the conversion of Cornelius. The key verses involved are:

10:2 Cornelius is described as "a devout man who feared God with all his household."

---

[50] See *Barnabas* 11:11 where baptism is described as "we descend into the water" and "we rise up." See also the *Shepherd of Hermas* 4.31 where in baptism they "descended into the water."

10:24 "Cornelius was expecting them and had called together his relatives and close friends."
10:44,46–48 "While Peter was still saying these things, the Holy Spirit fell on all who heard the word.... For they were hearing them speaking in tongues and extolling God. Then Peter declared, 'Can anyone withhold water for baptizing these people, who have received the Holy Spirit just as we have?' And he commanded them to be baptized in the name of Jesus Christ."
11:14 Cornelius is told that Peter "'will declare to you a message by which you will be saved, you and all your household.' As I began to speak, the Holy Spirit fell on them just as on us at the beginning" (see also 1 Cor 1:16; 16:15).

The assumption that infants were part of Cornelius's household and that they were also baptized is often put forward by advocates of infant baptism. However, it should be noted that the "them" who are baptized in 10:48 and 11:17 are described as: having heard the word (10:44); having received the Holy Spirit (10:44–47; 11:15–17); having spoken in tongues (10:46) as at Pentecost (11:15); as believers (implied in 11:17); and having repented (11:18). One cannot exclude from the description of those who were baptized in 10:48 these other descriptions given by Luke. Thus, since infants cannot hear the word, speak in tongues, believe, and repent, it is evident that Luke does not intend for his readers to assume that infants were involved in the baptism described in 10:48.

The examples of Lydia ("And after she was baptized, and her household as well" [16:15a]) and Crispus ("Crispus, the ruler of the synagogue, believed in the Lord, together with his entire household" [18:8]) are also examples of household baptisms. The brevity with which Luke describes them is frustrating and warns against building a large theological practice of paedobaptism on them. Frequently paedobaptists make no distinction between the terms "children" and "infants/babies." To have children in one's family, however, does not mean that one has infants![51] Thus the argument that the households of Lydia and Crispus must have included children and that their baptism is an example of "infant" baptism is a *non sequitur*. Furthermore, concerning the baptism of the household

[51] See D. F. Wright, "The Origins of Infant Baptism - Child Believers' Baptism?" *ScotJT* 40 (1987): 2–3.

of Crispus, Luke specifically mentions that not only Crispus but his household became believers (18:8) and that many others heard, believed, and were baptized (18:8). There is no hint in the account that Luke intends for his readers to include infants with those who were baptized and, at the same time, to exclude infants from hearing and believing.

The final example of household baptism found in Acts involves the Philippian jailor and his family. In Acts 16:32–33 we read, "And they spoke the word of the Lord to him and to all who were in his house . . . and he was baptized at once, he and all his family." Once again it is assumed by proponents of infant baptism that the jailor's family included not only children but infants and these infants were baptized as well. Yet we need to remind ourselves that the terms "children" and "infants" are not synonyms, and Luke furthermore points out that the "word" was spoken to the entire household (16:32) and that the jailor ("he") and his entire household (*panoikei*) rejoiced in their new-found faith in God (16:34)! It is highly selective, on the one hand, to include infants in the baptism of the "entire family" of the jailor and then, on the other hand, to exclude them from the "entire family" that believes and rejoices in their new faith (16:34). This would be a clear case of special pleading. When one looks critically at the alleged evidence for infant baptism in the examples of household baptisms in Acts, there is good reason that "among New Testament scholars the view is increasingly widespread that infant baptism was not practiced in the New Testament Churches."[52]

Conclusion

Within the Book of Acts water-baptism "in/into the name of Jesus/Lord Jesus/Jesus Christ" is understood as an essential part of becoming a Christian. It is, however, one part of this process, and it is administered by the church, i.e., the individual receives Christ/is baptized. Through this experience he or she becomes part of the one body (2:41; see 1 Cor 12:12–13; Eph 4:6) of believers and devotes himself or herself to "the apostles' teaching and fellowship,

[52] Wright, "The Origins of Infant Baptism," 3.

to the breaking of bread and the prayers" (2:42). The individual's responsibility, which is always portrayed as preceding baptism, involves repentance, faith in Jesus Christ, and the confession of Jesus as Christ and Lord. The interrelatedness of this single, three-fold, response to the gospel message is such that often only one of these components of the individual's responsibility may be described in a particular account. Yet repentance always assumes the presence of faith and confession; faith always assumes repentance and confession; and confession always assumes repentance and faith. The intimate relationship of these three components are not understood in Acts as separate and isolated responses to the gospel but integral parts of "the" needed human response for becoming a Christian.

Along with this human response of repentance-faith-confession and the church's baptizing of the individual, God is also intimately involved in the conversion process. Thus, becoming a Christian involves a "trinitarian" relationship. In discussing the divine role in the conversion process, Luke is less interested in describing the prevenient work of the Spirit in bringing conviction and making possible repentance and faith (see, however, 2:37; 13:48; 16:14) than in describing the coming of the Spirit upon those who repent and believe. Because of the intimate relationship of repentance-faith-confession-baptism, the additional component of the gift of the Holy Spirit can be associated with any of these four components. In Acts it is associated at times with repentance, at times with faith, at times with baptism. Its association with baptism is such that the receiving of the Spirit can be referred to as "the baptism of the Holy Spirit" (Matt 3:11; Mark 1:8; Luke 3:16; John 1:33; Acts 1:5; 11:16; and 1 Cor 12:13). The relationship between the coming of the Spirit and baptism, however, should not be understood as automatic (*ex opere operato*) in Acts, because at times the Spirit is portrayed as coming before baptism. In the case of Cornelius, the prior reception of the Spirit legitimized and served as justification for Peter's baptizing him and his household (10:44–48; 11:17; see also 9:17–18), whereas the Spirit came upon Samaritan Christians some time after their baptism (see 8:12–13 and 17). Whereas we have pointed out that the conversion experience of the Samaritan Christians is most unusual and not meant to be understood as the normative pattern, it nevertheless reveals that baptism does not automatically convey the gift of the Spirit upon those baptized. The fact that all the components involved in conversion (faith, repentance, confession, the gift of the Spirit, baptism) took place on the same day, except in the unusual case of the Samaritan Christians, makes the issue of the exact order and timing of these various components somewhat irrelevant for Luke. It is a repentance-faith-confession-baptism that brings the gift of the Spirit. The debate over "baptismal regeneration" or whether infants at their baptism are given a gift of faith that later materialized in the church arose primarily from a situation in which these components, that in Acts all took place on the same day, were now isolated and separated in time. If Cornelius or the Philippian jailor in Acts were asked, "Do you remember when you received the Holy Spirit?," each could reply: "Yes, it was when I repented;" "Yes, it was when I put my faith in Jesus Christ;" "Yes, it was when I confessed Jesus Christ as my Lord;" "Yes, it was when I was baptized!" The separation of these components in time in the subsequent history of the church now makes this impossible and has resulted in much misunderstanding, confusion, and debate. If, however, we interpret the various NT texts on baptism in light of Luke's understanding of the integral relationship and unity of these components in becoming a Christian and note that all the five components took place on the same day, we will gain insight on how to interpret the texts about baptism in the NT.

Acts seems reasonably clear on the questions of the mode of baptism and of who should and can be baptized. With respect to the mode of baptism, immersion is suggested by (1) the comparison and relationship of Christian baptism with the baptism of John the Baptist, (2) the Ethiopian eunuch going down into the water to be baptized (8:38) and upon being baptized coming up out of the water (8:39), and (3) no evidence found in Luke-Acts for any other form of baptism being practiced. As to the question of who can be baptized, those baptized are portrayed as having heard the gospel preached, as responding with repentance and/or faith; and proceeding on their own to the place of baptism. No infant is described as being brought and experiencing baptism in Acts. The assumption that in the family conversions and baptisms in Acts infants were present and involved is ultimately unconvincing for they are not referred to in the description of the family, and those baptized in such family baptisms are described in various ways as having repented, believed, spoken in tongues, rejoicing in their new faith, etc.

BAPTISM IN THE EPISTLES:
AN INITIATION RITE FOR BELIEVERS

Thomas R. Schreiner[*]

Introduction

When a matter like baptism has been debated for so long without consensus among Christians, it is tempting to conclude that further discussion is fruitless. How can we advance the discussion when believers have been polarized for so many years? I do not believe, of course, that my essay will break up the logjam and produce consensus, and yet further study on baptism is still mandatory and helpful. If we are open to change, the Scriptures can correct, refine, or even confirm our previous understanding of a doctrine. And we should not avoid making judgments on controversial matters, for if we limited our doctrinal convictions to issues on which all Christians everywhere agreed, we would leave out many areas of teaching to which the Scriptures speak. Further, we are all responsible before God to understand the Scriptures to the best of our ability and to live in harmony with them. Indeed, in our churches we must decide how to order our life together as Christians. One way or the other we make a decision in our churches about how baptism should be practiced, and so every church implements some kind of theology of baptism. Surely all Christians would agree that we should strive to be as biblically faithful as we can in understanding and applying the scriptural teaching on baptism in our churches.

In this essay, I will explore afresh the epistolary teaching on baptism. The emphasis will be on Paul's teaching, since the other letters do not contain extensive teaching on the subject.[1] No attempt will

[*] Thomas R. Schreiner received his Ph.D. from Fuller Theological Seminary, and is the James Buchanan Harrison Professor of New Testament Interpretation and the Associate Dean for the Scripture and Interpretation Division at The Southern Baptist Theological Seminary in Louisville, Kentucky.

[1] Some scholars in the past argued that 1 Peter was a baptismal treatise. This view is not the consensus today and is not convincing. See T. R. Schreiner, *1, 2 Peter, Jude,* NAC (Nashville: Broadman & Holman, 2003), 42–43. In fact, the only other verse I will consider is 1 Pet 3:21.

be made to be comprehensive, but my essay will be divided into four areas: (1) exegetical comments on the main baptismal texts in the epistles; (2) comments on the mode of baptism and how baptism relates to washing and to sealing; (3) the relationship of baptism to redemptive history; and (4) the question whether baptism should be confined to believers.[2]

Baptismal Texts

The purpose of this section is not to fully exegete these texts but to focus on what they teach about baptism. The order in which the texts are discussed is not significant. I begin with those that emphasize the centrality of baptism (1 Pet 3:21; Eph 4:5; 1 Cor 12:13; 1 Cor 15:29; Gal 3:27), proceed to theologically weighty texts on baptism (Rom 6:3–4; Col 2:11–12), and conclude with texts that warn readers against overestimating baptism (1 Cor 1:13–17; 10:2).

It is striking that there is no sustained discussion of baptism in any of the epistles, presumably because the NT authors were writing to those who were already believers to whom the significance of baptism was explained upon their conversion.[3] When Paul does refer to baptism, he *assumes* that all believers are baptized. Hence, we cannot deduce from the infrequent references to baptism that baptism was unimportant. Schnackenburg rightly says, "Any limitation in the application of baptism, e.g., by postulating that it is not required at all times or for all people, is unknown to Paul. To him it is for every man the regular means of becoming a Christian."[4]

---

[2] Actually, some overlap will exist among the three areas since I will discuss the merits of infant baptism occasionally in the first section, and the essay is infused by my understanding of redemptive history.

[3] In NT scholarship, baptism has sometimes been understood to be borrowed from or influenced by mystery religions. For convincing criticisms of this hypothesis, see G. Wagner, *Pauline Baptism and the Pagan Mysteries: The Problem of the Pauline Doctrine of Baptism in Romans VI.1–11 in the Light of its Religio-Historical 'Parallels'* (Edinburgh/London: Oliver & Boyd, 1967); A. J. M. Wedderburn, *Baptism and Resurrection: Studies in Pauline Theology against its Graeco-Roman Background*, WUNT 44 (Tübingen: Mohr-Siebeck, 1987); S. Agnersnap, *Baptism and the New Life: A Study of Romans 6.1–14* (Aarhus: Aarhus University Press, 1999), 52–98. Hartman thinks there are similarities, but maintains that dependence cannot be demonstrated. L. Hartman, *'Into the Name of the Lord Jesus': Baptism in the Early Church*, Studies of the New Testament and Its World (Edinburgh: T. & T. Clark, 1997), 89–90.

[4] R. Schnackenburg, *Baptism in the Thought of St. Paul: A Study in Pauline Theology*, translat-

Centrality of Baptism

1 Peter 3:21. "Baptism, which corresponds to this, now saves you, not as a removal of dirt from the body but as an appeal to God for a good conscience, through the resurrection of Jesus Christ."[5]

The centrality of baptism strikes us upon reading 1 Pet 3:21, where we are told that "baptism now saves you." This verse occurs in one of the most difficult texts in the entirety of the NT (1 Pet 3:18–22). It is not my purpose here to resolve the many questions that arise in reading these verses that are unrelated to baptism, though I have explained elsewhere how I understand the entire context.[6] What is clear in these verses is that Christ through his death and resurrection has triumphed over angelic powers (1 Pet 3:18,22). He now reigns at God's right hand as the exalted Lord, and hence the suffering church can take confidence in his final victory.[7]

The survival of Noah and his family in the flood waters functions as a type (*antitypon*) of baptism. It seems that the waters of baptism are conceived of as a raging flood that destroy and kill. Such a view would fit with the notion that those submerged under water in baptism experience death, so to speak, under the baptismal waters. Just as Noah and his family survived the chaotic waters of death during the flood, so too believers in Jesus Christ have come through the baptismal waters alive.[8] Hence, Peter writes the surprising words, "baptism now saves you." On first glance, this statement seems to support a sacramental view of baptism where saving grace is auto-

---

ed by G. R. Beasley-Murray (Oxford: Blackwell, 1964), 125. As Beasley-Murray notes, it would have been incredible for first century Christians to conceive of becoming Christians without being baptized. G. R. Beasley-Murray, *Baptism in the New Testament* (Grand Rapids: Eerdmans, 1962), 298.

[5] Unless otherwise indicated, all Scripture quotations are from the ESV.

[6] Schreiner, *1, 2 Peter, Jude*, 179–98.

[7] Cross rightly argues from a related text that baptism here is integral to the gospel. A. R. Cross, "'One Baptism' (Ephesians 4.5): A Challenge to the Church," in *Baptism, the New Testament and the Church*, ed. S. E. Porter and A. R. Cross, JSNTSup 171 (Sheffield: Sheffield Academic Press, 1999), 192.

[8] The waters of the flood both saved and destroyed. Analogously, Jesus was destroyed by the flood of God's wrath (Mark 10:38–39; Luke 12:50) so that believers would be preserved through the waters of baptism. See D. G. McCartney, "The Use of the Old Testament in the First Epistle of Peter" (Ph.D. diss., Westminster Theological Seminary, 1989), 177–178.

matically conferred through baptism. In order to understand Peter's statement, however, we must carefully attend to the context.

Peter repudiates an *ex opere operato* view of baptism,[9] for he immediately qualifies the statement that baptism saves. It does not save mechanically or externally as if there are magical properties in the water. Peter comments that the mere removal of dirt from the body does not bring salvation, demonstrating that the water itself does not save. Baptism is only saving if there is an appeal to God for a good conscience through the resurrection of Jesus Christ. In other words, baptism saves only because it is anchored to the death and resurrection of Jesus Christ. The waters themselves do not cleanse as is the case when a bath removes dirt from the body.[10] Indeed, the objective work of Jesus Christ in his death and resurrection does not save unless there is a subjective element as well. The one receiving baptism also appeals to God for a good conscience, which means that he asks God to cleanse him of his sins on the basis of Christ's death and resurrection.

Many scholars, however, understand Peter to say that believers "pledge" (*eperōtēma*) to maintain a good conscience at baptism.[11] It is difficult to determine whether believers "appeal" to God for a good conscience or whether they vow before God to maintain a good conscience. Whatever one decides on this question, the subjective appropriation of God's grace is in view. Whether Peter speaks of an appeal or a pledge, baptism does not save apart from the commitment of the one being baptized. It seems to me that the notion of appeal is slightly preferable since it: (1) fits with the verbal form of the word (*eperōtaō*)[12]; (2) does not focus on the promise to live a godly life but on God's saving work based on Christ's cross and resurrec-

[9] *Ex opere operato* means that baptism (or any other sacramental action) saves by virtue of the action itself being performed. Incidentally, when referring to *ex opere operato* views of baptism, I am not implying that evangelical Presbyterians promote such a view.

[10] It is unlikely that Peter refers to circumcision here (see Schreiner, *1 Peter,* 195).

[11] E.g., P. J. Achtemeier, *First Peter,* Hermeneia (Minneapolis: Fortress, 1996), 270–72; J. H. Elliott, *1 Peter,* AB (New York: Doubleday, 2000), 679–80. Colwell argues, somewhat implausibly, that both prayer and promise are intended. See J. E. Colwell, "Baptism, Conscience and the Resurrection: A Reappraisal of 1 Peter 3.21," in *Baptism, the New Testament and the Church,* ed. S. E. Porter and A. R. Cross, JSNTSup 171 (Sheffield: Sheffield Academic Press, 1999), 224.

[12] E.g., Matt 12:10; Mark 7:5; Luke 8:9; John 9:23; Acts 23:34; Rom 10:20; 1 Cor 14:35. The verb occurs fifty-six times in the NT.

tion; and 3) fits with what occurs at the inception of the Christian life—the forgiveness and cleansing of sin. Still, in either case, what is said here does not fit with infant baptism, for infants cannot appeal to God for a good conscience or pledge to maintain a good conscience before God. Peter exalts the work of Christ in saving his people, but that work produces an effect in the consciousness and life of the believer. The teaching of 1 Peter on baptism, then, fits with the notion that baptism was not applied to infants.

Ephesians 4:5. "One Lord, one faith, one baptism."

The importance of baptism is also evident upon reading Eph 4:1–6. Believers are urged to maintain the unity of the Spirit that they already enjoy as believers in Jesus Christ (Eph 4:3). The basis of this unity is explicated in vv. 4–6 where Paul identifies seven realities that believers have in common. One of the realities held in common is "one baptism" (Eph 4:5).[13] Baptism here designates an initiation rite shared in common by all those belonging to the church of Jesus Christ.[14] Baptism, as in Gal 3:28 and 1 Cor 12:13, is mentioned to underscore the unity of believers. They have all shared a common saving experience by being immersed into Christ, and Paul assumes that all believers have been baptized.

1 Corinthians 12:13. "For in one Spirit we were all baptized into one body, whether Jews or Greeks, whether slaves or free, and we were all made to drink of one Spirit."[15]

This verse underlines the participation of all believers in baptism, and hence its centrality. It probably teaches that Christ is the baptizer, and he baptizes or immerses his people "in one Spirit." Some have suggested that the Spirit is the one who does the baptizing, but if we look at the parallel passages in the NT, the element into

---

[13] Hartman says, "The unity of the baptism thus seems to depend on the fact that it is a baptism into the one Christ" (*Baptism in the Early Church*, 104).

[14] Cross rightly argues that water and Spirit baptism should not be separated here ("One Baptism," 185–87). So also P. O' Brien, *Letter to the Ephesians*, PNTC (Grand Rapids: Eerdmans, 1999), 284. Best wrongly suggests a focus on water baptism rather than Spirit baptism, even though he says the two belong together. E. Best, *Ephesians*, ICC (Edinburgh: T. & T. Clark, 1998), 369.

[15] The translation here is mine. In defense of the interpretation adopted here, see G. D. Fee, *The First Epistle to the Corinthians*, NICNT (Grand Rapids: Eerdmans, 1987), 605–06. For a survey of scholarship on the verse, see A. C. Thiselton, *The First Epistle to the Corinthians*, NIGTC (Grand Rapids: Eerdmans, 2000), 997–1001.

which one is baptized is always communicated by the preposition "in" (*en*), whether the element into which one is plunged is water or the Holy Spirit (see Matt 3:11; Mark 1:8; Luke 3:16; John 1:33; Acts 1:5; 11:16).[16]

Paul is almost certainly speaking of the time of conversion here, for Jesus immerses in the Spirit so that his people are incorporated in the body of Christ. The second half of v. 13 expresses the same reality. At conversion, believers drink of one Spirit. The gift of the Spirit is the mark of induction into the people of God (Gal 3:1–5), and hence Jesus' work of baptizing with the Spirit occurs at the threshold of the Christian life. Once again we should not separate Spirit baptism from water baptism as if Paul were attempting to segregate the one from the other.[17] Conceptually they may be distinguished, but Paul himself was not interested in distinguishing them from one another in this verse since both are associated with the transition from the old life to the new.

Jesus' baptism with the Spirit is not restricted to only some believers. Paul emphatically teaches that all believers have been baptized regardless of their ethnic background or social status. Baptism in water and the Spirit is the signature event for Christians, marking them out as members of the people of God. It is difficult to see how infants could be said to be immersed in the Spirit, especially since Paul says elsewhere that the gift of the Spirit is received by faith (Gal 3:1–5). Those supporting paedobaptism would either have to argue

[16] O'Donnell argues that the verse most likely indicates that the Spirit is the agent of baptism rather than the element in which believers are baptized. See M. B. O'Donnell, "Two Opposing Views on Baptism with/by the Holy Spirit and of 1 Corinthians 12:13: Can Grammatical Investigation Bring Clarity?" in *Baptism, the New Testament and the Church*, ed. S. E. Porter and A. R. Cross, JSNTSup 171 (Sheffield: Sheffield Academic Press, 1999), 311–36. O'Donnell demonstrates that his view is a possibility, and it seems to me that his best argument is that the prepositional phrase precedes in 1 Cor 12:13 in contrast to Matt 3:11; Mark 1:8; Luke 3:16; John 1:33; Acts 1:5; 11:16. He has not convincingly shown, however, that his grammatical study is determinative, for the evidence is more ambiguous than his study suggests, and it seems more likely that the reference to the baptism of the Spirit would be understood similarly in all of these texts. Since Jesus is clearly the baptizer in the other verses, the same is likely the case here as well.

[17] Rightly Beasley-Murray, *Baptism in the New Testament*, 168–69; see the discussion in S. K. Fowler, *More Than a Symbol: The British Baptist Recovery of Sacramentalism*, Studies in Baptist History and Thought 2 (Carlisle: Paternoster, 2002), 170–73; against Dunn, *Baptism in the Holy Spirit*, 129–31; D. Wilson, *To a Thousand Generations—Infant Baptism: Covenant Mercy for the People of God* (Moscow, ID: Canon Press, 1996), 50–51.

that people are baptized without receiving the Spirit, which contradicts the meaning of the verse, or they would need to say that the Spirit is received without faith, but there is no warrant elsewhere in the NT for the Spirit being given without faith.[18]

1 Corinthians 15:29. "Otherwise, what do people mean by being baptized on behalf of the dead? If the dead are not raised at all, why are people baptized on their behalf?"

One of the most controversial and difficult texts in all of Pauline literature is the reference to baptism for the dead.[19] It is not my purpose to canvas the various interpretations proposed, nor does the view argued for in this essay depend in any way upon the interpretation proposed here. What the verse suggests, however, is that baptism was considered to be indispensable for believers. The plethora of interpretations indicates that the original meaning of the verse is not easily accessible to modern readers. The difficulty of the verse is not entirely surprising, for Paul does not explain the meaning of baptism here, but instead appeals to the baptism of the dead in support his theology of the resurrection. Any baptism performed for the sake of the dead is superfluous, Paul argues, if the dead are not raised. Strictly speaking, Paul does not praise or condemn the practice of baptism for the dead, and hence a theology of baptism for the dead can scarcely be established from this verse. It seems most likely, in my judgment, that baptism for the dead was practiced when someone became a believer and died very quickly thereafter—before baptism was possible.[20] What this verse suggests, despite its obscurity, is the importance of baptism. Baptism was considered to be the standard initiation rite for early Christians, and hence some believers at Corinth thought that baptism should be done for the sake of the dead.

Galatians 3:27. "For as many of you as were baptized into Christ have put on Christ."

---

[18] Nor is it convincing to posit here that infants exercise faith or that the faith of sponsors suffices.

[19] For a fuller discussion of this text with various interpretive possibilities, see Schnackenburg, *Baptism in the Thought of St. Paul*, 95–102; Thiselton, *First Corinthians*, 1240–49.

[20] If this view is correct, the death of those in view must have occurred very shortly after conversion since baptism was applied almost immediately after profession of faith during the NT period.

Paul's main theme here is not baptism. His point is that all believers are clothed with Christ. We see incidentally, however, that baptism was universal in the church (and hence central!), since all those who are clothed with Christ (i.e., all Christians) are baptized. Further discussion of this verse will be reserved for the discussion on salvation history.

Theology of Baptism

Romans 6:3–4. "Do you not know that all of us who have been baptized into Christ Jesus were baptized into his death? We were buried therefore with him by baptism into death, in order that, just as Christ was raised from the dead by the glory of the Father, we too might walk in newness of life."

If the first five texts we examined point to the centrality of baptism, the next two (Rom 6:3–4; Col 2:11–12) are particularly significant theologically relative to baptism (though the texts we just examined are theologically weighty too). In both texts, baptism is intimately linked with the believers' death to sin. The intention is scarcely to suggest that *only some Christians* have died to sin and been buried with Christ, namely, those who have been baptized. To say that those who are baptized have died with Christ is just another way of saying that *all* Christians have died with Christ. There was not a serious problem, as there is today, with Christians being unbaptized in the NT period. We are asking the wrong question, therefore, if we ask whether Spirit or water baptism is in view in Rom 6:3–4. Other Pauline texts suggest that water baptism and reception of the Spirit occurred at conversion. In my judgment Paul would have been initially puzzled if we asked him, "Do you mean Spirit or water baptism in these verses?" He would reply, when he understood the question, "Both."[21]

Those who restrict the reference to Spirit baptism in Romans 6 truncate the baptismal message, for separating water baptism and Spirit baptism introduces a false dichotomy into the Pauline argu-

---

[21] Again I am not denying that water baptism and Spirit baptism may be conceptually distinguished from each other, but J. D. G. Dunn's explanation of the text reveals the unnecessary complication involved in trying to make such distinctions (*Baptism in the Holy Spirit*, 140). See for a more satisfying explanation D. J. Moo, *Romans*, NICNT (Grand Rapids: Eerdmans, 1999), 359.

ment.[22] Paul does not drive a wedge between Spirit baptism and water baptism, as if the former is what really matters and the latter is superfluous. Such a viewpoint may suffer from reading the text through modern experiences in which water baptism often occurs significantly before or after conversion. When we recall that in Paul's day virtually all were baptized immediately after putting their faith in Christ, we grasp that both Spirit baptism and water baptism were part and parcel of the complex of saving events that took place at conversion.[23] When people are converted, they are baptized in water and the Spirit, and confess Jesus as Lord (Rom 10:9). Those who see a reference only to Spirit baptism and exclude water baptism put asunder what God meant to be joined together.[24]

Paul refers to baptism in Romans 6 and Colossians 2 because baptism recalls the conversion of the readers from the old life to the new. The grace of God secured their freedom from the power of sin at conversion, and the simplest and easiest way to recall the readers' conversion is to speak of their baptism. As Schnackenburg rightly says, "The baptized man is drawn into the once-for-all event of salvation accomplished in the cross and resurrection of Christ, and with Christ he goes through death and the grave to resurrection."[25]

Colossians 2:11–12. "In him also you were circumcised with a circumcision made without hands, by putting off the body of the

[22] Dunn emphasizes that baptism in Paul is metaphorical rather than literal (*Baptism in the Holy Spirit, passim*). For his reiteration of this view, see id., "'Baptized' as Metaphor," in *Baptism, the New Testament and the Church*, ed. S. E. Porter and A. R. Cross, JSNTSup 171 (Sheffield: Sheffield Academic Press, 1999), 294–310. But Dunn's view fails to convince, for Stein has shown in his essay on Acts in this volume that it was quite natural for the lines to be blurred between water and Spirit baptism since both were initiatory in the Christian life. For further support of the view supported here, see I. H. Marshall, "The Meaning of the Verb 'Baptize,'" in *Dimensions of Baptism: Biblical and Theological Studies*, ed. S. E. Porter and A. R. Cross, JSNTSup 234 (London/New York: Sheffield, 2002), 9.

[23] This point is argued convincingly and in detail by Cross in his essay where he posits that many references to baptism are an example of synecdoche where baptism stands for the entire process of Christian initiation. A. R. Cross, "Spirit- and Water-Baptism in 1 Corinthians 12.13," in *Dimensions of Baptism: Biblical and Theological Studies*, ed. S. E. Porter and A. R. Cross, (JSNTSup 234; London/New York: Sheffield, 2002), 120–48. Indeed, Cross's argument functions as support for the Baptist position, for it emphasizes that baptism is associated with conversion and saving faith (see p. 143).

[24] Hartman sees a fulfillment of God's eschatological promise of the Spirit in baptism (*Baptism in the Early Church*, 81).

[25] Schnackenburg, *Baptism in the Thought of St. Paul*, 111.

flesh, by the circumcision of Christ, having been buried with him in baptism, in which you were also raised with him through faith in the powerful working of God, who raised him from the dead."

The Pauline statement on baptism in Col 2:12 travels in the same orbit as Romans 6.[26] Colossians is designed to fend off those espousing a philosophy that minimizes Christ. Paul emphasizes the divine fullness of Christ and that believers enjoy Christ's fullness and hence need nothing other than Christ (Col 2:8–10). What Paul says about baptism fits with the themes of the pre-eminence and sufficiency of Christ that permeate Colossians. By virtue of their union with Christ, believers have received the only circumcision that is necessary (Col 2:11)—one made without hands, that is, accomplished by God himself. Literal circumcision, Paul implies, is made with hands (*cheiropoiētos*), implying that those who rely on physical circumcision are guilty of idolatry since false worship in the OT is regularly characterized as that made with human hands (see Lev 26:1,30; Isa 2:18; 46:6; Dan 5:4; so also Jdt 8:18; Wis 14:8). The true circumcision involves "the removal of the body of the flesh" (Col 2:11). This may refer to the same reality described in Romans 6 as the crucifixion of the old Adam (Rom 6:6).[27] Perhaps, however, a reference to Christ's death is slightly preferable since the words "the body of the flesh"[28] are repeated from Col 1:22 where the reference is certainly to Christ's death. The death of Christ is then described as the "circumcision of Christ."[29] At his death, so to speak, God cut off Christ's bodily life, just as the foreskin is removed in circumcision. The only circumcision believers need, then, is the circumcision they receive by virtue of their incorporation into Christ's death on the

---

[26] Hunt argues that the earliest patristic evidence does not support the notion that infant baptism was defended from the analogy with circumcision. Instead, the analogy from circumcision was introduced *after* infant baptism was introduced and practiced on other grounds. J. P. T. Hunt, "Colossians 2:11–12, The Circumcision/Baptism Analogy, and Infant Baptism," *TynB* 41 (1990): 227–44. Hunt also suggests that the analogy between infant baptism and circumcision was first "advanced as an argument for infant baptism in Italy or North Africa sometime in the second quarter of the third century" (p. 232).

[27] So Hartman, *Baptism in the Early Church*, 96–97.

[28] Col 1:22 and Col 2:11.

[29] So Hunt, "Colossians 2:11–12," 243; P. O'Brien, *Colossians, Philemon*, WBC (Waco: Word, 1982), 116–17; J. D. G. Dunn, *The Epistles to the Colossians and Philemon*, NIGTC (Grand Rapids: Eerdmans, 1996), 157–58.

cross. Circumcision was never intended to be a permanent rite for all of redemptive history; it pointed to the death of Christ on behalf of his people. The demand for (Deut 10:16; Jer 4:4) and promise of a circumcised heart (Deut 30:6) have now become a reality in the cross. Christ's cross is the true circumcision for believers. This accords with what we shall see in Galatians below where circumcision is fulfilled in the cross of Christ.

The message of Col 2:12 is rather similar in some respects to Romans 6. The benefits of Christ's death belong to believers because they were buried together with Christ in baptism. But in Colossians Paul explicitly connects baptism with being raised with Christ as well.[30] Some dispute this, maintaining that the words *en hō* in v. 12 refer to Christ rather than baptism. But baptism is the more likely antecedent since it occurs immediately prior to the words *en hō*.[31] It seems, then, that Paul unpacks here what was implied in Romans 6. By virtue of Christ's cross and resurrection, believers have been buried and raised with Christ. Baptism as the initiatory event in the lives of believers represents death to the old way of life and the birth of a new life.

Baptism, however, is not only an event in which the objective nature of Christ's saving work is applied to his people. It is also conjoined with the subjective appropriation of such salvation. Paul adds in v. 12 that the effectiveness of Christ's work is accessed through faith.[32] It is difficult to see, then, how infants can fit with what Paul says since they cannot exercise faith.[33] Those who support infant baptism rightly see the objective work of God's grace in Christ's death and resurrection that is applied in baptism, but they delay the subjective appropriation of God's gift by faith.[34] Such a view

[30] So also Hartman, *Baptism in the Early Church*, 97.
[31] So Beasley-Murray, *Baptism in the New Testament*, 153–54.
[32] Rightly Hartman, *Baptism in the Early Church*, 101. On the importance of faith, see Schnackenburg, *Baptism in the Thought of St. Paul*, 116, 122–27.
[33] For the indispensabililty of faith, see Beasley-Murray, *Baptism in the New Testament*, 156, 304.
[34] Cullmann falls into this error, for he celebrates God's objective work in baptism, and yet says that the effect of the work is nullified if *faith does not follow*. O. Cullmann, *Baptism in the New Testament*, trans. J. K. S. Reid (Philadelphia: Westminster, 1950), 32–37. But such a statement indicates that the objective and subjective elements should not be separated. The real indication that an objective work has occurred is the presence of faith in the one baptized.

truncates, as we have now seen in several texts, the fullness of the biblical witness.

Nor does the reference to circumcision constitute a parallel between infant baptism and infant circumcision, as is often claimed by paedobaptists.[35] Paul does not establish a connection between physical circumcision and baptism, but *spiritual circumcision and baptism*.[36] Indeed, he disavows emphatically any salvific efficacy in physical circumcision. A common problem in Israel is that people were physically circumcised but uncircumcised in heart (Deut 10:16; Jer 4:4; 9:23–24). What is necessary to belong to the redeemed people of God is a spiritual circumcision of the heart (Deut 30:6), which is promised in the new covenant work of God (Jer 31:31–34). Physical circumcision made one a member of Israel as God's theocratic people, but it did not ensure that one was regenerate. Hence, the need for the spiritual circumcision of the heart. The sign of the new covenant—baptism—is remarkably different, for those who are baptized have already undergone a spiritual change when they were buried and raised with Christ. The work of conversion has already been accomplished in their hearts, and this new work is received by faith. God's gracious work is not applied to infants who have no conception of what is happening; it is gladly received by those who trust in God for forgiveness of sins. Indeed, it is the forgiveness of sins that Paul celebrates in Col 2:13–14. Those who were dead in "the uncircumcision of their flesh" have now been made alive to God through the cross and resurrection of Jesus Christ. The typological antecedent to baptism, then, is not physical circumcision but spiritual circumcision.[37] Those who are baptized have died to their

---

Nor does it accord with the NT witness to speak of the faith of the congregation during baptism (against Cullmann, *Baptism in the New Testament*, 42–43, 55). Beasley-Murray rightly warns that some stress the objective nature of salvation to such an extent that they wrongly eliminate the subjective element (*Baptism in the New Testament*, 300).

[35] See e.g. M. E. Ross, "Baptism and Circumcision as Signs and Seals," in *The Case for Covenantal Infant Baptism*, ed. G. Strawbridge (Phillipsburg, NJ: P&R, 2003), 97–108. On p. 103 he assumes the circumcision here is spiritual in nature, but Paul specifically distinguishes spiritual from physical circumcision in Col 2:11. On this matter, see the definitive work of P. K. Jewett, *Infant Baptism and the Covenant of Grace* (Grand Rapids: Eerdmans, 1978).

[36] On this point, see Hunt, "Colossians 2:11–12," 243; D. F. Wright, "Children, Covenant and the Church," *Themelios* 29 (2004): 29.

[37] A dramatic example of this misreading is found in the work of Wilson, *To a Thousand*

old selves, are alive to God in Christ Jesus, and have put their faith in Jesus Christ for salvation. Baptism portrays what God has done for them in Christ. They have died and been buried with Christ and now have risen to a new life in him. Baptism functions as a pictorial representation of such, when believers are submerged under the waters and then emerge again.

Overestimating Baptism

1 Corinthians 1:13–17. "Is Christ divided? Was Paul crucified for you? Or were you baptized in the name of Paul? I thank God that I baptized none of you except Crispus and Gaius, so that no one may say that you were baptized in my name. (I did baptize also the household of Stephanas. Beyond that, I do not know whether I baptized anyone else.) For Christ did not send me to baptize but to preach the gospel, and not with words of eloquent wisdom, lest the cross of Christ be emptied of its power."

So far we have investigated central texts on baptism (1 Pet 3:21; Eph 4:5; 1 Cor 12:13; 1 Cor 15:29; Gal 3:27) and two texts that are particularly significant theologically (Rom 6:3–4; Col 2:11–12). Now we turn to two texts where Paul warns against overestimating baptism (1 Cor 1:13–17; 10:2). First Corinthians 1:13–17 also casts some interesting light on the practice of baptism. It seems evident that the baptism spoken of here occurred when Paul evangelized the Corinthians. Hence, it follows that baptism is an initiation rite

---

Generations, 59–80. Wilson continues to see covenantal significance in circumcision after the death and resurrection of Christ, though at the same time he argues that the practice fades away by AD 70. Wilson misconstrues here what the NT teaches about circumcision and the Mosaic covenant. Now that Christ has come the Mosaic covenant and law, and particularly circumcision (Gal 2:3–5; 5:2–6; 6:12–13; Rom 4:9–12; Phil 3:2–3; Col 2:11–12), have passed away. There is no evidence in the NT that circumcision continued to have any covenantal efficacy. Perhaps the Judaizers believed this, but Paul certainly did not. Paul did not circumcise Timothy for covenantal reasons in Acts 16:3, but for cultural and mission purposes, so that he could bring Timothy with him when he evangelized Jews in the synagogues. Nor does Acts 21:21–26 ascribe any covenantal significance to circumcision for Jews. The passage in question refers back to the apostolic council where it was determined that circumcision was not required for salvation (Acts 15:1–29). Circumcision continued to be allowed among the Jews for cultural reasons, but there is no evidence that it was practiced because of its alleged covenantal value. If Wilson were correct about circumcision, it is quite strange that it slowly faded away. For further defense of the view of the law and the covenant suggested here, see T. R. Schreiner, *The Law and Its Fulfillment: A Pauline Theology of Law* (Grand Rapids: Baker, 1993).

associated with their conversion. Furthermore, baptism must be understood in terms of the Pauline gospel. If baptism is placed outside the context of Christ crucified, it will inevitably be distorted.[38] Hence, Paul did not engage in mission primarily to baptize but to preach the gospel (1 Cor 1:17). Paul does not denigrate the practice of baptism per se, but baptism must be subordinated to the gospel so that it does not sabotage the gospel, that is, that Christ was crucified for sinners.[39] Indeed, those who view baptism casually or as insignificant veer away from Paul, for as Schnackenburg says, "Paul would not understand it if anyone refused to be baptized; to him such an attitude would no longer be genuine faith."[40] Verse 13 suggests the inextricable connection between baptism and Christ's self-giving on the cross. Twice Paul emphatically rejects the idea that the Corinthians were baptized in his name (1 Cor 1:13,15), implying instead that they were baptized into Christ's name. Paul is thankful, in light of the divisions in Corinth, that he had baptized few there, lest any imagine that their baptism somehow connected them in a special way to him (1 Cor 1:13). Instead, their baptism connected them to Christ and his cross (1 Cor 1:13,17). Though Paul does not work out the theology here, the relationship between baptism and the crucifixion anticipates what Paul explains in more detail in Romans 6 and Colossians 2.

1 Corinthians 10:2.   "And all were baptized into Moses in the cloud and in the sea."

The reference to baptism in 1 Cor 10:2 supports the idea that the gospel is fundamental so that baptism is understood within the context of the proclamation of the gospel. Here, in a rather surprising analogy, Paul maintains that the exodus generation was baptized into Moses in the cloud and the sea. The main purpose of the

---

[38] Hartman also argues that baptism is joined here with Jesus' death on behalf of believers (*Baptism in the Early Church*, 61). Fee nicely expresses Paul's concern here in saying that Paul does not "minimize Christian baptism" nor does he relegate it to a "secondary matter," but baptism does not "*effect* salvation" and comes after hearing and believing the gospel (*First Corinthians*, 63–64).

[39] See here Beasley-Murray, *Baptism in the New Testament*, 180. Fowler rightly sees that Paul does not view baptism negatively here, though he fails to note the priority of the gospel (*More Than a Symbol*, 162).

[40] Schnackenburg, *Baptism in the Thought of St. Paul*, 127.

section is to warn the Corinthians about the danger of apostasy (1 Cor 10:1–13). Israel was freed by God's grace from Egypt, and yet most of those liberated did not enter into the land of promise. Paul admonishes the Corinthians so that they do not fall prey to idolatry and thereby forsake the gospel that saved them. He finds parallels in Israel's experience for both baptism and the Lord's supper (1 Cor 10:2–4). It seems that the parallels to baptism and the Lord's supper are adduced to stave off any notion that they magically and inevitably protect the Corinthians from future judgment.[41] We have further evidence here that baptism must be interpreted in light of the gospel rather than vice-versa, for Paul rules out the notion that baptism functions *ex opere operato*.

Mode, Cleansing, and Sealing

So far we have examined some major baptismal texts in the epistles. Baptism is central in that it was the initiation rite for believers. Moreover, the theologically weighty texts (Rom 6:3–4; Col 2:11–12) show that baptism unites believers with Christ's death and resurrection. Finally, Paul also warns against overestimating baptism (1 Cor 1:13–17; 10:2). Christ and the gospel save, not baptism per se. In this second major section of the chapter, I will examine three matters that are loosely related: the mode of baptism, the significance of washing relative to baptism, and the relationship between baptism and sealing.

Mode of Baptism. Do Rom 6:3–4 and Col 2:12 specify the mode of baptism? Most scholars agree that immersion was practiced in the NT, and it is likely that both of these texts allude to the practice, even though baptism is not the main point of either text. [42]

[41] This is a common view; see Beasley-Murray, *Baptism in the New Testament*, 265; Hartman, *Baptism in the Early Church*, 91; Fee, *First Corinthians*, 443–44; D. E. Garland, *1 Corinthians*, BECNT (Grand Rapids: Baker, 2003), 446.
[42] I understand baptism in the NT period to be by immersion. Marshall maintains that the evidence is more ambiguous, saying that even though immersion was the norm, some evidence points to the practice of pouring. Marshall, "The Meaning of the Verb 'Baptize,'" 8–24. Space constraints forbid further discussion of Marshall's thesis here, but it seems to me that his evidence does not clearly point toward other modes being practiced in the NT period. For a further response to Marshall's view, see the remarks by Köstenberger in his chapter in this volume. R. L. Webb says John the Baptist practiced immersion (*John the Baptizer and Prophet: A Socio-Histori-*

Colossians 2:12 appears to teach immersion through a picture, for believers are buried with Christ in baptism, and also in baptism they are raised with Christ. Further, the picture provided by baptism in Rom 6:3–5 suggests immersion.[43] Death and burial are portrayed when the new believer is submerged under the water. The emersion from the water points to the new life that believers enjoy even now by virtue of Christ's resurrection.

It may be objected that many were buried above the ground in caves during the NT era, and hence the notion of burial *underground* as pictured in baptism does not clearly portray death.[44] The objection helps us to clarify the Pauline intention, but it does not succeed in terms of its main point. In saying that baptism pictures death and resurrection, the point is not that *death is always underground*. Baptism pictures death because *submersion* under water kills. The waters represent the flood of God's judgment on account of sin (see 1 Pet 3:20–21), and hence even Jesus himself, as Mark 10:38–39 explains, underwent a baptism in which he absorbed God's wrath on the cross for the sake of his people. Submersion under the water in baptism—which is in Jesus' name—indicates that the persons baptized have experienced God's judgment in Christ. That is, since they are incorporated in Christ, he has borne the judgment they deserved. Submersion under the water, then, does not specify that the dead are buried underground. The picture is not meant to be taken so literally. It does communicate, however, death and burial. Submersion is an apt picture because it demonstrates that death overwhelms and conquers its subjects. Pouring and sprinkling simply do not have the same effect. We all know that if we are held under water long enough we will die. Similarly, newness of life is represented by

cal Study, JSNTSup 62 (Sheffield: Sheffield Academic Press, 1991], 95, 179—81), and it is likely that Jesus' baptism employed the same mode. For a contrary view, see Wilson, *To a Thousand Generations*, 101–14.

[43] So Cullmann, *Baptism in the New Testament*, 14; Beasley-Murray, *Baptism in the New Testament*, 133. For a contrary view, see Dunn, *Baptism in the Holy Spirit*, 143–44; Agersnap, *Romans 6.1–14*, 268–69; J. Pipa, "The Mode of Baptism," in *The Case for Covenantal Infant Baptism*, ed. G. Strawbridge (Phillipsburg, NJ: P&R, 2003), 115–19, 124–26.

[44] Moo also argues that the preposition *dia* denotes the means of being buried with Christ rather than the place (*Romans*, 361). It seems, however, that there is no need to posit an either-or here.

emerging from the water. Believers now enjoy the resurrection life of Christ because they have been incorporated into him (Rom 6:4). I conclude, then, that the imagery used in Col 2:12 and Rom 6:3–5 points to *immersion* ("going into") and *emersion* ("coming out of").

Cleansing in Baptism. Baptism also signifies the cleansing believers received upon entering the body of Christ. We see the emphasis on cleansing and washing in three texts (1 Cor 6:11; Eph 5:26; Tit 3:5).[45] In 1 Cor 6:11 Paul says, "But you were washed, but you were sanctified, but you were justified in the name of the Lord Jesus Christ, and the Spirit of our God." Calling on his readers to avoid unrighteous behavior, Paul urges the Corinthians to live as new people since they were washed, sanctified, and justified. The prepositional phrases "in the name of our Lord Jesus Christ and the Spirit of our God" probably modify all three verbs, and hence the saving action of God has a trinitarian character since God is the implied subject of the passive verbs. Moreover, the three verbs denote what occurred at conversion. Paul uses metaphors of cleansing, of the cult, and the law court. Believers were washed or cleansed from their sins, set apart into the realm of the holy, and declared to be in the right before God.[46] In using the word "washing" Paul recalls baptism which symbolizes the cleansing of sin that occurs when believers come to faith.[47] Baptism signifies purification from the sin that characterized the former lives of believers. Because they are recipients of God's saving work in Christ and by the Spirit, they should live in a new way.

[45] In support of the view that all three texts relate to water baptism, see Beasley-Murray, *Baptism in the New Testament,* 162–67, 200–04, 209–16.

[46] Some are inclined to think that the verb "were sanctified" refers to progress in the Christian life, but Paul thinks here of definitive sanctification, i.e., the setting apart by God's grace that takes place at conversion. For the emphasis on definitive or positional sanctification in the NT, see the programmatic study by D. Peterson, *Possessed by God: A New Testament Theology of Sanctification and Holiness* (Grand Rapids: Eerdmans, 1995). In defense of such a meaning in this verse, see Fee, *First Corinthians,* 246; Thiselton, *First Corinthians,* 454.

[47] Many scholars place the emphasis only on the spiritual washing believers received at conversion (Fee, *First Corinthians,* 245–47; Dunn, *Baptism in the Holy Spirit,* 121–23; Thiselton, *First Corinthians,* 454). But it is quite unlikely that washing would not recall to mind water baptism as the initiatory event of conversion for the Corinthians. To play off water baptism from cleansing of sins is false dichotomy, as Garland rightly sees (*1 Corinthians,* 215–16).

Paul also refers to washing and cleansing in his instructions to husbands in Eph 5:22–33.[48] Husbands are to love their wives as Christ loved the church and tenderly care for and nurture them. Husbands are to model themselves after Christ who manifested his love for the church in giving his life on her behalf (Eph 5:25). The purpose of Christ's self-giving love on the cross is described in v. 26, "so that he should sanctify the church, by cleansing it with the washing of the water by the word." "Sanctify" here refers to the definitive sanctification accomplished at conversion where the church is set apart into the realm of the holy.[49] Verse 27 casts a glance forward to the final and eschatological sanctification on the day of the Lord. The definitive sanctification that occurs at conversion functions as the basis of and promise for future sanctification. The definitive sanctification that Christ accomplishes at conversion is further described metaphorically as a cleansing "by the washing of water." The language of the cult dominates this verse as is evident by terms like "sanctify," "cleansing," "washing," and "water." The emphasis is on the purity and spotlessness of believers through the atoning work of Christ. Paul again likely alludes to baptism since readers would naturally associate the cleansing received at conversion with the waters of baptism.[50] What Paul means by "the word" here is difficult and not decisive to our study. Paul may have in mind the baptismal declaration of faith by the person receiving baptism or a baptismal formula pronounced over the person receiving baptism. But since

[48] In support of a reference to baptism, see Hartman, *Baptism in the Early Church*, 105.

[49] Some argue that Paul thinks here of progressive sanctification. So J. R. W. Stott, *God's New Society: The Message of Ephesians* (Leicester: InterVarsity, 1979), 228. But Paul typically uses the verb "sanctify" to denote the definitive work of God at conversion (so Peterson, *Possessed by God*). In support of the notion that this verse refers to the sanctification that occurs at conversion, see Peterson, *Possessed by God,* 53; A. T. Lincoln, *Ephesians,* WBC (Waco: Word, 1990), 375; O'Brien, *Ephesians,* 421.

[50] In support, see Hartman, *Baptism in the Early Church*, 63–64. Many commentators see an allusion to the bridal bath of Ezek 16:8–14 rather than baptism (e.g., O'Brien, *Ephesians*, 422–23; H. H. Hoehner, *Ephesians: An Exegetical Commentary* [Grand Rapids: Baker, 2002], 753–54; Dunn, *Baptism in the Holy Spirit*, 162–65). But there is no need to posit an either-or here (rightly Hartman, *Baptism in the Early Church*, 106; Lincoln, *Ephesians*, 375–76; Beasley-Murray, *Baptism in the New Testament*, 201; F. F. Bruce, *The Epistles to the Colossians to Philemon and to the Ephesians*, NICNT [Grand Rapids: Eerdmans, 1984], 386–88). The participle *katharisas* does not denote antecedent action, but is coincidental with the main verb. So Lincoln, *Ephesians*, 375; O'Brien, *Ephesians*, 421–22.

Christ is the subject of the verb, it is preferable to see a reference to
the word of the gospel that effectively saves since Paul uses the same
term (*rhēma*) elsewhere to denote the gospel (Eph 6:17; so also Rom
10:8,17).

Titus 3:5 occurs in a paragraph that contrasts the former life of
believers with the new life that is theirs because of God's saving love
(Tit 3:3–7). Believers are not saved by their righteous works but
because of God's saving mercy. In v. 5 Paul teaches that believers
"were saved through the washing of regeneration and renewal from
the Holy Spirit." The Spirit "was poured out richly" on believers
through Jesus Christ, their Savior (Tit 3:6). Those who are justified
by his grace have become heirs of the hope of eternal life (Tit 3:7).
Not all scholars are convinced that this washing refers to baptism,
but again it seems most natural that believers would associate washing with their baptismal experience.[51] Two nouns modify "washing"
here: "regeneration" (*palingenesia*) and "renewal" (*anakainōsis*).
Both of these nouns point to the same reality: the new life granted to
believers upon conversion.[52] We see once again the initiatory character of baptism, in that it designates the boundary between the old
life and the new. The newness of life is also traced to the work of the
Holy Spirit,[53] for the Spirit is the genitive of source for both "regeneration" and "renewal." Both regeneration and renewal represent a
work of the Spirit, so that he is the one who grants new life to believers. The new life of believers is fittingly described in terms of washing, which recalls baptism where sins are washed away. Baptism in
Titus, then, is closely associated with the work of the Spirit,[54] as
it is in 1 Cor 12:13. Here the regenerating and renewing work of
the Spirit is central. Verse 7 shows that baptism is also linked with

[51] See Hartman, *Baptism in the Early Church*, 108–13. Against Dunn, *Baptism in the Holy Spirit*, 168–69.

[52] So Beasley-Murray, *Baptism in the New Testament*, 210; Dunn, *Baptism in the Holy Spirit*, 166. Paul does not draw upon mystery religions here. Mounce in a thorough study of the background of the term rightly concludes that the motif is a common one that was in the air and cannot be traced to any particular source. W. Mounce, "The Origin of the New Testament Metaphor of Rebirth" (Ph. D. diss., Aberdeen, 1981).

[53] Schnackenburg identifies it as a genitive of cause (*Baptism in the Thought of St. Paul*, 10). For the options available, see I. H. Marshall in collaboration with P. H. Towner, *A Critical and Exegetical Commentary on the Pastoral Epistles*, ICC (Edinburgh: T. & T. Clark, 1999), 316–17.

[54] See also Hartman, *Baptism in the Early Church*, 113.

justification ("being justified by his grace"), so that we have further evidence that baptism is associated with the decisive saving work of God that occurred at conversion.

Paul does not explicitly consider in the texts on washing whether baptism is fitting for infants. But a careful consideration of Tit 3:5–7 makes such a view unlikely. Baptism is closely associated here with the work of the Spirit in regenerating and renewing sinners so that they have new life. It is difficult to see how this can be true of infants unless one were to adopt an *ex opere operato* view of baptism. Such a view, however, is quite unlikely since justification is also mentioned in v. 7, and both baptism and justification occur at the inception of the Christian life. Indeed, Paul invariably links justification with believing (see Rom 3:22; 5:1; Gal 2:16).

Sealing and Baptism.   Many scholars see a reference to baptism when Paul speaks of sealing (2 Cor 1:22; Eph 1:13).[55] It is clear in both of these texts that sealing occurs at conversion when believers receive the Spirit, and hence the notion that baptism is a sealing accords with the notion that believers receive the Spirit when baptized. The reference to sealing, however, does not clearly refer to baptism, and hence we will not explore these texts in detail in this study. If sealing refers to baptism, it would not affect what is argued here in any case, for Paul clearly teaches that only those who have heard the gospel and believed in it are sealed with the Spirit (Eph 1:13).

Another text on sealing has played a significant role in the discussion on baptism. In Rom 4:11 Paul argues that Abraham's circumcision was a seal of the righteousness he already had by faith. It is quite common for paedobaptists to appeal to this verse to defend infant baptism, where it is argued that just as circumcision is a seal of God's work, so too baptism applied at infancy is a seal of God's promised work.[56] The fundamental flaw in this argument is that Paul does not

[55] E.g., Hartman, *Baptism in the Early Church*, 68.

[56] For this view of the seal, see P. C. Marcel, *The Biblical Doctrine of Infant Baptism: Sacrament of the Covenant of Grace,* trans. P. E. Hughes (London: James Clarke, 1953), 90, 210–11; Cullmann, *Baptism in the New Testament,* 45–46, 57, 64, 66; B. Chapell, "A Pastoral Overview of Infant Baptism," in *The Case for Covenantal Infant Baptism,* ed. G. Strawbridge (Phillipsburg, NJ: P&R, 2003), 15; C. P. Venema, "Covenant Theology and Baptism," in *The Case for Covenantal Infant Baptism,* ed. G. Strawbridge (Phillipsburg, NJ: P&R, 2003), 221–22. But for a more convincing explanation, see Jewett, *Infant Baptism and the Covenant of Grace,* 86–87.

speak of circumcision in general as a seal here. Rather, he argues that circumcision is the seal of *Abraham's righteousness by faith*. The text does not teach that circumcision in general is a seal, so that it functions as a defense of applying baptism before faith. What Paul emphasizes in Rom 4:9–12 is that circumcision is not necessary for salvation since Abraham *believed* and was right with God (Gen 15:6) *before* he was circumcised (Genesis 17). Circumcision in Romans 4 is a seal, ratification, or authentication of *a faith and righteousness Abraham already had*. How such an argument supports infant baptism is mystifying since faith precedes circumcision; it does not follow it. Circumcision functions as a seal because it documents and ratifies a faith and therefore a right-standing with God that already exists. If this verse is introduced into the debate on infant baptism, it clearly supports the Baptist view.

Baptism and Redemptive History

One of the main themes in Pauline theology is that the new age of fulfillment has arrived. With the coming of Christ "the ends of the ages have come" (1 Cor 10:11). The promises of the Old Testament have been realized in Christ. Or, at least the new age has been *inaugurated* by virtue of the death and resurrection of Christ (Gal 1:4), and it will be *consummated* at his second coming (1 Cor 15:20–28). Believers have the privilege of living under a "new covenant" (2 Cor 3:6). This new covenant brings righteousness, not condemnation; it is of the Spirit, not the letter, and it will last forever (2 Cor 3:7–11). Our understanding of Paul's theology of baptism will be enlarged when placed in the context of his view of redemptive history.

The Old Testament Scriptures promise that the new age will be one in which the Holy Spirit is poured out (Joel 2:28–29; Isa 44:3; Ezek 36:26–27). For Paul, one could not even be considered a Christian without possessing the Holy Spirit (Rom 8:9). In Gal 3:1–5 Paul argues that the rite of circumcision is not required to be a member of the church of Christ. God's granting of the Spirit to the uncircumcised proves that circumcision is unnecessary because the Spirit is the first-fruits of salvation, and those who insist upon circumcision are reverting back to the old evil age (Gal 1:4). Even though circumcision is a matter of indifference (Gal 5:6; 6:15), the Judaizers have failed to see that "a new creation" has dawned (Gal 6:15; cp. 2 Cor 5:17). The reality of the new creation is indissolubly linked with the gift of the Spirit.

It is instructive, then, to see that baptism is closely associated with the gift of the Spirit. We have seen that Tit 3:5 speaks of "the washing of regeneration and renewing by the Holy Spirit." Almost every word here has an eschatological import, signifying that the fulfillment of God's promises has begun. The reference to "washing" and the "Holy Spirit" evoke the promise of Ezek 11:19 and 36:25–27. The washing echoes Ezek 36:25, "I will sprinkle clean water on you, and you will be clean; I will cleanse you from all your filthiness and from all your idols." The Spirit and renewal are present in Ezek 36:26–27, "I will give you a new heart and put a new spirit within you," and "I will put my spirit within you." Indeed, Tit 3:6 speaks of the "pouring out" of the Spirit, which is an allusion to the promise in Joel 2:28–29 (cp. Isa 44:3). Baptism, then, is an initiation rite into the new age of redemption in fulfillment of the Old Testament promises. The granting of the Spirit demonstrates that the new age is inaugurated.

The eschatological thrust of baptism is also evident in Gal 3:27. Paul argues in Gal 3:15–4:7 that with the coming of Christ the covenant with Abraham has been fulfilled, and thus the covenant with Moses is no longer in force. Jesus is the seed promised to Abraham (Gal 3:16), and in him the pledges made to Abraham are realized. The age of childhood and infancy under the Mosaic law has ended (Gal 3:23–25), and now "you are all sons of God through faith in Christ Jesus" (Gal 3:26). What Paul means by "sons" is that all believers are now "adults" through faith in Christ; that is, they are no longer in the period of infancy under the Mosaic law. They are mature and grown up because the promises made in the Old Testament have come to fruition. Believers are the seed of Abraham because they "belong to Christ" (Gal 3:29). Since Christ is the only seed of Abraham (Gal 3:16), then belonging to Christ is the only means by which one can become part of the family of Abraham and receive the promises. How does one know that one belongs to Christ? Verse

26 says we know we are Christ's if we have faith. And v. 27 says that those who are baptized have clothed themselves with Christ. In other words, baptism signifies that one is united to Christ. And since Christ is the only seed of Abraham, then baptism signifies not only that we belong to Christ, but also that by belonging to Christ we become part of Abraham's family. The unity in Abraham's family is what Paul has in mind in Gal 3:28 when he says that we "are all one in Christ Jesus." In baptism we become part of Christ and become heirs to the eschatological promises made to Abraham.

So too, in Romans 6 and Colossians 2, death and burial with Christ indicate participation in the new age. When Paul speaks of death and sin in Romans 5, these refer to twin powers of the old era which exercise control over human beings. In Rom 5:12–19 Paul argues that Jesus Christ has conquered these two powers as the second Adam. The first Adam introduced sin, death, and condemnation into the world. The second Adam has overcome these powers and has granted righteousness and life to his people. Thus, Paul argues in Romans 6 that sin can no longer rule or master believers because they have died with Christ. When Jesus Christ died on the cross, he stripped death and sin of their authority forever (Rom 6:9–10). They can no longer exercise mastery and control over him. This triumph over death and sin is not a matter of historical interest relating only to Christ. Believers have died with Christ (Rom 6:3–4), so that his triumph over death and sin has become theirs. Baptism, therefore, functions as a reminder of the new eschatological reality that has been obtained with the death and resurrection of Christ.

Paul's theology of Christ as the second Adam is the key to understanding what is meant in Rom 6:6 when he says that "our old self was crucified with" Christ. Our old self is who we were in Adam, totally under the subservience of death and sin. Since believers are united with Christ, we are now in the second Adam. Our old self is no longer the fundamental reality of our lives. Death and sin have both been stripped of their power since we were united with Christ in both his death and resurrection.

When Paul speaks, then, of being baptized "into Christ" (Rom 6:3; Gal 3:27), he has in mind the union with Christ that is ours by virtue of our participating with him in his death and resurrection. Galatians 3:27 supports this by linking closely together being baptized into the name of Christ with being clothed with Christ (cp. 1 Cor 10:2). The central issue in Galatians was raised by outside teachers who insisted that Gentile believers must be circumcised to enter the people of God (Gal 5:2–6; 6:12–13; cp. 2:3–5). Paul counters these Judaizers by explaining who truly belongs to Abraham's family. Another way of putting it is that Paul defines true circumcision (see Phil 3:3). He insists that all those who trust in Jesus Christ for their salvation are members of Abraham's family (Gal 2:15–21). Those who have received the Spirit by faith are the true seed of Abraham. One does not become part of Abraham's family through circumcision, but through the one and only true seed of Abraham— Jesus Christ (Gal 3:16). True circumcision, according to Galatians, does not consist in the physical operation of removing the foreskin. The true circumcision occurred in the cross of Christ, for the cross represents the decisive saving act that inaugurated the new creation (Gal 1:4; 2:21; 3:1,13; 4:4–5; 5:12; 6:12,14,15). Galatians, then, runs along the same lines as Colossians, in that circumcision, rightly interpreted, points toward the cross of Jesus Christ.[57]

If Paul adopted the view customary in paedobaptist circles, we would expect him to say that circumcision is no longer required because baptism has replaced circumcision as the covenantal sign. Paul does not prosecute such an argument in Galatians or anywhere else in his letters, nor, incidentally, did the early church advance such an argument during the apostolic council of Acts 15. It would seem that the simplest argument Paul could make in Galatians would be as follows: "Of course, circumcision is not required, dear Galatians, because you all know that baptism has replaced circumcision as the initiation rite for the people of God."[58] Instead of making such an argument, however, Paul insists that demanding circumcision for salvation nullifies the cross of Christ. The cross of Christ

---

[57] Covenantal theology often makes the mistake of over-emphasizing the continuity between the old covenant and the new (rightly Beasley-Murray, *Baptism in the New Testament*, 337, 339).

[58] Chapell flatly argues that baptism has replaced circumcision ("Pastoral Overview of Infant Baptism," 17), failing to notice that Paul does *not* make this argument in Galatians, nor is it articulated at the apostolic council in Acts 15.

has inaugurated the new creation so that now, in the fullness of time, there is forgiveness of sins and redemption for those who trust in Jesus Christ (Gal 1:4; 4:4–5; 6:14–15).[59] Paul boasts only in the cross of Christ because it represents the crucifixion of the old world order and the introduction of a new life—indeed a new creation (Gal 6:14–15).

Paul's understanding of baptism, then, must be placed into the context of Galatians as a whole, and he only mentions baptism in one text (Gal 3:27), which emphasizes that in baptism believers are united with Christ. The close conjunction between v. 26 and v. 27 demonstrates that the group of those who are baptized into Christ is the same as those who *put their faith in Christ*. It follows that baptism is not solely an objective event apart from the subjective appropriation of that event by faith.[60] Sometimes paedobaptists celebrate the objective work of God's grace and complain that Baptists place too much emphasis on the human response, so that focus on God's grace is compromised. In some cases, of course, Baptists so emphasize the human response of faith that God's grace and power are obscured. But when Baptists rightly correlate the Pauline message in Galatians, both God's grace and the human response are included. Indeed, it is actually paedobaptists who have a truncated view of God's grace, since baptism in their scheme does not necessarily lead to faith and salvation. The so-called objectivity of faith ends up being a cipher if it does not have any effect in human beings. What Paul teaches in Galatians demonstrates, on the other hand, that God's grace produces the response of faith in human beings.

Immediately after mentioning baptism we find Paul's famous statement on the unity of the church in Gal 3:28. All believers are one in Christ, whether Jews or Gentiles, slaves or free, or male or female. Baptism as the boundary marker for the people of God also stresses the unity of the church. All of those baptized are members of God's people. Galatians 3:26 reminds us that the church is composed of the community of believers. To say that anyone is part of Abraham's seed by baptism at birth strays from Pauline categories,

---

[59] For an argument similar to what is being said here, see Dunn, *Baptism in the Holy Spirit*, 157.
[60] See especially Beasley-Murray, *Baptism in the New Testament*, 272–74.

for on this reading some are part of Abraham's seed without faith
and solely on the basis of an external covenantal sign. The church,
then, is united as a community of *believers*.[61]

Implications for Baptismal Regeneration and Infant Baptism

Baptism in the epistles is an initiatory event, representing the
boundary between the old life and the new. Those who are baptized
have received the Spirit, which is the indisputable mark of entrance
into the people of God (Gal 3:1–5). Paul does not sharply distinguish
between water baptism and Spirit baptism, for the two were closely
associated during the NT era and unbaptized Christians were unheard of. The issue of baptismal regeneration arose in later church
history when baptism was separated from faith, though those who
promoted baptismal regeneration rightly saw that baptism was irre-
trievably tied to initiation into the people of God in the NT. Hence,
NT writers did not specifically address the matter of baptismal regeneration since they never separated baptism from faith. We see
from 1 Cor 1:13–17 that baptismal regeneration is excluded since
baptism must be understood in light of the gospel rather than vice-
versa. What saves is the death and resurrection of Christ and the
gospel of grace, and hence NT writers did not conceive of baptism
in such a way that it contradicted the gospel of grace. When Peter
says baptism saves (1 Pet 3:21), he means that it is saves because in
baptism believers appeal for forgiveness of sins on the basis of the
work of the crucified and risen Lord. Furthermore, we find in Acts
that Cornelius received the Spirit before water baptism, indicating
that water baptism is not absolutely necessary for salvation (Acts
10:44–48).

For some believers today the connection of baptism to conversion seems odd, for they associate conversion with belief, making a
profession of faith, or even going forward at an evangelistic event.
Baptism is separated from conversion because many were baptized

---

[61] Wilson's own understanding of the covenants is such that he fails to see the implication
of this crucial difference between the covenants (*To a Thousand Generations*, 21–38). See further
the chapter by Stephen Wellum in this volume.

long before or after their conversion. But in the NT era it was unheard of to separate baptism from faith in Christ for such a long period. Baptism occurred either immediately after or very soon after people believed. The short interval between faith and baptism is evident from numerous examples in the book of Acts (Acts 2:41; 8:12–13; 8:38; 9:18; 10:48; 16:15,33; 18:8; 19:5).[62] It follows, then, that when Paul connects death to sin with baptism, death to sin takes place at conversion, for baptism as an initiatory event occurs at the threshold of one's new life.[63] Paul appeals to baptism because it dramatically represents the washing away of one's sins and the new life to which believers are called.[64]

We have, then, compelling grounds to reject infant baptism.[65] We have seen consistently that those who are baptized have been regenerated by or received the Spirit (Tit 3:5; 1 Cor 12:13). It is difficult to see how the reception of the Spirit could be predicated of infants since the Spirit is received by faith (Gal 3:2,5) and infants do not exercise faith. Moreover, the Spirit leads believers to a transformed life, so that they bear the fruit of the Spirit instead of the works of the flesh (Gal 5:16–26; cp. Rom 8:1–17), and it is not easy to see how one can speak of infants being transformed by the Spirit. In Rom 6:1–14 and Col 2:11–15 those who are baptized are said to be dead to sin and alive to God in Christ Jesus. The old Adam has been crucified or circumcised in Christ's death, and those who belong to

---

[62] For further support of this notion, see Robert Stein's essay in this volume.

[63] The believer's death to sin and conversion is anchored, of course, in history—in the death and resurrection of Christ. As Schnackenburg says, "The distance of time and the repetition of baptism for those who subsequently believe and come to baptism play no role in this view. All who attach themselves to Christ, irrespective of the time of their doing so, are taken up into the once-for-all event and in Him Himself" (*Baptism in the Thought of St. Paul,* 115).

[64] Baptism is inseparably joined with Christ's crucifixion. Schnackenburg rightly says, "Paul knows and recognizes only one source of salvation: the cross of Jesus Christ. He does not teach a miraculous effectiveness of holy signs and rites, isolated from the one great saving event on Golgotha" (*Baptism in the Thought of St. Paul,* 112).

[65] It is also instructive to see that David Wright, a paedobaptist, maintains that infant baptism was not practiced until much later than the apostolic era. He says, "Now the baptismal experience of the church of the early Fathers was largely of believer's baptism, or perhaps better conversion baptism. Historical study is steadily consolidating the conclusion that infant baptism did not really come into its own, as the common practice, until after Augustine, perhaps in the sixth century." So D. F. Wright, "Recovering Baptism for a New Age of Mission," in *Doing Theology for the People of God,* ed. D. Lewis and A. McGrath (Downers Grove: InterVarsity, 1996), 57. This quote was brought to my attention by Ardel Caneday.

Christ are new persons. Again, it is hard to grasp how infants might be dead to sin and alive to God in Christ Jesus, just as it is unclear how they could be regenerated and renewed by God's Spirit.

Indeed, Col 2:12 clarifies that those who have died and been raised with Christ have experienced these saving realities by faith. It is tempting to focus on God's grace in baptism, so that emphasis is placed only on the objective saving work of God. We have seen, however, that the epistles do not separate God's objective and subjective work. We should not separate what God has joined together. The grace of God is so powerful because it secures faith and trust in the heart of human beings. Galatians 3:27 clarifies that those baptized into Christ are those who are clothed with Christ, but those who are endowed with Christ are also those who have exercised faith (Gal 3:26). Since the NT does not speak of infants exercising faith, they should not be considered as candidates for baptism. In Tit 3:5–7, those who are baptized are those regenerated by the Spirit, but these same people are those who have been justified, and the signature of Paul's theology is that justification is by faith.

It is precisely here that the difference between the old covenant and the new shines forth. In the new covenant everyone knows the Lord (Jer 31:34), but in the old covenant physical circumcision did not necessarily translate into spiritual circumcision of the heart (see Deut 10:16; Jer 4:4 with Deut 30:6). Those who belonged to Israel were not necessarily spiritually regenerate. Physical circumcision was to be succeeded by spiritual circumcision and regeneration. But the new covenant community is the community of the Spirit. Only those who have the Spirit of God belong to God (Rom 8:9) and are his sons and daughters (Rom 8:14; Gal 3:26). Baptism is applied to those who have received the Spirit by faith (Gal 3:1–5), not to those whom it is hoped will receive the Spirit in the future. The Christian church is not tied to any nation or ethnic group, but comprises all believers in Jesus Christ everywhere. We have seen that baptism is a sign of unity in the church, but it is a unity among those who believe, as Gal 3:26–29 clarifies. Those who are the seed of Abraham believe like Abraham, and therefore they belong to Jesus Christ.

Those supporting paedobaptism often support their case by appealing to the parallel between baptism and circumcision in Col 2:12. The alleged parallel does not stand, however, because the connection is between baptism and *spiritual circumcision*, not physical circumcision. Hence, baptism is reserved, according to the argument of Colossians, for those with *regenerate hearts*. If Paul actually thought like our covenantal friends, he would have argued in Galatians that circumcision was no longer in force because baptism had replaced circumcision. Such an argument would have the merit of being compelling and clear. Instead, as we have seen, Paul argues in both Galatians and Colossians that circumcision points to the cross of Christ and the new creation inaugurated by him. Baptism, then, is tied to the saving work of the Spirit which produces faith in the lives of believers.

First Corinthians 7:14 cannot be rightly interpreted as a defense of infant baptism.[66] When Paul says that the children are "holy" through a believing parent, he does not mean that they are believers or part of the covenant.[67] In the same verse he says that the unbelieving husband or wife "is sanctified" through the believing spouse. But no one would argue that, therefore, the unbelieving spouse should be baptized or included in the covenant people even though they are "sanctified."[68]

---

[66] Contrary to G. W. Bromiley, *Children of Promise: The Case for Baptizing Infants* (Grand Rapids: Eerdmans, 1979); G. Strawbridge, "Introduction," in *The Case for Covenantal Infant Baptism*, ed. G. Strawbridge (Phillipsburg, NJ: P&R, 2003), 8; Ross, "Signs and Seals," 107; D. Wilson,"Baptism and Children: Their Place in the Old and New Testaments," in *The Case for Covenantal Infant Baptism*, ed. G. Strawbridge (Phillipsburg, NJ: P&R, 2003), 295; id., *To a Thousand Generations,* 17.

[67] Wilson in his essay ("Baptism and Children: Their Place in the Old and New Testaments," 286–302) argues from a number of texts on God's promises to children, and concludes from these that only infant baptism fits. Wilson's confidence in God's promises for our children is encouraging and biblical. Baptists also have every reason to be assured that God ordains his word to bear fruit in their children, but we believe that the scriptural witness demands that baptism be applied when there is *evidence* that God has so worked. Hence, Wilson's arguments do not clearly advance his thesis. Nor do we claim, as Wilson suggests, that every conversion must be dramatic, or that we can discern the precise moment of conversion in our children. But the Baptist does argue that baptism should only take place when there is evidence that God has indeed worked savingly in the heart of children. Not all Baptists follow this principle consistently, of course, but Baptists also need to continually reform their practice according to the word of God.

[68] Beasley-Murray rightly comments, "Above all it is to be recognized that the holiness of the child is commensurate with that of the unbelieving parent; a valid explanation of the former

Verse 16 indicates that the sanctification of the unbelieving spouse is not equivalent to salvation, for Paul says, "For how do you know, O wife, whether you will save your husband? Or how do you know, O husband, whether you will save your wife?" This would scarcely need to be said if the unbelieving spouse were already sanctified in the sense of being saved. So too, infants of believers are not "saved," but they are "holy."[69] I would suggest that this means that the possibility of their salvation is enhanced simply because they have believing parents.

Conclusion

Believer's Baptism is not essential for being an evangelical. We do not consider those who proclaim the gospel of justification by faith yet practice infant baptism to be heretics; we consider them brothers and sisters in the Lord. Still, it does not follow that the matter is unimportant. Those who allow infant baptism are allowing the unregenerate to be members of the church. But the church is the community of the Spirit, not the flesh. The church is properly composed of those who are members of the new covenant (Heb 8:8–13), not those who belong to the old age under Moses. The people of God are not a nationalistic or political entity as Israel was but rather the people of the Spirit. Baptism should not be given to those who have not received the Spirit, to those who have not died and risen with Christ, to those who have not trusted in Jesus for their salvation, and to those who have not been justified by faith so that they do not walk in newness of life. All of these realities are predicated of the baptized in the NT, for baptism does not belong to the old covenant but to the new. It is not applied with the hope that people will believe and receive the Spirit. It is applied because people have received the Spirit and believed.

must account also for the latter" (*Baptism in the New Testament,* 193). See also Jewett, *Infant Baptism and the Covenant of Grace,* 126, 131; Garland, *1 Corinthians,* 296. For a fine exposition of the verse that recognizes the parallel between children and the unbelieving spouse, see Fee, *First Corinthians,* 299–302.

[69] Suprisingly, Wilson appeals to the fact that children are "holy" (*hagios*) to support baptism, but places the verb "sanctify" (*hagiazō*) as it is used of unbelieving spouses in a different category (*To a Thousand Generations,* 17). The two words belong to the same semantic domain, however, and are used synonymously in this context. There is no warrant exegetically for Wilson to permit baptism for children who are holy and to deny it to spouses who are sanctified.

BAPTISM AND THE RELATIONSHIP BE-
TWEEN THE COVENANTS

Stephen J. Wellum[*]

Introduction

A t the heart of the advocacy and defense of the evangelical
Reformed doctrine of infant baptism is the argument that
it is an implication drawn from the comprehensive theological category of the "covenant of grace," a category which, it is
claimed, unites the Scriptures and without which the Bible cannot
be understood correctly. In many ways, all other arguments for infant baptism are secondary to this overall line of reasoning. If one
can establish the basic continuity of the "covenant of grace" across
the canon, then it is the belief of most paedobaptists that their doctrine is biblically and theologically demonstrated. It does not seem to
bother them that in the NT there is no express command to baptize
infants and no record of any clear case of infant baptism.[1] Rather,
as John Murray admits, "the evidence for infant baptism falls into
the category of good and necessary inference"[2] and ultimately this
inference is rooted and grounded in a specific covenantal argument.
Covenant theology, then, according to the paedobaptist, requires
infant baptism. In fact, specific details in their argument such as the
"mixed" nature of the church,[3] the relationship between circumci-

---

[*] Stephen J. Wellum received his Ph.D. from Trinity Evangelical Divinity School, and is
Professor of Christian Theology at The Southern Baptist Theological Seminary in Louisville,
Kentucky.

[1] Most paedobaptists acknowledge this point. See for example, J. Murray, *Christian Baptism*
(Phillipsburg, NJ: P&R, 1980), 69; L. Berkhof, *Systematic Theology* (1941; reprint, Grand Rap-
ids: Eerdmans, 1982), 632; R. L. Reymond, *A New Systematic Theology of the Christian Faith*
(Nashville: Thomas Nelson, 1998), 936.

[2] Murray, *Christian Baptism*, 69. The language of "good and necessary inference" is drawn
from the *Westminster Confession of Faith* 1:6. For a helpful Baptist discussion of this point see
F. Malone, *The Baptism of Disciples Alone: A Covenantal Argument for Credobaptism Versus Paedobaptism* (Cape Coral, FL: Founders Press, 2003), xvii–xix, 18–47.

[3] The "mixed" nature of the church refers to the belief that under both the old and new
covenants, the locus of the covenant community and the locus of the elect are distinct; hence
the "visible" church, by its very nature, is constituted by both believers and unbelievers or, as

sion and baptism, and various NT passages utilized to support their
view such as the household texts, are all dependent on their understanding of the continuity of the covenant of grace across redemptive history. Ultimately, if Baptists want to argue cogently against
the paedobaptist viewpoint and for a believer's baptism, we must, in
the end, respond to this covenantal argument.

The goal of this chapter is to do precisely this and I will proceed
in a twofold manner. First, I will outline and then unpack briefly the
covenantal argument for infant baptism as given by the proponents
and defenders of the view. Second, I will attempt to evaluate their
argument, albeit in a summary fashion, both in terms of critique and
positive construction.

The Covenantal Argument for Infant Baptism

An Outline of the Argument

Let me first sketch the overall argument for infant baptism from
the continuity of the "covenant of grace" before I unpack it in more
detail. Two examples will suffice to give the basic outline of the argument, even though many more examples could be given.[4]

Our first example is taken from a former Baptist, Randy Booth,
who has written a popular defense of paedobaptism in *Children of
the Promise*. Booth succinctly summarizes under five major headings

covenant theologians like to say, "believers and their children"—children who may or may not
constitute the elect. Baptist theology, on the other hand, argues that the NT church, by definition, is constituted by a regenerate community, so that under the new covenant the locus of the
covenant community and the elect are the same. This difference between a paedobaptist and
credobaptist understanding of the church will be discussed in greater depth below.

[4] In addition to the books already mentioned see for example, J. Calvin, *Institutes of the Chris-
tian Religion* (Philadelphia: Westminster, 1960), 2:1303–1359; F. Turretin, *Institutes of Elenctic
Theology*, trans. G. M. Giger, ed. J. T. Dennison, Jr. (Phillipsburg: P&R, 1997), 3:377–420; C.
Hodge, *Systematic Theology* (Grand Rapids: Eerdmans, 1982), 3:526–611; B. B. Warfield, *Se-
lected Shorter Writings*, ed. J. E. Meeter (Phillipsburg: P&R, 1970), 1:325–331; G. W. Bromiley,
Children of Promise: The Case for Baptizing Infants (Grand Rapids: Eerdmans, 1979); H. Hanko,
We and Our Children: The Reformed Doctrine of Infant Baptism (Grand Rapids: Reformed Free
Publishing Association, 1981); R. C. Sproul, *Essential Truths of the Christian Faith* (Wheaton:
Tyndale House, 1992), 225–229; E. Clowney, *The Church* (Downers Grove: InterVarsity, 1995),
276–284; D. Wilson, *To a Thousand Generations: Infant Baptism—Covenant Mercy for the People
of God* (Moscow, ID: Canon, 1996); G. Strawbridge, ed. *The Case for Covenantal Infant Baptism*
(Phillipsburg: P&R, 2003).

what he believes is the biblical case and theological warrant for the practice of infant baptism.

> 1. *Covenant Theology.* Throughout the Bible, God relates to his people by way of a covenant of grace. Covenant theology provides the basic framework for rightly interpreting Scripture.
> 2. *Continuity of the Covenant of Grace.* The Bible teaches one and the same way of salvation in both the Old and the New Testaments, despite some different outward requirements.
> 3. *Continuity of the People of God.* Since there is one covenant of grace between God and man, there is one continuous people of God (the church) in the Old and New Testaments.
> 4. *Continuity of the Covenant Signs.* Baptism is the sign of the covenant in the New Testament, just as circumcision was the sign of the covenant in the Old Testament.
> 5. *Continuity of Households.* Whole households are included in God's redemptive covenant.[5]

Along with most defenders of the Reformed view of paedobaptism, Booth is clear that infant baptism does not entail any kind of *ex opere operato* view[6] of the sacrament or ordinance.[7] Just because an infant receives the covenant sign, whether in the OT or NT, does not entail that the infant is regenerated, nor does it guarantee a future regeneration, that is, a kind of presumptive regeneration. Rather, as Booth contends, "the covenant sign was God's indication that its recipients were *set apart* for his special blessing and use. They therefore stood in need of cleansing, regeneration, and justification. The benefits of the covenant were to be appropriated by faith in the promised Redeemer."[8] Hence, to be a "child of the covenant" does not necessarily guarantee one's salvation. Rather, it makes available to the infant all the benefits and privileges of the covenant which must, in the end, be appropriated by faith; otherwise this same "cov-

---

[5] R. R. Booth, *Children of the Promise: The Biblical Case for Infant Baptism* (Phillipsburg: P&R, 1995), 8.

[6] *Ex opere operato* means that baptism (or any other sacramental action) saves by virtue of the action itself being performed.

[7] Historically, evangelicals have differed over whether to apply the term "sacrament" to baptism and the Lord's Supper.

[8] Booth, *Children of the Promise*, 9. There is some dispute within the paedobaptist community over whether infant baptism leads to a kind of "presumptive regeneration." See D. J. Engelsma's seven articles entitled, "A Candid Confession of the Character of a Conditional Covenant," in *The Standard Bearer* (January 1–April 1, 1997).

enant child" will be found to be a covenant breaker and thus stand under the covenantal curse, namely, the condemnation and judgment of God.

Our second example is Reformed theologian, Louis Berkhof. In a similar fashion to Booth, Berkhof lays out five summary propositions—all of which are intimately related to his understanding of the "covenant of grace" across redemptive history—which he believes supports and warrants the claim that infant baptism is a biblical doctrine.[9]

> 1. Although the Abrahamic covenant had national aspects to it, at its heart, it was a *spiritual* covenant which signified spiritual realities, including its sign and seal, that is, circumcision.
> 2. The Abrahamic covenant is still in force and is essentially identical with the "new covenant" of the present dispensation. The unity and continuity of this *one* covenant of grace in both testaments follows from the fact that the Mediator is the same; the condition of faith is the same; and the blessings are the same, namely, regeneration, justification, spiritual gifts, and eternal life.
> 3. By God's appointment, infants share in the benefits of the Abrahamic covenant and therefore received circumcision as a sign and seal. Since the "new covenant" is essentially identical with the Abrahamic covenant, infants of believing parents who receive the sign of the covenant are not excluded from covenant or church membership.
> 4. Even though the Abrahamic covenant is essentially identical with the new covenant there are some changes that have taken place. In the new dispensation, baptism is by divine authority substituted for circumcision as the initiatory sign and seal of the covenant of grace. Baptism corresponds with circumcision in *spiritual* meaning so that both signs signify the washing away of sin and the need for regeneration. Furthermore, given the essential unity of the covenant across the ages, baptism, as the new sign and seal of the new covenant age, does not exclude infants of believing parents.
> 5. Although the NT contains no direct evidence for the practice of infant baptism in the church this is due more to the fact that the apostolic age was primarily a missionary period which focused on the baptism of adults. But, given the unity of the covenant of grace, there is also no text in the NT which specifically abrogates the demand that the covenant sign be applied to the infants of believing parents in the new covenant era. Household baptisms probably, though it cannot be established with certainty, bear witness to this fact.

By briefly outlining the basic argument for infant baptism, it should now be clear that at the heart of the Reformed polemic for paedobaptism is an explicit view of the covenants. For defenders of

---

[9] The following summary points are taken from Berkhof, *Systematic Theology*, 632–34.

infant baptism, central to their argument is the essential continuity of the "covenant of grace" across redemptive history and the entailments that they believe result from this continuity such as the essential unity of the people of God (Israel and the church) and the covenant signs (circumcision and baptism). In the final analysis, this particular understanding of the covenants provides the primary basis for the defense of paedobaptism as a biblical doctrine. Booth states it well when he admits, "There are also other evidences in the pages of Scripture that support the truth of infant baptism. Nevertheless, *the foundation of the argument consists of the unified covenant of grace evident in the Scriptures of the Old and New Testaments.*"[10]

Now with that basic argument in mind, we will direct our attention to three interrelated aspects of the paedobaptist argument: their understanding of the nature of the covenant community, whether that community is Israel or the church, and to whom the covenantal signs should be applied today. The foundation for their argument in each of these three arenas is their understanding of the covenants.

The Nature of the "Covenant of Grace" and Infant Baptism

As already stated, the heart of the defense of infant baptism centers on a particular understanding of the covenant of grace. As B. B. Warfield memorably responded to Baptist theologian A. H. Strong, "The argument in a nutshell is simply this: God established His church in the days of Abraham and put children into it. They must remain there until He puts them out. He has nowhere put them out. They are still then members of His Church and as such entitled to its ordinances."[11]

We notice in Warfield's response a twofold conviction regarding the subject of the covenant. First, we discover the belief that one of the most important unifying themes of Scripture is God's redemptive work across the ages through the biblical covenants. Most people would not dispute this point.[12] Secondly, however, we

---

[10] Booth, *Children of the Promise*, 10 (emphasis his).

[11] B. B. Warfield, "The Polemics of Infant Baptism," in *Studies in Theology* (1932; reprint, Grand Rapids: Baker, 1981), 9:408. See the citation in C. P. Venema, "Covenant Theology and Baptism" in Strawbridge, ed., *The Case for Covenantal Infant Baptism*, 201.

[12] For an excellent treatment of how God's saving plan progresses across the ages through

also notice the conviction that the biblical *covenants* are merely an expression of the *one* covenant of grace. It is this latter contention, which is at the heart of covenant theology, that is under dispute in the baptism debate. Why? Because covenant theology has attempted to conclude from this particular understanding of *the* covenant of grace a fairly strict continuity between God's saving work across redemptive history, regardless of the specific covenant in question. This is especially true in regard to their understanding of the nature of the covenant community (Israel and the church) and the essential similarity and application of the covenant signs (circumcision and baptism) to the covenant community throughout the ages.

Let us examine the main contours of covenant theology. The "covenant of grace" is contrasted to the first covenant made with Adam, the "covenant of works."[13] The covenant of works was made with Adam as the head and representative of the entire human race. To him and his entire posterity, eternal life was promised upon the condition of perfect obedience to the law of God. However, due to his disobedience, he, along with the entire human race, was plunged into a state of sin, death, and condemnation (see Rom 5:12–21). But God, by his own sovereign grace and initiative, was pleased to make a second covenant—the covenant of grace—with human beings (specifically, the elect),[14] wherein the God of grace freely offered to sinners life and salvation through the last Adam, the covenantal head of his people, the Lord Jesus Christ (*West. Conf.* 7.2–3).[15] Thus the

---

covenants, see W. J. Dumbrell, *Covenant and Creation: A Theology of the Old Testament Covenants* (1984; reprint, Carlisle: Paternoster, 1997) and S. G. Dempster, *Dominion and Dynasty: A Theology of the Hebrew Bible* (Downers Grove: InterVarsity, 2003).

[13] On the teachings and variations of covenant theology, see P. Golding, *Covenant Theology: The Key of Theology in Reformed Thought and Tradition* (Ross-shire, Scotland: Christian Focus, 2004); G. Vos, "The Doctrine of the Covenant in Reformed Theology," in *Redemptive History and Biblical Interpretation*, ed. R. B. Gaffin, Jr. (Phillipsburg: P&R, 1980), 234–67; J. Murray, "Covenant Theology" in *Collected Works* (Carlisle, PA: Banner of Truth, 1982), 4:216–40; and O. P. Robertson, *The Christ of the Covenants* (Phillipsburg: P&R, 1980).

Not all covenant theologians accept a "covenant of works." See G. Van Groningen, *From Creation to Consummation* (Sioux Center, IA: Dordt College Press, 1996), 98. Robertson, *Christ of the Covenants,* 54–57; Dumbrell, *Covenant and Creation,* 44–46.

[14] Within covenant theology there is a dispute over the identification of the parties of the covenant of grace. Does God covenant only with the elect or does he covenant with believers and their children? On this issue see below.

[15] Within covenant theology there is also a distinction made between the "covenant of grace"

covenant of grace began immediately after the Fall with the promise of grace in Gen 3:15. This promise was then progressively revealed and fulfilled in history through variously administered covenants with Noah, Abraham, Israel, and David. Ultimately it was brought to fulfillment in the new covenant inaugurated by Jesus Christ in his victorious cross work on our behalf.

But it is important to stress that for covenantal theologians even though there are different covenants described in Scripture, there is, in reality, only *one* overarching covenant of grace. That is why one must view the relationships between the covenants in terms of an overall continuity. Booth underscores this point in his comments on the "newness" of the covenant inaugurated by our Lord. He states, "The new covenant is but a new—though more glorious—administration of the same covenant of grace."[16] Thus, under the old covenant, the one covenant of grace was administered through various promises, prophecies, sacrifices, rites and ordinances (e.g., circumcision) that ultimately typified and foreshadowed the coming of Christ. Now in light of his coming, the covenant of grace is administered through the preaching of the word and the administration of the sacraments. But in God's plan there are not two covenants of grace, one in the OT and the other in the NT, but one covenant differing in administration but essentially the same across the ages (see *West. Conf.* 7.6).

This brief overview of covenant theology raises several issues that we will address in four points. First, how is the new covenant new? Second, is the covenant of grace conditional or unconditional? Third, who are the parties to the covenant of grace? Fourth, what is the relationship between the covenant of grace and the Abrahamic covenant? Examining these four issues will show us the rigorous logic of covenant theology's argument for paedobaptism.

The "Newness" Of The New Covenant. Covenant theology does acknowledge that there are changes that have come about due to the coming of the "new covenant." However, these changes are only

---

and the "covenant of redemption. On this distinction see Hodge, *Systematic Theology*, 2:354–73; Berkhof, *Systematic Theology*, 265–83; and Murray, "Covenant Theology," 216–40.

[16] Booth, *Children of Promise*, 9. For the same emphasis also see Murray, "Covenant Theology," 223–34.

changes that God himself has explicitly revealed to us and even in these changes there is a basic underlying continuity from age to age. Thus, for example, the sign of baptism is one of the several administrative changes that have taken place under the new covenant. As Randy Booth admits, "under the older administrations of the covenant of grace, circumcision was the sign and seal of covenant admission. Under the final administration of the covenant of grace (the new covenant), water baptism has replaced circumcision as the sign of covenant admission."[17] But even though the form of the covenant sign has changed, given the underlying continuity of the covenant of grace, the *spiritual* significance of the covenant sign has not changed and hence the meaning and application of the sign is essentially the same in all eras.

Of course, this discussion raises an important question: What is "new" about the new covenant? What is the main difference, if any, between the older and newer administrations of the covenant of grace given the basic continuity of the covenant? Within Reformed theology the answer to these questions is not monolithic.[18] However, despite various nuances, most covenant theologians agree that the main difference is that of "promise and fulfillment" (or "shadow and substance"). In other words, what the older administration promised through types, ceremonies, and sacrifices have now come to fulfillment in Jesus Christ. It is with this understanding that most covenant theologians view the "newness" of the new covenant in terms of a *renewal* rather than a replacement or such a strong sense of fulfillment that would lead to a discontinuity between the covenants.[19] That is why most argue that the new covenant administration simply expands the previous era by broadening its extent and application and bringing with it greater blessing. Yet it leaves intact

[17] Booth, *Children of Promise*, 10.

[18] For differences within Reformed theology over the "newness" of the new covenant see, for example, the chapters in Strawbridge, ed. *Case for Covenantal Infant Baptism*, by J. D. Niell, "The Newness of the New Covenant," 127–55, and R. L. Pratt, Jr. "Infant Baptism in the New Covenant," 156–74. Also see Robertson, *Christ of the Covenants*, 271–300; Wilson, *To a Thousand Generations*, 21–38; and Booth, *Children of Promise*, 49–95.

[19] See for example, Booth, *Children of the Promise*, 51; Niell, "Newness of the New Covenant," 127–55; W. C. Kaiser, *Toward Rediscovering the Old Testament* (Grand Rapids: Zondervan, 1987), 25–26.

the fundamental elements of the covenant of grace—hence the assertion of the continuity of the covenant of grace across the ages.[20]

But covenant theology's discussion of "newness" fails to reckon that in the coming of Christ the *nature and structure* of the new covenant has changed, which, at least, entails that *all* those within the "new covenant community" are people, by definition, who presently have experienced regeneration of heart and the full forgiveness of sin (see Jer 31:29–34). Obviously this view of "newness" implies a discontinuity at the structural level between the old and new covenant—a view which is at the heart of the credobaptist position—but which covenant theology rejects. So, for example, paedobaptists continue to view the nature of the new covenant like the old, namely, as a mixed covenant which includes within it both the elect (covenant keepers) and the non-elect (covenant breakers) simultaneously. Suffice it to say, how one understands the nature and structure of the new covenant vis-à-vis the previous biblical covenants takes us to the heart of the baptismal divide.

The Nature of the "Covenant of Grace": Conditional or Unconditional? This present discussion raises two related issues that are crucial to understand why paedobaptists consider that the covenant of grace *requires* infant baptism. The first issue has to do with the *nature* of the covenant of grace. Even though it is difficult to define the exact meaning of the word "covenant," most within

[20] Specifically, but not limited to these points, covenant theology views the "newness" of the new covenant in the following ways.

1. On the basis of Christ's finished cross work and through the application of that work to us by the Holy Spirit a greater power of obedience is possible in the new covenant.

2. An extension of the knowledge of God to all nations. Under the new covenant more people will know more about the Lord which fulfills the Abrahamic promise of blessings to the nations.

3. The promise of redemption is now accomplished in Christ with the full payment of sin. The old Levitical administration, along with the ceremonial law, has now been fulfilled.

4. The new covenant is the final manifestation of God's redemptive plan. There are no more covenant administrations to be revealed.

These points are taken from a variety of sources. See Booth, *Children of the Promise*, 63–66; Wilson, *To a Thousand Generations*, 22–34; Niell, "The Newness of the New Covenant," 127–74; Pratt, "Infant Baptism in the New Covenant," 127–74; G. W. Bromiley, "The Case for Infant Baptism," *CT* 9:1 (1964): 7–10; Berkhof, *Systematic Theology*, 299–301; and R. S. Clark, "A Contemporary Reformed Defense of Infant Baptism," http://public.csusm.edu/public/guests/rsclark/Infant_Baptism.html, 1–29.

covenant theology are pleased to define it somewhat as O. Palmer Robertson proposes: "a bond in blood sovereignly administered."[21] In a covenant, especially a biblical covenant, God promises to be our God by his own sovereign initiative and grace. In response to God's grace, we promise to be faithful to the Lord in terms of covenant obligations, namely, repentance, faith, and obedience. But this raises a thorny issue as to the *nature* of the covenant, especially whether the covenant is conditional or unconditional.

On the one hand, covenant theology has rightly argued that the covenant is *unconditional*. God acts in a sovereign and unilateral fashion to establish the covenant. Furthermore, he not only sovereignly establishes the covenant relation but he maintains and fulfills completely the promises that he makes to his people. In the end, everything God demands of his people in terms of repentance, faith, and obedience, he graciously grants them by sovereign grace in Christ and by the power of the Spirit. As Cornelius Venema nicely summarizes:

> Not only are the covenant's obligations preceded by God's gracious promise, but these obligations are fulfilled for and in believers by the triune God—Father, Son, and Holy Spirit—in their respective operations. God's demands are born of grace and fulfilled in us by grace. In these respects, the covenant of grace is unconditional, excluding every possible form of merit, whereby the faith and obedience of God's people would be the basis for their obtaining life and salvation.[22]

On the other hand, covenant theology has also argued that the covenant is *conditional* in at least two senses. First, the blessings of the covenant are totally dependent upon the work of Christ, since the last Adam fulfilled the conditions of obedience first set down in the covenant of works as both the representative and substitute of his people. Second, in order to benefit from the covenant, we are obli-

---

[21] See Robertson, *Christ of the Covenants*, 3–15. For a further discussion regarding the biblical meaning of "covenant" in Scripture see M. G. Kline, *By Oath Consigned* (Grand Rapids: Eerdmans, 1968), 13–25; T. E. McComiskey, *The Covenants of Promise* (Grand Rapids: Baker, 1985), 15–93; P. A. Lillback, "Covenant," in *NDT*, ed. S. Ferguson, et al. (Downers Grove: InterVarsity, 1988), 173–76; J. H. Walton, *Covenant* (Grand Rapids: Zondervan, 1994), 13–23; P. R. Williamson, "Covenant" in *NDBT*, ed. T. D. Alexander, et al. (Downers Grove: InterVarsity, 2000), 419–29; D. L. Baker, "Covenant: An Old Testament Study," in *The God of Covenant*, ed. J. A. Grant and A. I. Wilson (Leicester: InterVarsity, 2005), 21–53.

[22] Venema, "Covenant Theology and Baptism," 211.

gated to believe and obey. No doubt, these covenant obligations are not viewed as meritorious conditions; rather they are "necessary responses to the covenant's promises" and, as such, are "instrumental to the enjoyment of the covenant's blessings."[23]

Most covenant theologians contend that the covenant of grace always involves a "conditional promise." Thus, every biblical covenant, as part of the *one* covenant of grace, carries with it a conditional promise *"with blessings for those who obey the conditions of the covenant and curses for those who disobey its conditions."*[24] In other words, in principle every biblical covenant, including the new covenant, is conditional in the second sense described above and is thus *breakable.*[25] It is precisely at this point that most covenant theologians argue for the "mixed" nature of the people in the covenant of grace. That is, the covenant community is comprised of both covenant-keepers and covenant-breakers. So the circle of the covenant community, whether in the old or new era, is wider and larger than the circle of election.[26] Thus paedobaptists argue that, in principle, there is nothing objectionable in viewing unregenerate people as part of the covenant community and applying the covenant sign to them.[27]

The Parties of the Covenant. This understanding of the nature of the covenant leads to another important and related issue that also pertains to the subject of infant baptism. Given the question of whether the covenant of grace is conditional, with whom does God covenant in the covenant of grace? In other words, who are the parties of the covenant? Does God covenant with the elect only, or does he covenant with "believers and their children"—children who may or may not be the elect? One might suppose, given what has been stated above, that the unanimous answer would be the latter because of the mixed nature of the covenant community. However,

---

[23] Venema, "Covenant Theology and Baptism," 211. For a further discussion of this point see Berkhof, *Systematic Theology*, 280–81 and Murray, "Covenant Theology," 223–34.

[24] Booth, *Children of the Promise*, 24 (emphasis his).

[25] For a development of the "conditional" and "breakable" nature of every biblical covenant including the new covenant see Wilson, *To a Thousand Generations*, 81–96; Pratt, "Infant Baptism in the New Covenant," 169–74.

[26] On this point see Venema, "Covenant Theology and Baptism," 214.

[27] Also see Pratt, "Infant Baptism in the New Covenant," 170, for an affirmation of this point.

within covenant theology, there has been a significant debate over this question. For example, the *Westminster Confession of Faith* (7.3) and the *Westminster Larger Catechism* (question 31) opt for the first option, namely that God covenants with the elect only in the covenant of grace. Venema succinctly summarizes the Confession at this point when he writes, "In the strictest sense of the covenant as a saving communion with God, the parties of the covenant of grace are the triune God and his elect people"[28] and the condition of reception into that covenant is repentance and faith. Thus, all those who reject the free offer of the gospel stand *outside* the covenant of grace and it would also seem to imply, the covenant community.

But if this is so, then a legitimate question must be asked: How does a commitment to this understanding of the "covenant of grace," specifically that the parties of the covenant are God and his elect people, *require* a doctrine of infant baptism, as many paedobaptists contend? Would it not be legitimate to conclude that, if the parties of the covenant are God and the elect, the covenant sign, especially in the new covenant era, should only be applied to those who are actually members of the covenant community since God's sovereign grace has brought them to faith in Christ? On this issue, nothing in the formulation of the *Westminster Confession of Faith* leads us to think otherwise. However, covenant theology does not stop at this point. It further states that the parties of the covenant of grace also include "all believers and their children"—children who, we know in reality, are not necessarily brought to saving faith and thus may constitute the non-elect. This is what is referred to as the "dual aspect" of the covenant. As Venema correctly notes, "These theologians, while acknowledging that the life and salvation promised in the covenant of grace are inherited only by the elect, argue that the covenant promise, together with its accompanying obligation, is extended to Abraham and his seed."[29] This latter emphasis on the parties of the covenant including "believers and their children" is central in the baptism discussion. That is why a standard contention of

[28] Venema, "Covenant Theology and Baptism," 212.
[29] Ibid., 214. For a further discussion of this "dual aspect" see Berkhof, *Systematic Theology*, 272–89.

paedobaptists is that "the children of believers were always included in the covenant of grace under the older covenant administrations. In deference to this established biblical pattern, *we must assume that, apart from explicit biblical warrant to the contrary*, the children of believers are still included in the covenant of grace."[30] Thus, infants, like their adult believing parents, are to be circumcised and baptized because they are both members of the covenant community.

The Relationship between the Abrahamic Covenant and the Covenant of Grace. For our purposes, what is crucial to note in this debate within covenant theology is how covenant theologians, in reality, understand the relationship between the biblical *covenants* vis-à-vis the *one* covenant of grace. Generally speaking, covenant theology tends to equate the "covenant of grace" (an overarching theological category) with the Abrahamic covenant (a specific historical covenant which includes within it national, typological, and spiritual aspects). Covenant theology does this by reducing the national (physical) and typological aspects of the Abrahamic covenant to the *spiritual* aspects, which then becomes the grid by which all other biblical covenants are viewed, specifically the new covenant. Thus, to speak of the "covenant of grace" is really to speak in terms of the Abrahamic covenant reduced to its spiritual aspects alone. That is why in the discussion regarding the parties of the "covenant of grace," Reformed theologians can speak of the "dual aspect" of the parties of the covenant, even though "believers and their children" is a genealogical formula specifically tied to the Abrahamic covenant (primarily interpreted in physical terms). This genealogical principle is certainly picked up in later covenants but, as I will argue below, it is also modified in light of the fulfillment which has now come in Christ (now reinterpreted in spiritual terms).

Examples of this equation abound. For example, Louis Berkhof admits, at least in theory, that the Abrahamic covenant has both national and spiritual aspects to it,[31] but in reality the national aspects of the covenant fall by the wayside and the *spiritual* aspects are treated as primary. That is why he can say that circumcision is "the initia-

[30] Booth, *Children of the Promise*, 10 (emphasis mine).
[31] See Berkhof, *Systematic Theology*, 632.

tory sign and seal of *the covenant of grace*" (when in truth it is the sign of the Abrahamic covenant and not all the biblical covenants) and that "this [Abrahamic] covenant is still in force and is *essentially identical* with the "new covenant" of the present dispensation."[32] He shows little regard for the redemptive-historical *distinctions* between the biblical covenants. Similarly, John Murray argues that we are under divine command, derived from the continuity of the covenant of grace, to baptize our infant children because "the new covenant is the fulfillment and unfolding of the Abrahamic covenant," and "the covenant made with Abraham included the infant seed and was signified and sealed by circumcision," and "circumcision is the sign of the covenant in its deepest spiritual significance."[33] The infant children of believing church members, therefore, are full members of the church. In the end, what Berkhof, Murray, and most covenant theologians do is to strip the Abrahamic covenant of some of its aspects, identify it as a pure gospel covenant, and then equate it, almost in a one-to-one fashion, with the new covenant inaugurated by our Lord Jesus Christ.

To anticipate my argument below, this understanding of the relationship between the biblical covenants vis-à-vis the "covenant of grace" may produce the desired continuity the covenant theologian requires for his defense of infant baptism. But, in the end, it fails to do justice to the biblical *distinctions* between the covenants

[32] Berkhof, *Systematic Theology*, 633 (emphasis mine). In fact, Berkhof argues that what is normative for Christians today is not the Mosaic (Sinaitic, old) covenant, but that of the Abrahamic covenant (interpreted in light of its spiritual aspects). The Sinaitic, argues Berkhof, "is an interlude, covering a period in which the real character of the covenant of grace, that is, its free and gracious character, is somewhat eclipsed by all kinds of external ceremonies and forms, which, in connection with the theocratic life of Israel, placed the demands of the law prominently in the foreground, see Gal. 3. In the covenant with Abraham, on the other hand, the promise and the faith that responds to the promise are made emphatic" (296–297). In a similar fashion, R. Scott Clark argues that the new covenant is "new" because it is contrasted with Moses (old covenant), but not with Abraham (or Adam), and it is the covenant with the latter that continues in the new covenant ushered in by our Lord Jesus Christ. See "A Contemporary Reformed Defense of Infant Baptism," 4.

[33] See J. Murray, "Baptism," in *Collected Writings of John Murray* (Carlisle: Banner of Truth, 1977), 2: 374. Also see this same emphasis in Venema, "Covenant Theology and Baptism," 222, and B. Chapell, "A Pastoral Overview of Infant Baptism," in *Case for Covenantal Infant Baptism*, 11–18.

which lead us to affirm some crucial covenantal *discontinuities*—all of which have massive implications for the baptismal discussion.

Before I turn to that critique, however, I want to continue to unpack the paedobaptist position by turning to the second pillar of their argument, namely their view of the nature of the church, that the circle of the covenant community is wider than the circle of election.[34] This view of the nature of the church, which is also an implication of their understanding of the covenant of grace, is foundational to their advocacy and defense of infant baptism.

The Nature of the Church and Infant Baptism

Intimately related to the unity of the covenant of grace is the unity of the people of God across the ages. Instead of viewing the relationship between OT Israel and the NT church in ways that preserve an emphasis on both continuity and discontinuity, covenant theology tends to emphasize the element of *continuity* at the expense of discontinuity, even though it must be admitted that there are fine nuances within covenant theology.[35] Randy Booth, for example, strongly asserts that a Reformed and covenantal understanding of the people of God entails that "God has had one people throughout all the ages. Although this *one church* has developed through various stages, she is still the *same church* from age to age."[36] Obviously, one of the crucial implications drawn from this view for infant baptism is the argument that if God, in the OT, included "believers and their children" into the membership of the covenant community (Israel) then nothing has changed in the NT era (in the church). Booth draws this exact conclusion when he states, "*Since God has not changed the terms of church membership, new covenant believers and their children are likewise included in his church.*"[37]

---

[34] For this statement see Venema, "Covenant Theology and Baptism," 214.

[35] See for example the very nuanced discussion of the relationship between OT Israel and the NT Church in E. Clowney, *Church*, 27–70, and O. P. Robertson, *Christ of the Covenants*, 271–300, and id., *The Israel of God: Yesterday, Today, and Tomorrow* (Phillipsburg: P&R, 2000), 33–51.

[36] Booth, *Children of the Promise*, 73 (emphasis mine). For this same point see Hodge, *Systematic Theology*, 3:549–52; Berkhof, *Systematic Theology*, 565–72; Bromiley, "Case for Infant Baptism," 8–9; and Murray, *Christian Baptism*, 31–44.

[37] Booth, *Children of the Promise*, 73 (emphasis his). In the same vein, remember the re-

This stress on the *continuity* of the people of God throughout the ages takes us back to an earlier observation: covenant theology not only views the OT covenant people of God (Israel) and the new covenant people of God (church) as one people, but it also views the NT church, in its very nature, to be like Israel of old. It is a "mixed" community comprised of believers and unbelievers simultaneously. Thus, parallel to OT Israel, the circle of the church is wider than the circle of true believers, born of the Spirit of God, united to Christ by faith, justified, and sanctified.

The Invisible And The Visible Church. At this point in the discussion covenant theology employs the famous "invisible/visible" distinction in relation to the church. The *invisible* church refers to the church as God sees it, that is, the elect. It is those from all times and places whom the Lord knows are his and his alone, perfectly and infallibly. In this sense, the church, whether in the OT or NT era, is a spiritual entity, invisible to the natural eye. It is the one people of God throughout the ages. Louis Berkhof states it this way:

> The Church is said to be invisible, because she is essentially spiritual and in her spiritual essence cannot be discerned by the physical eye; and because it is impossible to determine infallibly who do and who do not belong to her. The union with Christ is a mystical union; the Spirit that unites them constitutes an invisible tie; and the blessings of salvation, such as regeneration, genuine conversion, true faith, and spiritual communion with Christ, are all invisible to the natural eye—and yet these things constitute the real *forma* (ideal character) of the Church.[38]

However the invisible church manifests itself in history in a *visible*, local form. As John Murray reminds us, "The church may not be defined as an entity wholly invisible to human perception and observation. The church is the company or society or assembly or congregation or communion of the faithful."[39] The church is a divinely created bond between God and his people and between other human beings. It becomes visible in the ministry of the word, in the

---

sponse of B. B. Warfield to A. H. Strong quoted above on the subject of the validity of infant baptism.

[38] Berkhof, *Systematic Theology*, 566. For a similar discussion of the invisible/visible distinction as applied to the church see Booth, *Children of the Promise*, 88–90, and Murray, *Christian Baptism*, 31–33.

[39] Murray, *Christian Baptism*, 32.

practices of the sacraments, and in external organization and government.[40] But as a visible entity it is a "mixed" one including within it both believers and unbelievers.

This view of the *nature* of the church differs substantially from a Baptist view and from those who identify themselves as part of the believer's church tradition. In a Baptist view, at least in the one I will defend, even though there is only one people of God throughout the ages, there is a redemptive-historical difference between OT Israel and the NT church. No doubt, there is a significant amount of continuity in the one people of God, but there is also a significant amount of discontinuity as well, by virtue of our Redeemer's work which has inaugurated the entire new covenant age and who has brought to fulfillment all the promises, types, and covenants of the OT. That is why in a Baptist view of the church, what is unique about the nature of the new covenant community is that it comprises a regenerate, believing people, not a mixed people like Israel of old. Therefore, Baptists only view as true members of the new covenant community those who have actually entered into union with Christ by repentance and faith and as such are partakers of all the benefits and blessings of the new covenant age. Furthermore, for Baptists, it is for this reason that baptism, which is the covenant sign of the new covenant church, is reserved for those who have entered into these glorious realities by the sovereign work of God's grace in their lives. However, in contrast to a Baptist view, the paedobaptist argues for the "mixed" nature of the church. The members of the visible church are all those who "are marked out by baptism and actual membership in a local church"[41]—which, in the end, includes "all believers and their children."

What does this understanding of the nature of the church have to do with infant baptism? Everything. As the argument goes, since, in the OT, infants of believing households were included in the "visible church" (Israel) by their circumcision *prior to a personal profession of faith* and, additionally, by that act they were considered full members of the covenant community even though they were not

---

[40] See Berkhof, *Systematic Theology*, 566.
[41] Booth, *Children of the Promise*, 88.

yet regenerate, the same is true under the new covenant. Hence, the covenant sign of baptism is applied to the infants of believing parents even though these infants have not yet exercised faith, and even though this practice disrupts the biblical order of baptism in the NT—first, repentance towards God and faith in Christ, and second, a confession of that faith publicly in water baptism.[42]

Evidence for the Paedobaptist View of the Church. What evidence is given for the paedobaptist view of the church? There are at least three pieces of biblical and theological evidence often cited.[43]

1. *The most foundational evidence is the paedobaptist appeal to the essential continuity of the covenant of grace across redemptive history.* For them, this entails two truths: first, there is only *one* people of God throughout the ages, and second, the nature of the covenant community is essentially the same. Hence, what may be said about the nature of the covenant community with Abraham and his children and the nation of Israel is also true of the nature of the new covenant community, the visible church, which includes within it both believers and unbelievers.

It must be acknowledged that most people today, whether they are credo- or paedobaptists, would have no problem affirming that Scripture teaches that there is only *one* people of God throughout the ages.[44] Appeal to textual data which supports such a claim is not

---

[42] On the issue of the biblical order of baptism, namely, first conversion then baptism, and the close relationship between the two see the excellent treatment in G. R. Beasley-Murray, *Baptism in the New Testament* (Grand Rapids: Eerdmans, 1962), 93–305, and R. H. Stein, "Baptism and Becoming a Christian in the New Testament," *SBJT* 2:1 (1998): 6–17.

[43] These three pieces of evidence are fairly standard in paedobaptist literature. See for example, Berkhof, *Systematic Theology*, 632–35; Murray, *Christian Baptism*, 31–68; Booth, *Children of the Promise*, 71–95; and Wilson, *To A Thousand Generations*, 13–96.

[44] Historically, certain varieties of Dispensationalism (namely, classic) might disagree with this point, but even within Dispensationalism, as represented by Progressive Dispensationalism, this point would not be disputed. For more on the differences between those who identify themselves as Dispensationalist see C. A. Blaising and D. L. Bock, *Progressive Dispensationalism* (Wheaton: Bridgepoint Books, 1993), 9–56; id., ed. *Dispensationalism, Israel and the Church: The Search for Definition* (Grand Rapids: Zondervan, 1992); and R. D. Moore, *The Kingdom of Christ: The New Evangelical Perspective* (Wheaton: Crossway, 2004). At this point, it must also be stated that in contemporary paedobaptist literature there is often a sad caricature of Baptist theology. For the most part, Baptist theology is put in the category of classic Dispensationalism without any recognition that even within Dispensational theology there are fine nuances which distinguish positions (e.g. Revised and Progressive) and that there are many Baptists, such as the present author, who are neither Dispensational nor Covenantal (in the paedobaptist sense of the

really at dispute. For example, when the language of "assembly" (*qāhāl* and *ekklēsia*) is applied to Israel and the church (e.g., Deut 4:10; Josh 24:1,25; Isa 2:2–4; Matt 16:18; 1 Cor 11:18; Heb 10:25), or when OT language describing Israel (e.g., Exod 19:6; Isa 43:20–21; Hos 1:6,9; 2:1), or OT texts that were applied to Israel (e.g., Jer 31:31–34; Hos 1:10–11) are now applied to the church (e.g., 1 Pet 2:9–10; Heb 8:6–13; Rom 9:24–26), this is strong evidence in favor of the claim that there is only one people of God throughout the ages. However, what is at dispute between credo- and paedobaptists is the nature and structure of the covenant community as one moves across redemptive-history and whether the nature of the church is a "mixed" community like Israel of old or whether it should be described as a regenerate, believing community. This leads to the second piece of evidence often cited.

2. *The corroboratory evidence often given to support the claim that the new covenant community is a "mixed" community like Israel of old, is an appeal to the warning passages of Scripture, especially those warnings that speak of the possibility of apostasy* (e.g., Heb 6:4–6; 10:28–30). These texts are cited because, it is argued, they seem to imply that it is possible for a person to be a member of the new covenant community (i.e., the visible church), but then, sadly, to depart from the faith, thus demonstrating that they never were a regenerate, believing person even though they were externally and objectively members of the covenant community. Thus, whether one thinks of the nature of the covenant community in the OT (Israel) or NT (church), it is essentially the same in both eras. That is why OT Israel and the NT church may include within them the elect and non-elect, believers and unbelievers, that is, those who by receiving the covenant sign (circumcision or baptism) are externally brought into covenant membership but who may never exercise saving faith. Given this situation, so the paedobaptist argues, there is nothing objectionable in applying the covenant sign of baptism to infants

term). It does not further discussion to treat all Baptist theology with the same brush, to erect a straw man, and then attempt to shoot it down. Probably the clearest example of this reductionistic treatment of Baptist theology and hermeneutics is R. Booth, *Children of the Promise*, 14–30.

and viewing them as full members of the church apart from explicit faith in Christ.

Obviously, at this point someone could dispute this particular interpretation of the warning and apostasy passages. In fact, one could contend that this line of argument leads to the interpretation that it is possible for true, regenerate Christians to lose their salvation. After all, has not Arminian theology repeatedly argued this exact point from these texts?[45] Needless to say, most paedobaptists, especially those in the Reformed tradition, counter by arguing that the Arminian understanding of these texts is unbiblical *as applied to the elect*.[46] The Bible does not teach that true Christians (the elect) can lose their salvation. Ironically, however, paedobaptists agree with the Arminian exegesis and conclusion *as applied to full covenant members who are not the elect*. Thus, in the hands of Reformed paedobaptists, these texts do not imply that it is possible for the elect to lose their salvation; rather, they demonstrate that "unregenerate members of the visible church can be covenant breakers in the new covenant"[47] and that the new covenant is a breakable covenant like the old. In commenting on the implications of the warning texts for understanding the nature of the church, Douglas Wilson confidently asserts, "The *elect* and the *covenant members* are not identical sets of people."[48] Hence, according to the paedobaptist, the warning texts of Scripture are corroboratory evidence supporting their view that the covenant community across the ages is a "mixed" community. Wilson nicely summarizes the debate between credo- and paedobaptists:

> The baptistic assumption is that the covenants are *unlike* in this respect. Some Old Covenant members were regenerate, some were not. All New Covenant members are regenerate. The paedobaptist assumption is that the covenants are *alike* in this respect. Some Old Covenant members were regenerate, some were not. Some New Covenant members are regenerate, some are not. The paedobaptist holds that the *difference* between the cov-

---

[45] For example see C. Pinnock, ed. *Grace Unlimited* (Minneapolis: Bethany House, 1975) and id., *The Grace of God and the Will of Man* (Grand Rapids: Zondervan, 1989).

[46] See Berkhof, *Systematic Theology*, 545–49; Reymond, *New Systematic Theology*, 781–94; cp. W. Grudem, *Systematic Theology* (Grand Rapids: Zondervan, 1994), 788–809.

[47] See G. Strawbridge, "Introduction," in *The Case for Covenantal Infant Baptism*, 4–5.

[48] Wilson, *To a Thousand Generations*, 34.

enants is that the promises in the New are much better—meaning that the ratio of believer to unbeliever will drastically change. The history of the New Israel will not be dismal like the Old Israel.[49]

What does all this have to do with infant baptism? Simply this: if membership in the covenant community (Israel, church) is essentially the same in all ages, then this provides the needed rationale to view and apply the covenant signs in a similar manner, regardless of which covenant is in view. In other words, even given the NT pattern of baptism (repentance, faith, and baptism) and the lack of any specific NT command to baptize infants, the paedobaptist believes that the covenant provides the biblical grounds to practice infant baptism in the church. To be sure, the covenant sign does not save an individual, but it does mean that those who receive the sign—including infants—are viewed objectively as covenant members in the body of Christ.

3. Further supporting evidence to buttress the data already cited is claimed in the promise given in Acts 2:39—"for you and your children"—as well as in the household theme across the canon and the household baptisms in the NT (see Acts 16:15,32–33; 18:8; 1 Cor 1:16). These passages are held to provide a strong biblical warrant to ground the practice of infant baptism. Wilson is emphatic at this point. He believes that when all the data is considered, it does not lead us merely to affirm that infant baptism is consistent with Scripture, nor even that a biblical case may be made for it. Rather, he believes that all the evidence combined demonstrates beyond question that the Scriptures *require* the practice of infant baptism.[50] For, as many paedobaptists assert, it is almost unthinkable that infants would not be considered part of the church through the covenantal sign of baptism given the continuity of the covenant of grace and given the importance of households and family solidarity in the OT. Infants in the church, especially of Jewish-Christian parents, would naturally be regarded as subjects of baptism, just as they were of circumcision in the OT. Since infants of believers were always included in the covenant under older covenant administrations, then we must

---

[49] Wilson, *To a Thousand Generations*, 34–35.
[50] Ibid., 9.

assume that apart from explicit biblical warrant to the contrary, infants of believers are still included in the church today. We do not need a specific command to baptize infants nor do we need any unambiguous example of infant baptism in the NT. The principle of continuity leads us to assume that infants are included in the church unless we are explicitly told they are not. As John Murray states,

> Are we to believe that infants in this age are excluded from that which was provided by the Abrahamic covenant? In other words, are we to believe that infants now may not properly be given the sign of that blessing which is enshrined in the new covenant? Is the new covenant in this respect less generous than was the Abrahamic? Is there less efficacy, as far as infants are concerned, in the new covenant than there was in the old? . . .
>
> If infants are excluded now, it cannot be too strongly emphasized that this change implies a complete reversal of the earlier divinely instituted practice. So we must ask: do we find any hint or intimation of such reversal in either the Old or the New Testament? More pointedly, does the New Testament revoke or does it provide any intimation of revoking so expressly authorized a principle as that of the inclusion of infants in the covenant and their participation in the covenant sign and seal? . . .
>
> In the absence of such evidence of repeal we conclude that the administering of the sign and seal of the covenant to the infant seed of believers is still in operation and has perpetual divine warrant.[51]

Covenantal paedobaptists believe we have an explicit endorsement of the place of believers' children as recipients of the covenant promise in Acts 2:39. Joel Beeke and Ray Lanning state its importance in this fashion: "Peter's words in Acts 2:39 are therefore a covenantal formula. 'Unto you, and to your children' simply restates 'between me and thee and thy seed after thee' (Gen 17:7). These words assert the identity of the covenant of grace under all dispensations and the continuity of the covenant pattern in which promises made to believers are extended to their children."[52] The burden of proof, then, we are told, is upon anyone who wants to overturn what was previously given.

[51] Murray, *Christian Baptism*, 48–50.

[52] J. R. Beeke and R. B. Lanning, "Unto You, and to Your Children," in *The Case for Covenantal Infant Baptism*, 56. Also see in *The Case for Covenantal Infant Baptism*, J. M. Watt, "The Oikos Formula," 70–84, and D. Wilson, "Baptism and Children: Their Place in the Old and New Testaments," 286–302; and, cp. Booth, *Children of Promise*, 120–52.

Obviously, this standard argument has important implications for how one views the nature and function of the covenant signs. In the paedobaptist view, given the continuity of the covenant of grace and the covenant community, it is assumed that the covenant signs (circumcision and baptism) signify the same realities. Let us now turn to this last point.

The Nature of the Covenantal Signs: Circumcision and Infant Baptism

In order to make a biblical case for the doctrine of infant baptism, one must not only demonstrate the continuity of the covenant of grace and the covenant community across the ages, one must also establish that the covenant signs carry essentially the same meaning. In paedobaptist polemics, the relationship between circumcision and baptism is viewed in terms of *replacement*. No doubt, in replacing circumcision, baptism signifies that the promised era of the OT has now been fulfilled in Christ. In this sense, the new covenant brings with it change. However, the basic underlying meaning and significance of circumcision and baptism are essentially the same.[53]

The two covenantal signs primarily signify entrance into the covenant community and all the blessings pertaining thereto. Thus, for example, paedobaptists argue that in the OT circumcision was the outward "sign and seal" of entrance into the covenant of grace and the covenant community. It was a "sign" in the sense that it signified something; it was a "seal" in that it confirmed the binding nature of the covenant, grounded in God's promises to his covenant people.[54] Circumcision was administered to all infant male children when they were eight days old, but it was not effective on its own in any kind of *ex opere operato* fashion. It had to be combined with faith. If it was not, then one showed himself to be covenant-breaker instead of a covenant-keeper. That is why many Israelites, who were circumcised externally, in the end showed themselves to be "cov-

[53] For examples of this assertion see Booth, *Children of the Promise*, 96–119; Murray, *Christian Baptism*, 45–68; Wilson, *To a Thousand Generations*, 39–80; and Bromiley, "Case for Infant Baptism," 8–9.

[54] For a helpful discussion of "sign and seal" see Booth, *Children of the Promise*, 98–99.

enant-breakers," precisely as they did not believe and persevere in an obedient faith. That is why, as already noted, within the covenant community of Israel, one could legitimately distinguish between the covenant members (those who were externally circumcised) and the spiritual remnant or elect (those who were externally circumcised and internally regenerated). In the same way, so the argument goes, what may be said about circumcision is also true of baptism. In the NT, baptism *replaces* circumcision as the covenant "sign and seal." In baptism, as with circumcision, we are brought into the *visible* church, identified with Christ, and considered full covenant members. But, as with circumcision, baptism does not effect a saving union in and of itself. It is only by God's grace, when God's Spirit makes us alive, grants us faith and repentance, and unites us with Christ that we experience true salvation—the reality to which baptism points. That is why, parallel to the OT, even if infants are baptized under the new covenant and considered covenant members, they are only truly the remnant or part of the *invisible* church if they exercise saving faith in our Lord and persevere in following him.

The Spiritual Meaning Of Circumcision. Most of the paedobaptist discussion of circumcision attempts to demonstrate the *spiritual* meaning and significance of the rite. Why? Because central to the paedobaptist argument is the *continuity* of the covenantal signs—a continuity that seeks to point to the *spiritual* realities of such things as: regeneration, justification, union with Christ, and ultimately the cross work of Christ. Hence, for baptism to *replace* circumcision, as the paedobaptist argument demands, it must be shown that both circumcision and baptism signify the same realities. But, to anticipate my argument below, no one disputes the fact that baptism signifies *spiritual* realities won by Christ and applied to us as his people. The point of contention is whether circumcision, in its OT covenantal context, and baptism in the NT, convey identical realities. Does not circumcision also convey national and typological, as well as spiritual realities? If so, then circumcision and baptism may be similar in meaning but not identical. It is my contention, following the argument of Paul Jewett, that the paedobaptist attempt to reduce the meaning of circumcision merely to its *spiritual* significance is a classic example of reading new covenant realities into the old without first unpacking the OT rite in its own covenantal context and then carefully thinking through the issues of continuity and discontinuity between the covenantal signs.[55]

But first, we should note how paedobaptists limit and reduce the meaning of OT circumcision to its *spiritual* significance alone. For example, Berkhof admits that the covenant made with Abraham has a national aspect to it, but then he contends that the Abrahamic covenant must be viewed primarily as a *spiritual* covenant, parallel to the new covenant, including the rite of circumcision.[56] Or, as Booth contends, "The argument that circumcision had a purely natural or physical reference cannot stand the test of biblical teaching. Circumcision carried primarily a spiritual significance (i.e., justification by faith), and therefore may not be regarded as simply a physical sign of descent. It represented cleanliness (see Deut. 30:6; Isa. 52:1). Circumcision was an outward sign of the fact that God required a 'circumcised' or cleansed heart."[57] Or, as Murray writes:

> With reference to circumcision it must be fully appreciated that it was not essentially or primarily the sign of family, racial, or national identity. Any significance which circumcision possessed along the line of national identity or privilege was secondary and derived. . . . Circumcision is the sign and seal of the covenant itself in its deepest and richest significance, and it is the sign of external privileges only as these are the fruits of the spiritual blessings which it signifies.[58]

In paedobaptist literature the *spiritual* meaning of OT circumcision is usually understood in at least three ways—ways that ultimately link it to baptism under the new covenant, so that what may be said about circumcision may also be said about baptism.[59]

---

[55] For a development of this argument see P. K. Jewett, *Infant Baptism and the Covenant of Grace* (Grand Rapids: Eerdmans, 1978), 89–137.

[56] See Berkhof, *Systematic Theology*, 632–633. Berkhof writes, "The spiritual nature of this [Abrahamic] covenant is proved by the manner in which its promises are interpreted in the New Testament, Rom. 4:16–18; 2 Cor. 6:16–18; Gal. 3:8,9,14,16; Heb. 8:10; 11:9,10,13. It also follows from the fact that circumcision was clearly a rite that had spiritual significance, Deut. 10:16; 30:6; Jer. 4:4; 9:25,26; Acts 15:1; Rom. 2:26–29; 4:11; Phil. 3:2; and from the fact that the promise of the covenant is even called "the gospel," Gal. 3:8" (*Systematic Theology*, 633).

[57] Booth, *Children of the Promise*, 99–100.

[58] Murray, *Christian Baptism*, 46–47.

[59] For a discussion of these points see Murray, *Christian Baptism*, 45–68; Booth, *Children of*

1. *At the heart of the Abrahamic covenant is the covenantal formula—"I will be your God, and you shall be my people"—which speaks to the blessing of union and communion with the Lord.* As a sign of the covenant, circumcision signifies and seals this blessing. Objectively, it makes one a member of the covenant community. The same may be said of baptism, which signifies that the recipient has objectively entered into faith union with Christ in his redemptive work. As Booth summarizes, "Baptism unites believers and their children with God's promised Redeemer, Jesus Christ, and secures their position as his people."[60] Obviously, Booth is quick to add that baptism must also be followed by faith before covenant blessings may be appropriated. Failure to do so brings covenant curses instead of blessings. But note: like circumcision, baptism is viewed as a sign which promises and anticipates gospel realities; it does not, as credobaptists affirm, testify that these same gospel realities have already taken place in the recipient.

2. *Circumcision, as a physical act, signified the removal of the defilement of sin, the cleansing from sin, and it pointed to the need for a spiritual circumcision of the heart* (see Exod 6:12,30; Lev 19:23; 26:41; Deut 10:16; 30:6; Jer 4:4; 6:10; 9:25). Likewise, baptism is an outward sign of the inward, spiritual need for the grace of God in the heart of the covenant member—"it points to the necessity of spiritual regeneration."[61] It does not testify that regeneration has already taken place.

3. *Circumcision was the seal of the righteousness of the faith Abraham had while he was uncircumcised* (Rom 4:11). As such, in circumcision, "God signified and sealed the fact that he justifies believers by faith and considers us as righteous through faith."[62] Circumcision is not a guarantee that Abraham has faith, nor even that Abraham (or anyone else for that matter) has righteousness. Instead, "what circumcision guarantees is the word of God's promise: that *righteousness will be given on the basis of faith*."[63] The same may be said

---

the Promise, 96–119; M. E. Ross, "Baptism and Circumcision as Signs and Seals," in *The Case for Covenantal Infant Baptism*, 85–111.

[60] Booth, *Children of the Promise*, 107.

[61] Ibid., 107.

[62] Ibid., 102.

[63] Ross, "Baptism and Circumcision as Signs and Seals," 94 (emphasis his).

of baptism. That is why both circumcision and baptism testify to God's promise to justify the ungodly by faith. This is also why one can circumcise or baptize an infant before faith is present. The covenant sign is simply a promise that righteousness will be given when a person believes the promises of God.

The Parallel between Circumcision and Baptism. Thus, when thinking of the significance of circumcision and baptism, the defender of infant baptism argues that essentially they signify the same gospel realities, namely, regeneration (Col 2:11–12; Rom 2:29), union with Christ (Rom 6:4; Gal 3:27–29), and all the blessings related to that union (Acts 2:38). Because the signs are parallel in meaning and application, if it was legitimate in the OT to apply the sign to "believers and their children," then the same is true in the new covenant era. In fact, Booth draws such a tight relationship between circumcision and baptism that he emphatically contends, "This clear connection between the two covenant signs of circumcision and baptism creates a difficult problem for the opponents of infant baptism, for *any argument against infant baptism is necessarily an argument against infant circumcision.*"[64]

Wilson goes even further and argues that even up until AD 70, circumcision still continued to have covenantal significance for Jewish Christians as an initiatory rite. Wilson, in appealing to such texts as Acts 21:18–25, argues that the apostles permitted Jewish Christian infants to be circumcised under the new covenant, even though this was not required for Gentile Christians. For a period of time, according to Wilson, circumcision continued to be the means by which Jewish infants of believing parents were brought into the church. Paul himself, Wilson speculates, "if he had gotten married as a Christian, and if he had had a son, *he would have circumcised him*"[65] in a covenantally significant way. From this assertion, Wilson concludes that "*we know with certainty* that some first century Christian churches had infant members"[66] and that "the apostles approved and taught this practice"[67] during this time of covenantal transition.

[64] Booth, *Children of the Promise*, 109 (emphasis his).
[65] Wilson, *To a Thousand Generations*, 69 (emphasis his).
[66] Ibid., 71 (emphasis his).
[67] Ibid., 72.

Obviously these last points are highly debatable and not all paedo-baptists would agree with them, but they do nicely illustrate how infant baptists conceive of the parallel relationship between circumcision and baptism.

But one may legitimately ask why circumcision disappeared as a covenant sign, especially for Jewish Christians, if circumcision and baptism are parallel in significance? Most paedobaptists argue that the change was due to the greater blessings that the new covenant has ushered in, especially in terms of extending more blessings to more people than before (e.g., male and female, Jew and Gentile). As we have noted above, as we move from old to new covenant, we also move from promise to fulfillment. Now that Christ has come, some of the rites of the OT have been changed to reflect the completed work of Christ. Baptism has replaced the bloody rite of circumcision, just as the Lord's Supper has replaced the bloody Passover lamb.[68]

Conclusion

Here, then, is the basic argument for the doctrine of infant baptism. I have shown that the advocacy and defense of infant baptism as a biblical doctrine is rooted and grounded in an explicit view of the covenants. It is an argument which centers on a particular understanding of the relationship between the covenants across the canon and the amount of continuity and discontinuity between them. If this interpretation of the "covenant of grace" along with its understanding of the continuity between Israel and the church and the covenant signs can be maintained, then we have a strong case for the practice of infant baptism. However, if this understanding of these areas is faulty and inaccurate, then the entire biblical and theological warrant for the practice of infant baptism evaporates. It

---

[68] Some paedobaptists like Wilson, *To a Thousand Generations*, 59–80, even argue that the change occurred to show and maintain the unity of the church. Theoretically, he argues, even though the Jewish Christian could have kept circumcising and baptizing their infants in a cov-enantally significant way, for the sake of unity, what was required of Gentile Christians was now required of Jewish Christians as well. Once again this is a highly debatable point. It assumes that in the new covenant era, circumcision was allowed to be practiced among Jewish Christians in a covenantally significant way.

is my contention that the latter is true, and it is to this critique and evaluation of the covenantal argument which I now turn.

An Evaluation and Critique of the Covenantal Argument for Infant Baptism

Central to my critique of the covenantal argument for infant baptism is that it fails to understand correctly the proper relationships between the biblical covenants and the degree of continuity and discontinuity between them. Paedobaptists rightly emphasize the unity and continuity of God's salvific plan across the ages. They fail to do justice, however, to the progressive nature of God's revelation, especially in regard to the biblical covenants, the covenant community, and the covenant signs. In the end, this leads them to misunderstand the proper degree of discontinuity inaugurated by Christ's coming and to which the OT points, namely, the arrival of the promised new covenant age. I basically agree with many who argue that paedobaptists, due to their stress on continuity, tend to read new covenant realities into the OT and vice versa, without first unpacking the covenants, the nature of the covenant community, and the covenantal signs in their original redemptive-historical context before thinking carefully through the issues of continuity and discontinuity now that Christ has come.[69] In doing theology, it is imperative that we approach the Bible in its own categories and structure. When we do so, we observe that God's self-revelation, in word and act, involves historical progression, along a redemptive-historical storyline, ultimately centered in Jesus Christ (see Heb 1:1–2). What this entails for our reading of Scripture and doing theology is that we must do justice to the unity of God's plan without flattening the epochal changes that have occurred now that the Lord of Glory has ushered in the end of the ages.[70]

---

[69] See for example, Jewett, *Infant Baptism and the Covenant of Grace*, 69–137 and Malone, *The Baptism of Disciples* Alone, 23–135.

[70] On issues of theological method see the introductory articles in *NDBT*, 3–112; R. Lints, *The Fabric of Theology: Toward an Evangelical Prolegomenon* (Grand Rapids: Eerdmans, 1993); M. S. Horton, *Covenant and Eschatology: The Divine Drama* (Louisville: Westminster John Knox, 2002).

Specifically, my critique will follow my description of the paedobaptist viewpoint. In four steps I will evaluate their covenantal argument: first, their particular understanding of the covenant of grace; second, the relationship of the Abrahamic covenant to the other biblical covenants; third, the new covenant and the nature of the church; and finally a discussion of the relationship between the covenantal signs of circumcision and baptism.

The Use of the Theological Category, "The Covenant of Grace"

It is beyond question that the theme of the "covenant" is an important unifying theme in Scripture. As we have seen, paedobaptists have made the "covenant" a crucial organizing principle of God's relation to us. They have rightly used it to unpack the truth that God has one plan of salvation across the ages and that history is the working out of that plan centered in the coming and cross work of our Lord Jesus Christ (see Eph 1:9–10). I do not dispute this point at all. In fact, in one sense, all evangelicals regardless of whether they are more covenantal, dispensational, or somewhere in between, agree with this point. We believe that the storyline of Scripture moves clearly from Creation to Fall, from Abraham to David, and finally to Christ.

If we are not careful, however, the notion of *the* "covenant of grace" may be misleading, because Scripture does not speak of only one covenant with different administrations. Rather, Scripture speaks in terms of a *plurality* of covenants (e.g. Gal 4:24; Eph 2:12; Heb 8:7–13), which are all part of the progressive revelation of the one plan of God that ultimately is fulfilled in the new covenant. In reality, the "covenant of grace" is a comprehensive *theological* category, not a biblical one. This does not mean that it is illegitimate. In theology we often use theological terms that are not found specifically in Scripture (e.g., the Trinity). If the theological category, "the covenant of grace," is used to underscore the unity of God's plan of salvation and the essential spiritual unity of the people of God in all ages, it is certainly helpful and biblical. But if it is used to flatten the relationships and downplay the significant amount of progression between the biblical covenants, which then leads us to ignore specific covenantal discontinuities across redemptive-history, then it is unhelpful, misleading, and illegitimate.

In order to make headway in the baptismal divide and think biblically regarding the relationships between the covenants, we should place a moratorium on "covenant of grace" as a category when speaking of the biblical covenants and the relationships between them. In its place, let us speak of the one plan of God or the eternal purposes of God centered in Jesus Christ, for that is what the language of the "covenant of grace" is seeking to underscore. But when it comes to thinking of the "covenant," let us speak in the plural and then unpack the relationships between the biblical *covenants* vis-à-vis the overall eternal plan of God centered in Jesus Christ. We may then think more accurately about how the one plan of God, tied to the promises of God first given in Gen 3:15, is progressively revealed in history *through* the biblical covenants. To continue to speak of one "covenant of grace" too often leads to a flattening of Scripture; indeed, it results in a reductionism which has the tendency of fitting Scripture into our theological system rather than the other way around.

In fact, this flattening of Scripture is clearly taking place when the paedobaptist identifies and equates the Abrahamic covenant with the "covenant of grace" as though it actually were *that* covenant. Instead of first understanding the Abrahamic covenant in its own context, in all its diverse features (e.g., national/physical, typological, and spiritual), and then relating it to God's overall plan vis-à-vis the biblical covenants, the paedobaptist tends to reduce it merely to its spiritual realities while neglecting its other aspects. The paedobaptist thus reads new covenant realities into it and overlooks important differences between the Abrahamic and new covenant.

The Nature of the Abrahamic Covenant and its Relation to the Biblical Covenants

As noted above, the paedobaptist views the Abrahamic covenant as essentially identical with the new covenant, beyond a few explicit changes. In so doing, the paedobaptist tends to flatten the Abrahamic covenant by reducing it primarily to *spiritual* realities while neglecting its national and typological aspects, and then in turn he takes the genealogical principle operative in the Abrahamic covenant—"you and your seed" (Gen 17:7)—as applicable *in exactly the same way* across the canon without suspension, abrogation, and especially reinterpretation in the new covenant era. So the paedobaptist contends that baptism *replaces* circumcision and that the covenant sign, regardless of our location in redemptive-history, is for "you and your seed" (i.e., physical children). Even though the new covenant era is described as the *fulfillment* of the old, given the continuity of the covenant of grace interpreted in light of the genealogical principle of the Abrahamic covenant, the paedobaptist assumes that "believers and their children" are included in the church much as they were in Israel of old. This identification and equation of the Abrahamic covenant with the new covenant is particularly seen in the parties of the covenant. In arguing for the "dual aspect" of the covenant, namely, that in the "visible church" the parties of the covenant are "believers and their children," paedobaptists demonstrate that they view new covenant membership through the lens of the Abrahamic covenant, thus identifying the two covenants without acknowledging the redemptive-historical differences between them.

What, then, is the precise nature of the Abrahamic covenant? Should it be viewed primarily in spiritual terms or is this a reductionistic reading of it? How should we view the Abrahamic covenant in relation to the other biblical covenants? And is it correct to view the Abrahamic covenant as basically identical with the new covenant, especially in regard to the genealogical principle? Are there no differences as one moves from promise to fulfillment? I will attempt briefly to delineate the nature of the Abrahamic covenant and its relationship to the other biblical covenants in addition to noting a couple of implications for the baptismal debate.

Abrahamic covenant as paradigm of God's dealings with humankind. First, in agreement with much of covenant theology, I concur that Scripture presents the Abrahamic covenant as the basis for all God's dealings with the human race and the backbone for understanding the biblical covenants. Truly, it is through Abraham and his seed—ultimately viewed in terms of our Lord Jesus Christ (Gal 3:16)—that our Triune God fulfills his eternal purpose and promise to save a people for himself and to usher in a new creation. This is borne out, not only in terms of OT theology, but also in how the NT authors interpret the fulfillment of the Abrahamic promise in light of the person and work of Christ (e.g., Romans 4 and Galatians 3).

We must note the location of the Abrahamic covenant in the storyline of Scripture.[71] God's promises to Abraham of a great name, seed, and land (Gen 12:1–3; cp. Gen 15:4–5; 17:1–8; 18:18–19; 22:16–18) must be understood in view of the unfolding drama of Genesis 3–11, especially the promise given in Gen 3:15. As a result of the disobedience of Adam—the covenantal head of the human race—sin and death have entered God's good world. Unless God acts in grace and power, the original creation will stand completely under divine judgment. But, thankfully, God chooses to act on our behalf. He promises that his purposes for creation and the human race will continue through his provision of a Redeemer, the seed of the woman, to reverse the disastrous effects of the Fall. This promise continues in the Noahic covenant (Genesis 8–9) through the covenant mediator, Noah, and his family. But with Noah, like Adam, there is failure. By the time we reach Genesis 11, we have Genesis 3 all over again. The rebellious human attempt to make a name apart from God is set over against God's gracious calling and election of Abraham. But unlike the situation with Noah, where God destroyed everyone except Noah and his family, God does not destroy the human race as in the flood. Instead, God allows the nations to exist and then calls Abraham out of the nations. Ultimately, God's intent is to work through the covenant mediator, Abraham, and his seed to bring blessing to the nations. In this context, one must view the Abrahamic covenant as the means by which God will fulfill his promises for humanity. In this important sense, Abraham and his family

---

[71] For helpful resources on the nature of the Abrahamic covenant and its relation to other biblical covenants see Dempster, *Dominion and Dynasty*, 45–92; Dumbrell, *Covenant and Creation*, 47–79; and Blaising and Bock, *Progressive Dispensationalism*, 128–211.

constitute another Adam, a calling into existence of something new parallel to the original creation, but in this case a "new creation" (Rom 4:17). In Abraham and his seed, all God's promises for the human race will be realized—promises that God takes upon himself to accomplish in the inauguration of the covenant in Genesis 15. N. T. Wright summarizes well the importance of Abraham in this OT context when he writes, "Abraham emerges within the structure of Genesis as the answer to the plight of all humankind. The line of disaster and of the 'curse', from Adam, through Cain, through the Flood to Babel, begins to be reversed when God calls Abraham and says, 'in you shall all the families of the earth be blessed.'"[72]

Due to God's covenant promises to Abraham, the promise is confirmed and passed on to Isaac and Jacob (Gen 26:3–5; 28:13–15; 35:9–12). In addition, the promises made to Abraham are also the basis on which God delivers Israel from slavery in Egypt. God's calling and establishing his covenant with Israel through Moses is in fulfillment of the promises made to Abraham and his seed (Exod 3:6; cp. 2:24–25; Deut 4:36–38; 1 Chr 16:15–19; 2 Kgs 13:22–23). God did not set his love on Israel because they were better or more numerous than the nations (Deut 7:7). Neither was it for their righteousness that they were given the land of Canaan (Deut 9:4–6). The basis for God's calling of Israel was not to be found in them, but instead in God's sovereign choice and his covenant loyalty to Abraham (Exod 19:4; Deut 7:8). Once again, it is through Abraham and his family, now narrowed to the nation of Israel, that God purposes and plans to bring blessing to all nations. In this way, through Israel, which also serves as a kind of new Adam, God will bring about a resolution of the sin and death caused by the first Adam. Israel, as a nation, is the agent and means God uses to achieve the wider purposes of the Abrahamic covenant which ultimately leads us to Christ and the ushering in of a "new creation."

But it is not only the Mosaic covenant that is built on the backbone of the Abrahamic covenant; it is also the Davidic. The Davidic king of Israel is a son in relation to the Lord (2 Sam 7:14). He is the administrator and mediator of the covenant. As such, the Davidic

---

[72] N. T. Wright, *The New Testament and the People of God* (Minneapolis: Fortress, 1992), 262.

sons function as the Lord's representative to Israel. The sonship applied to Israel as a nation (Exod 4; cp. Hos 11:1) is now applied to David and his sons. But there is more: the Davidic king also inherits the role of Adam and Israel as son of God to humanity as a whole. As Walter Kaiser has rightly argued, the expression in 2 Sam 7:19b should read, "This is the charter by which humanity will be directed," indicating David's own understanding of the implications of the Davidic covenant for the entire human race, namely, that his role as covenant mediator would effect the divine rule in the entire world as God intended it for humanity in the original situation.[73] In this, the Davidic covenant is linked to the Abrahamic, which in turn is linked to God's earlier promises. Thus, under the Davidic king, the Abrahamic promise of the great nation and great name come together. In this sense, the ultimate fulfillment of the Abrahamic covenant coincides with the ultimate fulfillment of the Davidic covenant. The Abrahamic blessings, linked back to Noah and creation, will only be ultimately realized through the Davidic son. Indeed, the final fulfillment of the Abrahamic promise of blessing in a promised land will take place under the rulership of the Davidic king. In this important sense, the Davidic king becomes the mediator of covenant blessing, tied back to Abraham, ultimately tied back to Adam, as the covenant head of the human race.

In the OT none of the covenant mediators—whether Adam, Noah, Abraham, Moses, or David—fulfilled their role and brought about the promise; they only typified and anticipated the one to come (Rom 5:14). Only our Lord Jesus Christ, the God-man, fulfills the roles of the previous covenantal mediators and brings about the promises stretching back to Gen 3:15. That is why the NT presents Christ as nothing less than the Lord as well as the last Adam, the true seed of Abraham, David's greater Son, who ushers in a new covenant—a covenant which all the previous covenants anticipated and typified. In Christ, all the promises of God are yes and amen (2 Cor 1:20). That is why in Jesus and his cross work, the desperate

---

[73] See W. C. Kaiser, Jr., "The Blessing of David, The Charter for Humanity," in *The Law and the Prophets*, ed. J. H. Skilton (Nutley, NJ: P&R, 1974), 311–14. Also see the unpublished paper by P. J. Gentry, "The *hasdê dāwîd* of Isa 55:3: A Response to Hugh Williamson," and Dumbrell, *Covenant and Creation*, 151–52.

plight begun in Eden now finds its solution as the last Adam, the obedient Son, has accomplished his saving work. The promise that God himself must be the Savior of his people is fulfilled for he himself is the Lord. Indeed, the death of Jesus, the crime of all crimes, is nevertheless determined by the divine plan (Acts 2:23). Why? To bring to fulfillment what God had promised through the prophets, that the Messiah would suffer (Acts 3:18) in order to save his people from their sins (Matt 1:21). In Jesus Christ, the prophetic anticipation of God's coming to save in and through David's greater Son is fulfilled. Indeed, as D. A. Carson reminds us, "the promise that through Abraham's seed all the nations of the earth will be blessed, gradually expanded into a major theme in the Old Testament, now bursts into the Great Commission, the mushrooming growth of the Jewish church into the Gentile world, the spreading flame reaching across the Roman Empire and beyond, in anticipation of the climactic consummation of God's promises in the new heaven and new earth."[74]

Here in summary is something of the relationship of the Abrahamic covenant vis-à-vis the other biblical covenants. It is beyond question that the Abrahamic covenant is the basis for all God's dealings with the human race as it unfolds the promise and leads us to Christ. But in this overall summary of the covenants and their relationships there is something crucial that we must not miss: as we move from Abraham to Christ, there is a significant progression and advance that takes place. The Abrahamic covenant sets the context and anticipates the coming of the new covenant, but promise and type are not the same as fulfillment and antitype. No doubt continuity exists between the covenants, but there is also significant discontinuity. This has implications for how we view the nature of the covenant community and the significance of the covenant signs. It is this last observation that leads me to my second point regarding the nature of the Abrahamic covenant first in its own canonical context and then in its relation to the new covenant.

The Various Aspects of the Abrahamic Covenant. Second, as we think about the nature of the Abrahamic covenant in its own histori-

---

[74] D. A. Carson, *The Gagging of God* (Grand Rapids: Zondervan, 1996), 263.

cal context it is important that we do not reduce it merely to its *spiritual* aspects alone. To do so is to read new covenant realities into the old era *too fast*. We must first understand the Abrahamic covenant in its own canonical context before we relate it to what has now come in Christ. Surely the Abrahamic covenant ultimately leads us to the new covenant, but what is the nature of that covenant first in its own historical context? It is my contention that the Abrahamic covenant is very diverse; it encompasses not only spiritual elements that link us to the new covenant, but it also consists of national and typological elements that result in significant discontinuity as the era of fulfillment is inaugurated. This can best be illustrated if we think of the different senses Scripture gives to the genealogical principle—to "you and your seed" (Gen 17:7). As we have noted above, paedobaptists understand to "you and your seed" as "you and your physical seed" (i.e., believers and their children)—a principle that continues without suspension or change from Abraham to Christ. But does this understanding do justice to the Abrahamic covenant in its own context, let alone in light of the fulfillment in Christ? My answer is no. We see this by answering the important question, Who is the seed of Abraham? Who is the true heir of God's promise? Scripture teaches that there are four senses that must be distinguished and not confused. Let us look at each of these in turn.[75]

1. The "seed of Abraham" first refers to a *natural* (physical) seed, namely, every person who was in any way physically descended from Abraham such as Ishmael, Isaac, the sons of Keturah, and by extension Esau, Jacob, etc. In each case, all of these children of Abraham received circumcision even though many of them were unbelievers, and even though it was only through one of the "seeds," Isaac, that God's promises and covenant was realized (Gen 17:20–21; cp. Rom 9:6–9). Circumcision also marked out those who were not physically Abraham's descendants, but who were related to him either through a household birth or purchased as a slave (Gen 17:12). In the latter case, circumcision enabled those who were not biologi-

---

[75] On this point see T. D. Alexander, "Seed," in *NDBT*, 769–73; J. G. Reisinger, *Abraham's Four Seeds* (Frederick, MD: New Covenant Media, 1998); and R. F. White, "The Last Adam and His Seed: An Exercise in Theological Preemption," *TJ* 6 ns:1 (1985): 60–73.

cally related to Abraham to become his children and thus benefit from the divine blessing mediated through him.[76]

2. The "seed of Abraham" also refers to a *natural, yet special* seed tied to God's elective and saving purposes, namely Isaac, and by extension Jacob and the entire nation of Israel. As God enters into covenant relationship with Israel, they are a special, chosen people (Deut 7:7–10). As in the case of the natural seed, they too are marked as Abraham's seed by circumcision. But as a nation, they are a "mixed" entity comprising believers and unbelievers—Elijahs and Ahabs simultaneously—even though all males within the covenant nation, regardless of whether they were spiritually regenerate, were marked by the covenant sign of circumcision. In fact, being God's chosen people did not guarantee that they would receive God's ultimate redemptive blessings (see Matt 3:9; Luke 3:8; 16:19–31; John 8:31–39; Rom 9:1–15).[77] Instead, their being marked with the covenant sign not only showed their relationship to Abraham, but also, unlike the mere natural seed (Ishmael), allowed them the supreme privilege of bringing God's blessing to all nations through the coming of the Messiah.

3. The Messiah is the third sense of the "seed of Abraham." In Gal 3:16, Paul argues that the singular use of "seed" in Gen 12:3

---

[76] G. Strawbridge, "The Polemics of Anabaptism from the Reformation Onward," in *The Case for Covenantal Infant Baptism*, 277–80, disagrees with this assertion. Contrary to all biblical evidence he speculates that Ishmael and the sons of Keturah possibly were people of faith, like their father Abraham. Thus, for them, circumcision did not signify a physical demarcation, but a spiritual one. He appeals to the fact that circumcision cannot be viewed as a "national sign" since Ishmael was not part of the nation of Israel and so it must mean that in Ishmael's case (as well as Keturah's sons), circumcision carried a spiritual significance. But this misses the point. Strawbridge fails to distinguish between the physical and physical/special seed of Abraham who were both linked to Abraham and that is why they received the covenant sign, regardless of their personal faith. In fact, the entire household of Abraham was to be circumcised showing a "physical" link to Abraham, and Scripture gives no evidence that in their case, circumcision had a spiritual meaning. One cannot deny that circumcision marks out a physical seed (Ishmael, Isaac, Israel) and nowhere is there evidence in the case of this physical seed that their circumcision necessarily carried a spiritual significance. No doubt, more must be stated about circumcision, but this point cannot be dismissed.

[77] We must be careful that we do not equivocate on the term "redemption." In the OT context, it can simply refer to God's deliverance of the nation from Egypt without the full NT sense of redemption from sin and ultimate salvific blessings. To speak of the nation of Israel as a "redeemed" people does not necessarily mean that they were all redeemed in the same sense that the church is the "redeemed" people of God. No doubt there are typological relations, but the type is not the same as the antitype.

and other places is a reference to the *true/unique* "seed of Abraham," namely Christ.[78] Here Paul is picking up the promise theme from Gen 3:15, traced through a distinctive line of seed, beginning with Adam, running through Noah, Abraham, Isaac, Israel, David, and eventually culminating in Christ. In Christ, we have the promised seed, the mediator of God's people, the one who fulfills all God's promises, not least the Abrahamic promises. Hence, he is the true seed of Abraham, the true Israel, and David's greater Son. In this important sense, then, Jesus is the unique seed of Abraham both as a physical seed through a specific genealogical line and as the antitype of all the covenant mediators of the OT. What is crucial to note at this juncture is how in Christ, viewed as the true seed of Abraham and the mediatorial head of the new covenant, there is a significant typological advance as we move across the covenants which has implications for understanding the expression "to you and your seed." This is clear in the fourth sense of the "seed of Abraham."

4. In this last sense of the "seed of Abraham," the NT emphasizes its *spiritual* nature now that Christ has come. It includes within it both believing Jews and Gentiles in the church. Given the new era that Christ has inaugurated, the way into Abraham's family is not dependent on circumcision or the Torah, but it comes through faith and spiritual rebirth. Only those who have experienced conversion are those who are Abraham's "seed" in this *spiritual* sense. To be a member of Abraham's family now is not tied to a specific physical lineage, nor circumcision, nor any kind of physical links to other believers. Rather, one becomes a part of Abraham's family only through faith union in Christ brought about by the Spirit (Gal 3:26–29). Thus, in the coming of Christ, a new era of redemptive history has dawned where the structures, types, and shadows of the old have given way to the reality and fulfillment of what the OT was all along pointing to.

Implications of the Abrahamic Covenant for Baptism. At least two important implications follow this discussion of the baptismal issue. First, it is illegitimate to identify and equate the Abrahamic

[78] See Alexander, "Seed," in *NDBT*, 769–73 and T. R. Schreiner, *Paul: Apostle of God's Glory in Christ* (Downers Grove: InterVarsity, 2001), 73–85.

covenant with the new covenant without noting the diverse aspects within it (national/physical, typological, spiritual) and the discontinuity that results as we move from Abraham to Christ. For example, to identify and equate the *natural/special* seed (Israel) with the *spiritual* seed (church) as well as to equate the covenant signs of circumcision and baptism is a mistake often made by paedobaptists. It not only fails to do justice to the diverse aspects of the Abrahamic covenant, but also to the way that covenant is ultimately fulfilled in Christ. So Israel, as a nation, is a type of the church. But this is the case, not because the church is merely the replacement of Israel, but because Christ, as the true seed of Abraham and the fulfillment of Israel, unites in himself both spiritual Jews and Gentiles as the "Israel of God" (Gal 6:16). There is continuity, but also important discontinuity. Now that Christ has come, only those who have faith and have experienced spiritual rebirth are his people and part of his family. In the OT era, the people of God were both a nation and the spiritual people of God; circumcision signaled one's affiliation with the nation. But even though circumcision marked one as a *natural* seed of Abraham and brought one into the nation of Israel, not all who were part of Israel were the *spiritual* seed (see Rom 9:6). This, as I will argue below, is *not* the same in regard to the new covenant people of God. The new covenant people of God are all those, regardless of ethnicity or circumcision, who have confessed Christ as Lord, the *true/spiritual* seed of Abraham. It includes all those who believe in Christ and who have been born of his Spirit. That is why, in the end, Scripture teaches that we should only baptize those who are Christ's covenant children—those who are actually in the covenant by God's grace through regeneration and saving faith.[79]

A second implication is that the genealogical principle of the Abrahamic covenant is reinterpreted as we move from promise to fulfillment.[80] Under the previous covenants, the genealogical principle, that is, the relationship between the covenant mediator and his seed was *physical* (e.g., Adam, Noah, Abraham, David). But now, in

---

[79] For more on this point see Jewett, *Infant Baptism and the Covenant of Grace*, 93–104; Malone, *The Baptism of Disciples Alone*, 71–79.

[80] For more on this point see White, "The Last Adam and His Seed," 60–73; Reisinger, *Abraham's Four Seeds*.

Christ, under his mediation, the relationship between Christ and his seed is no longer physical but *spiritual*, which entails that the covenant sign must only be applied to those who in fact are the *spiritual* seed of Abraham. Is this not what is at the heart of the *promise* of the new covenant in Jeremiah 31 now fulfilled in Christ? That the Lord will unite himself with a *spiritually* renewed covenant people, *all* of whom will know him, in contrast to the "mixed" nation of Israel who broke the covenant? And that *all* of these new covenant people will be marked by the knowledge of God, the forgiveness of sins, and the reality of a circumcised heart which will allow them to be covenant-keepers, not covenant-breakers. In other words, in failing to grasp the significant progression in the covenants across redemptive-history, particularly in terms of the relationship between the covenant mediator and his seed, paedobaptists fail to understand correctly how the genealogical principle has changed from Abraham to Christ. Ultimately they do not acknowledge the "newness" of the new covenant. Their emphasis on the continuity of the covenant of grace has led them to flatten the covenantal differences and thus to misconstrue the nature of the new covenant community. It is to this point that I now turn.

The Newness of the New Covenant and the Nature of the Church

As already noted, how one understands the nature and structure of the new covenant vis-à-vis the previous biblical covenants takes us to the heart of the baptismal divide. In arguing for the continuity of the covenant community across the ages, paedobaptists argue that the new covenant community (church) is essentially the same as the old (Israel) in that both communities are "mixed" entities. As in Israel, so in the church, there is a distinction between the locus of the covenant community and the elect (remnant), with circumcision, and now baptism, being the sign of entrance into the former. That is why the covenantal signs may be applied in exactly the same way, even to those who have not yet exercised saving faith.

Baptists, on the other hand, disagree with this understanding of the nature of the new covenant community. Credobaptist theology, at least the view I will defend, argues for more redemptive-historical discontinuity between Israel and the church, especially in regard to the nature of the church. No doubt there is only one people of God throughout the ages; that is not in dispute. However, in the OT promise of the new covenant (Jer 31:29–34) and its fulfillment in Christ (see Luke 22:20; Heb 8–10), the nature of the covenant communities are not the same, which entails a difference in the meaning and application of the covenant sign. Specifically, the change is found in the shift from a *mixed* community to that of a *regenerate* community with the crucial implication that under the new covenant, the covenant sign must only be applied to those who are in that covenant, namely, believers. The covenant sign of circumcision did not require faith for all those who received it, for a variety of reasons, even though it marked a person as a full covenant member. However, the same cannot be said of baptism. Because the church, by its very nature, is a regenerate community, the covenant sign of baptism must only be applied to those who have come to faith in Christ. It is at this point that we see the crucial discontinuity between the old and new covenant communities, a point the paedobaptist fails to grasp.

This is why paedobaptists consistently interpret the new covenant in "renewal," rather than "replacement," or better, "fulfillment" categories. The new covenant, they maintain, is "new" because it expands the previous era, broadens its extent, yields greater blessings, but the basic continuity is still in place, particularly in regard to the nature of the covenant community. Additionally, this is why paedobaptists argue that the new covenant, like the old, is a *breakable* covenant which includes within it "covenant-keepers and covenant-breakers." Recently, there have been attempts to defend the paedobaptist understanding of the new covenant by Jeffrey Niell and Richard Pratt, Jr. Interestingly, these two attempts, even though they have much in common, are quite different in approach. Both, though, acknowledge the centrality of this discussion for the baptismal debate. Pratt, for example, grasps the point correctly when he admits,

Evangelical paedobaptists consistently stress that baptized children are in
the new covenant, but that they are not automatically or necessarily saved.
In effect, infant baptism introduces unregenerate, unbelieving people
into the new covenant community. But this practice appears to contradict
Jeremiah's prophecy that salvation will be fully distributed in the new covenant. How can it be right for infants to receive the covenant sign of baptism
when they often do not and may never "know the Lord"?[81]

This is precisely the issue at stake—the *nature* and *newness* of the
new covenant.

Niell contends, in his discussion of the new covenant (Jer 31:31–
34; Heb 8–10), that the *new* covenant is *not* really new in comparison with the old. For example, he notes that there is no radical
separation between the people of God across the canon: many OT
saints were regenerate, knew the Lord, and experienced forgiveness
of sins in the same way as those under the new covenant. And regardless of the covenant in question, God must take the initiative in
grace to redeem, and when he does, he establishes the same relationship with his people. Given these similarities, then, what is "new"?
According to Niell, the "newness" is found in the fact that Christ
has brought to an end the ceremonial law and the Levitical priesthood—a priesthood that was "especially engaged in teaching and
representing the knowledge of the Lord to the people."[82] In fact, he
interprets the "knowledge" of Jer 31:34 (see Heb 8:11) as only referring to the special knowledge of the Levitical priest, not, as most
would contend, a salvific knowledge. He argues that v. 34 is only
addressing "the removal of the ceremonial aspects of the law and refers to the knowledge that is possessed and published by the priests.
This is true whether or not they were elect before the foundation of
the world."[83] But, in the end, other than Christ's fulfilling all that is
associated with the ceremonial law, the "new" covenant is the same
as the old, especially in that both were breakable and "mixed" in
regard to membership.[84]

---

[81] Pratt, "Infant Baptism and the New Covenant," 161.
[82] Niell, "The Newness of the New Covenant," 153.
[83] Ibid., 153, n 37.
[84] See ibid., 153.

In contrast to Niell, Pratt (with most covenantal paedobaptists) rightly argues that Jeremiah's new covenant promise does relate to the soteriological nature of the community since Jeremiah anticipates that

> God himself will bring about deep internal transformation of his covenant people. . . . Jeremiah did not see entrance into the new covenant community as entrance into an external environment, but as undergoing a spiritual, inward change. . . . It is apparent that the law of God often regulated the lives of the people of Israel as little more than an external code. Obedience often came reluctantly and resulted from external pressures. But Jeremiah promised that the new covenant would bring this situation to an end. In this regard, Paul echoed Jeremiah's words when he contrasted the old covenant "ministry . . . which was engraved in letters of stone" (2 Cor 3:7) with the "new covenant . . . ministry of the Spirit . . . that brings righteousness" (2 Cor 3:6,8–9).[85]

Also, in contrast to Niell, Pratt rightly contends that v. 34 refers to a *saving* knowledge.

> In this sense, "knowing the Lord" means "properly acknowledging and recognizing him." This is why Jeremiah 31:34 concludes, "For I will forgive their wickedness and will remember their sins no more." In a word, to know God as Jeremiah spoke of it would be to receive eternal salvation. In the covenant of which Jeremiah spoke, salvation would come to each participant. There would be no exceptions.[86]

In other words, what the promise anticipates is a *regenerate* community, not merely a mixed one. Pratt's understanding of Jeremiah 31, which is in direct opposition to Niell's, raises serious issues for paedobaptists. How can they speak of baptized infants as participating in the external aspects of the covenant (i.e., the visible church) without an inward heart transformation? Pratt attempts creatively to skirt this issue. He appeals to the important "already-not yet" tension associated with inaugurated eschatology to argue that the ultimate fulfillment of the new covenant is not until the consummation.[87] No doubt, the new covenant is "already" here in the church, but the perfect fulfillment of it envisioned in terms of a regenerate community is still "not yet." Thus, it is not until the consummation of this age that the church will be a regenerate community; at pres-

---

[85] Pratt, "Infant Baptism and the New Covenant," 159–60.
[86] Ibid., 161.
[87] See ibid., 169.

ent it is only a "mixed" community constituted by covenant-keepers and covenant-breakers. Pratt writes,

> We can have confidence that after Christ returns in glory, everyone in the new creation will have the law of God written on his or her heart. . . . In this sense, we expect Jeremiah's prophecy to find complete fulfillment when Christ returns. At the present time, however, this expectation is only partially fulfilled. . . . Until the consummation, the new covenant will continue to be a mixture of true believers and sanctified unbelievers.[88]

Space permits only a brief response. First, paedobaptists fail to do justice to the biblical data, specifically the promise of Jeremiah 31 and its fulfillment in the NT. Second, due to that failure, they wrongly view the nature of the church as a "mixed" entity. Let us briefly address both of these issues in seven steps by first turning to Jeremiah 31 and then to the nature of the church.

1. In response to paedobaptists like Niell, most Baptists, at least those writing in this volume, do *not* deny what Niell thinks we deny namely, "that the internal operations of divine grace were not present for the old covenant saint,"[89] as if all Baptists understand the relations between the covenants within a framework of complete discontinuity.[90] I agree that OT saints were saved by grace through faith, were regenerate, knew the Lord, and experienced forgiveness of sins under the old covenant structures in anticipation of the fulfillment of those types and shadows in Christ. This is simply not the issue at debate. As James White rightly notes, "The point is that for Niell, the 'counterpoint' to which he is responding is an either/or situation: either the elements of the New Covenant described in Heb. 8:10 were *completely* absent in the Old Covenant . . . or they were present *and hence cannot be definitional of what is 'new' in the New Covenant.*"[91] What, then, is the real point of contention? This leads me to my second point.

2. The real issue centers on whether there is a fundamental change in the *structure* and *nature* of the new covenant community in con-

---

[88] Ibid., 171, 173.

[89] Niell, "The Newness of the New Covenant," 134.

[90] Here is another example of how paedobaptists often caricature Baptists as being classical Dispensationalists without acknowledging the diversity of viewpoint within Baptist theology.

[91] J. R. White, "The Newness of the New Covenant: Part 2" *Reformed Baptist Theological Review* 2:1 (2005): 88.

trast to the old.[92] Let us think first in terms of *structural* changes in the new covenant which, I would contend, become the basis for understanding the church as the "priesthood of all believers." Under the old covenant, as D. A. Carson has noted, God dealt with his people in a mediated or "tribal" fashion.[93] Despite remnant themes and an emphasis on individual believers, the OT pictures God working with his people as a "tribal" grouping whose knowledge of God and whose relations with God were uniquely dependent on specially endowed leaders. Thus, the strong emphasis on the Spirit of God being poured out, not on each believer, but distinctively on prophets, priests, kings, and a few designated special leaders (e.g., Bezalel). Given this hierarchical structure of the covenant community, when these leaders did what was right, the entire nation benefited. However, when they did not, the entire nation suffered for their actions. But what Jeremiah anticipates is that this tribal structure is going to change, "In those days people will no longer say, 'The fathers have eaten sour grapes, and the children's teeth are set on edge.' Instead everyone will die for his own sin; whoever eats sour grapes—his own teeth will be set on edge" (Jer 31:29–30).[94] As Carson observes,

> In short, Jeremiah understood that the new covenant would bring some dramatic changes. The tribal nature of the people of God would end, and the new covenant would bring with it a new emphasis on the distribution of the knowledge of God down to the level of each member of the covenant community. Knowledge of God would no longer be mediated through specially endowed leaders, for *all* of God's covenant people, would know him, from the least to the greatest. Jeremiah is not concerned to say there would be no teachers under the new covenant, but to remove from leaders that

---

[92] There is debate over the meaning of the word, "new" (Heb., *ḥādās*; LXX, *kainos*). Some argue that the word only means "renewed" (e.g. Lam 3:22–23) and others argue that it means "new" in a qualitatively different sense (Exod 1:8; Deut 32:17; 1 Sam 6:7; Eccl 1:10). Ultimately the "newness" of the new covenant must be contextually determined. On this debate see Dumbrell, Covenant and Creation, 175; J. R. White, "The Newness of the New Covenant: Part 1" *Reformed Baptist Theological Review* 1:2 (2004): 144–52; C. B. Hoch, Jr., All Things New (Grand Rapids: Baker, 1995), 105–107.

[93] See D. A. Carson, *Showing the Spirit: A Theological Exposition of 1 Corinthians 12–14* (Grand Rapids: Baker, 1987), 150–58; see id., "Evangelicals, Ecumenism, and the Church," in *Evangelical Affirmations*, ed., K. S. Kantzer and C. F. H. Henry (Grand Rapids: Zondervan, 1990), 347–85.

[94] All quotations from Scripture come from the NIV.

distinctive mediatorial role that made the knowledge of God among the people at large a secondary knowledge, a mediated knowledge.[95]

Related to this anticipation is the OT promise of the gift of the Holy Spirit and his empowering work in the new covenant era (Ezek 11:19–20; 36:25–27; Joel 2:28–32; cp. Num 11:27–29).[96] Under the old covenant, the "tribal" structure of the covenant community meant that the Spirit was uniquely poured out on leaders. But what the prophets anticipate is a crucial change: the coming of the new covenant era would witness a *universal* distribution of the Spirit (see Joel 2:28–32; Acts 2). God would pour out his Spirit on *all* flesh, namely, *all* those within the covenant community. Thus, *all* those "under the new covenant" enjoy the promised gift of the eschatological Holy Spirit (see Eph 1:13–14). In the NT, the Spirit is presented as the agent who not only gives us life but also enables us to follow God's decrees and to keep God's laws, thus making us covenant-keepers and *not* covenant-breakers. The role which Israel was supposed to play is now fulfilled in us, the church, by the Spirit.[97] It is precisely the dawning of this new age that John the Baptist announces (Matt 3:11), which is signaled at Pentecost, and which is grounded in the triumphant cross work of our Lord (John 7:39; 16:7; Acts 2:33). All these events are associated with the inauguration of the new covenant era. That is why it came to be understood that the new covenant era, the Messianic age, would also be the age of the Spirit. In this age, the Spirit is sent to *all* believers and thus becomes the precious seal, down-payment, and guarantee of the promised inheritance of the last day. To be "in Christ" is to have the Spirit for, as Paul reminds us, "if anyone does not have the Spirit of Christ, he does not belong to Christ" (Rom 8:9). What is the point of all this? It is simply this: one cannot understand the *new* covenant without acknowledging the massive *structural*

[95] Carson, *Showing the Spirit*, 152. It is clear from the context that the knowledge spoken of here is a salvific knowledge. See Dumbrell, *Covenant and Creation*, 177–78; Pratt, "Infant Baptism in the New Covenant," 159–61; P. R. House, *Old Testament Theology* (Downers Grove: InterVarsity, 1998), 317–21.

[96] On this point see Max Turner, "Holy Spirit," in *NDBT*, 551–58; D. F. Wells, *God the Evangelist* (Grand Rapids: Eerdmans, 1987), 1–4; G. Vos, "The Eschatological Aspect of the Pauline Conception of the Spirit," in *Redemptive History and Biblical Interpretation*, 91–125; A. A. Hoekema, *The Bible and the Future* (Grand Rapids: Eerdmans, 1979), 55–67.

[97] On this point see T. R. Schreiner, *Romans*, BECNT (Grand Rapids: Baker, 1998), 395–468.

changes that have taken place. It is simply *not* correct to think of the new covenant as merely a "renewed" version of the old; it brings with it significant change.

3. The new covenant results not only in *structural* change, but also change in the *nature of the covenant people.* Jeremiah signals this in two ways. First, he contrasts the new covenant with the old, "It will not be like the covenant I made with your forefathers . . . because they broke my covenant" (Jer 31:32). But, secondly, he tells us why this covenant will *not* be like the old due to a change in the very *nature* of the covenant community. Under the new covenant *all* will know the Lord, not in a mediate but immediate fashion, and *all* will have the law written on their hearts and experience the full forgiveness of sin. In fact, it is these last two aspects of the new covenant which highlight the incredible change that is anticipated and which is now a reality in the church.

Certainly the expression "law written on the heart" is very close to the language of "circumcision of heart" (see Deut 10:16; 30:6; Jer 4:4; 9:25), which can refer to nothing less than regeneration. This does not mean that no one in the OT ever experienced a "circumcision of the heart." Rather it is signaling the change that is taking place in the nature of the *entire* covenant community. Instead of the people being a "mixed" entity, now the entire community will experience a "circumcision of the heart." The change that is emphasized is nothing less than the change from a "mixed" to a *regenerate* people.[98] Jer 31:32 is clear: this is in direct contrast to the OT people of God. No doubt within national Israel there were many believers. But as an entire community not "all Israel was Israel" (Rom 9:6). Within the national community, there was a distinction between the physical and spiritual seed of Abraham. Under the old covenant both "seeds" received the covenant sign of circumcision and both were viewed as full covenant members in the national sense. However, it was only the believers—the remnant—who were the spiritual seed of Abraham, the "true Israel" in a salvific sense. As White reminds us, built within the very nature of the old covenant community "for every David there were a dozen Ahabs; for every

[98] See House, *Old Testament Theology*, 317–21.

Josiah a legion of Manassehs. Unfaithfulness, the flaunting of God's law, the rejection of the role of truly being God's people, the rejection of His knowledge, and the experience of His wrath, were the *normative* experiences seen in the Old Covenant."[99] But this is *not* what is anticipated of those under the new covenant. Thus White correctly observes that "Quite simply, there is no 'remnant' in the New Covenant, and all those with whom God makes this covenant experience its fulfillment. This is why it is better, and hence proves the author's [Hebrews] apologetic presentation of the supremacy of Christ over the old ways."[100]

Furthermore, this change is also evident in the promise that the Lord will no longer "remember" our sin (v. 34). White rightly notes that the entire presentation of Jeremiah 31 in Hebrews is "inextricably linked with this demonstration of the supremacy of Christ's priesthood *and salvific work* (7:22–25; 9:15,23–25; 10:10–18)."[101] The "better" nature of the new covenant is seen in light of the perfection of Christ's work which is *qualitatively* better than all that has preceded. It has better promises and better sacrifices and therefore is a *better* covenant. What is the *better* nature of the covenant? It is this: because of who the Redeemer is and what he offers as a sacrifice we now have a *more effective* sacrifice and thus a *more effective* covenant; indeed, we have a covenant that "is not susceptible to the breach perpetrated in the past."[102] Is this not the glory of what Christ has accomplished for us? Due to his work, he has brought about a full, effective, and complete salvation unlike the types and shadows of the old (see Heb 7–10). In the OT, forgiveness of sin is normally granted through the sacrificial system; however, the OT believer, if spiritually perceptive, was fully aware that it was not the blood of bulls and goats that forgave sins. Salvation ultimately had to be found in God's provision of his own Son. But in the new covenant the types and shadows of the

---

[99] White, "The Newness of the New Covenant: Part 2," 88.

[100] White, "The Newness of the New Covenant: Part 1," 160. See W. L. Lane, *Hebrews 1–8*. WBC (Dallas: Word, 1991), 200–11 and G. H. Guthrie, *Hebrews*, NIVAC (Grand Rapids: Zondervan, 1998), 286–87.

[101] White, "The Newness of the New Covenant: Part 1," 147 (emphasis his).

[102] A. I. Wilson, "Luke and the New Covenant: Zechariah's Prophecy as a Test Case" in *The God of Covenant*, ed. J. A. Grant and A. I. Wilson (Leicester: InterVarsity, 2005), 163.

old have reached their *telos*. Due to our covenant mediator, sin will be forgiven and "remembered no more." Clearly, the concept of "remembering" in the OT is not simple recollection (see Gen 8:1; 1 Sam 1:19). In the context of Jer 31:34 for God "not to remember" means that no action will need to be taken in the new age against sin. In the end, to be under the terms of *this* covenant entails that one experiences a full and complete salvation.[103]

4. When does this "new covenant" begin? The NT is clear: it was inaugurated and ratified by the sacrificial death of Christ (Luke 22:20; cp. 1 Cor 11:25; 2 Cor 3:7–18). Hebrews unambiguously applies Jeremiah to the church (Heb 8–10). As D. A. Carson notes, this means that whatever complex relationships obtain between Israel and the church, at least, in this context, it is a typological connection since the promise of the new covenant in Jeremiah is made to "the house of Israel and with the house of Judah" (v. 31).[104] Contrary to Pratt's view, Hebrews establishes the reality of the new covenant in the church without any hint that the full establishment of a regenerate community is yet future.[105] No doubt, we still await the "not yet" aspects of our redemption, but this does not entail that the community is not "already" a regenerate people. The perfect passive use of the verb in Hebrews 8:6—he "has enacted"—emphasizes the completed action even though the full ramifications may be future. As White rightly comments,

> There is nothing in the text that would lead us to believe that the full establishment of this covenant is yet future, for such would destroy the present apologetic concern of the author; likewise, he will complete his citation of Jer. 31 by asserting the obsolete nature of the first covenant, which leaves one to have to theorize, without textual basis, about some kind of intermediate covenantal state if one does not accept the full establishment of the New Covenant as seen in the term νενομοθέτηται.[106]

In fact, one cannot understand the argument of Hebrews without seeing that what Jeremiah anticipated has now come to pass in the

[103] On this point see Dumbrell, *Covenant and Creation*, 181–85.
[104] See D. A. Carson, "Evangelicals, Ecumenism, and the Church," 361.
[105] For a more detailed and helpful critique of Pratt, see White, "The Newness of the New Covenant: Part 2," 97–103.
[106] White, "The Newness of the New Covenant: Part 1," 157.

church. In Christ's coming, the new age is here, the Spirit has been poured out on the entire community, and we now experience our adoption as sons including the full forgiveness of sin (see Rom 8), even though we long for the end.

5. Everything that has been stated regarding the new covenant is also supported in the NT's instruction regarding the nature of the church. Once again, I do not dispute that Scripture teaches that there is only *one* people of God throughout the ages. However, what is at debate is whether the *nature* of the covenant community changes in Christ, specifically whether the church is a "mixed" community like Israel of old. As with the previous discussion, whole books have been written on this subject, so the discussion here is necessarily abbreviated. But the crucial point to note in regard to baptism is that the NT church everywhere is viewed as a regenerate, believing community. As Jeremiah anticipated and the NT proclaims, the people of the new covenant are *all* those who have the law written on their hearts, *all* of whom know the Lord salvifically, for *all* of them have experienced the forgiveness of sin. Unlike Israel of old, the locus of the covenant community and the locus of the redeemed is one in the new covenant.

What has brought about this change? Ultimately the answer is rooted in Christology. The person and work of Jesus, the new covenant head, requires a change. As we progress across the canon, we move from type to antitype, from covenant heads such as Adam, Noah, Abraham, and David to Christ; and with Christ, we have change.[107] This is *the* reason why it is *not* correct to view the church, as paedobaptists do, as simply the replacement of Israel, a kind of "renewed" instantiation of it. Rather the church is *new*. Because of her identification with Christ, the head of the new creation, she is a "new man" (Eph 2:11–22). This is why the church is identified with the "age to come" and not the structures of the old era, or what have been called "this present age." This is why the church is viewed as the community empowered by the Spirit in which *all* have been born of the Spirit.[108]

[107] For a development of this point see White, "The Last Adam and His Seed," 60–73.
[108] On this point see Carson, "Evangelicals, Ecumenism, and the Church," 362–63.

In fact, this is why the church is described as an eschatological and "gathered" (*ekklēsia*) community.[109] In this regard, the church as identified with the "age to come" is an illustration of the running tension between the "already" and the "not yet." It is the "gathered" people of God in a singular sense—"*the* church" (Col 1:18; cp. Heb 12:22–24)—because even *now* Christians participate in the heavenly, eschatological church of Christ as the beginnings of the new creation. As Carson reminds us, what this entails for our understanding of the church is that,

> each local church is not seen primarily as one member parallel to a lot of other member churches, together constituting one body, one church; nor is each local church seen as the body of Christ parallel to other earthly churches that are also the body of Christ—as if Christ had many bodies. Rather, each church is the full manifestation in space and time of the one, true, heavenly, eschatological, new covenant church. Local churches should see themselves as outcroppings of heaven, analogies of "the Jerusalem that is above," indeed colonies of the new Jerusalem, providing on earth a corporate and visible expression of "the glorious freedom of the children of God.[110]

But if this is so, then what is crucial to note is that *this* understanding of the church presupposes that it is a *regenerate* community—a community in faith union with Christ, born of his Spirit, those who have been raised and seated with Christ in the heavenly realms (Eph 2:5–6; Col 2:12–13; 3:3). It is unpersuasive to think of the church as a mixed entity. As Carson rightly notes, if this biblical and theological understanding of the church is basically right, "then the ancient contrast between the church visible and the church invisible, a contrast that has nurtured not a little ecclesiology, is either fundamentally mistaken, or at best of marginal importance."[111] Why? Because the NT views the church as a *heavenly* (i.e., tied to the "age to come" and the new creation, not "in Adam" but "in Christ") and *spiritual* community (i.e., born of and empowered by the Spirit in faith union with Christ), living her life out now while she awaits the

---

[109] See Carson, "Evangelicals, Ecumenism, and the Church," 363–67, as well as the helpful discussion in E. Clowney, *The Church*, 27–33.

[110] Carson, "Evangelicals, Ecumenism, and the Church," 366. Also see P. T. O'Brien, "Church," in *DPL*, 123–31.

[111] Carson, "Evangelicals, Ecumenism, and the Church," 367.

consummation, literally "the outcropping of the heavenly assembly gathered in the Jerusalem that is above."[112]

All this understanding of the church is basic NT ecclesiology.[113] And all of it is true because Christ Jesus has come and through his cross work has inaugurated the new covenant age. He, as the fulfillment of Adam, Abraham, Israel, and David, has brought covenantal and epochal change. And we, as the new covenant people of God, receive the benefits of his work in only one way—through individual repentance toward God and faith in our Lord Jesus Christ. By God's grace and power we are then transferred from being "in Adam" to being "in Christ" with all the benefits of that union. And the NT is clear: to be "in Christ" and thus in the new covenant, a member of his gathered people (church), means that one is a regenerate believer. The NT knows nothing of one who is "in Christ" who is not regenerate, effectually called of the Father, born of the Spirit, justified, holy, and awaiting glorification.[114]

6. Given what has been stated, Baptists insist that the covenant sign of the new covenant age, namely baptism, must only be applied to those who have repented of their sins and believed in Christ. This is precisely the pattern we find in the NT. In fact, as other chapters in this book have argued, the most fundamental meaning of baptism is that it signifies a believer's union with Christ, by grace through faith, and all the benefits that are entailed by that union. It is for this reason that, throughout the NT, baptism is regarded as an outward sign that a believer has entered into the realities of the new covenant that Jesus sealed with his own blood on the cross. J. I. Packer captures this point well when he writes,

> Christian baptism . . . is a sign from God that signifies inward cleansing and remission of sins (Acts 22:16; 1 Cor 6:11; Eph 5:25–27), Spirit-wrought regeneration and new life (Titus 3:5), and the abiding presence of the Holy Spirit as God's seal testifying and guaranteeing that one will be kept safe in Christ forever (1 Cor 12:13; Eph 1:13–14). Baptism carries these meanings because first and fundamentally it signifies union with Christ in his death,

---

[112] Ibid., 371.

[113] See Clowney, *The Church*, 27–70; D. J. Tidball, "Church," *NDBT*, 407–11; Schreiner, *Paul*, 331–44. Cp. S. Motyer, "Israel (nation)," *NDBT*, 581–87.

[114] On the biblical teaching regarding union with Christ see S. B. Ferguson, *The Holy Spirit* (Downers Grove: InterVarsity, 1996), 93–138, and Grudem, *Systematic Theology*, 840–50.

burial, and resurrection (Rom 6:3–7; Col 2:11–12); and this union with Christ is the source of every element in our salvation (1 John 5:11–12). Receiving the sign in faith assures the persons baptized that God's gift of new life in Christ is freely given to them.[115]

In fact, so close is the association between baptism and new covenant blessings in Christ that in the NT baptism "functions as shorthand for the conversion experience as a whole."[116] Evidence for this is quite apparent. For example, in Gal 3:26–27, Paul can say, "You are all sons of God through faith in Christ Jesus, for all of you who were baptized into Christ have been clothed with Christ." The language of being "clothed" with Christ refers to our union with him.[117] But what is interesting about Paul's statement is how Paul can ascribe union with Christ both to faith (v. 26) and to baptism (v. 27). How can Paul do this? Does he have in mind an *ex opere operato* view of baptism? No, he is not referring to those who have been baptized but have not believed; that would go against the clear statement of v. 26. Rather, he is referring to those who have been converted: all such have clothed themselves with Christ and have been united with him through faith. Thus, baptism, by metonymy, can stand for conversion and signify, as an outward sign, that a believer has entered into the realities of the new covenant as a result of his union with Christ through faith.[118]

We find something similar in Rom 6:1–4, where Paul sees the initiation rite of baptism as uniting the believer to Jesus Christ in the redemptive acts of his death, burial, and resurrection. In this text Paul is not primarily giving a theological explanation of the nature of baptism, but rather unpacking the significance of baptism for the Christian life. Paul is deeply concerned to rebut the charge that the believer may "remain in sin" in order to underscore grace.

---

[115] J. I. Packer, *Concise Theology* (Wheaton: Tyndale, 1993), 212.

[116] D. Moo, *The Epistle to the Romans*, NICNT (Grand Rapids: Eerdmans, 1996), 355. Moo, agreeing with James Dunn, notes that it is not as if baptism effects regeneration, but it is assumed that faith leads to baptism, and baptism always assumes faith for its validity. This observation underscores the importance the New Testament places on baptism, without denying the priority of salvation by grace through faith. See J. Dunn, *Baptism in the Holy Spirit* (London: SCM Press Ltd., 1970), 139–46; Moo, *Romans*, 366; Beasley-Murray, "Baptism," *NIDNTT*, 1:146–48.

[117] See R. Y. K. Fung, *The Epistle to the Galatians*, NICNT (Grand Rapids: Eerdmans, 1988), 170–75; Beasley-Murray, *Baptism*, 146–51; Clowney, *The Church*, 280.

[118] See Fung, *Galatians*, 173–74; Beasley-Murray, "Baptism," *DPL*, 62; and R. N. Longenecker, *Galatians*, WBC (Dallas: Word, 1990), 154–56.

Accordingly he uses the language of "realm transfer"[119] to show how inconceivable this suggestion really is. Christians, Paul affirms, have "died to sin" (v. 2b). We have been transferred from the realm of Adam (sin) to the realm of Christ (life, resurrection, grace), and as such, it is quite impossible for us to still live in sin; its power in us has been decisively broken due to our union with Christ in his death. When did this realm transfer, this "death to sin," take place? Significantly in vv. 3–4 Paul connects "death to sin" with our baptism, meaning that when we were "baptized into Christ Jesus" we were "baptized into his death" (v. 3). We have died to sin because we have become one with the Lord who died and rose for the conquest of sin and death. Furthermore, "We were buried with him through baptism into death in order that, just as Christ was raised from the dead . . . we too may live a new life" (v. 4). In this sense, then, baptism serves as the instrument by which we are united with Christ in his death, burial, and resurrection.[120] Once again, Paul's point is *not* to say that the practice of baptism itself unites us to Christ. Rather, as in Galatians 3:26–27, baptism functions as shorthand for the whole conversion experience. Thus, Douglas Moo is right in concluding that "just as faith is always assumed to lead to baptism, so baptism always assumes faith for its validity. In vv. 3–4, then, we can assume that baptism stands for the whole conversion-initiation experience, presupposing faith and the gift of the Spirit."[121] In truth, if we understand Paul's argument, it is *not* baptism which is the primary focus at all; rather, the redemptive events themselves are what Paul is stressing. Baptism is *only* introduced to demonstrate that we were united with Christ in his redemptive work, and now all the new covenant blessings that our Lord has secured for us are ours by virtue of our relationship with him. As Beasley-Murray states, "Through the faith expressed in baptism, what was done outside of us (*extra nos*) becomes effective faith within us. In Christ we are the reconciled children of God."[122]

---

[119] Moo, *Romans*, 354 (also pp. 351–52). See H. Ridderbos, *Paul: An Outline of His Theology*, trans. J. R. de Witt (Grand Rapids: Eerdmans, 1975), 44–181.

[120] Moo, *Romans*, 353–67.

[121] Ibid., 366.

[122] Beasley-Murray, "Baptism," in *DPL*, 62. Col 2:11–12 is another text which is parallel

Other texts could be multiplied to make this same point,[123] but suffice it to say that in the NT baptism is so closely linked with the gospel itself that it is not enough to say that baptism is merely a symbol. Instead, in the words of Beasley-Murray, it is also a "divine-human event."[124] One must not think of this either as *ex opere operato* or as implying the absolute necessity of baptism for salvation. The NT is clear: the benefits that come to us in baptism are tied to faith and faith alone. That is why faith and baptism do not enjoy the same logical status of necessity. But with that said, it is significant that Scripture links all the gracious benefits of the believer's being united to Christ with water baptism. But if this is so, we cannot conceive how the new covenant sign of baptism may be applied to anyone who does not have faith.

7. What do paedobaptists say in response? The most significant response is an appeal to the warning and apostasy passages of Scripture in order to demonstrate that the church is still a "mixed" community (e.g., Heb 6:4–6). Once again, we can only simply note a number of problems with this approach. First, the paedobaptist interpretation of these texts assumes the "covenant theology" it must first demonstrate. In order for their argument to carry any weight, they must first prove that the nature of the covenant communities is essentially the same throughout the canon. But I have already given reasons why I think this is not correct. Second, the paedobaptist interpretation of these texts is inconsistent with biblical teaching regarding the nature of the new covenant church.[125] Third, even

---

to Rom 6:1–4. On this text see below as well as P. T. O'Brien, *Colossians and Philemon*, WBC (Waco: Word, 1982), 114–21.

[123] For example see 1 Pet 3:21. On this text see T. R. Schreiner, *1, 2 Peter, Jude*, NAC (Nashville: Broadman & Holman, 2003), 193–97 and W. Grudem, *1 Peter*, TNTC (Grand Rapids: Eerdmans, 1988), 164–65.

[124] Beasley-Murray, "Baptism," *NIDNTT*, 1:148.

[125] Paedobaptist literature commonly asserts that our own experience sadly confirms what the NT says about the possibility of apostasy. This fact demonstrates to paedobaptists that the church must be viewed as a mixed community like Israel of old. Proof is offered from such texts as Matt 13:24–30 (the parable of the wheat and the tares—even though the parable portrays the kingdom of God in the world and not the constitution of the church), the vine imagery of John 15 and Romans 11, and the warning texts of Hebrews (e.g. 6:4–6). But the nature of the new covenant community makes this interpretation highly unlikely. We cannot deny Scripture's description of how the new covenant people of God has incredibly changed. Furthermore, the fact of apostasy and the status of the one who commits it are not the same. No one disputes the fact of apostasy in the new covenant age, but the status of those apostates is disputed. Are they

though their understanding of these texts is a "possible" reading, other legitimate ways of reading these texts (in light of a better way to understand the relations between the biblical covenants, the nature of the new covenant community, and what it means for someone to be in union with Christ) can do justice to *all* the Scriptural data.[126] The true test for anyone's theology is this: Does it do justice to *all* the biblical data? I have argued that paedobaptism fails in this regard.

The Relationship between Circumcision and Baptism

The final area to investigate is the relationship between circumcision and baptism. Assuming the continuity of the covenant of grace and the covenant community, paedobaptism contends that circumcision and baptism carry essentially the same *spiritual* meaning and that in the new covenant era baptism is the *replacement* of circumcision as a covenant sign. Neither covenant sign is effective apart from faith; they are merely entry markers signifying that one is part of the covenant community, at least in the external sense. They promise and anticipate the gospel, pointing forward to the need for a "circumcision of the heart," testifying to God's promise of righteousness by faith. Somehow they signify union with Christ and all the blessings related to that union without necessarily implying that one is regenerate in the full salvation sense of the word.[127]

"covenant breakers" (assuming they were once full covenant members), or those who professed faith and identified with the church, but who demonstrate by rejecting the gospel that they were never one with us (see 1 John 2:19)? The NT teaches the latter. Apostasy leads us, sadly, to reevaluate a person's former profession of faith and his covenant status. But this situation is unlike unbelievers in the old covenant who were still viewed as covenant members, even though they were unbelievers. As R. Fowler White, "The Last Adam and His Seed," 72, n. 19, asserts, "Unlike apostates from the Mosaic covenant (Heb 3:7–11,16–19) who had heard God say of them that he had (fore)known them in their mediatorial forebears (see Deut 4:37; 7:6–8; 10:15), apostates from the Messianic covenant will hear the Lord of the covenant say to them, 'I never knew you' (see Matt 7:23; cp. 2 Tim 2:17–19)." Trying to discern true saving faith is merely a human epistemological problem, and we do our best to discern whether one's profession of faith is genuine. But this is a far cry from baptizing where there is no faith.

[126] The best treatment of the warnings passages in Scripture showing how they function in the Christian life, which does *not* conclude that they entail that the church is a "mixed community" is T. R. Schreiner and A. B. Caneday, *The Race Set Before Us* (Downers Grove: InterVarsity, 2001).

[127] There is an equivocation of terms in the paedobaptist position. What does it mean for

Of course, the crucial question in the baptismal debate is this: Does circumcision signify the exact same spiritual realities as baptism? My answer is no. No doubt they are parallel in a number of ways, but they ought to be viewed as covenantal signs tied to *different* covenants. Circumcision is an OT ordinance established in a specific redemptive-historical context, and the same is true of baptism in the NT. To equate the two in a one-to-one fashion is a significant error, as I will seek to demonstrate.

1. In its OT context, circumcision is first instituted in Genesis 17 where it is clearly tied to the Abrahamic covenant. Up to that point in time, no covenant sign existed to mark God's people, even though God's promise was in the world (Gen 3:15). In fact, this point is stressed in Rom 4:9–12 where Paul correctly argues that God's declaration of Abraham's righteousness took place before the institution of circumcision, thus demonstrating the priority of faith over circumcision in our justification. Interestingly, paedobaptists often appeal to Romans 4 to argue that circumcision, as a sign and seal of Abraham's faith, is applied to infants as a sign and seal to them as well, which is then carried over in baptism.[128] But this is not Paul's point in this text. Instead, Paul is presenting Abraham as the paradigm for all believers, both Jew and Gentile. To Abraham and to him alone, circumcision was a covenantal sign attesting that he had already been justified by faith apart from circumcision. The text is not giving a general statement about the nature of circumcision for everyone who receives it. After all, Ishmael was also circumcised the very same day, but there is no evidence that Rom 4:11 applied to him in the same way as it did to Abraham. The text seems to indicate that one must first believe *before* one receives the covenantal sign.

one to be united to Christ apart from faith, or to affirm that one has entered into new covenant realities apart from faith, regeneration, and forgiveness of sin? In fact, what does infant baptism effect apart from faith? Reformed paedobaptists are not clear at this point, even though they attempt to provide some kind of explanation. See the helpful discussion of this problem in D. F. Wright, "Recovering Baptism for a New Age of Mission," in *Doing Theology for the People of God*, ed. D. Lewis and A. McGrath (Downers Grove: InterVarsity, 1996), 51–66. For an example of a confusing use of the word "regeneration" as it relates to what infant baptism effects, see R. Lusk, "Do I Believe in Baptismal Regeneration?" http://www.auburnavenue.org/Articles/DO%20I%20BELIEVE%20IN%20BAPTISMAL%20REGENERATION.htm.

[128] For example, see B. Chapell, "A Pastoral Overview of Infant Baptism," 14–15, and C. Venema, "Covenant Theology and Baptism," 221–22.

Thus, for Abraham (and those who have a faith like Abraham) circumcision served as a sign and seal of righteousness, but for others, it signified other realities.[129]

2. What else did circumcision signify? In the context of the Abrahamic and Mosaic covenants, the primary purpose of circumcision was to mark out a physical seed in preparation for the coming of Messiah.[130] The marking purpose of circumcision may be viewed in two complementary ways. First, circumcision marked out a national entity. With the inauguration of the Abrahamic covenant, God chose one man and his seed to grow into a nation to prepare the way for the coming of Christ. Now that Christ has come, God deals with all nations directly through his Son. We must, then, view the period from Abraham to Christ as a unique time in redemptive-history, a time of preparation in which Israel, as a nation, was used in the plan of God to bring forth the Messiah. Circumcision was integral to that purpose. It served as a physical sign to mark out a nation and to distinguish them as his people. In this regard, it did its job well, but now that Christ has come, its job is complete and the NT has abrogated it as a covenantal sign. What promises were signified by circumcision? *All* the promises tied to the Abrahamic covenant, which included not only salvific promises but also national ones, particularly the land promise (e.g., Gen 12:7; 15:12–21; 17:8). *All* these promises in different ways lead us to Christ, but we must not reduce all of them merely to their spiritual sense. Second, circumcision marked out a male line of descent from Abraham to David to Christ. That is why, in a typological way, every Jewish male child, specifically those in Judah's line, was a type of Christ who anticipated the day when the true/unique seed of Abraham would come.[131]

---

[129] For more on this issue see the helpful treatment in Schreiner, *Romans*, 222–33.

[130] On a general discussion of circumcision see the following: P. D. Woodbridge, "Circumcision," *NDBT*, 411–14; Robertson, *Christ of the Covenants*, 147–66; P. R. Williamson, "Circumcision" in *Dictionary of OT: Pentateuch*, ed. T. D. Alexander and D. W. Baker (Downers Grove: InterVarsity, 2003), 122–25; Jewett, *Infant Baptism and the Covenant of Grace*, 82–104.

[131] Circumcision also traces out the source of our moral corruption. Adam, as the head of the human race, is held responsible for sin. We were not corrupted through Eve but through Adam, and circumcision reminds us of this as well as the need for a radical spiritual surgery—hence it speaks of the need for a "circumcision of the heart." See Robertson, *Christ of the Covenants*, 148–52, and G. Vos, *Biblical Theology* (1948; reprint, Grand Rapids: Eerdmans, 1988), 88–90.

3. As circumcision was incorporated into the Mosaic covenant (see Lev 12:1–5; Josh 5:1–9), it served a number of purposes. It continued to mark and delineate the nation, which, by its very nature, was constituted as a spiritually mixed entity. Even in the darkest moments of Israel's history, the prophets never questioned Israel's right to circumcise their sons even though they reminded them that physical circumcision was not enough. What was ultimately needed was faith in the promises of God tied to a circumcised heart, but physical circumcision was never called into question.[132] In fact, one cannot find in Israel the idea that circumcision was only for "*believers and their children*" since many unbelieving Jews circumcised their infant boys and were still considered part of the covenant nation. The paedobaptist understanding already reads into circumcision a meaning that is not there.

But under the Mosaic covenant, there was also another purpose of circumcision which begins to point to spiritual and typological realities. In this regard, physical circumcision pointed to the need of a spiritually circumcised heart which would result in a wholehearted devotion to the Lord (Deut 30:6; cp. Jer 4:4). Indeed, the new covenant promise in Jer 31:33 of the "law written on their hearts" combined with Ezek 36:25–27 pointed forward to the day when the entire covenant community would be circumcised in heart. This emphasis picks up the teaching of the prophets that physical circumcision only availed the one who had been spiritually circumcised (see Rom 2:25–29). In this sense, circumcision serves as a type that finds its fulfillment and replacement in regeneration.

4. In the NT, it is beyond question that circumcision is abrogated as a sign of membership in the church. Circumcision, in light of Christ's coming, is no longer a covenantally significant sign and thus is not required for believers, whether they are Jewish or Gentile (see Acts 15:1–35; Gal 1:6–9; 2:11–16; 6:15; 1 Cor 7:18–19). In Christ, the previous covenants have come to fulfillment, and, as such, the covenant sign of circumcision is no longer necessary; it has served its purpose. Now, in Christ, and the creation of the "new man" (Eph 2:11–22), the law-covenant has been fulfilled and the God-given di-

---

[132] On this point see Jewett, *Infant Baptism and the Covenant of Grace*, 93–104.

visions tied to that law-covenant have been removed so much so that Paul can proclaim, "Neither circumcision nor uncircumcision means anything; what counts is a new creation" (Gal 6:15). In this new era, a new covenantal sign, baptism, has been established to testify of the gospel and to identify one as having become the spiritual seed of Abraham, through faith in Messiah Jesus. But unlike circumcision, baptism is *not* a sign of physical descent, nor is it a sign that anticipates gospel realities. Rather it is a sign that signifies a believer's union with Christ and all the benefits that are entailed by that union. No doubt, baptism is analogous to circumcision in that it is an initiatory rite, but it is not a mere replacement of it. Nowhere does the NT say that circumcision is now unnecessary because baptism has replaced it. That would have been the most logical answer to the Judaizers, if the paedobaptist position was correct.[133] This answer is never given because baptism is a new rite, applied to each person who has repented and believed, who has been born of the Spirit, united to Christ, and has demonstrated that he has entered into the new covenant realities inaugurated by our Lord.

5. Circumcision, then, in light of the entire canon, ought to be viewed as signifying at least two truths. Most important, it marks out a physical people and nation. Second, it serves as a type anticipating NT realities that have now come to fulfillment in Christ. We may view circumcision as a type in two ways. First, circumcision is a type in that it anticipates Christ. As noted above, the "seed of Abraham" has a number of nuances including its reference to Christ (Gal 3:16). In a typological way, then, every male offspring of Abraham—specifically through the line of Isaac, Judah, David—was a type of Christ and thus anticipated his ultimate coming. In this regard, Luke 2:21 is important. Jesus' circumcision is not a minor event; it marks the fulfillment of circumcision in its purpose of preserving a line of descent from Abraham to Christ and marking out the one in whom all the promises of God have reached their fulfillment. In Christ, Abraham's true seed is now here, and as such, circumcision is no longer necessary and was soon to be abrogated. In this sense, Jesus' circumcision is the last significant covenantal

---

[133] See Jewett, *Infant Baptism and the Covenant of Grace,* 228–32.

circumcision recorded in Scripture. Other circumcisions, such as Timothy's (Acts 16:3), were only done for principled pragmatic concerns in order to win Jews for the sake of the gospel.[134]

Second, circumcision is a type in that it anticipates the need for a "circumcision of the heart," a reality which all new covenant people have experienced. In us, the spiritual meaning of circumcision is fulfilled (Rom 2:25–29; Phil 3:3). That is why true believers, regardless of whether they have been physically circumcised are called "the true circumcision." Due to Christ's cross work and the Spirit's work within us, we have now received a circumcision without hands that gives us our new covenant status as God's people and thus makes us heirs and co-heirs with Christ.

In fact, this is the point of Col 2:11–13, the only text in the NT that brings together circumcision and baptism. But as it has repeatedly been shown, the connection in these verses is *not* between physical circumcision and baptism, as if the latter replaces the former, but *spiritual circumcision* tied to union with Christ and *baptism*.[135] As Paul reminds these believers, they are complete in Christ not because they were physically circumcised but because they were circumcised in "the circumcision of Christ." The "circumcision of Christ" refers either to "a Christian circumcision of the heart"[136] or to Christ's death on the cross. This means that the only circumcision believers need is that which has been done by our being united into Christ's death on the cross.[137] Either way, circumcision finds its fulfillment in being joined to Christ and experiencing the promises associated with the inauguration of the new covenant age. But note how the text says even more: v. 12 makes it clear that we participate by baptism in the burial of Christ, and through it "a real death has

---

[134] Against Wilson, *To a Thousand Generations*, 59–80, in the NT there is no covenantal significance in circumcision after the cross work of Christ. Just because Paul circumcises Timothy or other Jewish believers circumcised their children (Acts 21:21–26) does not mean that circumcision continued to have covenantal efficacy. Paul only circumcised Timothy for mission purposes, what I have called "principled pragmatic concerns." For a helpful treatment of this issue see D. A. Carson, "Pauline Inconsistency: Reflections on 1 Corinthians 9.19–23 and Galatians 2.11–14," *Churchman* 100:1 (1986): 6–45.

[135] For example, see Ridderbos, *Paul*, 404–405, n 38.

[136] See M. J. Harris, *Colossians and Philemon*, EGGNT (Grand Rapids: Eerdmans, 1991), 101–105.

[137] See O'Brien, *Colossians and Philemon*, 114–21.

occurred and the old life is now a thing of the past. Those who have been buried with Christ 'through baptism into death' (Rom 6:4) can no longer go on living as slaves to sin."[138] It is clear that Paul does not view baptism in an *ex opere operato* fashion for he clearly stresses the instrumentality of faith. But he does argue that in baptism the objective realities of having died to sin and being made alive in Christ have actually taken place—something which cannot be applied to infants unless one affirms some kind of baptismal regeneration. All of this is to say that circumcision, as a type, *pointed to* a spiritual regeneration. Baptism, on the other hand, testifies that by faith *these realities have occurred*. Baptism marks and defines the children of God, those who believe in Messiah Jesus. That is why we baptize only those who have confessed Jesus as Lord, who have experienced his power, who are, by faith and spiritual rebirth, Abraham's true spiritual seed.

6. What does baptism signify? As already stated, it signifies a believer's union with Christ, by grace through faith, and all the benefits that result from that union. It testifies that one has entered into the realities of the new covenant and as such, has experienced regeneration, the gift and down-payment of the Spirit, and the forgiveness of sin. It graphically signifies that a believer is now a member of the body of Christ (Eph 4:22–25). It is our defining mark of belonging as well as a demarcation from the world (see Acts 2:40–41). It is an entry into the eschatological order of the new creation which our Lord has ushered in. Through baptism, we are united with Jesus Christ, by faith, and sealed with the Holy Spirit for the day of redemption (Eph 4:30).[139]

What is crucial to note in this description of Christian baptism is that what it signifies cannot be said of circumcision; they carry two different meanings. Circumcision, in a typological way, may anticipate and point to these new covenant realities, but it does not testify that all these realities are true of us. Baptism, in contrast to circumcision, is a NT ordinance, commanded by our Lord (Matt

---

[138] O'Brien, *Colossians and Philemon*, 118; cp. Beasley-Murray, *Baptism in the New Testament*, 152–60.

[139] For a theological summary of Christian baptism see Beasley-Murray, *Baptism in the New Testament*, 263–305.

28:18–20). It is a covenantal sign for the new covenant age. And as a covenantal sign, it communicates the grace of God *to those who have faith*, something which could not be said of circumcision of old. Baptism, in the end, is a new rite for the new covenant people of God; it is not the replacement of circumcision. To argue in a contrary fashion, is fundamentally to misunderstand not only the relations between the biblical covenants and the nature of the new covenant community, but also to confuse promise with fulfillment and type with antitype.[140]

Concluding Reflections

More can be said regarding the covenantal argument for infant baptism. In truth, the baptismal question is a major test-case for one's entire theological system since it tells much about how one puts the entire canon together. The Reformed paedobaptist argument is grounded in an explicit view of the covenants; if this understanding of the "covenant of grace" can be sustained, it provides a strong warrant for the position. However, if this understanding is inaccurate, then the entire biblical and theological warrant for the practice of infant baptism evaporates. In this chapter, albeit in a preliminary way, I have argued that the latter is the case. At the heart of the paedobaptist problem, I contend, is a failure to understand correctly the proper relationship between the biblical covenants. In fact, a truly *covenantal* approach to Scripture, preserving the proper biblical emphasis on continuity and discontinuity between the covenant communities of the old and new testaments, as well as between the covenant signs, demands an affirmation of believer's baptism.

But the baptism issue must not remain merely at the level of theological debate. Much unites credo- and paedobaptists, but there are also profound differences, and it is not helpful to blur the differences merely for the sake of unity. Ultimately baptism is linked to the proclamation of the gospel itself as it proclaims the glories of our Lord Jesus Christ and the full realities of the gospel of sovereign grace. To get baptism wrong is not a minor issue. It not only mis-

---

[140] For an in-depth treatment of this point see Jewett, *Infant Baptism and the Covenant of Grace*, 93–104, 219–43.

construes our Lord's command and instruction to the church, it also leads to a misunderstanding of elements of the gospel, particularly in regard to the beneficiaries of the new covenant and the nature of the church. It may even lead, if we are not careful, to a downplaying of the need to call our children to repentance and faith. Often Baptists are charged with not appreciating the place of their children in the covenant community.[141] Not only does this charge miss the mark in fundamentally misunderstanding the nature of the new covenant community, but it also runs the danger of what is truly imperative—to call all people, including our children, to faith in our Lord Jesus Christ. It is only then that the promise of the new covenant age becomes ours, for the promise is not only for us, but for our children and "for all who are far off, as many as the Lord our God will call" (Acts 2:39). Baptism, as a new covenant sign, even though it does not bring us into a state of grace, has been ordained by our Triune God as a proper means of grace that we ignore, distort, or downplay to the detriment of our spiritual life and mission.

---

[141] This is a constant charge against credobaptists. Obviously it only carries weight if the paedobaptists can sustain their entire argument, which I have attempted to disprove. For a helpful response see Malone, *The Baptism of Disciples Alone*, 173–85.

BAPTISM IN THE PATRISTIC WRITINGS

Steven A. McKinion*

I n order to present the early Christian views regarding the recipients of Christian baptism, we will examine patristic writings in which the Church Fathers specifically addressed the ordinance of baptism, including the purposes for which baptism was to be administered. We will seek to determine what the attitudes were toward the notion of baptizing only believers.[1]

Baptism was practiced universally in the early church from the NT forward. For those Christians who came after the NT period, baptism remained an essential component of the church's life and practice.[2] Christians celebrated baptism to mark a new convert's confession of faith in Jesus Christ as Savior. The rite of baptism also served as a means of initiation into the community of believers, the church. Use of the Triune Name in the administration of baptism assisted the church's faithful handing on of the faith once for all delivered to the saints by confessing the saving work of all three Persons of the Godhead.[3] Baptism had special meaning not just for the believer but for the entire Christian community; it was an ordi-

---

* Steven A. McKinion received his Ph.D. from King's College, University of Aberdeen, and is Associate Professor of Historical Theology and Patristic Studies at Southeastern Baptist Theological Seminary in Wake Forest, North Carolina.

[1] In Christian history the time following the deaths of the apostles until approximately AD 596 is called the patristic period. "Patristic" is derived from the Latin term for "father" and thus refers to the period of the so-called Church Fathers.

[2] See S. A. McKinion, *Life and Practice in the Early Church: A Documentary Reader* (New York: NYU Press, 2002), 5–41. Also A.W. Argyle, "Baptism in the Early Christian Centuries," *Christian Baptism*, ed. A. Gilmore (Philadelphia: Judson, 1959), 187–222; E. Ferguson, ed. *Conversion, Catechumenate, and Baptism in the Early Church*, Studies in Early Christianity (New York: Garland, 1993); G. Kretschmar, "Recent Research on Christian Initiation," *Studia Liturgica* 12 (1977): 87–106; G. W. H. Lampe, *The Seal of the Spirit. A Study in the Doctrine of Baptism and Confirmation in the New Testament and the Fathers* (London: Longmans, Green, 1952).

[3] Jesus' command in Matt 28:19 to baptize "in the Name of the Father, the Son, and the Holy Spirit" became, for early Christians, the formula used in baptism ceremonies. This passage of Scripture, and its derived formula, played an important role in Athanasius of Alexandria's explication of the Trinity against the Arians. See Athanasius, *Letters to Serapion* in *The Letters of St. Athanasius Concerning the Holy Spirit*, trans. C. R. B. Shapland (New York: Philosophical Library, 1951).

nance of the church. Baptism's role in the early church was central to the formation and discipline of the body of believers.

Our purpose is limited, in that our focus is on the extent to which the early church practiced believer's baptism. Some clarification of this purpose is in order as it relates to early Christianity. Believer's baptism is the practice of baptizing *only* those who profess faith in Jesus Christ for their salvation, having repented of their sins. An essential element of the practice is that baptism is subsequent to repentance and faith.[4] Adherents narrowly define baptism as an act that follows salvation. Consequently, believer's baptism excludes infant baptism because it denies that the rite professes *future* faith.[5]

The question we are then seeking to answer is, "Is there a consensus in the patristic writings that accepts believer's baptism as the ancient and normative practice of the church?" In other words, do we discover in early Christian history an attitude toward baptism that, in an ideal setting, the church would baptize children and adults who have *first* repented of their sins and professed faith in Jesus Christ? Does baptism follow salvation or precede (or even produce) it?

A *Debate over* Infant *Baptism*

We can readily dismiss the notion that normative baptism was exclusively *adult* baptism. As our investigation will demonstrate, the early church baptized children, but these children were not infants, had at least some understanding of the faith, and had accepted Christianity's tenets. What we know of baptism from the patristic writings is that the question was really not about the age of the one being baptized. Rather, the question was about that person's state in relation to faith in Jesus Christ and repentance from sin. We will see that the debates in the early church were not over adult baptism versus infant baptism, but believer's baptism versus paedobaptism.[6]

---

[4] Generally ascribed to Peter's statement in his Pentecost sermon recorded in Acts 2:38: "Repent and be baptized for the remission of sins." We will see that Patristic writers often insisted that baptism was inseparable from repentance.

[5] Many forms of paedobaptism exist, each with different opinions regarding the purpose and effect of baptism; believer's baptism requires that the ordinance follow active, saving faith.

[6] See D. F. Wright, "The Origin of Infant Baptism—Child Believers' Baptism?" *SJT* 40

Christian writings from the third and fourth centuries show a difference of opinion over the practice of baptizing infants. There is no doubt that infant baptism was practiced quite early in the church's history, but the prevalence of the practice, its significance, and its origin are a matter of contention. The sources are, in many ways, themselves unclear. Two questions emerge from an examination of the documents, as we shall see. First, does the existence of infant baptism in the third century necessarily mean that the practice is ancient? If the practice began in the third century rather than in apostolic times, one might wonder why there is no fanfare accompanying a change of such magnitude in one of Christianity's most central components. The absence of any debates in the literature of the second century could lead one to conclude that the practice was a tradition received from the apostles rather than an innovation. Despite the appearance of infant baptism in the patristic writings of the third century and beyond, there is no necessary attribution of antiquity to the practice. One might just as likely conclude that the practice is novel as that it is ancient. Second, do the debates regarding infant baptism in the fourth and fifth centuries indicate a rejection of the ancient practice of paedobaptism in favor of something novel, or do the documents show a continued resistance to the innovative practice of infant baptism over and against a more ancient believer's baptism? These questions will be crucial to our investigation.

To lay a foundation for the discussion of believer's baptism in early Christianity, we will briefly survey the classic debate between Joachim Jeremias and Kurt Aland regarding the origin of paedobaptism in early Christianity.[7] Three short volumes, the first by Jeremias, a challenge by Aland, and a final reply by Jeremias, comprise the scholarly debate. Jeremias's first volume, *Die Kindertaufe in den ersten vier Jahrhunderten*, appeared first in 1938, then in a re-

---

(1987): 1–23 and "At What Ages Were People Baptized in the Early Centuries?" *StPatr* 30 (1997): 389–394.

[7] J. Jeremias, *Infant Baptism in the First Four Centuries* (Philadelphia: Westminster, 1960); K Aland, *Did the Early Christian Church Baptize Infants?*, trans. G.R. Beasley-Murray (London: SCM Press, 1963); J. Jeremias, *Origins of Infant Baptism* (London: SCM Press, 1963). Also E. Ferguson, "Inscriptions and the Origin of Infant Baptism," *JTS*, n.s. 30 (1979): 37–46; A. N. S. Lane, "Did the Apostolic Church Baptise Babies? A Seismological Approach," *TynBul* 55.1 (2004): 109–30.

vised German edition in 1958. An English translation was published as *Infant Baptism in the First Four Centuries* two years later. Much of the study is concerned with baptism in the apostolic period and the NT. This material, while of great importance to the question of the origin of infant baptism, is addressed in earlier chapters in the present volume and will therefore not be addressed in detail here. However, some important elements of Jeremias's conclusions from the first century merit discussion here, due to the direct correlation he sees between first century practice and later practice.

Jeremias examines the practice of infant baptism in the first four centuries of the church's existence. He addresses the apostolic period in two chapters, then has one chapter on developments in the second and third centuries, and one on infant baptism in the fourth century. He begins with the question, "Were the children of converts [in the NT period] baptized along with their parents?" To answer this question Jeremias turns to the NT statements regarding the baptism of converts and to the origin of Christian baptism.

First Jeremias focuses attention on the *oikos* formula found in several NT passages.[8] In these, converts and their "households" are baptized. Jeremias contends that these households include all the children of the house, regardless of age. To support his conclusion, Jeremias reads the NT *oikos* statements in the light of Old Testament references to a "household" meaning all those living in the home, including infant children. He concludes, "The New Testament *oikos* formula was adopted from the Old Testament cultic language (and in particular, we may say, from the terminology of circumcision) and introduced into the formal language employed in the primitive Christian rite of baptism."[9] In addition, Jeremias's reading of the *oikos* passages is based on "family solidarity" in the ancient world.[10] In the Jewish-Christian church, Jeremias contends, unbaptized members of the family are not allowed to join in table-fellowship. He finds it highly unlikely that parents would not baptize their children and thus exclude them from family meals! When the NT states

---

[8] Jeremias, *Infant Baptism in the First Four Centuries*, 19–24.
[9] Ibid., 21.
[10] Ibid., 22–23.

that because of the faith of one member of the family the entire family, including any infant children, is baptized (e.g., his reading of Acts 16:30–34), it is because, "the faith of the father who represents the household and the faith of the mother also embraces the children."[11]

The second part of Jeremias's answer to the question of whether the infant children of converts were baptized along with them is his examination of baptism's origins. Jeremias argues that Christian baptism is the offspring of proselyte baptism. He claims that "the only possible conclusion is that the rites are related as parent [Jewish proselyte baptism] and child [Christian baptism]."[12] Specifically, Christian baptism is derived from Jewish proselyte baptism in its terminology, its outward administration, and its theological understanding.[13] The final point is most appropriate for our discussion: when Gentile adults converted to Judaism, "the children, even the smallest children, were admitted with their parents to the Jewish faith."[14] Jeremias contends that because Jewish proselyte baptism is the progenitor of Christian baptism then "with the admission of Gentiles to Christianity children of every age, including infants, were baptized also."[15] He asserts that infant baptism was the normal practice in the Christian church from the apostolic period onwards.

These two conclusions—that the *oikos* formula for baptism in the NT necessarily included infants, and that proselyte baptism, which included infants, is the progenitor of Christian baptism—form the basis for Jeremias's reading of the later evidence. He reads the church orders, inscriptions, and other documents from this perspective, and the remainder of his study is based on these conclusions.

Chapter Three moves beyond NT times and up to the "crisis" of the fourth century. Jeremias surveys evidences for infant baptism in both East and West. Accounts of martyrs' lives written in the second century describe believers as faithful to Christ from childhood. Jeremias takes these as indirect evidence of infant baptism.

[11] Ibid., 24.
[12] Ibid., 36.
[13] Ibid., 24–40.
[14] Ibid., 39.
[15] Ibid.

Polycarp, born in the first century, claimed to have served Christ for over eighty years. Jeremias conjectures that he must have been baptized as an infant.[16] Aland, however, demonstrates that the evidence may just as likely be read as referring not to infant but to *child* baptism.[17]

Jeremias's reading of the inscriptions and patristic writings is guided by his belief that there is a difference in early Christianity between "missionary" baptism and the later practice that included the baptism of believers' children. Missionary baptism, reflected almost exclusively in the NT baptism accounts, signified the entrance of converts into Christianity from non-Christian religions. These early instances of baptism involved adult converts and their now-Christian children, including infants. Jeremias reads the catechetical instructions regarding baptism as intended for these converts to Christianity. In addition to this missionary baptism, Jeremias contends that the church, from the NT on, baptized the infant children of believers in a practice parallel with Jewish circumcision. He then reads later evidence in the light of this two-fold practice.

Who was Baptized in Early Christianity

In this section, we will survey chronologically the relevant discussions of baptism in the patristic writings. We will discover a shift in the discussions in the third century, when the question of infant baptism arose. There is no defense of infant baptism prior to the third century. In fact, each instance of instruction regarding baptism supports a conclusion that the baptism of believers only was the normative practice in the second century, with the possible exception of emergency baptisms of mortally ill infants later in the century.[18] This novel practice became widespread in the third century, leading Origen to conclude that, at least in Palestine, infant baptism was the standard practice of the church. The debate over the innovation of infant baptism continued into the fourth century where

---

[16] Ibid., 62–63.

[17] Aland, *Did the Early Christian Church Baptize Infants?*, 70–74.

[18] Ferguson has argued that these instances, deduced from funerary inscriptions, demonstrate that Christians who believed in the importance of baptism began to baptize infants in emergency situations as an accommodation ("Inscriptions and the Origin of Infant Baptism").

Gregory, Bishop of Nazianzus, allowed infant baptism in emergency situations but otherwise rejected it on the grounds that infants have no sins to confess and therefore do not need baptism since baptism is properly related to repentance.

Several types of documents inform us of early Christian attitudes toward baptism. There are works dedicated to the topic, such as Tertullian of Carthage's *On Baptism* or Cyprian of Carthage's *Epistle 58* announcing an African synod's decision regarding baptism. There are also references to the Christian practice of baptism that are intended to clear up misunderstandings or instruct those who are perhaps outside of the church about the practice, as is a paragraph in Justin Martyr's *First Apology*. A third and important type of writing is the church manual, such as the late first- or early second-century *Didache*. These manuals tell us about prevailing attitudes toward practices in the church, while also giving us a glimpse into liturgical tradition. What is most helpful is that church manuals are intended to project current practice into the past, while also influencing future church practice. These are important both for what they say and for what they omit.[19] Finally, there are works that provide instruction to the catechumen, the person preparing for baptism. Normally, new believers, including children, would spend a considerable amount of time being taught the fundamental beliefs of Christianity, including the meaning of the baptism for which they were preparing. These writings, such as Cyril of Jerusalem's *Catechetical Lectures*, are enlightening.

Second Century

Three sources from the second century are significant for our study; the *Didache*, Justin Martyr's *First Apology*, and Aristides' *Apology*.[20] A church manual written just after the turn of the sec-

---

[19] As an example, were a manual in the second century to mandate one element of practice that is missing from a later manual, one might reasonably conclude that the practice fell out of favor, particularly if a competing description of the practice is given in the later work. As this type of writing intends to make current practice normative, it may or may not be helpful in conveying accurately *past* practice. However, this fact makes church manuals all the more important to our study: they tell us what was happening at a given time in a given area.

[20] See J. Lewis, "Baptismal Practices of the Second and Third Century Church," *ResQ* 26 (1983): 1–17.

ond century, *The Teaching of the Lord through the Twelve Apostles*, known usually by the first word of the Greek title, the *Didache*, detailed contemporary practice regarding the ordinance of baptism.[21] First, the manual stated that the Triune Formula was to be used in baptism: one should be baptized in the Name of the Father, the Son, and the Holy Spirit. Second, the church was to use running water when available, though standing water, such as a pool, was acceptable. Presumably, this instruction was to make Christian baptism parallel to Christ's baptism, which was in a river of running water. The candidate should be immersed in water, provided enough was available. Where there was not water deep enough for immersion, water could be poured over the recipient's head three times. Most important for our study was the requirement that the person being baptized (along with the one doing the baptism and the rest of the church) was to fast for one or two days before the baptism. In fact, the *Didache* stated that the one being baptized should be instructed in this regard. "Instruct the one being baptized to fast one or two days before" implies that the one being baptized was of the age and mental capacity to comprehend and obey the instruction. It would seem entirely unlikely that an infant would be able to obey this command. Moreover, if the *Didache* envisioned an instance in which infant baptism would be practiced, instructions for such a ceremony would surely have been included in the manual. The absence of specific instructions for baptizing infants in the liturgies and church orders into the fourth and fifth centuries imply that infant baptism was a liturgical innovation that did not find universal acceptance.

In his *First Apology*, written in the middle of the second century, Justin Martyr sought to explain the rite of Christian baptism so that his readers might understand the meaning of the ordinance.[22] Consistent with the command of the *Didache*, Justin claimed that Christian baptism was done in the Name of the Father, Son, and Holy Spirit.[23] Four elements of Justin's exposition relate directly to

[21] *The Didache* 7 in *Ante-Nicene Fathers* (hereafter *ANF*) vol. 7, ed. A Cleveland Coxe (reprint, Peabody, MA: Hendrickson, 1994). See A. H. B. Logan, "Post-Baptismal Chrismation in Syria: The Evidence of Ignatius, the *Didache* and the *Apostolic Constitutions*," *JTS* 49.1 (1998): 92–108.
[22] Justin Martyr, *First Apology* 61 in *ANF* vol. 1.
[23] In fact, this Triadic Confession is referenced twice in the same chapter.

the topic at hand. First, Justin, like the *Didache*, stated that those who were to be baptized were those who had been "persuaded and believe that what we teach and say is true, and undertake to live accordingly."[24] Clearly believers were in mind here. They have already believed the truthfulness of Christianity and have made the commitment to live a Christian life. Justin presented these candidates for baptism as already having begun to live according to their faith. Infants could not be included in Justin's description of those coming to baptism on either of these counts.

Second, they were to fast and pray for the remission of past sins.[25] As with the *Didache* one is hard-pressed to consider infants fasting and praying for the remission of their past sins. In fact, as will become clearer, many of the patristic writers denied that infants were guilty of any sins that needed forgiving.[26] Once again, Justin appears not to have been calling infants to prepare for their baptisms by fasting and praying. These were instructions reserved for older children and adults.

Third, Justin described candidates for baptism as those who "choose and repent."[27] This was consistent with the command in Peter's Pentecost sermon (Acts 2:38) to "repent and be baptized for the forgiveness of sins." Justin is in a long line of patristic writers to follow the NT lead of linking repentance and baptism. As was previously the case, he could not have been referring to infants as having chosen to become believers and repented. Even if one accepts the need for infants to receive forgiveness for original sin (a theme in the third century and in the West even after), the subjects of baptism for Justin could not have included infants.

Finally, Justin said that those who are illuminated in their understanding were the ones who were to be washed in baptism.[28] Were Justin an advocate of paedobaptism he would have at least allowed for one to be washed and then, at a later time, illuminated. This is

---

[24] Justin Martyr, *First Apology* 61.

[25] Ibid.

[26] This is distinctly unbiblical and should not be used by Baptists as a polemic against paedobaptism.

[27] Justin Martyr, *First Apology* 61.

[28] Ibid.

the argument of later writers who advocate infant baptism. Their claim is that the washing may in the case of believers' children precede the awakening to faith, and perhaps even aid its coming. For Justin, though, candidates for baptism were those who had been awakened already to their need for salvation.

A passage in the *Apology* of Aristides is also important for a second-century picture of baptism.[29] The passage in which the apologist described Christian behavior as superior to others in the empire speaks of how Christians acted toward the servants and children of Christians who were persuaded to become Christians themselves. After the servants or the children became Christians they were called "brothers and sisters without distinction."[30] In other words, it was only after their conversion that the children of believers were considered a part of the community of faith. Such a statement appears to contradict directly the notion of "household" baptisms, for clearly Aristides did not have "missionary" baptism in mind. These were the children of believers. As Aland rightly notes, Aristides' *Apology* "indirectly excludes infant baptism."[31]

Even Jeremias acknowledges no *direct* evidence of infant baptism in the second century. However, he does assert that patristic references to believers who have served Christ faithfully from a young age qualify as indirect evidence of infant baptism.[32] These references, mainly from biographical statements about martyrs such as Polycarp, who is said to have served Christ for 86 years, can all be grouped together as efforts by patristic writers to highlight a believer's faithful devotion to Christ from "youth." Such statements do not necessarily mean, however, that the subject was baptized as an infant. It is just as likely that the martyr, or other believer, was baptized as a young child, or even an older child, as it is that she or he was baptized as an infant. Such "evidence," important as it is to Jeremias's cause, does not appear to pose a serious threat to the claim that infant baptism was not the norm in second century Christianity.[33]

---

[29] Aristides, *Apology* 15, in J. R. Harris, *The Apology of Aristides* (Cambridge: 1891).

[30] Ibid., 15.

[31] Aland, *Did the Early Christian Church Baptize Infants?*, 58.

[32] Jeremias, *Infant Baptism in the First Four Centuries*, 59–61.

[33] Anecdotally, for many years my own description of my conversion (or testimony) began,

In the second century, then, there is no direct reference to the baptism of the infant children of converts or believers. The evidence from the second century argues more convincingly for one common practice of baptizing believers after their repentance from sin. The methods described in patristic writings, along with the description of those who were to be baptized, furnish direct evidence of believer's baptism as the normative practice of the church in the second century.

Third Century

Tertullian of Carthage, apologist and founder of Western Theology, wrote the earliest extant treatise on the subject of baptism. His work, *On Baptism*, is the only surviving treatise on the ordinance of baptism from the time before the First Ecumenical Council (Nicaea, AD 325).[34] The treatise was written in response to the innovative practice of infant baptism, prior to his conversion to the Montanist sect. Tertullian claimed that the church's act of baptism was remarkable because of its simplicity: a person was immersed in water.[35] Once baptized, the individual was no cleaner than before the baptism. However, the result was a spiritual cleansing that far exceeded any physical cleansing one might desire. While the washing with water was a mere external act, the cleansing from sins was spiritual and eternal.[36]

Tertullian advised patience when determining to whom the ordinance was to be administered.[37] The apologist was offering an alternative to a practice already in existence, the practice of baptizing infants. The practice, Tertullian argued, was fraught with danger. In the first place, the message conveyed by paedobaptism was that the

"I was raised in a Christian home." Someone writing of my view of baptism a hundred years from now would be mistaken to conclude either that I was baptized as an infant or that I believed in household baptisms. A lifelong Baptist, I was baptized as a twelve-year-old believer, and have never intended by my earlier statement to imply that I was a Christian prior to my conversion.

[34] The work was written between AD 200 and 206.

[35] Tertullian, *On Baptism* 2, in *ANF* vol. 3.

[36] Ibid., 7.

[37] Ibid., 18.

infant was in need of salvation, which Tertullian denied.[38] Moreover, those who served as "sponsors" for the infant being baptized might not be able to ensure that the one baptized would grow up to live in accordance with the promises made at baptism.[39] In other words, Tertullian recognized that inherent in the ordinance of baptism is both a repentance from sins and a commitment to right living. Infants had not sinned, and therefore were not responsible for the former. The "sponsors" were incapable of keeping the latter, and could not therefore be responsible for it. Why should the church have done something that was both unnecessary and irresponsible? "Why does the innocent period of life hasten to the 'remission of sins?'"[40] Tertullian's concern was that paedobaptism committed infants to the Christian life without their compliance. On their behalf the church was determining that they would be responsible to live faithful Christian lives. He reminded his readers that infants were not given adult responsibilities in "worldly" matters, so they should not be given the responsibility of living a Christian life (the presumed result of baptism) when they were not ready.[41] As we saw earlier with Justin Martyr, the one being baptized was expected to commit to live a Christian life, a commitment that a very young child could not be expected to make or keep. Moreover, infants were "innocent," and therefore free from sin. They were consequently not in need of "remission of sins." Tertullian also asked, "Why should sponsors be thrust into danger if baptism is not necessary for salvation?"[42] Clearly, for Tertullian, baptism was not a requirement for salvation. Were that to be the case, indeed one might argue for the validity of paedobaptism. Such a conclusion is unwarranted because infants were innocent from sin.

Tertullian concluded chapter eighteen with two strong statements. First, "If any understand the weighty importance of baptism they will fear its reception more than its delay."[43] Tertullian was re-

38 Ibid.
39 Ibid.
40 Ibid.
41 Ibid.
42 Ibid.
43 Ibid.

ferring to the great responsibility of post-baptismal Christian living. Baptism was not to be undertaken lightly, for a grave responsibility comes with it. Second, and most importantly, Tertullian claimed that "sound faith is secure of salvation."[44] No stronger statement could be made to divorce the rite of baptism in itself from saving faith.[45] Salvation was not procured by baptism, but faith was the sure indicator of salvation. In other words, for Tertullian salvation was by faith alone, even when the believer lacked baptism.

What can we glean from this text about the role of baptism for the believer? First, baptism should come subsequent to agreement with Christian belief and commitment to Christian practice, as with Justin. Baptism was the occasion when believers confessed their "past sins," and would "lay beforehand the foundation of defenses against the temptations which will closely follow."[46] In other words, baptism was an act related to both the remission of the believer's prior sins and the prevention of the believer's post-baptismal sins. Delaying baptism simply due to the danger of post-baptismal sins would be contrary to Tertullian's understanding of the role of baptism for the believer. Second, faith, not baptism, was the means to salvation. Third, the baptized person was held to a higher standard of Christian moral practice, presumably because of his or her identification with the church. While catechumens possessed salvation because of their saving faith, they were not "Christians" in the sense of being identified with the church. This identification came with baptism.

In the following chapter Tertullian turned to the significance of baptism. Passover was the best time for baptism, he argued, because we are baptized into the death of Christ (Rom 6:1). Interestingly, Tertullian referred to Jesus' statement to his disciples to watch for a man carrying water as a reference to baptism, since water was associated with the Passover. The second most solemn occasion for baptism was Pentecost because it was at that time that the promised Spirit descended on the disciples. Tertullian was quick to add that

---

[44] Ibid.

[45] Against J. N. D. Kelly, *Early Christian Doctrine*, rev. ed. (San Francisco: Harper & Row, 1978), 209.

[46] Tertullian, *On Baptism*, 20.

every day is the Lord's, and every hour is apt for baptism. Though the solemnity might differ, the significance would not.[47]

In the next chapter, Tertullian described what was to be done at the baptismal ceremony itself and how one should prepare for it. In preparation, the candidate was to "pray with repeated prayers, fasts, and bending of the knee."[48] Of course, none of these acts of preparation were appropriate for infants. Only older children and adults could respond to these instructions. More significantly, in preparation "there should be vigils all through the night accompanied by the confession of all past sins."[49] Obviously, infants could not hold vigils throughout the night confessing their sins.

Baptism was tied inextricably to "satisfaction of former sins" and to a defense against "temptations which will closely follow."[50] The catechumen, already possessing saving faith, would come to the font having confessed former sins. But baptism, besides its role relative to past sins, also served as a source of strength for the believer to overcome future sins. Baptism was the foundation, or beginning point of the Christian's life of obedience in the sense that the sins committed prior to the exercise of saving faith had been "washed." Temptations coming after repentance and baptism were like those of Christ, who was tempted immediately following his own baptism. What was the lesson to be learned? At Christ's baptism, the Spirit is said to have descended on him "as a dove." So too the anointing following the believer's baptism was representative of the Spirit's anointing. Tertullian emphasized not only the Spirit's work in the remission of sins, but also in overcoming temptation following conversion.[51] Baptism was useful in aiding the believer in the struggle against post-baptismal sins by providing the believer with defenses against temptation.

Tertullian's primary concern was that infant baptism negated the church's practice, already seen clearly in the documents from the second century, of a time of preparation for baptism which included

[47] Ibid., 19.
[48] Ibid., 20.
[49] Ibid.
[50] Ibid.
[51] Ibid.

repentance from sin, fasting, and prayer. None of these necessary precursors to baptism was possible for infants. Each was possible, however, for young children and those who were older. Tertullian argued that the practice of triple immersion was a long-standing tradition, but was not commanded in Scripture or handed down from the apostles.[52] For him to defend this practice as traditional, while rejecting infant baptism without making a similar argument, indicates that he did not know infant baptism as a traditional practice, but as a novel one.

Following Tertullian chronologically is the mid-third century *Apostolic Tradition* of Hippolytus.[53] In chapter 42 Hippolytus stated that there is to be a three-year period from conversion to baptism in which the catechumen was to be tested regarding his or her faith and Christian lifestyle. This period was also to be a time of instruction in the faith of the church. In the following chapter the *Tradition* instructed that catechumens were to attend worship and participate fully in the life of the church, with the exception of taking the Eucharist, from which they were excluded.[54] The next chapter was concerned with catechumens who were martyred before they had been baptized. Their martyrdom served as their "blood baptism."[55] Chapter 45 detailed the final preparation for baptism, including the use of witnesses to the catechumen's faithfulness, then Scripture reading, fasting, and prayer. Then, in chapter 46, Hippolytus instructed that children who were catechumens were to be baptized. Clearly, he meant those children who had gone through the process described in the preceding chapters. Next, he made allowance for those little ones who could not speak for themselves to profess their faith. Allowance was made for a believing parent or other believing family member to confess on behalf of the child. Following the children, the adult catechumens were baptized.

What is one to make of Hippolytus's allowance for children who could not speak for themselves? It is possible that the text is a later

---

[52] Tertullian, *On the Chaplet* 3 in *ANF* vol. 3.

[53] C. M. Edsman, "A Typology of Baptism in Hippolytus Romanus," *StPatr* 2 (1957): 35–40.

[54] Hippolytus, *Apostolic Tradition* 42, in G. Dix, *The Treatise on the Apostolic Tradition of St. Hippolytus of Rome, Bishop and Martyr* (London: Alban Press, 1992). See also chaps. 48, 50, 62.

[55] Hippolytus, *Apostolic Tradition* 43.

interpolation.[56] Even if it is original, it only confirms that infant baptism was permissible in Hippolytus's context. It cannot be an example of Jeremias's missionary baptism, as the children were baptized *before* the adults. In Hippolytus, the order of baptism is infants first (i.e., the children who could not speak for themselves) and subsequently the newly converted adults. The infants being baptized were certainly not the children of those catechumens waiting to be baptized after their children, because in Jeremias's argument only the infants of baptized converts would have been baptized in early Christianity. The essence of missionary baptism is that new converts and their children would have been baptized. Hippolytus may be allowing for the baptism of believers' children, but he is not articulating a pattern of paedobaptism for the infants of new converts. No distinction would need to be made between children who could speak for themselves and children who could not, if paedobaptism was the norm. It appears that paedobaptism was the exception, provided the text in question is not an interpolation. Hippolytus describes the baptism of believers who had previously demonstrated fidelity to Christianity and the Christian community during the period of instruction preceding baptism, with an allowance for the baptism of infants.

Cyprian of Carthage's *Epistle 58* was written to announce the decision of an African synod in AD 253 to require the baptism of infants. The addressee of the letter believed that baptism should be performed on the eighth day, commensurate with the practice of circumcision. The synod did not make a pronouncement on this, because of the disagreement among the bishops over the relationship between baptism and circumcision. One might wonder whether some of the bishops rejected the belief that infant baptism is the Christian replacement of Jewish circumcision. Cyprian's announcement does not state this categorically, but simply claims that the "law of circumcision" (i.e., baptism on the eighth day) was not required. It might be surmised that if the bishops were united in their belief that baptism was a replacement for circumcision, they would

---

[56] Aland, *Did the Early Christian Church Baptize Infants?*, 49–50.

have been much more prone to follow instructions regarding its application much more closely.

What is apparent is that while church leaders in this part of North Africa might have disagreed over circumcision as the origin of infant baptism, they affirmed *in solidum* that infant baptism was proper for the church. That a synod would even need to meet to decide this matter suggests that paedobaptism was not universally practiced. In fact, were it merely a few who opposed it, such as Tertullian, would an African synod be necessary? Whatever the background to the council, its decision is significant. "No one," the council decided, "should be hindered from baptism and from the grace of God."[57] Baptism, for Cyprian and the council on which he reported, was a means of grace because its recipients received "divine mercy."[58] Moreover, baptism was even more important for infants, Cyprian argued, because they would enjoy the help, mercy, and grace of God from the very beginning of their lives, helping them to overcome sin.[59] A shift from Tertullian to Cyprian is clear. Whereas Tertullian emphasized baptism's relationship to the believer's past sins as well as future ones, Cyprian emphasized only its relationship to the future. For Tertullian, baptism was administered to a believer who had repented of past sins; for Cyprian, it could also be administered to an infant who would need its benefits for a future Christian life.

Writing in the middle of the third century, Origen of Alexandria on three occasions defended the practice of baptizing infants.[60] In each instance Origen had one purpose in mind: to explain how infant baptism could be the practice of the church without infants needing the forgiveness of sins. Origen was apparently responding to the challenge that infant baptism was unnecessary, as infants have committed no sins.[61] Origen concluded that while infants themselves have committed no sins, they shared in the universal stain of Adam's

[57] Cyprian of Carthage, *Epistle* 58.2, in *ANF* vol. 5.
[58] Ibid., 58.6.
[59] Ibid.
[60] The works in view date from Origen's time in Caesarea in Palestine (c. 231–250).
[61] Origen, *Homilies on Leviticus* 7, in *Fathers of the Church*, Vol. 83, trans. G. W. Barkley (Washington, DC: Catholic University of America Press, 1992).

sin, and were thus benefited by baptism.[62] It was for this reason that infant baptism was the "custom of the Church,"[63] a custom Origen claimed was handed down from the apostles.[64] Origen's claim that the church in Palestine, or at least some of it, practiced paedobaptism demonstrates only that the practice was contemporary with Origen. There is no need to conclude that the practice of paedobaptism in third-century Palestine is proof of its apostolic origin. It is plausible that had infant baptism arisen in Palestine in the late second century it could easily have found widespread acceptance in the churches of the region by the time Origen wrote around 250.[65]

In the third century we see the beginning of paedobaptism as normative for parts of the church. The practice was not universal, as Tertullian's aggressive defense of believer's baptism and Origen's need to mount an apology for infant baptism both attest. Despite Origen's statement that paedobaptism was an ancient practice in the church, his argument on behalf of baptizing infants rests primarily on baptism's intended outcome rather than its apostolic origin. In the third century a debate evidently raged between those who advocated infant baptism and those who resisted it. Defenders of baptizing infants relied primarily on the argument that the sacrament was needed to cleanse infants of the stain of original sin. The evidence from the third century points to the origin of infant baptism in the practice of baptizing mortally ill infants due to an increasing belief that baptism was necessary for the salvation of the child.[66] The opposing viewpoint, found in Tertullian's argument against paedobaptism, was that faith was sufficient for salvation, despite his equivocation in allowing infant baptism in times of "necessity."

---

[62] Origen, *Commentary on Romans* 5.9, in Origen, *Commentary on the Epistle to the Romans, Books 1–5,* in *Fathers of the Church,* vol. 103, trans. T. P. Scheck (Washington, DC: Catholic University of America Press, 2001).

[63] Origen, *Homilies on Leviticus* 7.

[64] Origen, *Commentary on Romans* 5.9.

[65] Aland, *Did the Early Christian Church Baptize Infants?,* 48–49.

[66] Ferguson, "Inscriptions and the Origin of Infant Baptism."

Fourth and Fifth Centuries

The *Apostolic Constitutions*, written near the end of the fourth century, is a compilation of portions of earlier church manuals, including the *Didache* and Hippolytus's *Apostolic Tradition*.[67] Christ's command in the Great Commission to baptize served as the explicit basis for the practice in the church.[68] In the ceremony, the bishop was to anoint the head of the one to be baptized, both men and women. A presbyter then was to immerse them in water in the Name of the Father, Son, and Holy Spirit. If the baptized person was a man, a male deacon was to receive him out of the water. A woman would be received by a deaconess to preserve modesty.[69]

One was baptized into the death of Christ, the immersion being followed by an anointing that was a "confirmation of the confession." The author states that "the descent into the water *represents* the dying together with Christ, and the ascent out of the water the rising again with him."[70] This is the clearest example thus far of the symbolic character of baptism, though we have seen it implicitly elsewhere. The Trinitarian profession of belief in and association with Father, Son, and Holy Spirit was the means to the true sharing in the death and resurrection of Christ.[71] Baptism was a graphic representation of that death and resurrection.

The representative character of baptism is sensible considering that the one being baptized was to "be free of all [past] iniquity."[72] As we have seen, baptism was contingent upon the confession of past sins and was subsequent to repentance and faith. The one being baptized was to be already a "son of God."[73] Later, the author reiterated that baptism was to follow conversion and that "the water is the symbol of the death of Christ."[74] The one being baptized has

---

[67] On baptism in the fourth century, see T. M. Finn, "Baptismal Death and Resurrection: A Study in Fourth Century Eastern Baptismal Theology," *Worship* 43 (1969): 175–89; E. Yarnold, *The Awe-Inspiring Rites of Initiation: Baptismal Homilies of the Fourth Century*, 2d rev. ed. (Edinburgh: T&T Clark, 1994).

[68] *Apostolic Constitutions* 7.2.22, in *ANF* vol. 7.

[69] Modesty was necessary since the baptisand was nude. Ibid., 3.2.16.

[70] Ibid., 3.2.17 (emphasis added).

[71] Ibid., 7.3.41.

[72] Ibid., 3.2.18.

[73] Ibid., 3.2.18. See 7.3.41.

[74] Ibid., 7.2.22.

already repented, has been cleansed of sin, and has died with Christ. Baptism symbolized the conversion of one who already possessed faith.

Before baptism the candidate was to fast.[75] Jesus fasted after, rather than before, his baptism, but the author explained that since Jesus had no sins to confess, no cleansing was needed. Moreover, Jesus was not baptized into his own death and resurrection, as his baptism looked forward to these events. Thus, fasting followed baptism. For believers, baptism looked back to participation in the death and resurrection of Christ by faith, and fasting thus preceded baptism. Jesus' baptism was to confirm John's message, whereas the believer's baptism was performed in recognition of having received the message of Christ.

Church manuals such as the *Apostolic Constitutions* and its constituent documents indicate both contemporary church practice and what their authors wished to be standard practice; thus, they are invaluable to our study. Just as important are the works of theologians who sought to justify or explain the church's practice, or to challenge certain practices. Gregory of Nazianzus (fourth-century) explained the church's baptismal practice and joined earlier third-century opponents of the innovation of infant baptism. Gregory is one of the so-called Cappadocian Fathers, along with Gregory of Nyssa and his brother Basil the Great.[76] Interestingly, none of the three, despite being the children of Christian parents, was baptized while an infant. Gregory of Nazianzus, whose father was a bishop, was not baptized until he was about 30 years old.[77] He dedicated his *Oration* 40 to the topic of baptism. He explained that in baptism one symbolized outwardly what is an inward reality.[78] Baptism was an outward type of the inner cleansing of the soul. Water was an outward cleansing of the body, but the inward cleansing of the soul occurred "apart from the body."[79]

---

[75] Ibid., 7.2.22.

[76] E. Ferguson, "Preaching at Epiphany: Gregory of Nyssa and John Chrysostom on Baptism and the Church," *CH* 66.1 (1997): 1–17.

[77] Zosimus, *Historia Romana*, 4.39, ed. L. Mendelssohn (Leipzig, 1887).

[78] Gregory of Nazianzus, *Oration* 40.8, in *Nicene and Post-Nicene Fathers* (hereafter *NPNF*) series 2 vol. 7, ed. W. Sandy (repr., Peabody, MA: Hendrickson, 1994).

[79] Ibid., 40.8.

Gregory was generally opposed to infant baptism, except where there was a danger of death.[80] Where this imminent danger existed, it was better for the infant to depart "unconsciously sanctified" than "unsealed and uninitiated."[81] But what did he mean by "uniniti-ated"? While it is possible that he meant "unsaved," he may have meant "not initiated into the life of the church." With the emphasis on the corporate and initiatory effects of the act of baptism on the believer, transferring the believing catechumen from "outsider" to "insider" status, one might plausibly find Gregory accommodating infant baptism as a pastor leading the community into closer communion with grieving parents.

Reading Gregory's allowance for infant baptism as a pastoral accommodation is supported by his immediate appeal to avoid the practice in other than emergency circumstances.[82] Only children who were old enough to understand the "basic outlines" of the faith should be baptized. Children were responsible for their lives when their reason had matured to the point that they recognized a need for forgiveness. Until that time, Gregory said, they had no account to give for sins of ignorance.[83] His instruction is consistent with the contention that paedobaptism arose among Christians in response to infant mortality, a conclusion supported by evidence from the inscriptions.[84]

In the year 350, Cyril of Jerusalem delivered a series of *Catechetical Lectures* to explain Christian belief and practice to catechumens in preparation for their initiation by baptism into full participation in the life of the church.[85] In lectures 19 and 20 he described the baptism ceremony in which they would participate, explaining its various elements. The description was detailed, instructing the one being baptized to face west, to renounce Satan and his ways, and to

---

[80] Ibid., 40.28.

[81] Ibid.

[82] Ibid.

[83] Ibid.

[84] See Ferguson, "Inscriptions and the Origin of Infant Baptism."

[85] H. M. Riley, *Christian Initiation: A Comparative Study of the Interpretation of the Baptismal Liturgy in the Mystagogical Writings of Cyril of Jerusalem, John Chrysostom* (Washington, D.C.: Catholic University of America Press, 1974).

commit to live an obedient Christian life.[86] The emphasis was on the ceremonial display of one's conversion, repentance, and faith in Jesus Christ. Lecture 20 explained that those being baptized would be naked, "imitating Christ, who was stripped naked on the cross."[87] Immersion in water symbolized death and burial; arising from the water pictured the believer's sharing in the resurrection of Jesus Christ.[88] All these instructions were evidently intended for those old enough to understand, believe, and obey them. It is fair to say, then, that Cyril had believers in mind.

Augustine of Hippo is one of the most revered theologians in the Western Christian tradition. He has influenced Protestants and Catholics, paedobaptists and Baptists in similar and strikingly different ways. He spoke of baptism in writings directed against two of his staunchest opponents, Pelagius and the Donatists. In his *On Baptism against the Donatists*, Augustine argued that the practice of baptizing infants was "the invariable custom of the church handed down from the apostles."[89] Augustine defended the practice on the grounds both of its antiquity and its meaning. He argued that the apostles instructed the church to baptize infants because baptism was "a parallel of circumcision."[90] God's covenant with the church was both symbolized and effected through the administration of baptism to the children of believers, themselves heirs of the promise of God's salvation.

Against Pelagius, Augustine's main concern was the need of cleansing from original sin and the imbuement of life by Christ to the infant. His answer to the question why infants should be baptized was an exposition of the effects of original sin on all humanity.[91] All who were born of Adam were subject to Adam's condemnation. Those regenerated in Jesus Christ, however, received eternal life. Participation in Christ was by means of baptism, which Augustine

---

[86] Cyril of Jerusalem, *Catechetical Lecture* 19.1–6, in NPNF 2.7.
[87] Cyril of Jerusalem, *Catechetical Lecture* 20.2, in NPNF 2.7.
[88] Ibid., 20.2, in NPNF 2.4.
[89] Augustine, *On Baptism Against the Donatists* 4.32, in NPNF 1.4.
[90] Ibid.
[91] Augustine, *On the Merits and Forgiveness of Sins, and on the Baptism of Infants* 2.43, in NPNF 1.5.

called "the sacrament of regeneration."[92] Because infants were born of Adam, and thus were condemned with him, they too were in need of the regeneration through baptism. "Without it [baptism] the infant would have an unhappy exit out of this life."[93] Since infants shared in the guilt of Adam's sin, they must find cleansing in baptism, which was "administered for the remission of sin."[94]

Augustine's primary defense of the practice of baptizing infants was the work that baptism accomplished in the life of the one being baptized. In his *Enchiridion* Augustine wrote, "From the newborn infant to the elderly man bent by age, no one is closed off from baptism, so there is none who in baptism does not die to sin."[95] Baptism's effect—the remission of sins—was available to infants just as adults. This was needed because infants, as well as adults, were in need of the forgiveness of sin. Unlike advocates of infant baptism in the East, Augustine rejected the innocence of infants; even newborns needed forgiveness, though it was the forgiveness of original sin, not sins "added to the sin they brought with them."[96]

What one finds in the fourth and fifth centuries is that the church remained divided about the propriety of paedobaptism, as it had been in the third century. Some writers, such as Augustine, argued that infant baptism was to be the rule and requirement of the church. Those from the West who defended infant baptism typically did so on the basis of the need to deal with original sin: baptism cleansed infants from original sin, thus establishing their salvation. In the East, however, writers defended paedobaptism without attributing sin to infants. Instead, infants, though innocent and without need of the forgiveness of sins, still benefited from baptism through a reception of "sanctification, justice, filial adoption, inheritance, that they may be brothers and members of Christ, and become dwelling places of the Spirit."[97] Even an Eastern writer such as Gregory

---

[92] Ibid.

[93] Ibid.

[94] Ibid., Also Augustine, *On the Grace of Christ, and on Original Sin* 44, in NPNF 1.5.

[95] Augustine, *On the Merits and Forgiveness of Sins, and on the Baptism of Infants* 2.43, in NPNF 1.5.

[96] Ibid.

[97] John Chrysostom, *Baptismal Instruction* 3.6, in NPNF 1.9.

of Nazianzus, however, who allowed infant baptism in emergency situations and even attributed some benefit to baptized infants (although he, the son of a bishop, was not baptized until adulthood), still preferred believer's baptism because of the proper connection of baptism with repentance.

In the East, therefore, there was a clear picture of believer's baptismal practice and theology being adopted for infants. Importantly, though, in the East baptism was not believed to remit the sins of the infants. There were other benefits articulated by theologians, however. Gregory of Nazianzus did not attribute original sin or guilt to infants.[98] Rather, he argued that infants who died without baptism were not punished.[99] Chrysostom[100] similarly assumed the innocence of newborns, stressing numerous blessings beyond merely the forgiveness of sins: the infant received sacramental membership in the body of Christ, the indwelling presence of the Spirit, and other spiritual benefits.[101] In the West, things were much different. Cyprian wrote, "The infant approaches much more easily the reception of the forgiveness of sins in baptism because the sins remitted are not his own, but those of another."[102] Western theologians defended paedobaptism because the guilt of original sin needed to be forgiven.

Conclusions and Implications

We can draw several conclusions from our investigation. Baptism in the patristic writings had less to do with the age of the baptized person than with the role of repentance, profession of faith, and entrance into the full life of the church. In each period we surveyed, the emphasis was on the catechumen who began a new stage in her

---

[98] Gregory of Nazianzus, *Oration* 22.13, in *NPNF* 2.7.

[99] Ibid., 40.

[100] Ferguson, "Preaching at Epiphany"; T. M. Finn, *The Liturgy of Baptism in the Baptismal Instructions of St. John Chrysostom* (Washington, D.C.: Catholic University of America Press, 1967); T. Harjunpaa, "St. John Chrysostom in the Light of his Catechetical and Baptismal Homilies," *LQ* 29.2 (1977): 167–95; L. L. Mitchell, "The Baptismal Rite in Chrysostom," *AThR* 43 (1961): 307–403; P. Pleasants, "Making Christian the Christians: The Baptismal Instructions of St. John Chrysostom," *GOTR* 34.4 (1989): 379–92.

[101] Chrysostom, *Baptismal Instruction* 3.6.

[102] Cyprian, *Epistle* 64.5, in *ANF* 5.

or his life as a believer: having demonstrated a commitment to the teachings and lifestyle of the church, the catechumen was initiated into full communion with the church through the rite of baptism. The normal order of conversion, preparation for church life, and baptism is reflected, not only in direct references from the second and third centuries, but in the church orders both ancient and later. The practice of infant baptism, arising most likely in the second century, required accommodation of the church's baptismal liturgy to the innovative practice, and is not reflected in the early manuals.[103] Prior to the third century, there are no patristic advocates for paedobaptism. Even if the inscriptions reflect an early practice of emergency baptism (which they do), they do not constitute an explicit rejection of a normative practice of believer's baptism.

In the West, the patristic writings show a defense of infant baptism that corresponds with a more refined view of original sin. In Augustine, for example, baptism is the means by which original sin is removed. Because infants are guilty of this sin, and in need of forgiveness, baptism is logically extended to them. Tertullian was aware of this view in the third century but rejected it on two counts: first, infants are innocent, guiltless, and not in need of forgiveness; second, faith alone is sufficient for salvation. Baptism should follow faith. Since young children do not need forgiveness and cannot possess faith, baptism is unnecessary.

We found no support for the view of missionary baptism advanced by Jeremias. Nothing in the patristic writings prior to the third century either states or implies that the church conceived of two different baptisms: paedobaptism for the infant children of believers and missionary baptism for converts from Judaism or paganism.

The baptismal ceremony we find in the church manuals typically considers only the baptism of adults and children old enough to believe. It would seem that emergency baptism and the development of the church's understanding of the doctrine of original sin drove the desire to institute paedobaptism. It is hard to imagine how the patristic descriptions and instructions regarding baptism would have developed within a church that already and regularly prac-

---

[103] A possible exception is Hippolytus, but even this evidence is debatable.

ticed infant baptism. Why is there no description of how this would happen? Why, even in the fourth and fifth centuries, do the documents not even hint at how infant baptism might be performed? It seems that the ancient practice of baptizing only believers was subsequently adjusted to allow for the baptism of non-believing infants in addition to believing children and adults.

Jeremias's arguments notwithstanding, the most plausible conclusion is that the disagreement which was present in the third century continued into the fourth. Though paedobaptism was allowed in emergency situations, and even as a rule in some churches, it was never the universal practice of the church. Tertullian's position continued to have supporters even into the fourth and fifth centuries. There is no legitimate reason to dismiss such a conclusion so easily, as Jeremias does.

The ancient practice of the church was to baptize only those who had repented of sin, placed their faith in Jesus Christ, and committed to a life of faithful Christian service following a time of instruction and testing. Catechumens were Christians but were not considered fully-participating members of the church (they did not participate in the Lord's Supper, for example). Due to the dual pressures of infant mortality and evolving views of the sinfulness of even newborn infants, the novel practice of baptizing infants became widespread by the third century. This practice was not accepted as universal even by the fourth century, as infants' need for forgiveness continued to be questioned.[104] In both the third and fourth centuries, some theologians continued to argue for only the baptism of believers. These writers ended up where Peter, in his Pentecost sermon began: "Repent and be baptized." The account in Acts then records, "Those who received his word were baptized."

---

[104] Though we agree that infant baptism was an innovation, we are not endorsing the view that children are born innocent and without sin.

"CONFESSOR BAPTISM": THE BAPTISMAL DOCTRINE OF THE EARLY ANABAPTISTS

Jonathan H. Rainbow[*]

O n May 1, 1523, the day of the saints Philip and James, two men, Ulrich Zwingli and Balthasar Hubmaier, stood by the moat of Zurich and discussed the topic of baptism.[1] Both were educated men, pastors who had broken with the Roman Catholic church. Both were championing the Bible as the sole source of Christian truth and practice. And both, according to Hubmaier's account, agreed that day that the practice of infant baptism should be discontinued.[2]

But the discussion by the moat was only a snapshot, and a poignant one, for Zwingli would go on to become a ferocious persecutor of those who rejected infant baptism as well as the originator of a unique theological defense of infant baptism. Hubmaier, for his part, would continue to question infant baptism, eventually taking the decisive step of "rebaptism"—though for him and his party what their opponents called "rebaptism" was not rebaptism but simply true baptism—and would become the first systematic defender of the practice of "believer baptism" in the Reformation period. As Zwingli and Hubmaier diverged theologically, their personal rift became total. Several years after the conversation by the moat, Hubmaier was stretched on a rack in Zurich, with Zwingli's knowledge and compliance. Shortly thereafter, in 1528, Hubmaier met his death at a stake in Austria.

This short history has an illustrative purpose, for my aim in this essay is to set out Balthasar Hubmaier's doctrine of baptism, not so much at close range or in systematic detail, but as part of a larger theological event: the early Protestant response to the medieval

---

[*]Jonathan H. Rainbow received his Ph.D. from the University of California at Santa Barbara, has pastored two churches, and is currently a High School Instructor in Visalia, California.

[1] Reprinted with minor changes from the *American Baptist Quarterly* VIII (Dec. 1989): 276–290, with permission of the American Baptist Historical Society, Valley Forge, PA 19482.
[2] Balthasar Hubmaier, *Ein Gespräch* (1526), in *Quellen zur Geschichte der Täufer* (Gutersloher: Verlagshaus Gerd Mohn, 1962), 9:186.

Roman Catholic doctrine of baptism. The 1520s were a tumultuous decade. People were reading the Bible, thinking new thoughts, questioning long-unquestioned traditions, and starting new churches. And the old practice of infant baptism had to be dealt with again, as in fact it was —in diverse ways.

We will look first at Martin Luther, whose thinking on baptism was a conservative readjustment of the medieval legacy. Then we will turn to the radicals, Zwingli and Hubmaier, each of whom in his own way dismantled the medieval doctrine of baptism. In the course of this comparison, the theological uniqueness of the Anabaptist doctrine will emerge in sharp focus.

But first, it is necessary to understand something of the Roman Catholic thinking that preceded the Reformation.

The Medieval Legacy: Faith, Baptism, and Infants

The baptismal theology inherited by the Reformers from the medieval Roman Catholic church was characterized by tension. On the one hand, Catholic theologians recognized and tried to honor the biblical teaching that faith and baptism belong together and that faith is prerequisite to baptism (e.g., Mark 16:16, 1 Peter 3:21). On the other hand—and this was the source of the tension—they took the practice of infant baptism as a given. There were, in other words, three things that had to be combined: faith, baptism, and infants. There was no tension between faith and baptism, nor between baptism (considered simply as the application of water) and infants. The tension lay in the conjunction of faith and infants. So Catholic theologians had to answer this question: how can infants be said to have faith?

As was so often the case, Roman Catholic theology got its starting point from Augustine (d. 430), who defended infant baptism at a time when it had become the only kind of baptism that most Catholics ever witnessed—in short, an unquestioned institution. Augustine recognized that faith is the prerequisite for baptism and that infants cannot fulfill this prerequisite for themselves. He proposed as a solution the concept of *fides aliena*, the faith of others. At the baptism of an infant, the church believes for the infant. "So, when the others answer for them, in order to fulfill for them the celebration of the sacrament, it certainly avails for their consecration, since they themselves are not able to answer."[3] The church is the "mother" who offers her "maternal mouth for her children . . . for they cannot as yet with their own hearts believe unto righteousness, nor with their own mouths confess unto salvation."[4]

Later medieval theologians explored the doctrine of *fides aliena* with proverbial scholastic thoroughness. If *fides aliena* solves the problem of the infant's lack of faith, it opens up a new question: who actually does the believing? The early scholastics reckoned with the possibility that parents or sponsors may not really believe. In this case, the act of believing devolves upon the church as a whole, as Augustine had said. But what if the entire church was in error? Then, said the early scholastics, it is the faith of the *ecclesia triumphans*, the church already in heaven, that suffices. But the church triumphant does not need faith; how can it "believe"? Answer: its faith is on deposit in the treasury of merits. So the theologians spun out the strands that came from the Pandora's box that Augustine had opened.

Fides aliena turned out to be slippery ground, and the unsatisfying implications of it eventually sent some Catholic thinkers searching in another direction. Beginning with Peter Lombard, the center of gravity in the discussion shifted from the believing act of the church to the power of baptism itself to bestow faith on the infant. By about 1200, the dominant viewpoint was that faith is *virtus infusa baptisme*, a virtue or power infused by baptism.[5] While the doctrine of *fides infusa* avoided the casuistry of *fides aliena* by making baptismal faith the infant's own, it opened up again the problem that *fides aliena* had solved, namely, the requirement of NT texts that describe faith as the prerequisite for baptism. Clearly, faith cannot be both the prerequisite for baptism and the gift bestowed by baptism.

[3] Augustine, *De Baptismo* 7.4.24.

[4] Augustine, *De Peccatorum Meritis et Remissione* 1.25.

[5] One historian of medieval theology judges the doctrine of *fides infusa* to be the distinctive contribution of scholastic theology to the old question of faith and baptism. A. M. Landgraf, *Dogmengeschichte der Frühscholastik, Dritter Teil: Die Lehre von den Sakramenten* (Regensburg: Verlag Friedrich Pustet, 1954), 323.

So both doctrines continued to find support in Catholic theology into the Reformation period, and their coexistence was symbolic of the unresolved tension. How do infants believe? Through the faith of others *before* baptism? Through infused faith *at baptism*? Each answer carried its own liabilities. But it is crucial, especially for modern Baptists, to observe that, in the medieval discussions, baptism was always regarded as the *sacramentum fidei* (Augustine's term), the sacrament of faith. Nobody discarded faith; nobody said that baptized infants simply do not believe. The NT continued to exert its influence. And this conviction that faith must somehow be present in baptism was preserved liturgically for all to see on frequent occasions, in the baptismal ceremony, when the priest asked the infant: "Do you believe in God the Father Almighty? . . . Do you believe in Jesus Christ his only Son, our Lord, who was born and suffered? . . . Do you believe in the Holy Spirit, the holy Catholic Church, the remission of sins, the resurrection of the flesh?"[6] To which questions the sponsor(s), replying for the infant, answered: "I believe." The ceremony clearly harks back to the time when baptismal candidates were adults, capable of confessing their own faith in the creed. By ca. 500, the liturgy had to make certain adjustments for the fact that almost all recipients of baptism were infants and could not answer the faith questions, but the liturgy still proceeded as if they believed. The theological nexus of faith and baptism, though encumbered and compromised, was still visible in the baptismal liturgy, just as it was preserved in the doctrines of the theologians.

Martin Luther: The Faith of Infants

Although Martin Luther affirmed in one of his early blasts against the papacy that baptism was the one thing that Rome had not ruined, the medieval theology of baptism did not escape adjustment at his hands. Luther set forth a doctrine of baptism that took into account two of his prominent emphases, faith and the Word.

---

[6] These questions were present in the baptismal liturgy as early as the Gelasian Sacramentary, which dates to ca. 500. The Gelasian Sacramentary is essentially the liturgy of the Roman church, which became the pattern for the entire western church. For a helpful study of medieval baptismal practice, see J. D. C. Fisher, *Christian Initiation: Baptism in the Medieval West. A Study in the Disintegration of the Primitive Rite of Initiation* (London: S.P.C.K., 1965).

Just as Luther proclaimed the centrality and sufficiency of faith for justification, so he accentuated with new power the role of faith in the reception of the sacraments. He declared that a sacrament apart from faith is empty; in reference to baptism he said: "Unless faith is present, or comes to life in baptism, the ceremony is of no avail."[7]

In light of this, the medieval concept of *fides aliena* was bound to be questioned. When Luther insisted on faith, he meant the faith of the person being baptized, *fides propria*. Faith, which is the true priestly office, "permits no one else to take its place."[8] The principle of individuality which applies to the mass ("No one can observe or hear mass for another, but each one for himself alone"[9]) applies also to faith in baptism: "Who should receive baptism? The one who believes is the person to whom the blessed, divine water is to be imparted."[10] Building on the ancient baptismal liturgy, which he kept largely intact in his creation of the "German Mass," Luther affirmed that grace does not come to the baptized infant *quia baptizatur, sed quia credit*—not because he is baptized, but because he believes.

That Luther meant that infants truly believe is clear from his exchanges with Andreas Bodenstein von Carlstadt and the Bohemian Brethren in the early 1520s. Carlstadt and other radical followers of Luther, building on Luther's premise that "faith and baptism belong together"[11] and the common sense observation that infants cannot believe, were moving towards the rejection of infant baptism itself. Luther struck back with clarity: "In baptism the infants themselves believe and have their own faith."[12] To the Bohemian Brethren, who were still baptizing infants but only on the basis of future faith, Luther replied with an appeal to the baptismal liturgy: "When the baptizer asks whether the infant believes, and it is answered 'Yes' for

[7] Martin Luther, *On the Babylonian Captivity of the Church*, in *Martin Luther: Selections from His Writings*, ed. John Dillenberger (Garden City, NY: Doubleday, 1961), 293.

[8] Martin Luther, *A Treatise on the New Testament, that is, the Holy Mass*, in *Luther's Works*, 54 vols: (Saint Louis: Concordia, 1958–67), 35:101.

[9] Luther, *A Treatise on the New Testament*, in *Luther's Works*, 35:94.

[10] Luther, *A Treatise on the New Testament*, in *Luther's Works*, 51:185.

[11] K. Brinkel, *Die Lehre Luthers von der fides infantium bei der Kindertaufe* (Berlin: Evangelische Verlagsanstatt, 1958), 38.

[12] Quoted by Brinkel, *Die Lehre Luthers*, 41.

him, and whether he wants to be baptized, and it is answered 'Yes' for him . . . therefore it must also be he himself who believes, or else those who answer must be lying when they say 'I believe' for him."[13] According to Luther, the infant's *credo*, even though not spoken by his own lips, is truly his own.

So infant faith for Luther was truly faith. He ignored the scholastic distinction between *fides in usu* (adult faith, consciously exercised) and *fides in habitu* (faith present but unexercised in infants). He rejected all viewpoints which, in his opinion, linked faith with the exercise of reason. Carlstadt, the Bohemian Brethren, and, later, the Anabaptists, saw faith as an intelligent response to an understood gospel message. Luther saw reason as a hindrance to faith. Indeed, Luther considered infants more receptive to the Word because of their lack of reason than adults, "better capable of faith than the old and the reasonable, for whom reason always lies in the way."[14]

Luther's emphasis on faith in baptism cannot be understood, however, without the recognition of his emphasis on the role of the Word of God. Faith and the Word were always in tandem for Luther, whether in the case of the "reasonable" adult taking communion, or the infant being baptized. For Luther, as for Augustine, faith was no human work, but the gift of the grace of God. And the faith which Luther insisted was necessary in baptism was faith granted, created, and bestowed through the Word itself, specifically, the gospel Word spoken in the baptismal ceremony. That an infant cannot reasonably understand the Word is no obstacle to the Word; the Word performs its work of creating faith without our cooperation. In baptism the infant comes under the hearing of the Word, which penetrates his heart and creates faith; he answers the baptismal questions through the mouths of his sponsors.

Luther retained from the medieval doctrine of baptism the fundamental link between faith and baptism. He also retained the practice of infant baptism. He left behind the idea of *fides aliena*, at least in

---

[13] Brinkel, *Die Lehre Luthers*, 44.
[14] Brinkel, *Die Lehre Luthers*, 40.

its classic meaning,[15] and insisted that faith be personal, even in the case of infants. He retained a kind of *fides infusa*, with a strong focus on the Word of God as the power that creates or infuses faith.

We cannot leave Luther without giving some attention to his 1528 tract *On Rebaptism*, where he came directly to grips with Anabaptist theology as he perceived it. In *On Rebaptism*, Luther moved on to somewhat different ground from that expressed in his baptismal teaching of the early 1520s. When facing Roman Catholic sacramental objectivity, Luther had been at pains to emphasize the necessity of personal faith as generated by the Word. Now, facing a perceived Anabaptist "subjectivity" (i.e., the insistence on personal and intelligent confession of faith as prerequisite to baptism), Luther emphasized the objectivity of baptism. "Whoever bases baptism on the faith of the one to be baptized can never baptize anyone."[16] "Since there is no difference in baptism whether faith precedes or follows, baptism does not depend on faith."[17] "True, one should add faith to baptism. But we are not to base baptism on faith."[18] Such statements have a decidedly different tone from the statements we examined earlier. One could argue that the difference is simply one of emphasis.[19] But then one would have to reckon with this: "Even if they could establish that children are without faith, it would make no difference to me."[20] Was this the same Luther who said, earlier, "Unless faith is present, or comes to life in baptism, the ceremony is of no avail"?

It is difficult to decide whether the tract of 1528 was just an especially glaring instance of Luther's tendency to overstatement or whether Luther's baptismal theology was actually moving in the di-

---

[15] Luther once utilized the concept of *fides aliens* (*Babylonian Captivity* of 1520). Perhaps Brinkel is correct that Luther is simply saying that the church aids the infant by bringing him under the hearing of the word (*Die Lehre Luthers*, 41).

[16] Martin Luther, *On Rebaptism*, in *Luther's Works*, 40:240.

[17] Luther, *On Rebaptism*, in *Luther's Works*, 40:248.

[18] Luther, *On Rebaptism*, in *Luther's Works*, 40:252.

[19] J. Pelikan ("Luther's Defense of Infant Baptism," in *Luther for an Ecumenical Age* [St. Louis: Concordia, 1967]) sees no significant conflict between *On Rebaptism* and Luther's earlier theology. Brinkel asks whether Luther changed his theology in *On Rebaptism* (*Die Lehre Luthers*, 57), and concludes that the very different thought of Luther's tract against the Anabaptists is due to a "dialectical viewpoint."

[20] Luther, *On Rebaptism*, in *Luther's Works*, 40:246.

rection of making faith unimportant for baptism. If the latter, then the connection between Word and faith which had structured his earlier doctrine had been broken. The Word, instead of creating faith, had swallowed it up and made it exiguous. It is true, as we have noted, that Luther had long stressed the gracious nature of faith as a gift of God; but it is also true that he had described faith as something given at baptism. If Luther was indeed moving away from that emphasis, then he was also moving away from the medieval tradition, and in the direction that Ulrich Zwingli had already pointed. If the former (and I think this is more likely), then what we have in *On Rebaptism* is Luther overreacting to the Anabaptist insistence on personal faith as expressed in confession by virtually emptying baptism of its subjective dimension. This, I believe, was an impoverishing of Luther's earlier doctrine. Even more disturbing is how Luther, in his strenuous effort to remove any human contribution to the grace of baptism, comes dangerously close to implying that faith is a work—as if the faith of an adult recipient of baptism who confesses Christ with his or her own mouth is any less the gracious gift of God than the faith of an infant.

Assuming, then, that *On Rebaptism* was not a substantial shift in his baptismal theology, we can conclude that Luther's understanding of baptism in its relationship to faith moved within the same general orbit as the doctrine which Roman Catholic theologians had developed since Augustine: that faith and baptism belong in some sense together, and that infants must be said in some sense to believe.

Ulrich Zwingli: Covenant and Circumcision

Luther adjusted the medieval synthesis of faith, baptism, and infants; Zwingli shattered it. Luther had ambiguously suggested the idea that baptism need not be linked with faith; Zwingli boldly embraced and championed it. In 1525, Zwingli announced his revolution in the essay *De Baptismo*:

> In this matter of baptism—if I may be pardoned for saying it—I can only conclude that all the doctors have been in error from the time of the apostles. This is a serious and weighty assertion, and I make it with such reluctance that had I not been compelled to do so by contentious spirits, I would

have preferred to keep silence. . . . At many points we shall have to tread a different path from that taken either by ancient or more modern writers or by our own contemporaries.[21]

Zwingli was fully aware of the novelty of his doctrine. He also acknowledged the important role that his theological conflict with the Anabaptists, whom he called "contentious spirits," had played. This is the all-important historical fact: Zwingli, unlike Luther, had Anabaptists at his doorstep, proclaiming their doctrine of baptism within Zurich, debating Zwingli before the city council. Many of them, including Balthasar Hubmaier, were erstwhile disciples and friends. And Zwingli, much more clearly than Luther, realized that the traditional linkage of baptism and faith pointed towards the rejection of infant baptism—unless, of course, one was willing to accept *fides aliena, fides infusa,* or Luther's *fides infantium,* all of which Zwingli considered ludicrous. Early on, Zwingli toyed with the rejection of infant baptism, but in the end maintained it with the aid of two novel strokes, one destructive and the other constructive.[22]

Zwingli did what nobody had yet done: he severed baptism from faith. His willingness to take this step grew out of one of the fundamental premises of his theological thinking: the cleavage between the material and the spiritual. Most traditional Christian theology distinguished matter and spirit but allowed for some degree of interpenetration; Zwingli divorced them. Applying this premise, Zwingli identified baptism as an "external" material thing and faith as an "internal" spiritual thing, and concluded that the traditional theology had been guilty of mingling and confusing them. "All the doctors

---

[21] Ulrich Zwingli, *Of Baptism,* in *Zwingli and Bullinger,* Library of Christian Classics, vol. 24, trans. G.W. Bromiley (Philadelphia: Westminster, 1953), 130.

[22] Zwingli mentions his flirtation with baptistic theology in *Of Baptism,* 139. Scholars debate whether Zwingli changed his doctrine because of the Anabaptist challenge. Martin Brecht has answered in the affirmative ("Herkunft und Eigenart der Taufanschauung der Züricher Täufer," *Archiv für Reformationsgeschichte,* 64 [1973]:147–65); R. Walton argued that Zwingli's baptismal understanding was firmly in place even before the Anabaptist challenge (*Zwingli's Theocracy* [Toronto: Toronto University Press, 1967], 171). Walton's case is weak; it seems clear to me that Zwingli's doctrine of baptism evolved in the conflict. In any case, I find it strange that scholars so often try to protect their favorite thinkers from accusations of change in the face of challenge. If anything, it is a credit to Zwingli that he perceived the heart of the Anabaptist position and took radical measures to refute it.

have ascribed to the water a power which it does not have."[23] "No external thing can make us pure or righteous."[24] In Zwingli's estimation, the papists on the one hand and the Anabaptists on the other had ascribed too much importance to a mere external rite.[25] And the Anabaptist Hubmaier, according to Zwingli, was on the horns of a dilemma: either baptism saves, or it does not, and if it does not (which was Hubmaier's position) then it is a mere, dispensable external thing.[26] So Zwingli asked in effect, Why all the fuss about keeping faith and baptism together?

What, then, of the biblical passages which join faith and baptism? Zwingli handled these by asserting that Scripture uses the term "baptism" in various ways, sometimes of the outer symbol and sometimes of the inner reality of faith and salvation. In his terms, there are both an outer baptism and an inner baptism. This hermeneutic enabled Zwingli to deal with any biblical text. In 1 Pet 3:21, for example, which had historically been a key proof-text for the necessity of faith in baptism, the term "baptism" according to Zwingli signified "the inward faith which saves us," not the water.[27] Obviously, when this hermeneutical knife is unsheathed, there is no way to argue for the traditional conjunction of faith and baptism: any text in which baptism is linked with faith and salvation (and the NT bulges with them) cannot be speaking of the external rite of water baptism.

Baptism and faith, therefore, are apples and oranges; there is no necessity that they be together. By the ruthless application of the separation of the material and the spiritual, Zwingli cut baptism loose from faith, and himself from the whole baptismal tradition.

Zwingli's second stroke was constructive. Having set baptism apart from salvation, he had to find a new way to argue for the baptism of infants. He found this way in the doctrine of the covenant and the

---

[23] Zwingli, *Of Baptism*, 130.

[24] Ibid.

[25] Ibid., 156. "The Anabaptists themselves set too great store by the baptism of water, and for that reason they err just as much on the one side as the papists do on the other."

[26] *Antwort über Balthasar Hubmaiers Taufüchlein*, in *Huldreich Zwinglis Sämtliche Werke*, ed. Emil Egli et al (Leipzig: Verlag von Heinsius Nachfolger, 1927), 4:617.

[27] "Here the words 'washing of the body with pure water' are a figurative saying" (*Antwort*, 4:619).

analogy of circumcision, which he developed most fully in his final polemic against the Anabaptists, *The Refutation of the Anabaptist Tricks* (1527).[28] There is one covenant spanning all of redemptive history, explained Zwingli, which is the external relationship God has established with a visible people, whether Abraham, Israel, or the church.[29] Logically, one covenant means one covenant people.[30] And if there is one covenant people, then the external signs that mark that people—circumcision in the Old Testament and baptism in the New—must be parallel, indeed identical, in meaning. Zwingli concluded that just as "the Hebrews' children, because they with their parents were under the covenant, merited the sign of the covenant, so also Christians' infants, because they are counted within the church and people of Christ, ought in no way to be deprived of baptism, the sign of the covenant."[31]

None of this, be it remembered, had anything necessarily to do with salvation or true faith in Zwingli's theology; the covenant, the church, and baptism were external things. Faith and regeneration flowed from God's inscrutable election and the Spirit's invisible work in the heart.

What Zwingli achieved was a marvelously clever and persuasive way to reject the suspicious devices of previous paedobaptist argumentation, *fides aliena, fides infusa, fides infantium,* and the like, and at the same time to maintain infant baptism against the Anabaptists. But this solution had as its price the integrity of Zwingli's exegesis of the baptismal passages of the NT and the very significance of baptism itself. For if baptism is a mere external thing, disconnected from salvation, why practice it at all?

---

[28] Ulrich Zwingli, *In catabaptistarum strophas elenchus, Sämtliche Werke,* Band VI, (Zurich: Verlag Berichthaus, 1961), translated as *Refutation of Baptist Tricks* in *Ulrich Zwingli Selected Works,* ed. S. M. Jackson (Philadelphia: University of Pennsylvania Press, 1972).

[29] Zwingli, *Refutation,* 233.

[30] Ibid., 227.

[31] Ibid., 236. Zwingli was not, of course, the first theologian to bring circumcision into the discussion of infant baptism. (See Steven McKinion's chapter on "Baptism in the Patristic Writings.") But until Zwingli, circumcision had played "only an ancillary place in giving propriety to infant baptism" (P. Jewett, *Infant Baptist and the Covenant of Grace* [Grand Rapids: Eerdmans, 1978], 81). For Zwingli it was the central thing—the only thing.

Meanwhile, prodding Zwingli and being prodded by him, Balthasar Hubmaier was dismantling the old synthesis of faith, baptism, and infants in a different but equally radical manner.

Balthasar Hubmaier: Confessor Baptism

The story of the relationship of Ulrich Zwingli and Balthasar Hubmaier, as we have seen, is a sad one of friendship turned to enmity, a kind of microcosm of the bitter rift that came to separate the magisterial Reformers from the Anabaptists. At the center of this rift was the Anabaptists' defiant rejection of infant baptism, with all that was ecclesiastically and socially attached to the act, and their insistence that in order to be baptized, one must both believe in Christ and be able to say so with one's own mouth. This is the baptism that Balthasar Hubmaier laid out so clearly in the few years between his (re)baptism and his death.

At the core of Hubmaier's doctrine was the conviction that the inner reality of faith and conversion and the outer sign of water baptism belong together. Hubmaier was trained as a scholastic theologian; he knew exactly where the heart of the difference between Zwingli and himself lay. He knew that precisely at the point where Zwingli was using a knife, he wanted to use a clamp. He distinguished the inner from the outer, but he insisted that in the rite of baptism they must be held together.

> [Baptism] is nothing other than a public confession and testimony of an inward faith and commitment.[32]

> Although the confession of sin be expressed outwardly in baptism, after the event, nevertheless, it has already taken place inwardly in the heart.[33]

> The baptism in water is called a baptism in remissionem peccatorum (Acts 2), that is, in the pardon of sins. Not that through it or by it sins are forgiven, but by virtue of the inward "yes" of the heart, which a man openly witnesses to on submitting to water baptism, declaring that he believes and feels in his heart that his sins are forgiven through Jesus Christ.[34]

[32] Balthasar Hubmaier, Concerning the Christian Baptism of Believers, in W. R. Estep, ed. Anabaptist Beginnings (1523–33): A Source Book (Nieuwkoop: De Graaf, 1976), 69.

[33] Ibid., 74.

[34] Ibid., 80.

Hubmaier had completely abandoned the medieval Catholic conception of baptism ex *opere operato;* sinners must come "with honest hearts, in complete trust, cleansed in their hearts from an evil conscience [here the insistence on the inward]. And this must, must, must [Hubmaier repeats the imperative three times] be accompanied by the washing of the body in pure water."[35] The reader will perhaps recognize that Hubmaier was here expounding the classic text, 1 Peter 3:21.

Thus far, Hubmaier clearly stood with the ancient tradition, which had held the faith-baptism nexus as a given, over against Zwingli, who had destroyed it. But instead of delving into speculations on how infants can fulfill the requirement for faith, as Augustine and the medieval theologians and Luther had done, Hubmaier simply discarded infant baptism. He was not, of course, alone in this momentous step, nor were the 16th-century Anabaptists the first to do so. There is evidence that throughout the medieval period, and especially after 1000, voices of protest arose against the practice of infant baptism, but the evidence is available only indirectly, through the arguments of Catholic theologians and the inquisitorial records.[36] But the antipaedobaptist movement for which Hubmaier spoke was by far the biggest thing of its kind since the days of the apostles, and it had something that the medieval antipaedobaptists had not: the printing press.

Hubmaier's was a simple, bold stroke, as was Zwingli's. But because it was in its time an ecclesiastical, social, even political statement to reject infant baptism, Hubmaier's was, unlike Zwingli's, a lethal one. One could dismantle an ancient idea and only the experts would notice, but one who spurned Catholic infant baptism was an intolerable subversive, fit only to be jailed, drowned, and burned.

Hubmaier himself resented both Zwingli and Luther, because he felt that their own teaching about the nature and centrality of faith had opened the way to end the practice of infant baptism. Zwingli, as we have already noted, passed briefly through a period of doubt

---

[35] Ibid., 84.

[36] Landgraf's account of the development of the Catholic doctrine makes it clear that medieval Catholic theologians were often answering objections posed by real people: Cathars, Henricians (12th-century followers of Henry the Monk), Waldensians, or just generic "heretics."

about the validity of infant baptism. His early trumpet-call that all belief and ecclesiastical practice must be based on Scripture had a powerful impact on those who would shortly become Anabaptists, including Hubmaier. Hubmaier was also quick to point out that Luther's early writings, particularly those in which he had maintained the necessity of personal faith for the reception of the sacraments, had seemed to him to imply the end of infant baptism. As late as 1526, Luther could write with characteristic candor of his desire for something that resembled very much the kind of church the Anabaptists were trying to achieve:

> [They] should sign their names and meet alone in a house somewhere to pray, to read, to baptize, to receive the sacrament, and do other Christian works. According to this order, those who do not lead Christian lives could be known, reproved, corrected, cast out, or excommunicated, according to the rule of Christ, Matthew 18. Here one could also solicit benevolent gifts to be willingly given and distributed to the poor, according to St. Paul's example, II Corinthians 9. Here would be no need of much and elaborate singing. Here one could set out a brief and neat order for baptism and the sacrament and center everything on the Word, prayer, and love.[37]

Granted, Luther did not in this passage jettison infant baptism, but we can with justice ask whether the polity of Luther's little gathered church does not demand such a step. The Anabaptists of the 1520s felt that the reformers had pointed the way, and then turned back. Scholarly admirers of Luther and Zwingli still argue that this was not the case, and historians debate whether the magisterial Reformation ended up as a kind of retrenchment against the logical and radical outworking of Reformation theology. But there was no question among the Anabaptists themselves: the Reformers had just chickened out.

Hubmaier, then, kept the old baptismal *theology* (faith plus baptism) and abandoned the *practice* of infant baptism. His baptismal ceremony, the *Form zu taufen*,[38] resembled closely in liturgical form the heart of the Roman Catholic ceremony: the recipient was asked the same questions from the Apostles' Creed ("Do you believe . . . ?") that had been asked of candidates for more than a millennium. But

---

[37] Martin Luther, *The German Mass and Order of Service,* in *Luther's Works,* 53:53 ff.
[38] *Quellen zur Geschichte der Täufer,* 9:350.

his answers to this series of questions reflected the revolution that had taken place in the early sixteenth century, for he answered in his own language (*Ich glaub* instead of *credo*), which announced the end of a sacerdotal language and the coming of the word of God to men and women in the common languages, and he answered with his own lips, which announced the end of infant baptism.

Hubmaier's doctrine can be encapsulated thus: only the person who confesses faith in Christ may be baptized. The term "believer baptism" does not really suffice, for as we have seen, both Catholics and Lutherans maintained that baptized infants are believers. It is the requirement that the baptismal candidate *himself* or *herself* be able to say "I believe" that makes the Anabaptist position unique. In short, what Hubmaier was calling for was *confessor baptism*.

Toward a Deeper Understanding of Baptist Theology

What can modern Baptists learn from the Anabaptists of the 16th century, and from Hubmaier in particular?

Unlike Hubmaier and his Anabaptist comrades, contemporary Baptists are usually ignorant of what the paedobaptist traditions actually teach. Through his theological education and the priesthood, Hubmaier knew the Roman Catholic position. Through his voracious reading of Luther, he knew the Lutheran position; and through his personal controversies with Zwingli, he knew the Reformed covenant-plus-circumcision position. Consequently, his own doctrine had a depth, a three-dimensionality, that contemporary baptist doctrine often lacks.[39] All too often, among modern baptists, one encounters the ignorant notion that all paedobaptists are "baptismal regenerationists" (i.e., people who believe in some crude sense that the act of baptism saves the infants), the cavalier notion that since the antipaedobaptist position is so obviously right anyone who thinks otherwise must be somehow stupid or perverse, and worst of all, a baptismal doctrine that is only an atrophied fragment of that propounded by men like Hubmaier when the antipaedobaptist struggle was young. It is my hope that the bit of comparative

---

[39] I lower-case "baptist" to include not only Baptists but Mennonites, Brethren, and other modern groups carrying on the tradition of the believers' church.

historical theology we have done in this essay might open the way to a fairer dialogue with representatives of the paedobaptist traditions, and a better doctrine of baptism for baptists.

First, baptists need to understand something of the complexity of paedobaptist theology. The paedobaptist position is not one monolithic thing, but a variety of approaches to the question of infant baptism. Baptists may argue—accurately, in my opinion—that this complexity is the result of a false starting point. But baptists may not, with integrity, simply lump all paedobaptists together and lambast them with identical (and sometimes facile) arguments. As our sketch of the 1520s shows, we have to ask: *which* paedobaptists are we talking to? Not until we are able to do that will we earn the respect of our Roman Catholic, Lutheran, or Reformed friends.

Specifically, baptists need to reckon with something that will come as a surprise: they do not have a corner on the concept of "believer baptism." As we have seen, both the medieval Catholic tradition and Luther's revision of it maintained staunchly that faith is necessary for baptism. And that places them in the "believer baptism" camp along with baptists. Once baptists have grasped this fact, they will be prodded to examine more exactly the specific point at which they part ways (for part ways they definitely do!) with Roman Catholics and Lutherans. It is not the insistence that baptismal recipients be believers that distinguishes baptist theology, but the definition of a "believer" as a person who confesses Christ freely and intelligently with his or her own mouth. Given the history of the doctrine, the best descriptive term for the position of both Anabaptists and baptists is not "believer baptism" but "confessor baptism."

Along with this, there is also the strange fact that on the doctrine of baptism, baptists are separated by a great gulf from the paedobaptist tradition to which they are otherwise closest, namely, the Presbyterian-Reformed. If the continental baptists of the 16th century are the "grandfathers" of modern baptists, the English Puritan Separatists, Reformed theologians all of them, are the fathers. Yet, as we have seen, it was Reformed theology, beginning with Zwingli, that boldly cut the link with the past and left the "believer baptism" camp. In dialogue with Reformed paedobaptists, baptists often have that strange "so close and yet so far away" feeling. The theological history helps explain why.

Finally, and most importantly, our look at the 1520s may help baptists to recover a full-bodied doctrine of baptism instead of the minimalistic view that is often heard in baptist circles today. A real devaluation of baptism takes place when baptists, overresponding to the perceived overvaluation of baptism in the paedobaptist churches (which is often the fruit of misunderstanding on the part of baptists), begin to talk about baptism as if it were a marginal, optional, not-very-significant thing. What is really important, we often hear in baptist churches, is what happens in the heart, in the conversion experience as it is transacted between God and the soul. Baptism is "just" a symbol—like a wedding ring, nice but dispensable, a mere external ceremony. So what is usually left as the compulsion for baptism among baptists? Obedience. Why do it? Because Jesus did it and the NT commands it. So baptism, instead of being a cataclysmic gateway from death to life, becomes merely the first of many acts of discipleship. The sense of drama is gone, the sense of baptism having some real contact with salvation is gone, and baptism has been reduced to an act of sheer obedience. The real drama is elsewhere, in the private enclave of the heart.

The reader who has followed our argument in this essay will recognize that, to the extent that this conception of baptism influences modern baptist thought and practice, we are dealing with the same bifurcation of matter and spirit that we saw in the baptismal doctrine of Ulrich Zwingli. Among baptists today, as with Zwingli, there is a fear of allowing water baptism to come too close to the work of grace in the sinner's heart; there are raised eyebrows and puzzled looks at the NT texts that closely associate baptism with salvation; many would rather not baptize at all than leave room for the impression that baptism is an integral part of the conversion experience. But baptists should understand that when they think in this direction, they move away from historic baptist doctrine, and towards the quasi-platonic baptismal doctrine of Zwingli. It was Zwingli, remember, who accused Hubmaier, the baptist, of *making too much of baptism*. And it was Hubmaier who demanded that the inner work of the Spirit "must, must, must" be accompanied by the outward washing of water. It was Hubmaier who wrote (in a letter to the reformer Oecolampadius, January 1525):

> We ourselves have indeed earlier taught as well that according to the ordinance of Christ, the very young should by no means receive baptism. . . . Why, then, do we baptize the very young? Baptism, the saying goes [referring to Zwingli and Leo Jud], is a *naked sign*. Why is it that we dispute so fiercely over this "sign"? The sign is assuredly also a "symbol." . . . [T]he bonding signified by that sign and symbol (whereby for the sake of the faith and in hope of the resurrection to life eternal one binds oneself to God even unto death) should be valued more seriously than the sign itself.[40]

For Zwingli, baptism was a *mere sign*. For Hubmaier, it was *more than a sign*. Baptists historically belong in the high baptismal tradition which sees baptism as the expression and embodiment of the saving work of God, the *sacramentum fidei,* not just an act of obedience tacked on. Baptists historically have known how to embrace Peter's declaration, "Baptism now saves you" (1 Pet 3:20), not because they ascribe a crude, magical saving power to the rite as such, but because they consider, on the basis of an open and personal confession, that the person coming to the water believes in Jesus Christ, and that there is an inner reality to which the baptism corresponds. Baptism is not magic, but it is more than a sign. That is the heart of what the Reformation Anabaptists were saying.

---

[40] Balthasar Hubmaier, "A Letter to Oecolampad," in *Balthasar Hubmaier: Theologian of Anabaptism,* ed. and trans. H. W. Pipkin and J. H. Yoder (Scottdale, PA: Herald, 1989), 70 (emphasis mine). Editors' note: In Rainbow's original article, the source of this quotation was not cited. The quotation here cited comes from a later translation of the letter Rainbow referenced.

BAPTISM AND THE LOGIC OF REFORMED PAEDOBAPTISTS

Shawn D. Wright*

Introduction

Our task in this chapter is to understand and examine the internal logic of the Reformed paedobaptist position. This is no simple task, however, as even our paedobaptist brethren admit. For example, Frank James, a Presbyterian professor, candidly states the difficulty of grasping the logic of the Reformed paedobaptist position:

> If I may hazard a generality (a generality, however, based on years of training pastors for Presbyterian ministry), I am quite convinced most Presbyterians, whether in the pulpit or the pew, do not understand clearly why they baptize their infants. If asked to explain why Presbyterians baptize infants, . . . I would expect that many Presbyterians would stumble and blunder the explanation.[1]

In our attempt to understand our Reformed brethren, we will look at the arguments of three prominent Reformed evangelical paedobaptists whose defenses of paedobaptism are still used today: John Calvin's powerful sixteenth-century exposition, and John Murray's and Pierre Marcel's popular twentieth-century statements.[2] By focusing on the thought of just these three thinkers, we will be able to see the inner logic of the Reformed paedobaptist position. We will examine their thought under six headings, which are the chief points of their apology for the baptism of the infants of at least one

---

* Shawn D. Wright received his Ph.D. from The Southern Baptist Theological Seminary and is Assistant Professor of Church History at The Southern Baptist Theological Seminary in Louisville, Kentucky.

[1] F. A. James, "Introduction: The Covenantal Convictions of a Compassionate Calvinist," in L. B. Schenck, *The Presbyterian Doctrine of Children in the Covenant: An Historical Study of the Significance of Infant Baptism in the Presbyterian Church* (1940; reprint, Phillipsburg, NJ: P&R, 2003), xvi.

[2] The three dealt with here are representative of the majority opinion for paedobaptism among evangelicals. Meredith Kline's idiosyncratic apology is effectively treated by Duane Garrett's chapter in this volume.

believing parent. First, we will examine their doctrine of the sacraments. Second, we will consider their definition of baptism and
compare it to their practice of baptizing infants. Third, we will look
at their belief that the church is inevitably a mixed body of believers
and unbelievers. Fourth, we will look at their construct of the "covenant of grace," which is the bedrock for their practice of paedobaptism. Fifth, we will examine their use of the NT as a justification for
the practice of infant baptism. Finally, we will note that their practice of paedobaptism fits uncomfortably with their belief that salvation is by faith alone. Taken as a whole these points that buttress
paedobaptism display that paedobaptism lacks biblical support and
should be untenable for evangelical Christians. We will therefore
conclude the chapter with an appeal for biblical consistency.

The Doctrine of the Sacraments

Reformed paedobaptists are inconsistent in relating their practice
of baptism to their definition of the sacraments.[3] They define the
sacraments carefully and biblically. Then they contradict their own
definition by their insistence that believers' infants should be baptized. In this section we will examine their inconsistency by noting
Calvin's and Marcel's discussions.[4] Our discussion will be brief since
in the next section we will consider specifically the paedobaptist
definition of the sacrament of baptism. We will conclude that the
credobaptist practice of baptizing only those who are followers of
Jesus Christ is actually the consistent application of the paedobaptist definition of the sacraments.

Calvin

Calvin argues that there are only two biblical sacraments since
they alone "clearly present Jesus Christ to us."[5] Indeed, according

---

[3] When I use the word "sacrament" in this chapter, I am referring to the same thing Baptists
typically call an "ordinance." Paedobaptists usually label it "sacrament," so I will use that term
as well. But I intend nothing "sacramentarian" by its use.

[4] On Murray's view see J. Murray, "The Sacraments," in Collected Writings of John Murray
(Carlisle, PA: Banner of Truth, 1977), 2:366–69.

[5] F. Wendel, Calvin: The Origin and Development of His Religious Thought, trans. P. Mairet
(New York: Harper and Row, 1963), 317. See R. S. Wallace, Calvin's Doctrine of the Word and

to Wilhelm Niesel, bringing persons into relationship with Christ is "the heart of the Calvinistic doctrine of the sacraments."[6] Calvin says a sacrament "is an outward sign by which the Lord seals on our consciences the promises of his good will toward us in order to sustain the weakness of our faith; and we in turn attest our piety toward him in the presence of the Lord and of his angels and before men."[7] For our purposes, it is essential to note that Calvin stresses the individual's active participation in the sacraments as we "attest our piety" to the Lord.[8]

According to Calvin, the sacraments serve two purposes. First, they are "seals" that confirm to us what is written in God's Word.[9] Paul teaches in Rom 4:11 that Abraham was justified through his faith; then the promise of God to him was sealed in his circumcision. That is, his circumcision did not justify him but was the seal of the covenant in which he was already justified through his faith. So the promise of God is sealed by the sacraments.[10] Second, sacraments function as "signs" of God's covenant promise to his people. God gives his people tokens of his covenantal love for them in the sacraments, making them more certain of the trustworthiness of God's promissory word to them. Thus a sacrament, says Calvin, referencing Augustine, is a "visible word."[11]

Sacraments (London: Oliver and Boyd, 1953), 133, 143–52. Space limitations constrain me to focus my attention on Calvin's opinions as expressed in his final (1559) edition of the *Institutes*, his final, and most extensive, defense of baptism. I am aware that the ideal would be to read the *Institutes* in tandem with his other writings. See R. A. Muller, *The Unaccommodated Calvin: Studies in the Foundation of a Theological Tradition* (New York: Oxford University Press, 2000).

[6] W. Niesel, *The Theology of Calvin*, trans. H. Knight (Philadelphia: Westminster, 1956), 217; see also 220–21.

[7] J. Calvin, *Institutes of the Christian Religion,* ed. J. T. McNeill, trans. F. L. Battles, Library of Christian Classics, Vol. 21 (Philadelphia: Westminster, 1960), 4.14.1.

[8] On the centrality of "piety" in Calvin's thought see F. L. Battles, "True Piety According to Calvin," in F. L. Battles, *Interpreting John Calvin*, ed. R. Benedetto (Grand Rapids: Baker, 1996), 289–306, and J. R. Beeke, "Calvin on Piety," in *The Cambridge Companion to John Calvin*, ed. D. K. McKim (Cambridge: Cambridge University Press, 2004), 125–52.

[9] See Wallace, *Calvin's Doctrine*, 137–38.

[10] "The existence of the sacraments depended, in [Calvin's] view, upon a prevenient divine promise; for the sacrament was no more than a confirmation of the promise, to give us additional faith in it. The sacrament, therefore, adds nothing to the promise as such, but is only a means of making us believe in it" (Wendel, *Calvin*, 313). See A. M. Hunter, *The Teaching of Calvin: A Modern Interpretation*, 2nd ed. (London: James Clarke, 1950), 168.

[11] Calvin, *Institutes* 4.14.6. He also says, "Or we might call them mirrors in which we may

Three requirements are needed to make the sacraments effective
in a person's life: preaching, the Holy Spirit, and faith. First, preaching is essential, according to Calvin, because the Lord does not work
apart from his word.[12] It is necessary since our faith is weak and we
are ignorant of spiritual realities. Thus preaching is the substance,
and the sacrament is "a sort of appendix, with the purpose of confirming and sealing the promise itself. . . . By this means God provides first for our ignorance and dullness, then for our weakness."[13]
Second, the Holy Spirit must act in the sacraments since they do
not operate secretly or by some inherent power. In an effort to distance himself from Rome's *ex opere operato* notion,[14] Calvin says,
"The sacraments properly fulfill their office only when the Spirit,
that inward teacher, comes to them, by whose power alone hearts
are penetrated and affections moved and our souls opened for the
sacraments to enter in. If the Spirit be lacking, the sacraments can
accomplish nothing more in our minds than the splendor of the sun
shining upon blind eyes, or a voice sounding in deaf ears."[15] Third,
the individual must exercise faith to make the sacraments effective.
This is a result of God's grace, since "sacraments are truly named
the testimonies of God's grace and are like seals of the good will that
he feels toward us, which by attesting that good will to us, sustain,
nourish, confirm, and increase our faith."[16] Faith on the person's
part is absolutely essential, since both preaching and the sacraments
offer to the individual mercy and the pledge of God's grace. Yet they
are "understood only by those who take Word and sacraments *with
sure faith*, just as Christ is offered and held forth by the Father to

contemplate the riches of God's grace, which he lavishes upon us" (*Institutes* 4.14.6). On "signs"
and "seals" see E. Grislis, "Calvin's Doctrine of Baptism," *CH* 3 (1962): 223–24.

[12] See Wallace, *Calvin's Doctrine*, 135–36. Calvin quotes Augustine in this regard: "Let the
word be added to the element [of the sacrament] and it will become a sacrament." And in his
own words he asserts that "the sacrament requires preaching to beget faith" (*Institutes* 4.14.4).

[13] Calvin, *Institutes* 4.14.3; Niesel, *The Theology of Calvin*, 215.

[14] *Ex opere operato* (lit., "by the work performed") defines the Roman Catholic belief that the
sacraments are effective through the operation of the rite itself, conveying grace to the recipient
unless he or she "places a spiritual impediment (*obex*) in the way of grace." See R. A. Muller,
*Dictionary of Latin and Greek Theological Terms: Drawn Principally from Protestant Scholastic
Theology* (Grand Rapids: Baker, 1985), 108.

[15] Calvin, *Institutes* 4.14.9.

[16] Ibid., 4.14.7.

all unto salvation, yet not all acknowledge and receive him."[17] The sacraments are mere ceremonies without preaching, the Spirit, and faith. Again, we note Calvin's stress on the necessity of the individual's response to God's mercy expressed in the sacraments.

Marcel

Like Calvin, Marcel's definition of the sacraments highlights the importance of personal response and participation. As did Calvin, he begins by noting that the sacraments and the preaching of the word have the same content: Jesus Christ. "The content of the Word and of the sacraments is exactly the same," Marcel argues. "Word and sacraments contain, present, and offer the same Mediator, Jesus Christ, the same covenant of grace, the same benefits, the same communion with God, the same redemption."[18] Next he notes that a believer must put his trust in Jesus in order for the sacraments to be effective in his life. He thus asserts that the "respective contents [of the word and the sacraments] are appropriated *by the believer* in the same manner—*by faith*. Faith is the sole way in which the sinner can become a participant of the grace which is offered both in the Word and in the sacraments. Word and sacraments are identical as regards the mode and the organ of perception and reception: *faith alone*."[19] In another place Marcel drives home the point that "a sacrament received without faith confers nothing more than the Word heard without faith."[20] He echoes here Calvin's stress that one must exercise faith to receive the blessing of the sacraments.

Marcel proceeds to argue for the practice of paedobaptism, however, by stressing the objective efficacy of the sacraments. God makes the sacrament of baptism, like preaching, objectively efficacious even when it is not immediately received in faith. A person recollecting

---

[17] Ibid., 4.14.7 (emphasis mine).

[18] P. Marcel, *The Biblical Doctrine of Infant Baptism: Sacrament of the Covenant of Grace*, trans. P. E. Hughes (Cambridge: James Clarke & Co., 1953), 38.

[19] Ibid., 42 (emphasis his).

[20] Ibid., 49. Further: "In His Word and in His sacraments our heavenly Father offers His mercy, His good will, and His grace to us all. But this grace is only accepted by those who receive this Word and these sacraments with an assured faith" (p. 48). Citing Calvin, he notes that we must lift "our hearts and spirits up to Christ, who alone, through His Spirit, communicates these graces to us with the aid of external signs [i.e., the sacraments]" (p., 51).

his prior baptism and trusting in God's forgiveness offered through the sacraments warrants the prior baptism.[21] Just as we preach in the hope that the Word of God preached will later take root in the hearts of our listeners, so we should baptize infants hoping that faith will characterize them later in life. Thus Marcel writes, "The efficacy of the sacrament will only be perceived subjectively when the child, having believed the Word, will be able to relate himself to it by faith. The *remembrance* of the sacrament received will play a part of the greatest importance."[22] A time lag between the reception and the effect of the sacrament thus allows for paedobaptism, according to Marcel, due to God's decision to make it effective.

Evaluation

Calvin and Marcel define sacraments differently than they practice them in the church. They maintain that God graciously provides for his people and offers promises in the sacraments. These promises, on the one hand, are objective because they are made by the sovereign God. On the other hand, they note the subjective requirement that persons respond to the promises of God in the sacraments. Christians must put their trust in the God who graciously gives the sacraments to them in order to strengthen their weak faith and to reassure them of their union with Christ, for the Lord uses the tandem of preaching and the sacraments to assure them of his love. Such a theology of the sacraments is surely appropriate for believers as they receive the Eucharist or for believers who are baptized. Believers can "attest our piety toward" the Lord[23] at baptism; infants cannot. At baptism, believers can reflect on the love and care of God exhibited in the death of Christ on their behalf. But this same theology of the sacraments cannot easily be applied to infants who are baptized when they are unable to grasp Christ, to ascertain the truths of the gospel, or to exercise faith. Thus the paedobaptists' definition of the sacraments is more biblical than their practice.

[21] Ibid., 52.
[22] Ibid., 53 (emphasis his).
[23] Calvin, *Institutes* 4.14.1.

Their argument that one can look back on his baptism years later and be nourished spiritually by it and exercise faith in Christ certainly is plausible. One can reflect on a past experience and be edified by seeing the Lord's goodness in the incident and trusting in him anew. The question, though, is, Do the sacraments function this way in the NT? It seems not. Rather, the NT teaches that the sacraments are for those who have faith in Christ at the time of the sacrament (Acts 2:38–41; Col 2:11–12; 1 Cor 11:23–29).[24] Their argument also does not cohere (at least) with Calvin's doctrine of the Eucharist, which teaches that in the Supper the believer is raised with Christ to heaven to feed on him spiritually. Bread and wine are used because *as we eat* we are reminded of, and express, our dependence on Christ.[25] As the sacrament of the Eucharist is to nourish believers in the present, so it seems that the logical conclusion of the definition of the sacrament is to see the nourishment of baptism to occur in the present, when the individual is baptized. Therefore, the waters of baptism should be reserved for those who, in the present, put their trust in Jesus. Reformed paedobaptists appear to be caught in a quandary regarding the baptism of infants who never trust in Christ. Certainly subjectively these persons are culpable for failing to trust the promises of God in the gospel. But what has become of God's objective promise in the sacrament? A more consistent practice (and the one taught in the NT) is to reserve the sacraments for those God has saved (the objective side) who can attest their love for him when they receive the sacrament (the subjective side).

Definition of Baptism

Calvin, Murray, and Marcel are biblical in their definition and discussion of the significance of baptism, the ordinance we are considering here. Baptism, they say, is a sign of a person's regeneration and union with Christ, and it presupposes that the person baptized has exercised faith in Christ. Their interpretation of baptism—fu-

---

[24] See Robert Stein's chapter in this volume.

[25] See Calvin, *Institutes*, 4.17.1–5, 8–10, 18–19, 31–34, 38–39, 42; Wendel, *Calvin*, 334–55; and K. A. Mathison, *Given for You: Reclaiming Calvin's Doctrine of the Lord's Supper* (Phillipsburg, NJ: P&R, 2002), 3–48.

eled by a great deal of NT material—is commendable. This contrasts starkly with their paedobaptism, for their definition contradicts their practice of baptizing infants who are neither regenerate nor have exercised faith in Jesus.[26] Their definition of baptism is biblical; their practice of paedobaptism is not.

Calvin

Calvin defines *baptism* as "the sign of initiation by which we are received into the society of the church, in order that, engrafted in Christ, we may be reckoned among God's children." Fundamentally, then, it brings one into the membership of the church. But it does more than simply transport one into a mixed body of the visible church. It also marks one out as being united with Christ; that is, it identifies one as being a Christian. So baptism, in its nature as a sacrament, functions to give us confidence of our standing before God.[27] Additionally, Calvin notes that "baptism serves as our confession before men. Indeed, it is the mark by which we publicly profess that we wish to be reckoned God's people; by which we testify that we agree in worshiping the same God, in one religion with all Christians; by which finally we openly affirm our faith."[28] Indeed, according to Calvin, the exercise and confirmation of faith is one of the major purposes of baptism. Thus he says, "From this sacrament, as from all others, we obtain only as much as we receive in faith. If we lack faith, this will be evidence of our ungratefulness, which renders us chargeable before God, because we have not believed the promise given there."[29] Faith is central to receiving the blessing of baptism.

The exercise of a person's faith is obviously a subjective act. But that is not the only import of baptism, according to Calvin. Baptism also has three objective components, objective in the sense that they signify what God does to the one baptized. First, baptism is a to-

---

[26] Note the similar point in P. K. Jewett, *Infant Baptism and the Covenant of Grace* (Grand Rapids: Eerdmans, 1978), 140–41.

[27] Calvin, *Institutes* 4.15.1.

[28] Ibid., 4.15.13. Later Calvin notes that baptism "is given for the arousing, nourishing, and confirming of our faith" (4.15.14).

[29] Ibid., 4.15.15.

ken and proof of a Christian's cleansing.[30] Second, it is a token of a believer's mortification and renewal in Christ.[31] Third, baptism is a token of a disciple's union with Christ, as Calvin argues based on the symbolism of baptism:

> Our faith receives from baptism the advantage of its sure testimony to us that we are not only engrafted into the death and life of Christ, but so united to Christ himself that we become sharers in all his blessings. For he dedicated and sanctified baptism in his own body in order that he might have it in common with us as the firmest bond of the union and fellowship which he has deigned to form with us.[32]

Objectively, then, baptism marks the one baptized as being united with Christ.

Murray

Murray echoes Calvin's biblical definition of baptism, highlighting that baptism signifies the closest union possible between a person and Christ. He notes that "Baptism is an ordinance instituted by Christ and is the sign and seal of union with him. This is just saying that it is the sign and seal of membership in that body of which Christ is the Head."[33] There are two "import[s] of baptism"—union with Christ and purification from sin.[34] Union with Christ is the first and primary notion of baptism.[35] He argues that

> baptism signifies union with Christ in his death, burial, and resurrection. It is because believers are united to Christ in the efficacy of his death, in the

[30] Ibid., 4.15.1–4.

[31] Ibid., 4.15.5.

[32] Ibid., 4.15.6.

[33] J. Murray, *Christian Baptism* (1952; reprint, Phillipsburg, NJ: P&R, 1980), 31.

[34] Murray disagrees with some other Reformed thinkers who attempted to skirt such a definition of baptism by arguing that there are different meanings of baptism, one for adults and another for infants. These theologians (Murray cites nineteenth-century Scottish thinkers William Cunningham and James Buchanan) believed that although infants should be baptized, the fundamental meaning of baptism was different for adults than for infants. But Murray disagrees. The meaning of baptism, he says, is the same for both. It represents fundamentally union with Christ and secondarily the purification from sins. Murray's recourse at this point is to the unity of God's covenantal working throughout Scripture. See *Christian Baptism*, 85.

[35] "The emphasis must be placed," he says, "upon union with Christ. It is this that is central, and it is this notion that appears more explicitly and pervasively than any other. Hence our view of baptism must be governed by this concept" (ibid., 5). Union with Christ for Murray, as for Calvin, was "the central truth of the whole doctrine of salvation" (J. Murray, *Redemption Accomplished and Applied* [Grand Rapids: Eerdmans, 1955], 170).

power of his resurrection, and in the fellowship of his grace that they are
one body. They are united to Christ and therefore to one another. Of this
union baptism is the sign and seal. The relationship which baptism signifies is therefore that of union, and union with Christ is its basic and central
import.[36]

Second, baptism symbolizes the purification of sins.[37] According to
Murray, then, union with Christ and the cleansing of sins are the
fundamental meanings of baptism.

Marcel

Marcel similarly defines baptism biblically. He says that "baptism
is the established means whereby a man declares publicly that he is
a Christian. It is the mark of his Christian profession before men; it
assures to him the privileges of membership in the visible Church
and, if he is sincere and faithful, it is the pledge given by God that
he will participate in all the blessings of redemption."[38] Baptism signifies three things. It is, first of all, "the sign and the seal of the
remission of sins and, consequently, of our justification."[39] It also
acts as "the sign and the seal of regeneration, of the death of the old
man and of the resurrection of the new man, through communion
in the death and resurrection of Christ."[40] Finally, baptism "is the
sign and the seal of the believer's communion not only with Christ
Himself, but also with the Church which is His body."[41] According
to Marcel, then, baptism signifies a completed fact about the person
baptized; he or she has been redeemed. As he argues, "Baptism is the
sign and the seal that we are 'set apart,' 'saved from the midst of this
corrupt generation.'"[42] For Marcel, baptism represents an objective,
completed fact.

---

[36] Murray, *Christian Baptism*, 3. In his exposition of Romans 6:3–4, Murray echoes this
biblical definition of baptism. See J. Murray, *The Epistle to the Romans*, NICNT (Grand Rapids:
Eerdmans, 1968), 1:214–16.

[37] Murray, *Christian Baptism*, 4–5.

[38] Marcel, *The Biblical Doctrine of Infant Baptism*, 178–79.

[39] Ibid.

[40] Ibid., 144.

[41] Ibid., 148.

[42] Ibid., 149.

Evaluation

To baptize infants, Reformed paedobaptists are inconsistent with their own definition of baptism. With little variation Calvin, Murray, and Marcel define baptism as cleansing, mortification, and union with Christ. Significantly, they each appeal to the necessary response of faith on the part of the one baptized. Therefore, baptism, according to their careful NT exegesis, represents an individual's commitment to Christ.[43] Each of them goes on to argue, however, for the baptism of infants who have not exercised faith and therefore have not been cleansed of sin, have not mortified (or are not in the process of mortifying) the flesh, and are not united to Christ.

For example, how does Calvin stress baptism's role in uniting a believer with Christ and still advocate the baptism of infants, who lack faith and therefore are not united to Christ? François Wendel rightly notes that "Calvin seems to be making union with Christ dependent upon reception of baptism, whereas almost everywhere else he says that this union is given at the same time as faith, and independently of the sacrament, which, on the contrary, presupposes the existence of faith and therefore of union with Christ."[44] Calvin movingly, and rightly, stresses that the individual must exercise faith in God's promises to receive a benefit at baptism. The exception to this is Calvin's defense of paedobaptism. Karl Barth perceptively challenged Calvin's doctrine at this point, noting that the practice of infant baptism is irreconcilable with Calvin's own definition of baptism:

> According to Calvin's own and in itself excellent baptismal teaching, baptism consists not only in our receiving the symbol of grace, but it is at the same time, in our *consentire cum omnibus christianis*, in our public *affirmare* of our faith, in our *iurare* in God's name, also the expression of a human *velle*. This without doubt it must be, in virtue of the cognitive character of the sacramental power. But then, in that case, baptism can be no kind of infant-baptism. How strange that Calvin seems to have forgotten this in his

[43] D. F. Wright perceptively notes that Calvin's discussion of baptism in 4.15 of the *Institutes* "defines baptism in such terms that it might almost have been written of believers' baptism only" ("Children, Covenant and the Church," *Them* 29/2 [2004]: 33). He goes on to show the huge problem in relating Calvin's definition of baptism in 4.15 with his practice of infant baptism in 4.16 (pp. 35–36).

[44] Wendel, *Calvin*, 321.

next chapter where he sets out his defence of infant-baptism, there commending a baptism which is without decision and confession![45]

In sum, Reformed paedobaptists define baptism as a rite for believers. They here echo the NT, which teaches that believers should express faith *at* their baptism, not when they look back on it years later.[46] Reformed paedobaptists' definition of baptism is better than their practice of baptizing infants.

The "Mixed" Character of the Church

One's doctrine of baptism affects one's view of the church. In this regard, J. I. Packer rightly notes that "the ongoing debate [between paedo- and credobaptists] is not about nurture but about God's way of defining the church."[47] We should note at the outset that evangelical paedobaptists and Baptists agree on a great deal about the church. For example, both agree that the membership of the church on earth (the visible church) is not coextensive with the membership of God's elect (the invisible church).[48] This is an important point to make, for it shows that for both paedobaptists and Baptists membership in a local church does not necessarily equal salvation. Some members may not actually be Christians. But how to deal with this less than ideal situation constitutes a major difference between the two groups. Evangelical paedobaptists note that the church will inevitably include unregenerate persons, and they proceed to receive into membership baptized infants who are unregenerate. Baptists

[45] K. Barth, *The Teaching of the Church Regarding Baptism*, trans. E. A. Payne (London: SCM Press, 1948), 48.

[46] Later Reformed confessions reflect this tension, defining baptism as taking place subsequent to faith but still advocating the baptism of infants. See T. George, "The Reformed Doctrine of Believers' Baptism," *Int* 47 (1993): 247. G. W. Bromiley notes differences in expression but is more sympathetic in his evaluation. See his "Baptism in the Reformed Confessions and Catechisms," in *Baptism, the New Testament and the Church*, ed. S. E. Porter and A. R. Cross, JSNTSup 171 (Sheffield: Sheffield Academic Press, 1999), 402–18. Also see Murray's discussion of the centrality of faith in salvation in *Redemption Accomplished and Applied*, 106–13.

[47] J. I. Packer, *Concise Theology: A Guide to Historic Christian Beliefs* (Wheaton: Tyndale House, 1993), 216. Compare B. B. Warfield's statement: "According as is our doctrine of the Church, so will be our doctrine of the Subjects of Baptism" ("The Polemics of Infant Baptism," in *Studies in Theology* [1932; reprint, Grand Rapids: Baker, 2000], 389).

[48] See, for example, J. L. Reynolds, *Church Polity or the Kingdom of Christ*, in *Polity: Biblical Arguments on How to Conduct Church Life*, ed. M. E. Dever (Washington, D. C.: Center for Church Reform, 2001), 311–23.

believe that the church should have as members only those who are regenerate. They argue that the church is a body of Christians who have been baptized as believers and have committed themselves to follow Jesus in communion with one another.[49] They will not intentionally receive unbelievers into the church's membership. When they recognize that a church member is not actually a believer in Christ, they will discipline that person in order to keep the church pure. The difference comes down to one of intentionality: should not the church do what it can to keep from admitting unbelievers as members? Infant baptism appears rather to do just the opposite.

The view of the church held by Reformed paedobaptists differs from that of Baptists. The defense of infant baptism leads the former to defend the mixed character of the church, a fellowship composed of both regenerate and unregenerate persons.[50] In this they are inconsistent with their prior commitment to the purity of the church. Baptists, however, note that the NT clearly speaks of the church as a holy people, a regenerate community of followers of the Lord Jesus Christ. Following this, they will baptize and admit to membership only those who are committed to following Jesus. One's view of baptism has definite ramifications for one's view of the church. In this section we will note Calvin's, Murray's, and Marcel's concession that the church will inevitably be a mixed body.

Calvin

Related to Calvin's doctrine of paedobaptism is his assumption that the visible church is composed of members who are both believers and unbelievers, although one must be a member of it for salvation.[51] On the other hand, the invisible church consists of those

---

[49] "The members of these churches are saints by calling, visibly manifesting and evidencing (in and by their profession and walking) their obedience unto that call of Christ; and do willingly consent to walk together, according to the appointment of Christ; giving up themselves to the Lord, and one to another, by the will of God, in professed subjection to the ordinances of the Gospel" (*Second London Confession*, 26.6, in W. L. Lumpkin, *Baptist Confessions of Faith* [Valley Forge, PA: Judson, 1969], 286).

[50] This is a standard paedobaptist argument. See, for example, G. Strawbridge, "The Polemics of Anabaptism from the Reformation Onward," in *The Case for Covenantal Infant Baptism*, ed. G. Strawbridge (Phillipsburg, NJ: P&R, 2003), 280–84.

[51] He says, "There is no other way to enter into life unless this mother [the church] conceive

who have been elected by God the Father and joined in union with Christ. Thus we must be a part of the invisible church in order to be saved.[52]

Baptism is essential, according to Calvin, because it "initiates" one into faith in Christ, thus bringing one into the communion of the saints in the church. This baptism is not a sure sign of salvation, however, since the fellowship one is initiated into, that is, the visible church, consists of both believers and unbelievers: "By baptism we are initiated into faith in [Christ]; by partaking of the Lord's Supper we attest our unity in true doctrine and love; in the Word of the Lord we have agreement, and for the preaching of the Word the ministry instituted by Christ is preserved. In this church are mingled many hypocrites who have nothing of Christ but the name and outward appearance."[53] One must be in the church because in it is the forgiveness of sins, and one is initially forgiven of sins through the cleansing of baptism. Thus he says, "We are initiated into the society of the church by the sign of baptism, which teaches us that entrance into God's family is not open to us unless we first are cleansed of our filth by his goodness."[54] Finally Calvin argues that as God had true believers even in the midst of primarily unfaithful Israel, so he has some elect people in the Catholic fold. Baptism is the sign indicating that the Lord has not abandoned his people in the Catholic church. Speaking of Israel, he says that "the Lord's covenant abode there. Their treachery could not obliterate his faithfulness, and circumcision could not be so profaned by their unclean hands as to cease to be the true sign and sacrament of his covenant." And even among the Catholic Church God "maintained baptism there, a witness to this covenant; consecrated by his own

---

us in her womb, give us birth, nourish us at her breast, and lastly, unless she keep us under her cares and guidance until, putting off mortal flesh, we become like angels. Our weakness does not allow us to be dismissed from her school until we have been pupils all our lives" (Calvin, *Institutes* 4.1.4).

[52] Ibid., 4.1.3.

[53] Ibid., 4.1.7. Calvin considered a pure church on earth a fiction, drawing on the thought of Cyprian (*Institutes* 4.1.19). His notion that the church consists of both "wheat and tares" (Matt 13:24–30,36–43) is thus in line with historic Catholic ecclesiology.

[54] Calvin, *Institutes* 4.1.20.

mouth, it retains its force despite the impiety of men."[55] So baptism is prominent in Calvin's mind for marking the true people of God even among a church that has many hypocrites.

Murray

John Murray also defines the church as a mixed body.[56] Murray says many things that credobaptists (i.e., those who insist that belief and confession of faith must precede baptism) can agree with. After pointing out that union with Christ is the hallmark of those who are part of the church,[57] he notes that no human can perfectly discern who the members of the church are.[58] He argues that the NT mostly speaks of the visible, not the invisible church, since union with Christ—*the* mark of being a Christian—should lead to an observable communion with other believers in the church.[59] Finally, he notes that the one condition of membership in the church according to the NT is "faith in Christ," requiring a credible profession of one's faith to gain entrance.[60] The church's leaders and the church as a whole need to be certain (as much as they are able) that the one who is accepted into the membership of the church is making a credible profession.[61]

[55] Ibid., 4.2.11.

[56] A helpful survey of Murray's argument for infant baptism, along with a critique, is found in F. Malone, *The Baptism of Disciples Alone: A Covenantal Argument for Credobaptism Versus Paedobaptism* (Cape Coral, FL: Founders Press, 2003), 3–22.

[57] The church, he says, comprises "those who are sanctified and cleansed by the washing of water by the Word, the company of the regenerate, the communion of the saints, the congregation of the faithful, those called effectually into the fellowship of Christ" (*Christian Baptism*, 31). Note the inconsistency of Murray's position. He here defines the church as a "company of the regenerate," but later he will commend the entrance of unregenerate persons into the church. Infant baptism leads him to this view.

[58] His biblical support for this point is John 8:31 (there were some following Jesus who were not truly his disciples) and John 15 (there are some externally united with Christ who are not really members of the vine). See Murray, *Christian* Baptism, 32.

[59] Murray, *Christian Baptism*, 33–34. In another place, Murray says, "The church is the company or society or assembly or congregation or communion of the faithful" (p. 33).

[60] In making this assertion, he cites Acts 2:38–42; 8:13,35–38; 10:34–38; 16:14–15,31–33 (*Christian Baptism*, 35). Murray's words could be echoed by many credobaptists: "It is by divine institution that the church, as a visible entity administered by men in accordance with Christ's appointment, must admit to its fellowship those who make a credible profession of faith in Christ and promise of obedience to him" (p. 36).

[61] Ibid., 38–39. Murray does not attempt to eliminate the inconsistency in his thinking between this assertion and his argument that I will examine next.

At the same time, however, Murray concedes that the church will be a mixed body composed of both unbelievers and believers. Some unregenerate persons will inevitably be admitted into the membership of the church because some will make a credible profession "who do not have true faith."[62] Thus we have the "anomaly" (as Murray labels it) of non-Christians in a church body that is supposed to be made up of Christians alone. Yet this situation is unavoidable: "This is an anomaly which must be fully appreciated and we must not make attempts to eliminate it."[63] Murray is left with a tension-filled definition of the church, since the congregation should be composed of believers alone[64] but will inevitably contain hypocritical unbelievers as well.[65] As a justification for this mixed composition, Murray, like Calvin, turns to God's people in the OT as the pattern for the NT church.[66] The parallel between Israel and the church is supported by Murray's conception of the covenant of grace: "It is this basic and underlying unity of the covenant of grace and of promise that establishes the generic unity and continu-

[62] Ibid., 36. He cites Acts 8:13,20–23 as proof.

[63] Ibid., 36–37. Later Murray refers to the same key text that Augustine and Calvin used to justify regarding the church as a mixed community, Matt 13:24–30,36–40. Referencing "the parables of the tares and the wheat and of the drag net," he notes that "there is a mixture in the kingdom, and Christ will at the end gather out of his kingdom all things that offend and them which do iniquity." Significantly, at one point Murray cites Calvin approvingly to make the point that "those who are not Christ's gain admission" into the church (p. 42, citing *Institutes* 4.1.7–8).

[64] Murray, *Christian Baptism*, 39. Credobaptists would agree with Murray's use of the salutations of Paul's epistles as proof that the church is made up of "those sanctified in Christ Jesus and called to be saints, and [Paul] does not conceive of the church in broader terms so as to distinguish between the church and those sanctified and called" (p. 40). His discussion includes Rom 1:7; 1 Cor 1:1–2; 2 Cor 1:1; Eph 1:1; Phil 1:1; Col 1:2; 1 Thess 1:1; and 2 Thess 1:1.

[65] He notes that "hypocrites may secure admission to the church. . . . There are disciples who are not truly disciples, and there are branches in the vine which are not vitally and abidingly in the vine. But while we fully recognise this fact we must at the same time distinguish between the constitutive principle in terms of which the church is defined, on the one hand, and the *de facto* situation arising from the way in which Christ has chosen to administer the affairs of his church in the world, on the other" (ibid., 41). But, he adds, "we may not revise the definition [of the church] in order to relieve the tension" (p. 42).

[66] Ibid., 43–44. He asserts (p. 43) that "full allowance must be made for the new form of structure and administration established by the death, resurrection, and ascension of Christ and the outpouring of the Holy Spirit at Pentecost. Nevertheless the distinction does not warrant the denial of the existence of the church under the Old Testament, nor of the generic unity and continuity of the church in both dispensations. . . . The church as it exists in the respective dispensations is not two organisms. It is likened to one tree with many branches, all of which grow from one root and stock and form one organic life (Rom. 11:16–21)."

ity of the church. In terms of covenant union and communion the church is but the covenant people of God in all ages and among all nations."[67] For Murray the church, as such, will inevitably contain both regenerate and unregenerate members.

Marcel

Pierre Marcel similarly argues that the people of God are fundamentally the same throughout biblical history due to covenantal continuity:[68]

> Since the covenant is the same in both Old and New Testaments, and the sacraments have the same fundamental significance, another conclusion urges itself upon us where the objective elements of the covenant are concerned, namely, that through the course of history *the Church has been and remains one: the nation of Israel was the Church; the Christian Church, since it also comes under the covenant of grace, is the same Church.*[69]

More succinctly, he asserts: "*No authentic definition of the Church can exclude the Church of the people of God in the Old Testament.*"[70] To Marcel, then, there is continuity in the make up of God's people throughout Scripture.

From this assertion Marcel draws two conclusions. First, he argues that the sacraments of the two covenants are essentially the same, as we shall see below. Second, Marcel argues that the church—that is, the people of God in both the OT and the NT—includes in its midst both believers and those who are hypocrites and will only be shown to be unbelievers on judgment day. The Lord alone knows those who are truly his, and the church has no warrant for attempting to make the church of the NT purer than the people of God were under the old covenant. Thus, he argues that "in the covenant . . . there are the called and the elect."[71] What was true of the old covenant is

---

[67] Ibid., 44.

[68] Malone reviews and critiques Marcel in *The Baptism of Disciples Alone*, 245–51.

[69] Marcel, *The Biblical Doctrine of Infant Baptism*, 95 (emphasis his).

[70] Ibid., 95 (emphasis his).

[71] Ibid., 116. Marcel's statement is based on his exegesis of John 1:12f. where he argues that "his own" is a reference to those within the covenant but that not all of them received Christ (p. 115).

also true of the new: "The visible Church is not and never has been composed of only converted and regenerate people."[72] Only for the grossest heresy or misbehavior, he says, does the church have the right to discipline church members.[73] Beyond that, the NT forbids us from judging men's hearts, for Christ "never committed to [the church] the task of separating the tares from the wheat. Judgment belongs to God."[74] There will be unregenerate church members, and the church can do little about it.

Since it is certain there will—and indeed must[75]—be unregenerate members of the church, receiving believers' infants into church membership through baptism is warranted.[76] The church must follow the NT's injunction to exercise "the judgment of charity" as well as the apostolic church's example of welcoming "with large-hearted charity and without suspecting their good faith those who desired baptism."[77] For Marcel, it is axiomatic that the church will be a mixed community.

Evaluation

Paedobaptists' presupposition that the NT church, like OT Israel, must inevitably contain both regenerate and unregenerate members is foundational to their apology for infant baptism. Each of those we surveyed argues for it at length. A church composed inevitably of both believers and unbelievers allows for the practice of infant baptism, which knowingly introduces unbelievers into the church's membership.[78] This is not only an instance of their importing an OT

---

[72] Ibid., 124.

[73] Ibid., 127. This is validated by the fact, he argues, that the church is composed not of "regenerate" persons but of "disciples," some of whom are unregenerate (p. 127).

[74] Ibid., 126. Once again, note the reference to the parable of the wheat and the tares in Matt 13:24–30,36–43. In another place, Marcel notes that the quest for a regenerate church membership is "contrary to the laws of the administration of the covenant, and . . . impracticable" (p. 184).

[75] Ibid., 231–32.

[76] Ibid., 129.

[77] Ibid., 185.

[78] Jewett rightly counters this notion, arguing that the new covenant community is only composed of the elect (*Infant Baptism*, 221–23). The Reformed paedobaptist response is typically that the NT (e.g., Heb 10:29) shows that there is such a thing as a "covenant breaker" in the new covenant, which demonstrates that the Baptist conception of the church is too idealized to fit reality. See, e.g., A. A. Hoekema, "Review of *Infant Baptism and the Covenant of Grace* by

construct into the NT with no warrant, however, but also involves a wrong understanding of the NT itself.

John Murray's exposition is a good example of the paedobaptist inconsistency. He argues with a great deal of NT support that the "constitutive principle" of the church means that it is made up of believers. He admits that defining the church as a mixed body results in tremendous problems for local churches. A church is faced with baptized members who are not believers. Murray calls them "confederate members," and he urges churches to take hold of their responsibility to discipline such "members" who do not live godly lives. Thus he comments:

> If the church is vigilant and faithful, confederate members will be constantly under the instruction of the church and, ordinarily, long before they have children of their own, will be confronted with their covenant responsibilities and privileges. They will be advised that the necessary implicate of the covenant relation, sealed by their baptism in infancy, is the open avowal and embrace of that covenant and the public confession of Christ as their only Saviour and Lord. . . . If, therefore, confederate members are not ready or willing to embrace the covenant of grace sealed by baptism and not willing to make the confession incident to it, then they are liable to discipline and, obviously, they are not in a fit state to receive baptism for their children.[79]

So Murray urges churches to require that members live according to the gospel. Such persons who exhibit godly lives are allowed to become "communicant members," namely, those who are permitted to receive the Eucharist.[80]

P. K. Jewett," *CTJ* 14 (1979): 102, and Strawbridge, "Polemics of Anabaptism," 280–84. Baptists respond that there are certainly those who *appear* to be believers who fall away from the faith; but their very leaving the fellowship of the church shows that they were never truly part of the church. They broke the new covenant because they were never truly part of it. On this see D. A. Carson, "Reflections on Assurance," in *Still Sovereign: Contemporary Perspectives on Election, Foreknowledge, and Grace*, ed. T. R. Schreiner and B. A. Ware (Grand Rapids: Baker, 2000), 260–69, and T. R. Schreiner and A. B. Caneday, *The Race Set before Us* (Downers Grove: InterVarsity, 2001).

[79] Murray, *Christian Baptism*, 79. He is here inconsistent with his prior admission of the inevitability, i.e., the "anomaly," of having unregenerate members in the church (*Christian Baptism*, 36–37).

[80] Murray, *Christian Baptism*, 78–79.

However, the NT never speaks in the categories of "communicant" and "confederate" members.[81] Rather, the NT everywhere assumes that those who are members of a local fellowship are believers. It is certainly the case that God's people in the old covenant included both "Jacobs and Esaus," that is, both believers and unbelievers. But the longing of the OT (e.g., Jer 31:31–34; Ezek 36:25–27), as well as the common assumption of the NT, is that when the new covenant became a reality God's people would be composed of those who are regenerate, that is, who have been born again by the Holy Spirit. Everywhere the NT addresses churches as those composed of "saints," who not only are regarded by the apostles as "holy" but who have had certain objective things done for them because of God's grace. For example, in Ephesians Paul argues that they have been elected by the Father, redeemed by the Son, and sealed by the Spirit (Eph 1:3–14). These things are true of all the saints, of all those in the fellowship. Others are not part of the church.[82]

The paedobaptist appeal to Jesus' use of the wheat and tares is poor exegesis, for the Lord says explicitly that "the world," not the church, is composed of these mixed elements (Matt 13:38).[83] This is no justification for a mixed church membership. Rather, when it becomes clear that some baptized members of the church are in fact unregenerate, the church must be diligent to discipline them and treat them as unbelievers (e.g., Matt 18:15–20; 1 Cor 5:1–5). Paedobaptism leads to pastoral problems in the local church because it admits to membership those who are definitely not "saints." The

[81] Not only is this an unbiblical concept, but it also results in practical problems at the level of the local church. We see this, for example, in the Presbyterian Church in America. Their *Book of Church Order* says, on the one hand, that the children of believing parents are "through the covenant and by right of birth, non-communing members of the church. Hence they are entitled to Baptism, and to the pastoral oversight, instruction and government of the church, with a view to their embracing Christ and thus possessing personally all benefits of the covenant" (6.1). On the other hand, it argues that the church "should encourage [baptized children], on coming to years of discretion, to make confession of the Lord Jesus Christ and to enter upon all privileges of full church membership" (28.3; *The Book of Church Order of the Presbyterian Church in America*, 6th ed., 2003, available at http://www.pcanet.org/BCO/index.htm). The NT does not speak in the categories of "non-communing members" who need to confess Christ and become "full church members."

[82] See Stephen Wellum's chapter in this volume.

[83] See D. A. Carson, "Matthew," in *EBC*, ed. F. E. Gaebelein (Grand Rapids: Zondervan, 1984), 8:325.

recourse to "communicant membership," which has no NT warrant, seems both fanciful and dangerous.[84] Credobaptists are correct in requiring credible evidence that a person is a believer before admitting him to baptism and to church membership.

Paedobaptists, however, do not agree. Murray, for example, excoriates credobaptists for attempting to play God when they judge people's hearts and discipline them. He does this in the context of noting the anomalous situation that exists in paedobaptist churches when they baptize those who are not the recipients of grace. Baptists face the same quandary, he says: "This anomaly does not concern infant baptism alone. . . . Antipaedobaptists must not think that they enjoy any immunity from this question, although they may sometimes naively consider that it is the exclusive problem of paedobaptists."[85] However, Murray does not acknowledge the tremendous difference between the practices of credo- and paedobaptists. Baptists, fallible as they are, are to examine the candidate for baptism to make sure the individual has a credible profession of faith. There is a principle in their system for determining one's relationship with the Lord before being baptized. There is no such check in a paedobaptist scheme.[86] Paedobaptist churches will *necessarily* admit unregenerate persons to the membership; credobaptists will only do so *accidentally*, and they can correct the fault by the exercise of church discipline.[87] So, although credobaptists may receive unbe-

---

[84] In another place Murray argues at length for restricting the Lord's Supper to "members" who are actually professing faith in Christ. See J. Murray, "Restricted Communion," in *Collected Writings of John Murray* (Carlisle, PA: Banner of Truth, 1977), 2:381–84. This pastorally wise paedobaptist practice, however, amounts to inventing an ordinance—confirmation—found nowhere in Scripture. Paedocommunionists are more consistent in their practice than is Murray. (on this point, see Jewett, *Infant Baptist*, 193–207). Credobaptists, though, are more consistent, and more biblical in their practice.

[85] Murray, *Christian Baptism*, 51. Warfield similarly argued: "The vice of this [Baptist] system, however, is that it attempts the impossible. No man can read the heart. As a consequence, it follows that no one, however rich his manifestation of Christian graces, is baptized on the basis of infallible knowledge of his relation to Christ. All baptism is inevitably administered on the basis not of knowledge but of presumption. And if we must baptize on presumption, the whole principle is yielded, and it would seem that we must baptize all whom we may fairly presume to be members of Christ's body" ("The Polemics of Infant Baptism," 390).

[86] For other unwarranted asides at Baptists see Murray, *Christian Baptism*, 52, 72.

[87] On this see R. A. Mohler Jr., "Church Discipline: The Missing Mark," in *The Compromised Church: The Present Evangelical Crisis*, ed. J. H. Armstrong (Wheaton: Crossway, 1998), 171–87.

lievers as members, they will not admit them to the church intentionally. Since they deny baptismal regeneration,[88] Reformed paedobaptists necessarily receive (at least some) unbelievers as members
via infant baptism. This is a tremendous difference from Baptists at
the level of the church.

The "Covenant of Grace": Foundation for Paedobaptism

The "covenant of grace" is the primary justification for the baptizing of infants offered by Reformed paedobaptists such as Calvin,
Murray, and Marcel. Under the umbrella of the covenant of grace,
the key elements are the unity of the people of God and the unity of
the purpose of the sacraments. The covenant of grace thus presupposes the intentional mixed character of the church we have already
reviewed. And it also explains the parallel that paedobaptists note
between circumcision and baptism, the key textual support being
Col 2:11–12. Since this is the major justification Reformed paedobaptists offer for their practice, we shall attempt to follow their logic
carefully.[89] We shall conclude, however, that the "covenant of grace"
is an illegitimate apology for infant baptism. Rightly emphasizing
God's gracious action in salvation, it fails to see the differences between the old and new covenants.[90]

Calvin

Calvin argues that the relationship between the covenants is the
"whole matter" of the discussion and clearly decides the baptismal

[88] Although see our discussion under the heading, "Salvation *sola fide*."

[89] For example, see the recent forthright admission of Mark Ross: "I would maintain that
the case [for paedobaptism] fundamentally rests on establishing two principal contentions: first,
that baptism and circumcision have essentially the same meaning; and second, that the covenant
community is similarly constituted in the Old and New Testaments (specifically, that children
are members of the covenant community in both)" (M. E. Ross, "Baptism and Circumcision as
Signs and Seals," in Strawbridge, *Case for Covenantal Infant Baptism*, 100). For an older, but just
as forthright, defense of the same point, see A. A. Hodge, *The Substance of Four Sermons on Infant
Baptism* (Fredericksburg, VA: n.p., 1857), 11–12.

[90] For a fuller critique along these lines, see Jewett, *Infant Baptism and the Covenant of Grace*,
75–137, and Stephen Wellum's chapter in this book.

issue in favor of the paedobaptistic position.[91] In his opinion covenantal continuity is the strongest biblical argument for paedobaptism. Infants in the OT were participants in the people of God and had received God's promise. Therefore, since "the covenant still remains firm and steadfast, it applies no less today to the children of Christians than under the Old Testament it pertained to the infants of the Jews." "This one reason," Calvin confidently concludes, "if no others were at hand, would be quite enough to refute all those who would speak in opposition. . . . since the Lord, without fixing the day, yet declares that he is pleased to receive infants into his covenant with a solemn rite, what more do we require?"[92] God's uniform way of receiving infants into his people across the covenants is thus Calvin's primary defense of the practice of paedobaptism.

Calvin defends paedobaptism because of the parallel he notes between circumcision in the OT and baptism in the NT.[93] The heart of Calvin's argument here is that the meaning of circumcision and baptism are the same in both covenants.[94] Baptism in the NT objectively represents cleansing from sin, mortification of the flesh, and union with Christ.[95] Circumcision in the OT served the same purpose: "A spiritual promise [was] given to the patriarchs in circumcision such as is given us in baptism, since it represented for them forgiveness of sins and mortification of flesh."[96] Although the visible ceremonies of

---

[91] Calvin, *Institutes*, 4.16.24. In the liturgy which Calvin wrote to be used in the Genevan churches for the baptism of infants, the covenantal argument was the central foundation of the practice. Once Calvin asserts this theological linchpin, the only biblical support he offers in support of the baptism of the baby is 1 Cor 7:14 and Matt 19:13–15. See *John Calvin: Writings on Pastoral Piety*, ed. and trans. E. A. McKee, *The Classics of Western Spirituality* (Mahwah, NJ: Paulist, 2001), 154–55.

[92] Calvin, *Institutes*, 4.16.5.

[93] Calvin's discussion here presupposes his view of the relationship between the OT and NT. On Calvin's "covenantal" views, see P. Helm, "Calvin and the Covenant: Unity and Continuity," *EQ* 55 (1983): 65–81; P. A. Lillback, *The Binding of God: Calvin's Role in the Development of Covenant Theology*, Texts and Studies in Reformation and Post-Reformation Thought (Grand Rapids: Baker, 2001); and Grislis, "Calvin's Doctrine of Baptism," 51. For a concise overview of Reformed covenantal thinking, see J. I. Packer, "On Covenant Theology," *The Collected Shorter Writings of J. I. Packer* (Carlisle: Paternoster, 1998), 1:9–22.

[94] For a spirited apology for Calvin's doctrine see P. A. Lillback, "Calvin's Covenantal Response to the Anabaptist View of Baptism," *Christianity and Civilization* 1 (1982): 185–232.

[95] See his comments to this effect in *Institutes* 4.16.2.

[96] Calvin arrives at this definition of the significance of circumcision in two ways. First, God's promise to Abraham in Genesis 17 shows that the point of circumcision was the forgive-

circumcision and baptism are distinct, they signify the same thing.[97] Thus Calvin argues:

> The promise . . . is the same in both, namely, that of God's fatherly favor, of forgiveness of sins, and of eternal life. Then the thing represented is the same, namely, regeneration. In both there is one foundation upon which the fulfillment of these things rests. Therefore, there is no difference in the inner mystery, by which the whole force and character of the sacraments are to be weighed. . . . We therefore conclude that, apart from the difference in the visible ceremony, whatever belongs to circumcision pertains likewise to baptism.[98]

Calvin employs two NT passages to justify the circumcision-baptism parallel. First, 1 Cor 7:14 teaches that "the children of Christians are considered holy." Therefore, in the same way that Abraham's children were considered "holy" under his covenant and were circumcised, so believers' children are holy and are to receive the sign of the covenant, infant baptism. Calvin concludes, "Seeing that the Lord, immediately after making the covenant with Abraham, commanded it to be sealed in infants by an outward sacrament, what excuse will Christians give for not testifying and sealing it in their children today" since "what was circumcision for them was replaced for us by baptism"?[99] Second, Col 2:11–12 answers his opponents' charge that the old covenant was primarily carnal with fleshly signs and fleshly promises.[100] This will not do, according to Calvin, because of the parallel that exists between the old and new covenants. Just as the promises associated with baptism are spiritual, so also were the promises associated with circumcision. If one denies the spiritual character of circumcision, one must also make baptism carnal. Thus in Colossians 2 Paul says:

> We were circumcised in Christ not by a circumcision made with hands, when we laid aside the body of sin which dwelt in our flesh. This he calls the "circumcision of Christ." Afterward, to explain this statement, he adds

---

ness of sins. Second, later commentary on circumcision in Deuteronomy 10 shows that "circumcision is the sign of mortification" (*Institutes* 4.16.3).

[97] Calvin's teaching here is founded on his earlier teaching of the relationship between the OT and NT. See *Institutes* 2.6.2–4; 2.10.

[98] Ibid., 4.16.4.

[99] Ibid., 4.16.4.

[100] Ibid., 4.16.10.

that in baptism we were "buried with Christ." What do these words mean, except that the fulfillment and truth of baptism are also the truth and fulfillment of circumcision, since they signify one and the same thing? For he is striving to demonstrate that baptism is for the Christians what circumcision previously was for the Jews.[101]

In Calvin's mind, then, the covenantal character of Scripture—along with its concomitant parallel between OT circumcision and NT baptism—warrants paedobaptism. It is the "whole matter" of the doctrine.

Murray

The covenant of grace is also Murray's primary defense of paedobaptism, as he points out several times. For instance, he notes at the beginning of his chapter, "Infant Baptism," that "the *basic premise* of the argument for infant baptism is that the New Testament economy is the unfolding and fulfilment of the covenant made with Abraham and that the necessary implication is the unity and continuity of the church."[102] Concluding this chapter, with reference to Acts 2:39 ("The promise is to you and to your children"), Murray says this covenantal working of God is the sole reason for baptizing infants:

It is precisely because there is such evidence of the perpetual operation of this gracious principle in the administration of God's covenant that we baptise infants. It is for that reason *alone* that we continue to baptise them. It is the divine institution, not, indeed, commended by human wisdom and not palatable to those who are influenced by the dictates of human wisdom, yet commended by the wisdom of God. It is the seal to us of His marvelous goodness that He is not only a God to His people but also to their seed after them.[103]

Murray sees this "divine institution," that is, God's command to baptize babies, expressed in God's covenant to Abraham, especially Gen 17:1–14, "the fullest account of the covenant made with Abraham,"[104] and in the corporate principle by which God works

---

[101] Ibid., 4.16.11.
[102] Murray, *Christian Baptism*, 45 (emphasis mine).
[103] Ibid., 68 (emphasis mine).
[104] Ibid., 46.

throughout redemptive history. The divine covenant in Genesis 17 is thus the ground of Murray's defense of infant baptism.

To Murray, as to Calvin, circumcision and baptism have parallel meanings. First, circumcision enabled one to have union with God.[105] Second, circumcision, the cutting off of a male's foreskin, was representative of cleansing from the defilement of sin. Third, circumcision was the seal of the righteousness that Abraham had because of his faith.[106] Thus, circumcision had deep spiritual significance: "Circumcision is the sign and seal of the covenant itself in its deepest and richest significance, and it is the sign of external privileges only as these are the fruits of the spiritual blessing which it signifies."[107] These three purposes of circumcision "indicate the deep soteric richness of the blessing that circumcision signifies and seals."[108] Since, therefore, circumcision is primarily spiritual and signifies fundamentally the same things as baptism, Murray concludes that just as all males of the old covenant community were circumcised so also all children of the church should be baptized.[109] The "divine institution" obliged Abraham to circumcise the male members of his household in the same way it obliges church members to have their children baptized.[110]

---

[105] Ibid., 46–47.

[106] Ibid., 47. Murray echoed Calvin's understanding of the "signs" and "seals" of the covenant. Additionally see Murray, *Romans*, 1:137–38.

[107] Murray, *Christian Baptism*, 47.

[108] Ibid., 48.

[109] Elsewhere Murray contends, "The most distinctive feature of covenant theology in connection with the sacraments is the inference drawn from the nature of the covenant in support of paedobaptism. The argument, reduced to its simplest terms, is that the seals of the covenant pertain to those to whom the covenant itself pertains. But that the covenant pertains to infants is clear from Genesis 17:7 and Acts 2:39. From God's ordinance his grace extends from parents to children. Since the things signified in baptism, namely, remission of sins, regeneration, and the kingdom of heaven, belong to infants, there is no reason why the sign should not also be added. . . . Of particular importance is the emphasis placed on the unity and continuity of the covenant. In covenant theology the argument for infant baptism falls into its place in the schematism which the organic unity and continuity of covenant revelation provided" ("Covenant Theology," in *Collected Writings of John Murray* (Carlisle, PA: Banner of Truth, 1982), 4:239–40.

[110] Murray, *Christian Baptism*, 48. He also argues that "the gospel dispensation is the unfolding of the covenant made with Abraham. . . . Abraham is the father of all the faithful. They who are of faith are blessed with faithful Abraham. . . . If children born of the faithful were given the sign and seal of the covenant and therefore of the richest blessing which the covenant disclosed, if the New Testament economy is the elaboration and extension of this covenant of which circumcision was the sign, are we to believe that infants in this age are excluded from that which

Marcel

The "covenant of grace" is essential to Marcel. He announces that "the doctrine of the covenant is the germ, the root, the pith of all revelation, and consequently of all theology; it is the clue to the whole history of redemption."[111] To Marcel the construct of the covenant of grace is primarily equated with God's will to save sinners. He notes, for example, "As revealed in time and in the course of history, this will of God to save man from ruin and to give him justification and life is given the name of the 'covenant of grace.'"[112] Three points encapsulate the importance of this salvific construct for Marcel. First, it is objective. Second, God works through the covenant of grace in families, not merely in individuals. Third, the covenant of grace is continuous throughout the Bible and is lived out consistently by God's people in both testaments. This third point is essential for Marcel's doctrine. By it he draws a parallel between the OT's practice of circumcision and the NT's rite of baptism. We will now examine these three points.

First, the covenant of grace is an objective fact. Marcel says this repeatedly. God is the actor in the covenant of grace; his grace is an objective given. The subjective responses of persons will vary and indeed may waver at times, but that does not deter from the fact that God will make his saving will take effect in persons. The Bible, he asserts,

> compels us to be most attentive on the one hand to the objectivity of the Word, of the promises and acts of God, and on the other hand to the realities of spiritual solidarity—realities which we experience *objectively*, realities which proclaim the revealed intentions of God—which never cease to throw into relief the unity of the family, of the nation of Israel, of the Church visible or invisible, and of the intimate communion which unites objectively those whom God calls, and not only those whom He elects, to the body of Christ.[113]

Marcel laments that many modern Christians have fallen prey to subjective, individualistic notions of faith. Certainly, subjective re-

was provided by the Abrahamic covenant?" No, for we must "remember that baptism, which is the sign of the covenant under the new economy as circumcision was under the old, bears essentially the same import as did circumcision" (*Christian Baptism*, 48–49).

[111] Marcel, *The Biblical Doctrine of Infant Baptism*, 72.

[112] Ibid., 66.

[113] Ibid., 23 (emphasis his).

sponses to God's grace may follow; but those are secondary.[114] The main characteristic of the covenant is its objective nature. The covenant of grace is "sovereignly objective."[115]

By labeling the covenant of grace "objective," Marcel stresses the sovereignty of God in salvation. But even more he stresses the sovereignty of God as the designer and initiator of the covenant. God acts first in the covenant and *then* sinners respond; it is never the other way around.[116] More than that, the sovereign, initiating God promises to do certain things in the covenant of grace for his people, and for their children: "The covenant contains *the promise* that God will be equally the God of the posterity of believers."[117] Thus children "born in the covenant" are heirs to the promises of the covenant.[118] This objective character of the covenant of grace, stressing as it does God's sovereignty and his promises, therefore becomes the bedrock of Marcel's apology. He argues that "since [the children of believers] participate in all the promises and all the spiritual realities signified and sealed in baptism, we say that they are fit to receive it; *there is no other reason for administering baptism to them.*"[119] The covenant of grace justifies infant baptism.

Second, Marcel stresses that in the covenant of grace God works not in individuals but through families. Children born into the covenant community receive understandable blessings such as hearing the gospel preached and receiving Christian nurture. More than that, though, as part of the covenant the children themselves should receive not only the blessings of the covenant but also the sign of being members of the community.[120] The Bible assumes the solidarity of the family throughout its pages. Not only do we see this in God's command to Abraham to circumcise his sons, but we see it as well in the NT, according to Marcel. Thus the widow's faith in Luke 7:11–17 demonstrates that "families were saved and attained faith

---

[114] Ibid., 212.
[115] Ibid., 191.
[116] Ibid., 101, 203–4.
[117] Ibid., 73 (emphasis his).
[118] Ibid., 107; see 209, 221–22.
[119] Ibid., 192 (emphasis his).
[120] Such children are "of" but not "in" the covenant because of their birth (ibid., 111).

through the faith of one of their members, generally the father, but also the mother when she is a widow."[121] The household baptisms in Acts equally show that "in God's eyes parents and their children are *one*."[122] This is of the utmost importance to Marcel. If God does not treat believers' families in solidarity, there is no justification for paedobaptism: "The legitimacy of infant baptism *depends entirely* on the question of the manner in which Scripture regards the children of believers and wishes us, consequently, to regard them."[123] So family solidarity in the covenant of grace justifies paedobaptism.

Third, the covenant of grace is continuous throughout the Bible. God has worked similarly—sovereignly, graciously, treating the children of his people as heirs of the promises of the covenant—throughout redemptive history. Beginning with God's dealings with Abraham, the Lord saves by the covenant he establishes with his people, and its benefits reach to their children. The promises are equally theirs. This promissory character of the covenant of grace began in Genesis 17, continued throughout the OT, and is in effect in the NT.[124] Although Marcel notes that there are differences in administrations of God's covenant with his people in different times, he is loath to see any differences between the Abrahamic and the new covenant.[125] In his view the "new" covenant is merely a right understanding of the old covenant. The new covenant is not "new" in the sense of being substantially different from the old; rather, fundamentally in the new covenant "we have a *new* attestation of the identity of the covenant in its accomplishment, of its newness in its permanence, and of its freedom in its trustworthiness."[126] This is an essential point for Marcel. Since there is no substantial difference between the old and new covenants, it logically follows that the sign and recipients of both covenants are substantially the same. Thus he argues that the problem the NT sees with the old covenant was the

---

[121] Ibid., 117.

[122] Ibid., 117 (emphasis his). He also appeals to 1 Cor 7:14, arguing that "children are not outside, they are *within* the circle of the elect people" (p. 120 [emphasis his]).

[123] Ibid., 189 (emphasis mine).

[124] Ibid., 67–72.

[125] Ibid., 75–76.

[126] Ibid., 77 (emphasis his).

Pharisees' abuse of the old covenant rather than anything intrinsic to that covenant. In other words, the problem "is not that of the covenant but in particular that of pre-Christian legalistic Judaism which misused the sign of circumcision. . . . The Apostle's criticisms are addressed to carnal Israel who have corrupted the spiritual covenant into a carnal covenant."[127] The covenant of grace is continuous throughout redemptive history.

The continuity of the covenant of grace implies a similar meaning of the sacraments throughout biblical history.[128] Circumcision in the old covenant is parallel in both meaning and application to baptism in the new. The sacraments indeed are what tie together the covenant of grace: "The sacraments—although differing in form—have essentially the same significance in the two dispensations, for the sacraments are always the signs and seals of the covenant of grace (Rom. 4.11; 1 Cor. 5.7; Col. 2.11f.). The covenant is to the sacraments what the palm of the hand is to the fingers."[129] God sovereignly and objectively works in the covenant of grace, and this is signified in the sacraments:

> All that we have today in our sacraments the Jews had formerly in theirs, namely, *Jesus Christ and His spiritual riches*. . . . [There is] a difference between the sacraments as regards outward appearance, but they are identical as regards their internal and spiritual significance. *The signs have changed, while faith does not change.*[130]

The parallel between the sacraments in the covenant of grace functions as the justification for paedobaptism since the purposes and significance of circumcision and baptism are parallel.[131] Circumcision had a spiritual, not just a physical, character, indicating that one had been cleansed from sin. Baptism has the same spiritual meaning as circumcision, thus showing the continuity of the covenant of grace throughout the testaments. For this reason Marcel notes that one of the keys to the debate between credo- and paedobaptists is

[127] Ibid., 75.
[128] Ibid., 86–94.
[129] Ibid., 79–80.
[130] Ibid., 90 (emphasis his).
[131] Marcel admits there are minor differences in the sacraments of the old and new covenants such as the OT's national character and its looking forward to the Messiah, but these are the only differences, and they are not substantial (ibid., 91–92).

the different value they place on circumcision. Credobaptists claim that physical circumcision was carnal, whereas paedobaptists label it spiritual.[132] Since circumcision had spiritual significance in the old covenant, and since baptism has spiritual significance, paedobaptism is proper in the new covenant. The covenant of grace warrants baptizing infants. As Israel was to circumcise male children within the community, so the church should baptize the children of its members.

Evaluation

Calvin, Murray, and Marcel wrongly interpret the covenantal character of Scripture, leading to their assumption of a parallel between circumcision and infant baptism.[133] God is gracious. Scripture is clear, from beginning to end, that God is sovereign in salvation, that he saves by grace, that he justly saves on account of the work of Christ for his people, and that the necessary role of his people is to trust him and humbly follow him in obedience. However, the Bible never calls God's salvific intention the "covenant of grace." Although we should not deny the validity of the phrase for this reason (lest we have to discard such biblically defensible terms as the "Trinity"), we must let Scripture define what we mean by such a label. The Lord has worked through various covenantal administrations throughout redemptive history. Specifically, the "new covenant" which Christ instituted (Luke 22:20) is different and "better" than the old covenant it was replacing (Heb 8:6–7,13). With Christ's death and resurrection a new age has dawned with tremendous ramifications for the identity of the people of God.

---

[132] Ibid., 94.

[133] B. B. Warfield argues similarly: "If the continuity of the Church through all ages can be made good, the warrant for infant baptism is not to be sought in the New Testament but in the Old Testament, when the Church was instituted, and nothing short of an actual forbidding of it in the New Testament would warrant our omitting it now" ("Polemics of Infant Baptism," 399–400). For a full rebuttal of the paedobaptistic covenantal argument from Baptists sympathetic with much of Reformed theology, in addition to chapters in this volume, see D. Kingdon, *Children of Abraham: A Reformed Baptist View of Baptism, the Covenant, and Children* (Haywards Heath, UK: Carey, 1973); Jewett, *Infant Baptism and the Covenant of Grace*; and Malone, *The Baptism of Disciples Alone*. Historically Baptists have been quick to show the inconsistencies of covenantal paedobaptists at this point. See Reynolds, *Church Polity*, 326–27.

By making Genesis 17 the primary justification for infant baptism, Calvin, Murray, and Marcel take three wrong steps. First, Gen 17:12–13 shows circumcision was not only to be given to male children but also to other male household members. The paedobaptists, though, are not faithful to the scope of the covenant, since they do not argue for a wider inclusion of those baptized. Second, each of them overspiritualizes circumcision. Circumcision was a physical marker of ethnic Israel identifying them as distinct from other nations. Yet the paedobaptists do not consider Paul's negative judgment of circumcision *per se* by comparison with the necessity of spiritual circumcision in Rom 2:25–29.[134] Third, they fail to see the significance of the Abrahamic covenant, as the NT reads it. The significance is that Abraham exercised *faith*, and *subsequently* he received the sign of circumcision. Thus Paul says, "Know then that it is those of *faith* who are the sons of Abraham" (Gal 3:7; see John 8:34–47). Similarly Rom 4:3,9–12 shows that faith, not circumcision, is primary to Paul. Reformed paedobaptists pay inadequate attention to the NT's interpretation of the "newness" and the "betterness" of the new covenant (Heb 8:6).

Reformed paedobaptists are convinced, however, that the parallel between the meaning of the sacraments across redemptive history is the one reason to continue the practice of paedobaptism. As we have seen, this leads Murray to note an "anomaly," the tension that we see when the sign of the covenant (either circumcision or baptism), which represents one's union with God, is given to those who are patently unregenerate. This anomaly appears in the circumcisions of Ishmael and Esau, whom God knew were not the children of the covenant (Gen 17:23).[135] Why should they receive the sign of the covenant with all its spiritual connotations? Murray's recourse is God's command to Abraham. This is the same ground as the practice of paedobaptism: "Divine institution governs its administration. That is the *ground*. And that is what constitutes for us the obligation to comply."[136] We reply, however, that there is no anomaly.

---

[134] See Murray, *Romans*, 1:85–90, and T. R. Schreiner, *Romans*, BECNT (Grand Rapids: Baker, 1998), 136–45.

[135] See Murray, *Christian Baptism*, 56.

[136] Ibid., 58 (his emphasis). In a previous discussion Murray states, "Baptised infants are to

Abraham received a divine command to circumcise his male heirs to mark them as physical Israelites. There is no such instruction in the NT, for it teaches instead that the sign of the covenant (baptism) is reserved for those who have trusted in Christ due to the work of the Spirit.[137]

Similarly, the Reformed paedobaptist argument for a parallel between circumcision and baptism is unconvincing. For example, Col 2:11–12 does not support paedobaptism. Paul is speaking here to believers (1:1–6,21–23) who are urged to follow Christ and not turn aside to false ways of thinking (2:6–8). Infants cannot fit this category of persons. Calvin, Murray, and Marcel do not elaborate on the nature of the relationship between the "circumcision of Christ" (2:11) and the circumcision of Genesis 17 and the Mosaic covenant. They assume continuity without demonstrating it. Yet their continuity thesis is opposed by Paul's insistence that the benefits of baptism are received "through faith" (2:12). In their use of Colossians 2 as support for baptizing infants, they do not even mention the necessity of faith. Colossians 2:11–12, then, refers to *spiritual*, not physical, circumcision, and hence the parallel between physical circumcision and Christian baptism fails.

God saves his people graciously throughout redemptive history, and he calls them to be members of his covenant community. But in the new covenant, members of God's people are believers in Jesus Christ, and only they should receive the sign of membership in the

be received as the children of God and treated accordingly" (p. 56). At this point he refers to the Westminster *Directory for the Public Worship of God*, which says, "That *children, by baptism, are solemnly received into the bosom of the visible church, distinguished from the world, and them that are without, and united with believers; and that all who are baptized in the name of Christ, do renounce, and by their baptism are bound to fight against the devil, the world, and the flesh*: That they are Christians, and federally holy before baptism, and therefore are they baptized" (p. 56, n. 31 [emphasis mine]). The actions that are claimed of those baptized fit naturally with Murray's (and the NT's) definition of the significance of baptism. Of course, infants cannot comply with the requirements; hence the incongruity of baptizing infants under such a definition of baptism.

[137] See D. C. Lane, "Was Circumcision the 'Seal' of the Abrahamic Covenant? With Implications for the Reformed Doctrine of Infant Baptism" (paper presented at Evangelical Theological Society, November 2004) and "Was Circumcision the 'Seal' of the Abrahamic Covenant? Part 2: How Covenant Theology Misunderstands and Misapplies Romans 4:11. With Implications for the Reformed Doctrine of Infant Baptism" (paper presented at Evangelical Theological Society, November 2005).

church. Yet Marcel states, "It is the covenant [of grace] that is the sole basis of [infant] baptism."[138] Since the construct of the "covenant of grace" fails to account for the movement of redemptive history and for the newness of the new covenant, the practice of infant baptism lacks warrant.

NT Justification for Paedobaptism

Although Calvin, Murray, and Marcel find their primary justification for infant baptism in the covenant of grace, they offer supplemental NT justification for paedobaptism to corroborate their argument. They are consistent in the NT passages to which they appeal. They are also consistently unconvincing in this NT appeal; for, as we shall see, the NT warrants credobaptism, not paedobaptism.

Calvin

Calvin appeals to 1 Cor 7:14 and Col 2:11–12 to prove covenantal continuity in baptism as we have seen already. Beyond that, he offers little NT support for infant baptism. His primary defense is Jesus' blessing of the children who came to him in Matt 19:14. Calvin notes, "But (someone will say) what does baptism have in common with Christ's embracing the children?" These opponents chide paedobaptists saying, "If we would follow [Christ's] example, let us help infants with prayers, but not baptize them." But Calvin asserts that Jesus concluded his welcoming of the children by explaining, "For of such is the Kingdom of Heaven." Baptism is not mentioned, but obtaining the kingdom of heaven is parallel to the purpose of baptism. "If the Kingdom of Heaven belongs to them, why is the sign denied which, so to speak, opens to them a door into the church, that, adopted into it, they may be enrolled among the heirs of the Kingdom of Heaven? How unjust of us to drive away those whom Christ calls to himself! To deprive those whom he adorns with gifts! To shut out those whom he willingly receives!" Lest one argue that the children had to be old enough to "come" to Christ, Calvin argues that the account in Luke 18:15 included "infants at the breast."

---

[138] Marcel, *The Biblical Doctrine of Infant Baptism*, 219.

So "come" means "have access to" Christ. Infants should have access to Christ in infant baptism.[139]

This is the bulk of the NT warrant offered. Because of covenantal continuity and Jesus' welcoming children, Calvin believes that paedobaptism rested on the "firm approbation of Scripture." Therefore, "infants cannot be deprived of [baptism] without open violation of the will of God."[140]

Murray

Although there is no NT command to baptize infants, Murray finds NT "Corroboratory Evidence."[141] Two important revelations come from this NT data. First, there is no repeal of the OT's inclusion of children in the covenant community, and, second, there is "positive evidence . . . that the same principle which gave meaning and validity to the circumcision of infants under the old economy is embedded and is operative in the administration of the covenant of grace under the new."[142] The positive evidence Murray sees is "the principle of representation, of solidarity, or corporate relationship" showing "that our Lord and his apostles taught and acted upon the recognition that the same principle which provided the basis of infant circumcision was to be applied to the administration of the kingdom of God and of the church."[143] The corporate nature of God's people, and of God's relationship to them, is paramount.

Murray appeals to five different NT passages supporting covenantal continuity. He first recalls Jesus' words in Matt 19:14 ("Suffer the little children and forbid them not to come unto me, for of such is the kingdom of heaven"), remarking that Jesus taught the king-

---

[139] Calvin, *Institutes* 4.16.7.

[140] Ibid., 4.16.8. At this point Calvin also introduces an argument that is part of the paedobaptist arsenal. As we allow women to take the Lord's Supper even without a clear scriptural example, so also we should allow infant baptism without an example. This is an invalid argument. Men and women may both be in Christ (Gal 3:28); both may be in the church. Therefore both men and women are among the church who are to receive the Eucharist (1 Cor 1:2; 11:17–34). One may not legitimately assume, though, that infants are members of the church without further proof.

[141] Murray, *Christian Baptism*, 58.

[142] Ibid.

[143] Ibid., 58–59.

dom of God truly belongs to little children of Christian parents.[144] From Jesus' words here we learn three principles "which lie close to the argument for infant baptism and without which the ordinance of infant baptism would be meaningless": first, infants are members of Christ's body; second, "they are members of his kingdom and therefore have been regenerated"; third, they are to be received into the fellowship of the church.[145] So infant baptism is appropriate in the church.

Second, Murray turns to Paul's instructions to children in Eph 6:1–4 and Col 3:20–21 and notes that, given the addressees of these letters, these children are assumed to be "saints." This means the children were baptized as infants.[146] Third, Murray discusses 1 Cor 7:14. After acknowledging that this text shows a special relationship between a believer and both an unbelieving spouse and a child, he argues that it teaches not the holiness "of regeneration" but the holiness "of connection and privilege." This is a

> "holiness" that evinces the operation of the covenant and representative principle and proves that the Christian faith of even one parent involves the embrace of the offspring in a relationship that is by divine warrant described as "holy." This is wholly consonant with the basis upon which the ordinance of infant baptism rests, just as it is counter to the moving principle of the antipaedobaptist contention.[147]

Fourth, Murray turns to the "household baptisms" in Acts. Having admitted that "we cannot prove conclusively that there were infants in these households," he argues that two factors lead us to assume infants were there.[148] First, one quarter of the only twelve instances

---

[144] Ibid., 59. "What Jesus is asserting here is rather that the kingdom of God belongs to little children and that they are members of it, not at all that the kingdom of God belongs to such as resemble little children" (p. 60). He supports his conclusion by the parallels found in Mark 10:14 and Luke 18:16.

[145] Ibid., 62. Murray does not attempt to deal with the inconsistency of his second conclusion. He argues elsewhere against notions of baptismal regeneration but here says that baptized infants have been regenerated.

[146] Ibid., 63–64. Of course, this is an argument from silence. There is no suggestion here of paedobaptism; it is at least equally as likely that these children were of age and had put their trust in Jesus. Indeed, these instructions cannot be directed to infants but must be addressed to children who can understand the Pauline admonitions.

[147] Ibid., 65.

[148] This, of course, is an assumption that cannot be proved. See Reynolds, *Church Polity*, 376.

of baptism in the NT are of households; we should reasonably assume that infants were included. Second, "household baptism would be a perfectly natural application" of the representative principle already enunciated.[149]

Fifth, Murray highlights Acts 2:38–39, especially Peter's statement that "the promise is to you and to your children." Genesis 17 alone, he maintains, makes sense of the fact that children are included in the promise here. Thus the divine institution again is the rationale for the practice of infant baptism.[150]

Marcel

Marcel similarly admits that the NT contains little direct evidence supporting the practice of paedobaptism.[151] Having admitted that, he proceeds to relate four major lines of NT evidence for the practice of infant baptism. All of this data assumes and confirms Marcel's *a priori* understanding of the covenant of grace. First, he notes that believers' children are born within the covenant of grace because of family solidarity. Thus they are viewed as distinct from the rest of humanity due to the objectivity of the covenant.[152] Second, Christ's regard for the little children in Matt 19:13–14, for example, shows they were "members of the covenant, members of His kingdom, and of the Church."[153] Third, Peter's and Paul's preaching in Acts 2:39 and 16:31 demonstrates that the "benefits [of the covenant] are extended to the children of believers."[154] Fourth, the household baptisms of Acts equally confirm the fact of the covenant, as does 1 Cor 7:14.[155]

[149] Murray, *Christian Baptism*, 66.

[150] Ibid., 67–68.

[151] The first section of his chapter on *The Baptism of Children* is titled "The Silence of the New Testament." Marcel begins by admitting, "We find ourselves immediately confronted with one of the most serious objections urged by the adversaries of infant baptism, namely, that in Scripture there is no explicit commandment requiring the baptism of the little children of believers. This is quite true" (*The Biblical Doctrine of Infant Baptism*, 187).

[152] Ibid., 191–92.

[153] Ibid., 192.

[154] Ibid., 194.

[155] Ibid., 194–96; see also 119–20. In addition to Tom Schreiner's treatment of 1 Cor 7:14 in this volume, see Jewett, *Infant Baptism*, 122–37.

Evaluation

Calvin, Murray, and Marcel each use the material of the NT to "corroborate" what they previously argued about the nature of the sacraments and the covenant of grace. When they define baptism alone, they rely on the NT. But when they try to apply this biblical definition of baptism to the practice of baptizing infants, they are unconvincing since the NT gives us no warrant for paedobaptism. When they seek to justify infant baptism, they disregard the NT epistolary material that teaches specifically what baptism represents. This may be because none of these passages (e.g., Rom 6:3–4, 1 Pet 3:21) mentions infants; indeed, their exclusion of infants is almost explicit since infants cannot be said to have faith in Christ. Thus the covenantal reading of the Bible by Reformed paedobaptists results in an importing of OT constructs into the NT contrary to NT teaching. Their understanding of the new covenant is not new enough.

First Cor 7:14 and Col 2:11–12 provide no warrant for infant baptism.[156] The "household baptisms" of Acts also do not justify the practice.[157] Here we need to focus on two additional NT passages consistently employed by paedobaptists to justify infant baptism. First, Calvin, Murray, and Marcel each turn to Jesus' welcoming of the little children in Matt 19:14 as justification for infant baptism. This incident from Jesus' ministry, however, has nothing to do with paedobaptism.[158] Certainly, this passage shows the Lord's love for children. But Jesus uses the little ones as an example of his requirement for childlike faith. Baptism is not in view at all. Thus, D. A. Carson notes:

> Jesus does not want the little children prevented from coming to him
> (v. 14), not because the kingdom of heaven belongs to them, but because
> the kingdom of heaven belongs to those like them (so also Mark and Luke,
> stressing childlike faith): Jesus receives them because they are an excellent
> object lesson in the kind of humility and faith he finds acceptable.[159]

---

[156] Referring to 1 Cor 7:14, G. Fee remarks that "one of the curiosities of the use of Scripture in the church has been the use of this text to support infant baptism" (*The First Epistle to the Corinthians*, NICNT [Grand Rapids: Eerdmans, 1987], 301 n. 27).

[157] See Robert Stein's chapter in this volume.

[158] See Jewett, *Infant Baptism*, 55–63.

[159] Carson, "Matthew," 8:420.

As Timothy George concludes, "Jesus took a special interest in children, received them into his arms, and blessed them. He did not baptize them."[160] So we should welcome, love, and nurture children, teaching them the gospel and calling them to repentance and faith. And after they have professed faith in Christ for salvation we may then baptize them and welcome them into the church.[161]

Second, the appeal to Acts 2:38–39 fails to read Peter's words in context.[162] Reformed paedobaptists assume that "the promise" here means the promise of God's blessing to those who are within the covenant community, including the children of believers, just as Abraham's offspring were blessed by their relationship to him. But that is not what Peter means by "the promise" here. The promise is specifically the promised new age inaugurated by the Holy Spirit (2:33), an age which is not marked by ethnic boundaries but by regeneration and commitment to the Lord (2:17–20). It is a promise of forgiveness for all who call on the name of the Lord (2:21). Just as in their exegesis of 1 Cor 7:14 paedobaptists are not consistent in their application of the verse to unbelieving spouses, so also in Acts 2:39 they inconsistently apply the promise to believers' children. But Peter does not. Rather, the promise is "for all who are far off" (leading to forced baptisms of everyone indiscriminately according to paedobaptist logic?), for "everyone whom the Lord our God calls to himself." Thus, the promise, with its accompanying sign of baptism (2:41), is for all who receive the gospel in faith and repentance. The promise is for those God calls who respond in faith. Christian parents should

[160] George, "The Reformed Doctrine of Believers' Baptism," 252.

[161] Wendel's evaluation of Calvin's theology of paedobaptism is cogent: "Since it was not possible for [Calvin] to adduce a single New Testament passage containing a clear allusion to infant baptism, he had to be content with indirect inferences and analogies drawn from circumcision and Christ's blessing of the children. . . . he himself seems to have been aware of the defects of his exegesis upon this point. He was debarred, however, from using any other, from the moment when he undertook to defend on scriptural grounds an institution of later date than the New Testament writings and to justify an ecclesiastical tradition after having proclaimed that all tradition, to be valid, must be based upon certain scriptural proof. By his having allowed for a degree of independence in the domain of external discipline and in ceremonies Calvin had, moreover, pointed to a way in which we may regret that he did not go farther (4.10.30). For that would have enabled him to come to the conclusion that infant baptism was useful to the Church and for the piety of the faithful, while frankly acknowledging that one cannot find an acceptable basis for it in the Scriptures" (*Calvin*, 328–29).

[162] Note Jewett's discussion of this text in *Infant Baptism*, 119–22.

pray that their children would so respond. They should use all means available to help their children understand their obligation to obey the gospel (Acts 17:30), but the church must wait until the children respond in faith before giving them the sign of faith, baptism.

At the crucial point of offering NT justification for infant baptism, then, Calvin, Murray, and Marcel are unconvincing, basing their practice on the theological construct of the "covenant of grace." They are caught in the bind of biblically defining a doctrine and then attempting to justify an unbiblical application of it. The NT neither assumes nor justifies infant baptism.

Salvation Sola Fide?

So far we have evaluated Reformed paedobaptists under five headings and found their conclusions biblically unwarranted and inconsistent. Their conclusions can nonetheless be held by evangelicals who believe that salvation is by faith alone (*sola fide*) in God's gracious gift of Christ the Savior. In one area, however, Calvin, Murray, and Marcel abandon their evangelical commitments in an effort to support paedobaptism. Each of them suggests that God may grant baptized infants salvation at the point of their baptisms.[163] They suggest and posit that God may save baptized infants "mysteriously," according to his sovereign power. Because of this, they can remain consistent with their definition of baptism that included the necessity of exercising faith in God's promises. In so arguing, though, they are closer to a Catholic *ex opere operato* conception of baptism than to their own evangelical commitments. To be fair to them, this is not a major plank in their support of paedobaptism. It is, though, another indication of the instability of the paedobaptist position. To support a practice (paedobaptism) with no biblical warrant, they offer a defense for it (the salvation of infants at the point of baptism) that is, to say the least, inconsistent with their evangelical belief that

---

[163] Note also the *Westminster Confession of Faith*: "The efficacy of Baptism is not tied to that moment of time wherein it is administered; yet notwithstanding, by the right use of this ordinance, *the grace promised is not only offered, but really exhibited and conferred by the Holy Ghost, to such (whether of age or infants) as that grace belongeth unto*, according to the counsel of God's own will in His appointed time" (28.6, emphasis mine). Grace is conferred to elect infants at their baptisms.

salvation requires the individual exercise of personal and conscious faith in Christ Jesus.

Calvin

Calvin maintains that God may work in infants even apart from their exercising faith.[164] John the Baptist's leaping in his mother's womb (Luke 1:15) proves that God can work savingly even in an infant. This is absolutely essential, Calvin argues, due to infants' connection to Adam in sin which makes them liable to the wrath of God. "Now it is perfectly clear," Calvin reasons, "that those infants who are to be saved (as some are surely saved from that early age) are previously regenerated by the Lord. For if they bear with them an inborn corruption from their mother's womb, they must be cleansed of it before they can be admitted into God's Kingdom, for nothing polluted or defiled may enter there."[165] But is not faith—with its prerequisite to understand that one is sinful and needs a Savior—the *sine qua non* of new life in Christ? Not necessarily, Calvin asserts, for "God's work, though beyond our understanding, is still not annulled."[166] We may not understand how God works in his elect infants, but he may unite them to Christ nonetheless. The lack of preaching-induced faith is not a deterrent to baptism. Rather, Calvin suggests that preaching is merely "the ordinary arrangement and dispensation of the Lord which he commonly uses in calling his people—not, indeed, prescribing for him an unvarying rule so that he may use no other way. He has certainly used such another way in calling many, giving them true knowledge of himself by inward means, that is, by the illumination of the Spirit apart from the medium of preaching."[167] Acknowledging

---

[164] Wendel notes that Calvin's argument beginning with the 1539 edition of the *Institutes* is different from his view of 1536. Previously Calvin had agreed with Luther that God gave faith to children when they were baptized. Later he argued that God works secretly in children (*Calvin*, 327). Calvin's argument here is different from the contention he made based on the promise of God: "The children of believers are baptized not in order that they who were previously strangers to the church may then for the first time become children of God, but rather that, because by the blessing of the promise they already belonged to the body of Christ, they are received into the church with this solemn sign" (*Institutes* 4.15.22).

[165] Ibid., 4.16.17.

[166] Ibid., 4.16.17.

[167] Ibid., 4.16.19. In another place he asserts, "In baptism, God, regenerating us, engrafts us into the society of his church and makes us his own by adoption" (4.17.1). Jewett perceptively notes that

that some measure of comprehension is essential for salvation, Calvin speculates that if it pleases God "why may the Lord not shine with a tiny spark at the present time on those whom he will illumine in the future with the full splendor of his light—especially if he has not removed their ignorance before taking them from the prison of the flesh?"[168] We certainly will not understand how the Lord effects this mighty work in infants, but that does not mean he cannot do it. Rather, "infants are baptized into future repentance and faith, and even though these have not yet been formed in them, the seed of both lies hidden within them by the secret working of the Spirit."[169] His desire to justify paedobaptism has moved Calvin to a place that logically calls into question the importance of personal repentance and faith for salvation.

Some scholars interpret Calvin's teaching at this point differently than I do. For instance, Henri Blocher has recently argued that "Calvin does not endorse the causative view" that baptism effects the salvation of infants. He notes that for Calvin "the sacraments confer as preaching does, as a visible word, so that God fulfills his promise if the promise meets faith in the recipient; more generally the efficacy of sacraments, which Calvin often extols, is that of sealing and confirming, not of causing grace as an instrument."[170] However, as I showed above, Calvin believed that God may mysteriously work to bring about (at least a spark or seed of) faith in the baptisms of elect infants. Of course, they would subsequently express that faith fully when they came of age if they lived that long;

Calvin's "powers of logical penetration seem at times to have driven him to the assertion that covenant children from the moment of birth are indeed the subjects of God's saving mercy and renewing grace in the full sense of New Testament inwardness. . . . Calvin does not say [in 4.15.20] that when believers' children grow up to be of a pious frame, God adopts them for his own; rather, the grace of salvation is secured to them before they are born. As they are 'in Adam,' so they are 'in Christ'; they are made partakers of him, with all his saving benefits" (Infant Baptism, 145–46).

[168] Calvin, Institutes 4.16.19. See Grislis, "Calvin's Doctrine of Baptism," 229–30, and J. Raitt, "Three Inter-related Principles in Calvin's Unique Doctrine of Infant Baptism," SCJ 11 (1980): 53.

[169] Calvin, Institutes 4.16.20. See in this regard Barth, The Teaching of the Church Regarding Baptism, 46–47, and Raitt, "Three Inter-related Principles," 59.

[170] H. A. Blocher, "The Lutheran-Catholic Declaration on Justification," in Justification in Perspective: Historical Developments and Contemporary Challenges, ed. B. L. McCormack (Grand Rapids: Baker/Edinburgh: Rutherford House, 2006), 209. Also see C. P. Venema, "Covenant Theology and Baptism," in Case for Covenantal Infant Baptism, 228–29; Jewett, Infant Baptism, 147–58.

nonetheless, they had at least a modicum of faith as infants and thus could be rightly baptized. This is inconsistent with Calvin's other views, but he offers it as a rationale for infant baptism none-theless.[171] Lewis Schenck has convincingly argued that Calvin's view (as I noted above) was that the church should assume that the baptized children of believing parents are truly regenerate; even if they do not understand how God does it, believers must trust in the secret working of God in the infants.[172] He argues that Calvin's view has been the historic view of the Reformed churches,[173] but that the ethos of revivalism in America beginning in the mid-eighteenth century challenged the presumptive regeneration view of Calvin and the Reformed tradition.[174] It seems to me, then, that contem-porary Reformed paedobaptists who assert that the church should assume the salvation of baptized infants are in the historic stream of Reformed churches,[175] even if there is still disagreement over this point among our paedobaptist brethren.[176]

[171] D. F. Wright has noted Calvin's inconsistency with his own thought when he posits a secret working of God in infants. Calvin believed that infants "are quite capable of being regen-erated, as Christ's own infancy demonstrates. Without regeneration, dying infants must surely perish" ("Children, Covenant and the Church," 35). See also K. Barth, *Church Dogmatics* IV/4, trans. G. W. Bromiley (Edinburgh: T&T Clark, 1969), 173–75, 187.

[172] Schenck, *Presbyterian Doctrine of Children in the Covenant*, 11–22, 134–36. Schenck includes a suggestion of how Calvin dealt with the charge that he was inconsistent with his own thought else-where that stressed the importance of individual trust in God in the sacraments (pp. 20–21).

[173] Ibid., 24–52.

[174] Ibid., 80–103. Revivalism assumed that children needed to evidence signs indicating that they had been converted to Christ, whereas the Reformed doctrine assumed that they were the children of God due to their baptisms. Schenck notes the heated debates between Charles Hodge of Princeton (who followed Calvin's presumptive view) and R. L. Dabney and J. H. Thornwell (both of whom argued that a baptized child was a child of the covenant but should not be presumed to be regenerate, p. 87).

[175] See, e.g., R. S. Rayburn, "The Presbyterian Doctrine of Covenant Children, Covenant Nurture and Covenant Succession," *Presbyterion* 22 (1996): 76–109; and these chapters in Strawbridge, *Case for Covenantal Baptism:* P. J. Leithart, "Infant Baptism in History: An Unfin-ished Tragicomedy," 246–62; D. Wilson, "Baptism and Children: Their Place in the Old and New Testaments," 286–302; and, R. C. Sproul Jr., "In Jesus' Name, Amen," 303–10. Venema notes how Reformed confessions use efficacious language when speaking of infant baptism (C. P. Venema, "The Doctrine of the Sacraments and Baptism according to the Reformed Confes-sions," *Mid-America Journal of Theology* 11 [2000]: 80–81).

[176] This other view is expressed in the article in Strawbridge's book by J. Beeke and R. Lanning who say, "Covenant promise is no substitute for personal regeneration. Parents who presume that their children are regenerate by virtue of the covenant may see no need to tell

Murray

Murray likewise suggests that God may work uniquely in the lives of infants at their baptisms. He notes that the little children of Matt 19:13–14 "are members of [Christ's] kingdom and therefore *have been regenerated*."[177] This assumption that by one's baptism the church can rightly assume the person is a Christian contradicts Murray's opposition to "presumptive regeneration."[178] Nevertheless he notes, "That which is signified by baptism, namely, union with Christ, regeneration, and justification, is not *in the case of infants* mediated by intelligent faith."[179] Even though adults are saved by their faith in Jesus, infants receive salvation differently. Murray argues that "in the case of adults intelligent repentance and faith are the conditions of salvation. But intelligent repentance and faith are not the conditions of salvation in the case of infants. They are not psychologically capable of such faith and its corresponding confession. It is so in reference to baptism."[180] In arguing this way, Murray seems to have changed his biblical emphasis on the requirement of faith in order to protect his notion of infant baptism.[181] His final word on the matter is that infants can be regenerated apart from what we normally refer to as "faith":

> Though infants are not capable of the intelligent exercise of faith, they are, nevertheless, susceptible to God's efficacious grace in uniting them to Christ, in regenerating them by His Spirit, and in sprinkling them with the blood of His Son. This grace, in the bonds of the everlasting covenant, infants may fully possess. This is what baptism signifies and seals, and no warrant can be

them that they must be born again" ("Unto You, and to Your Children," in *Case for Covenantal Infant Baptism*, 67).

[177] Murray, *Christian Baptism*, 62 (emphasis mine).

[178] Murray had argued against the idea of the presumptive regeneration of baptized infants, noting that the only ground for baptism is the divine command based on Genesis 17 (ibid., 54–55). Reformed paedobaptists, however, are not monolithic at this point. See, e.g., L. B. Shenck, "Review of *Christian Baptism* by John Murray," *Int* 7 (1953): 118, and K. J. Foreman, "Review of *Christian Baptism* by John Murray," *ThTo* 10 (1953–1954): 132.

[179] Murray, *Christian Baptism*, 85, n 45 (emphasis his).

[180] Ibid., 70–71.

[181] Murray's later discussion of the "sign" and "seal" nature of the sacrament does not make his view more biblical. He notes that "baptism is the sign and seal of a spiritual reality which is conceived of as existing. Where that reality is absent the sign or seal has no efficacy" (*Christian Baptism*, 83). He seems to suggest here that the baptism is efficacious only when faith is present. Before, however, he argued that God regenerates (elect) infants at their baptisms.

elicited for the assumption that in respect of efficacy this sign or seal has any other effect in the case of infants than in the case of adults.[182]

Since he says, "This grace . . . infants may fully possess," we must assume that Murray is not referring to a future time when, as adults, the infant possesses faith. Rather, they possess grace through God's regeneration *now*. Murray's thought is illogical and inconsistent with his prior discussion of both the NT's doctrine of baptism and the significance of infant baptism. Most importantly, his belief that God regenerates infants apart from faith is unbiblical.

Marcel

Marcel likewise argues in this fashion, which is equally inconsistent with his biblical views.[183] A couple of his statements will suffice to show his views:

> God Himself in His amazing goodness provides the divine and paternal answer, which confirms the whole biblical revelation of the plan of salvation: "Yes, it is My wish! I will be your God and the God of your posterity after you. You will be saved, together with your family."[184]

> The *promise* of the regeneration of the children of the covenant is sufficient for us. It is not for us to define whether this regeneration in view of salvation is found in the elect children before or at the moment of baptism, or sometimes even years afterwards.[185]

At one point Marcel, like Calvin, asserts that God regenerates infants mysteriously in their baptisms: "Although God's working is incomprehensible and hidden from us, we affirm, taking our stand on the covenant which contains the promise of regeneration, that God does not forbear to act in the little children of believers."[186] To prove this he maintains that "in the covenant regeneration and baptism cannot be dissociated from each other." The Bible supports his contention, as seen in Yahweh's calling of Jeremiah in his mother's womb (Jer 1:5), his working in John the Baptist (Luke 1:5), "and others"! We may not understand this mysterious working of God,

---

[182] Ibid., 87.
[183] See Malone, *The Baptism of Disciples Alone*, 249–51.
[184] Marcel, *The Biblical Doctrine of Infant Baptism*, 109.
[185] Ibid., 200. See also 110 n. 1, 198.
[186] Ibid., 221.

but it is *a reality of faith. God performs what He promises.*[187] So, he concludes:

> We refuse to impose on God the time or the means or the circumstances of His action in the heart of our children and to confine it within the categories of our reason. *He has promised: He acts: the thing is sure since we believe in Him!...* We believe and affirm that children as well as adults have a share in the benefits of His grace, that they are or will be regenerated by the Holy Spirit, and that baptism is also given to them as a sign, seal, and pledge of this regeneration.[188]

The infant who has been baptized is, or will be, or may be born again.[189] He is no longer a sinner connected to Adam and liable to God's wrath. Rather, he is "a child of God and a lamb in Christ's fold. . . . He no longer belongs to the race of Adam . . . He is placed under the direct protection of the Lord. . . . God loves him and regards him with affection." In other words, the child is an "heir presumptive of salvation."[190] So Marcel concludes that an infant's baptism should lead us to presume the gracious salvation of that child.

Evaluation

Such statements by Calvin, Murray, and Marcel about the presumed salvation of baptized infants are inconsistent with their previously examined doctrine of baptism, which emphasized the requirement of the person to exercise faith in God's promises. They are closer to Rome's *ex opere operato* view of baptism's efficacy than they are to the Protestant heritage. Much more importantly, though, such statements are a denial of the biblical imperative that salvation comes by faith in the gospel of Jesus Christ—by faith alone, not by

---

[187] Ibid., 222 (emphasis his). None of the "others" are named since Scripture is silent about them.

[188] Ibid., 223 (emphasis his).

[189] Marcel is objective in his understanding of the efficacy of baptism in marking the salvation of infants. Yet at the same time he did not believe that all who were baptized in infancy were necessarily saved. We merely note that inconsistency here. We wonder, of course, what the efficacy of the sacrament is for those baptized who are not elect. Marcel, it seems, would argue that nothing occurs in them since they are not some of God's elect. How, then, can he speak so certainly of God's sovereign working in the lives of "our children" who are baptized?

[190] Marcel, *The Biblical Doctrine of Infant Baptism*, 225.

means of one's baptism. The fact that these Reformed paedobaptists are forced to go to such unbiblical lengths to justify paedobaptism is a further indication of the unbiblical character of the rite.

Conclusion: A Plea for Biblical Consistency

In this chapter we have attempted to follow the internal logic of Calvin, Murray, and Marcel as they defend the baptism of the infants of believing parents. Their common defense includes a definition of the sacraments and baptism that is impossible to reconcile with their practice of paedobaptism, the concession that the church will be a mixed body of believers and unbelievers (differing from Baptists because they intentionally induct unbelievers, that is, infants, into the church), the use of the covenant of grace (with its parallel between circumcision and baptism) as the foundation of their doctrine and their hope in the mysterious work of God to regenerate baptized infants. Throughout we have found the biblical support for their position to be lacking. Their biblical exposition is oriented toward the OT with a lack of attention to the baptismal practice of the NT and to the NT's teaching on baptism, the church, or the old covenant. Lacking NT support for the practice, the evangelical paedobaptists we have surveyed argue that infant baptism is clearly inferred from the biblical text.

What recourse do we have to solve the debate between evangelical credobaptists and paedobaptists? The Bible alone can be the source of any rapprochement between the two positions. Murray and Marcel both employ arguments reminiscent of the *Westminster Confession of Faith*, which states, "The whole counsel of God concerning all things necessary for His own glory, man's salvation, faith and life, is either expressly set down in Scripture, *or by good and necessary consequence may be deduced from Scripture*: unto which nothing at any time is to be added, whether by new revelations of the Spirit or traditions of men."[191] After the discussion of some of his NT "corroboratory evidence," Murray concludes, "Surely the inference is one of good and necessary consequence that infants

---

[191] *Westminster Confession of Faith* 1.6 (emphasis mine).

should be given the sign and seal of that which, by the authority of Christ, they are to be accounted."[192] Later he announces that "the evidence for infant baptism falls into the category of good and necessary inference."[193] Similarly, Marcel claims that infant baptism is a "legitimate deduction" from Scripture that is "analogous to that of the admission of women to the Lord's supper."[194] The NT gives no example of either women taking the Eucharist or of infants being baptized, he argues, but that does not mean that either of these practices is illegitimate as we do theology, for "that which follows by legitimate deductions from scriptural norms is as exact as that which is explicitly stated."[195]

But paedobaptism is neither a "good" nor a "necessary" deduction from the biblical text, as we have noted throughout this chapter. Instead, evangelicals should follow the lead of Calvin and seek clear biblical support for their practice. "The divine will is the perpetual rule to which true religion is to be conformed," Calvin cautions in the *Institutes*.[196] The Bible must be the sole guide to the church's belief and practice. We are in danger when we institute a belief or practice not taught in Scripture. Calvin is right to argue that the church is bound in doctrine and practice by the clear teaching of the Bible.

We thus end by appealing to our evangelical brethren to be biblically consistent in their doctrine and practice of baptism. Baptists have historically maintained this point. The Baptist revision of the *Westminster Confession of Faith*, released in 1689, changes the wording of "good and necessary consequences" to highlight the primacy of Scripture: "The whole counsel of God concerning all things necessary for His own glory, man's salvation, faith and life, is either expressly set down *or necessarily contained in the Holy Scripture*; unto which nothing at any time is to be added, whether by new revelation

---

[192] Murray, *Christian Baptism*, 63.

[193] Ibid., 69.

[194] Marcel, *The Biblical Doctrine of Infant Baptism*, 189.

[195] Ibid., 189–90.

[196] Calvin, *Institutes*, 1.4.3; cp. 1.5.13; 4.10.23. This has come to be known as "the regulative principle" and is one of the hallmarks of the Reformed tradition of Protestants. See P. G. Ryken et al., eds., *Give Praise to God: A Vision for Reforming Worship* (Phillipsburg, NJ: P&R, 2003), 17–93.

of the Spirit or traditions of men."[197] May we all be conformed in thought and practice to God's word, which alone is trustworthy.

---

[197] *Second London Confession* 1.6 (emphasis mine).

MEREDITH KLINE ON SUZERAINTY, CIRCUMCISION, AND BAPTISM

Duane A. Garrett[*]

The Suzerainty Treaty Form

In 1954, building on the work of other scholars, George Mendenhall published "Covenant Forms in the Israelite Tradition." In this article, Mendenhall observed parallels between the formal structure of Israelite covenants and ancient Near Eastern suzerain-vassal treaties.[1] That is, ancient treaty documents between more powerful kings (suzerains) and less powerful kings (vassals) were structurally similar to the covenants between God (the suzerain) and Israel (the vassal) in the OT. Evangelical scholars quickly grasped the significance of these parallels for the issue of the date of the writing of Deuteronomy. If Deuteronomy follows the pattern of the late- to mid-second millennium BC treaties, the obvious implication was that Deuteronomy was in large measure composed at that time. This provided a powerful counter-argument to the dominant theory of pentateuchal origins, the documentary hypothesis, which argued that document D, the major source for Deuteronomy, was not composed until the time of Josiah of Judah in the late seventh century.

No evangelical exploited more thoroughly the parallels between biblical covenants and the ancient Near Eastern suzerain-vassal treaty than did Meredith Kline, who can be said to have made the concept of the suzerain-vassal covenant the centerpiece to his whole understanding of OT theology. This is the point where he begins his commentary on Deuteronomy, the aptly-named *Treaty of the Great King*.[2] More significantly, the suzerain-vassal treaty is also the start-

---

[*] Duane A. Garrett received his Ph.D. from Baylor University, and is the John R. Sampey Professor of Old Testament Interpretation at The Southern Baptist Theological Seminary in Louisville, Kentucky.

[1] G. E. Mendenhall, "Covenant Forms in the Israelite Tradition," *BA* 17 (1954): 50–76.

[2] M. G. Kline, *Treaty of the Great King; the Covenant Structure of Deuteronomy: Studies and Commentary* (Grand Rapids: Eerdmans, 1963).

ing point for *The Structure of Biblical Authority*,[3] a work that encapsulates Kline's understanding of biblical theology. For Kline, "The origin of the OT canon coincided with the founding of the kingdom of Israel by covenant at Sinai," and the concept of covenant, specifically after the pattern of the suzerain-vassal treaty, has worked itself out in the unfolding of biblical theology as seen in the growth of the canon itself. Not only Sinai and Deuteronomy, but the historical texts, the prophets, the Psalter, the wisdom texts, and finally the NT itself are all developments of the idea of a covenant between the divine suzerain and his vassal people. The prophets, for example, were primarily prosecutors sent by the divine sovereign to accuse his people in the "covenant lawsuit" motif.[4] Furthermore, the "psalms of praise... were a part of Israel's tributary obligations; they were the spiritual sacrifices of the lips offered to the Great King."[5] As for the wisdom texts, the "central thesis of the wisdom books is that wisdom begins with the fear of Yahweh, which is to say that the way of wisdom is the way of the covenant."[6]

Kline's understanding of how this works itself out in the NT is especially significant. Few will argue against the idea that "covenant" is of primary significance in the NT since, after all, the word "testament" is essentially synonymous with "covenant." But Kline's thesis goes beyond that. For him, the "New Testament belongs to that pattern of renewing covenants by the issuing of new treaty documents which is already found in the inner history of old covenant administration."[7] That is, and again following a pattern observed in ancient Near Eastern suzerain-vassal treaties, the NT is a re-issuance of the treaty between the divine sovereign and his vassals, albeit a re-issuance with changes in the stipulations that are in accord with changed circumstances. Kline sees analogy for this in the OT itself, in that, for example, Deuteronomy is an updated re-issuance of the Sinai covenant.[8] Kline is one of the major advocates of "covenant theol-

---

[3] M. G. Kline, *The Structure of Biblical Authority* (Grand Rapids: Eerdmans, 1972).
[4] Ibid., 58–9.
[5] Ibid., 63.
[6] Ibid., 64.
[7] Ibid., 68–9.
[8] Ibid., 69.

ogy," a school of evangelical biblical interpretation that emphasizes continuity between the Testaments. Through much of the twentieth century, covenant theology was in a struggle for the minds of evangelical theologians against "dispensationalism," a school of biblical interpretation which in its classic form maximized the *discontinuity* between the two testaments. All this bears on Kline's understanding of circumcision and baptism.

Before examining this, however, a few general remarks on Kline's approach are in order. First, he is to be commended for giving due attention to the historical context of Scripture. This was in marked contrast to many of his counterparts, who often read the Bible as though it had no historical or cultural context at all. Second, Kline was working at a time when a great deal of attention was given to biblical theology in its ancient Near Eastern context (the time of the "biblical theology movement"), and when the idea of covenant in particular was a focus of biblical studies. As Kline was developing his approach, for example, Walther Eichrodt's *Theology of the Old Testament* appeared, a work which also argued for the centrality of the covenant in the OT (albeit from a perspective quite different from Kline's).[9] This is not to dismiss Kline, but to observe that he, too, has a historical context.

At the same time, much of Kline's approach is open to question. The prominence he gives to the suzerain-vassal treaty form as the framework for biblical theology is unwarranted. As one reviewer has put it, Kline "is making the hypothesis of the suzerainty treaty bear a weight it can hardly sustain."[10] For instance, apart from the constraints of this model, it is hard to imagine anyone describing the Psalms as the work of vassals carrying out their treaty obligations to their suzerain. It is worth noting that the word "covenant" (*berith*) only occurs once in Proverbs, and that in a context of a woman's fidelity to her husband (2:17). Furthermore, the approach is reductionistic; it restricts our vision of what the OT is about. Wisdom literature, for example, deals with a wide range of practical issues and

---

[9] W. Eichrodt, *Theologie des Alten Testaments* (Stuttgart: Klotz, 1957; trans. Philadelphia: Westminster, 1961, 1967).

[10] F. L. Moriarty, "Review of *The Structure of Biblical Authority*, by Meredith Kline," *CBQ* 35 (1973): 247.

interacts significantly with ancient Near Eastern wisdom texts, but there is no observable tie to suzerainty treaties. One would seriously distort the messages of Job or Ecclesiastes, to say nothing of Song of Songs, by interpreting them via this model.

It is in the extension of this model to the NT, however, that the greatest problems appear. No one disputes that at the heart of the NT is the new covenant between God and man, but it is doubtful that it can be described as belonging to "the pattern of renewing covenants by the issuance of new treaty documents." The new covenant of Jeremiah 31 is precisely that—a *new* covenant; it is not an issuance of new treaty *documents* with a few modifications (NRSV):

> 31 The days are surely coming, says the Lord, when I will make a new covenant with the house of Israel and the house of Judah. 32 It will not be like the covenant that I made with their ancestors when I took them by the hand to bring them out of the land of Egypt—a covenant that they broke, though I was their husband, says the Lord. 33 But this is the covenant that I will make with the house of Israel after those days, says the Lord: I will put my law within them, and I will write it on their hearts; and I will be their God, and they shall be my people. 34 No longer shall they teach one another, or say to each other, "Know the Lord," for they shall all know me, from the least of them to the greatest, says the Lord; for I will forgive their iniquity, and remember their sin no more.

It is *not like* the covenant that God made with their forefathers at Sinai (Jer 31:32). The discontinuity and "newness" of the new covenant must be taken seriously here. This is not to embrace the kind of discontinuity envisioned in dispensationalism, which has serious problems of its own, but to recognize that the new covenant breaks with and abolishes the old. It is precisely in his understanding of the new covenant that Kline has made errors that lead to a seriously distorted understanding of circumcision and baptism, a subject to which we now turn.

Suzerainty, Circumcision and Baptism

Kline published his views on circumcision and baptism first in a two-part article for the *Westminster Theological Journal*,[11] which he then expanded into a book, *By Oath Consigned: A Reinterpretation*

---

[11] M. G. Kline, "Oath and Ordeal Signs," *WTJ* 27 (1965): 115–39 and *WTJ* 28 (1965): 1–37.

of the Covenant Signs of Circumcision and Baptism.[12] Kline is seeking to defend the practice of infant baptism, but he is aware of the primary shortcoming of all paedobaptist arguments: unless one is willing to assert that baptism actually creates faith and regenerates the infant, it is difficult to explain what spiritual blessing is conferred at baptism. A strong advocate of the reformation doctrine of *sola fide*, Kline can hardly go down the Roman Catholic route of asserting that there is a conferral of grace in the operation of the sacraments, from baptism through to confirmation and the first partaking of the Eucharist. But, absent such a theology, it is hard to see how baptism does anything at all for an infant.[13]

Kline thus strikes out in a new direction and proposes what may be the most original and provocative theory on baptism of the twentieth century: as a sign of the covenant, its primary function is not as a bestowal of grace but as a sign of judgment. He does this by exploiting the connection between circumcision and baptism in light of his understanding of the biblical ideal of the covenant as suzerainty treaty. In his words, "the traditional consensus that these sacramental symbols [circumcision and baptism] are primarily if not exclusively signs of divine grace and blessing is now called in question."[14]

Circumcision

Circumcision as a Sign of Malediction

Beginning his discussion of circumcision, Kline asserts that "circumcision is . . . an oath rite and, as such, a pledge of consecration and a symbol of malediction. That is its primary, symbolic significance."[15] To make this claim, he first argues that circumcision is a rite of covenant ratification. He draws primarily upon Genesis 17,

[12] M. G. Kline, *By Oath Consigned: A Reinterpretation of the Covenant Signs of Circumcision and Baptism* (Grand Rapids: Eerdmans, 1968).

[13] Roman Catholic theologians rightly point out the dilemma of Protestant paedobaptists, who baptize infants without a sacramental theology. See, for example, B. Neunheuser, "Baptism," *Sacramentum Mundi: An Encyclopedia of Theology*, ed. K. Rahner et al. (New York: Herder & Herder, 1968), 1:136–46.

[14] Kline, "Oath and Ordeal," 115.

[15] Kline, *By Oath Consigned*, 47–8.

the chapter that describes God's imposition of the rite of circumcision on Abraham and his extended household. This text builds upon Genesis 15 (the creation of the Abrahamic covenant), and Kline calls Genesis 17 a "historical narrative describing the ratification ceremony of the covenant."[16] For Kline, behind this event is the suzerain-vassal treaty, and in particular the stipulations of "blessings and curses." These are the promises of benefits for obedience and of catastrophe for disobedience that such covenants make to vassals. The primary biblical example of the same is in Deuteronomy 28, which promises every kind of horror for the Israelites if they abandon their covenant duty. Genesis 17, then, is a ritual that symbolically declares disaster for Abraham's descendants if they fail to keep the covenant of Genesis 15.

Kline cites ancient Near Eastern parallels for the ideology he sees in operation here. For example, citing the eighth century BC treaty between Ashurnirari V of Assyria (the suzerain) and Mati'ilu of Arpad (the vassal), he notes that the covenant ceremony called down a curse on Mati'ilu for failure to observe his vassal duties to Ashurnirari. In the ritual, a ram that had been head of a flock was separated from the herd and decapitated and dismembered as a sign of what would happen to Mati'ilu if he broke faith with his suzerain.[17] Kline sees a parallel in the "dismembering" ritual of Genesis 15, where sacrificial animals are cut in half.

In circumcision, the foreskin is cut off from the male genitals, and this, he argues, is to be read as a sign of what would happen to the Israelite who broke faith with the terms of the covenant. Gen 17:14 says, "Any uncircumcised male, who has not been circumcised in the flesh, will be cut off from his people; he has broken my covenant."[18] In Kline's analysis, "There the threat of the curse sanction sounds against the one who breaks the covenant by not obeying the command of circumcision."[19]

[16] Kline, *By Oath Consigned*, 39.
[17] A standard work on this topic is D. R. Hillers, *Treaty-curses and the Old Testament Prophets* (Rome: Pontifical Biblical Institute, 1964).
[18] Unless otherwise indicated, Scripture quotes are the author's translation.
[19] Kline, *By Oath Consigned*, 43.

Before proceeding further, and while acknowledging that "covenant ratification" is certainly an aspect of circumcision in Genesis 17, we must note that there are two significant problems in Kline's presentation. First, the splitting of the animals in Genesis 15 cannot be regarded as a threat against Abram and his offspring for the simple reason that Abram did not walk between the animal pieces—only God did, in the form of the pillars of cloud and fire as represented by the "smoking firepot" and "blazing torch" of Gen 15:17. That being the case, the *differences* between this and a typical suzerain-vassal treaty rather than the *similarities* are the main point. God takes the covenant obligation on himself; he does not threaten Abram with annihilation. This covenant is promissory and shows God laying the obligation on himself. It is also "by grace through faith," as implied in Gen 15:6 ("Abram believed in the Lord and it was credited to him as righteousness"). Kline's analysis of this text in terms of Deuteronomy 28, to say nothing of using Assyrian suzerainty treaties as the analogue, is problematic from the start.

Second, regarding Gen 17:14, it is noteworthy that the penalty of being "cut off" from the people is not applied to the one who first received the mark of the covenant and then violated it. Rather, it applies to the one who does not have the mark of the covenant at all, and who thus never enters into the covenant. Such a person is thus "cut off," apparently here referring not to execution but to permanent exclusion from the covenant community. In short, circumcision cannot here be said to mark the calling down of destruction upon oneself for violating the covenant, since the prescribed punishment is for someone who is uncircumcised. Circumcision is simply the mark of the covenant and thus, so to speak, is the I.D. card for membership in the community. It is not an "ordeal sign" in the sense that Kline argues.

If circumcision were the "ordeal sign" that Kline imagines, then one would expect the prophets to invoke this sign in their countless diatribes against Israel. These would read something like, "You took circumcision to your flesh as a sign of the covenant and so placed yourselves under a curse. Yet you violated the covenant and have called this curse down upon yourselves! Therefore, as your circumcision is a mutilation sign, now you will be mutilated! You will be cut off, Israel, in fulfillment of your circumcision!" But one never sees anything of the kind. This is because the Israelites did not regard circumcision as a mutilation of the flesh; to the contrary, they saw it as good and wholesome, a marked contrast to the uncircumcised state of the Gentiles.

Gentile lack of circumcision was proof enough, in Israelite eyes, that they were by and large dirty, uncivilized and unholy. Calling someone uncircumcised was the equivalent to a Greek calling someone a "barbarian." David, in disdainfully referring to his enemies as "uncircumcised Philistines," plainly does not regard circumcision as a sign of "malediction" (1 Sam 17:36). When Jeremiah calls to Jerusalem, "Circumcise your hearts" (4:4), he is reflecting the general attitude that circumcision is a positive and cleansing act. When Jer 9:25 declares that God will punish all who are circumcised only "in the flesh," the prophet again treats circumcision not as a ritual mutilation but as an act of purification and sanctification. Kline's notion that circumcision is a "sign of malediction" is profoundly wrong.

Circumcision as Consecration

Kline, citing Jer 4:4, acknowledges that circumcision is an act of consecration, but here again he sees it as a matter of being set apart for destruction. The primary example is Isaac, who was consecrated to God in circumcision (Gen 21:4) and then laid before God as a human sacrifice (Genesis 22). In Kline's view, God's command that Isaac be sacrificed was meant "to perfect Isaac's circumcision by cutting him off altogether from among the living."[20] That is, he sees a direct theological connection between Isaac's circumcision and his being sacrificed. His rationale is that Isaac is an accursed son of Adam, and thus his consecration requires nothing less than his destruction as a burnt-offering. To be sure, Isaac is not actually sacrificed. But this is not because the circumcision/consecration does not require death. It is because God himself provided an alternative

---

[20] Ibid., 44.

sacrifice: the ram caught in the thicket (Gen 22:13), which is of course a type of Christ. But the fact that God has provided a substitute sacrifice, in Kline's view, should not obscure the basic theological equation behind this text: circumcision = consecration to God = destruction of the sinner.

Kline then argues that Isaiah 53 affirms the above equation in that it speaks of the "cutting off" of the Messiah, affirming the link between circumcision and the human sacrifice: "The prophet who later wrote of the messianic Servant that 'he was cut off out of the land of the living, stricken for the transgression of my people' (Isa. 53:8b) might have articulated this Old Testament identification faith in some such assurance to the faithful as this: You were cut off with the Servant in circumcision."[21]

Kline further argues that we can see the same line of thinking in Colossians 2, where Paul asserts the linkage between circumcision and crucifixion: "In him also you were circumcised with a spiritual circumcision, by putting off the body of the flesh in the circumcision of Christ; when you were buried with him in baptism, you were also raised with him through faith in the power of God, who raised him from the dead" (vv. 11–12, NRSV). Circumcision here clearly equals death, according to Kline, because the text has the sequence of circumcision, burial, and resurrection.[22] In summary, Kline asserts that in circumcision, "a man confessed himself to be under the juridical authority of Yahweh and committed himself to the ordeal of his Lord's judgment for the final verdict on his life. The sign of circumcision thus pointed to the eschatological judicial ordeal with its awful sanctions of eternal weal or woe."[23]

The notion that Isaac in Genesis 22 is in a sense everyman, worthy of death before God, and that the ram that was sacrificed is a type of Christ, our substitutionary sacrifice, is as old as Christianity itself and need not detain us. What is novel here is that Kline sees the sacrifice of Isaac as a necessary fulfillment of his circumcision. Two facts are worthy of note: first, Genesis 22 never mentions cir-

[21] Ibid., 46.
[46] Ibid., 46.
[23] Ibid., 48.

cumcision in connection with the sacrifice of Isaac, nor for that matter does any other biblical text. Second, the comment that Isaac was
circumcised on the eighth day (Gen 21:4) is itself unremarkable and
may be included for no other reason than to complete the picture
of Abraham's entire household having been circumcised (17:26–27;
Isaac was not yet born when the circumcision of Abraham's household took place). The idea that Isaac's circumcision was behind
God's command that he be sacrificed is conceivable, but no biblical
author explicitly makes the connection.

Similarly, it is not clear that Isaiah regards the death of the servant of the Lord as the fulfillment of the Israelite practice of circumcision. The verb in Isa 53:8 to which Kline appeals is *gāzar*, meaning
to "split in half" or "cut off." It is used for the splitting of the baby in
Solomon's verdict in the dispute between the two prostitutes (1 Kgs
3:25), for the splitting of the Red Sea in Ps 136:13, for being cut off
from God or from worship in Ps 31:22 (Hebrew v. 23) and in 2 Chr
26:21, and for cutting down trees in 2 Kgs 6:4. It is never used with
the meaning of or even in the context of circumcision, and there is
no reason to suppose that the Hebrew reader would make a connection between *gāzar* and circumcision.[24] Kline claims that "the
prophet might have articulated" the connection between circumcision and the death of the Messiah with words such as, "You were
cut off with the Servant in circumcision," but the simple fact is that
Isaiah said no such thing.

Kline argues that Col 2:11–12 connects circumcision and consecration to death, but is that really Paul's meaning? The text, translat-
ing very literally, says, "In whom also you were circumcised with a
circumcision not done by hands, in putting off the body of the flesh
in the circumcision of Christ; having been buried with him in baptism, in whom also you were also raised through faith in the power
of God, who raised him from the dead." Obviously there is a connection between our circumcision in Christ and our baptism/death and
resurrection in him (note the uses of "in whom" in each verse). But

[24] The noun *gezer* "half," is used to refer to the pieces of the sacrificed animals in Gen 15:17, but this has no bearing on Kline's case since circumcision does not appear in Genesis 15.

what is the connection? Is our death and resurrection in Christ the fulfillment of our circumcision in him?

The believer's burial with Christ in baptism cannot be the *fulfillment* of his circumcision in Christ, as though the *ordo salutis* were circumcision, burial, and resurrection. Unbelieving, uncircumcised Gentiles (the Colossians) were in no manner circumcised to God *prior* to their identification with Christ's death and resurrection through the gospel. One could argue, however, as Kline does, that circumcision and baptism are both metaphors of being crucified with Christ: "Paul affirms the union of the Christian with Christ in his circumcision-crucifixion."[25]

There are two basic interpretations of "in putting off the body of the flesh in the circumcision of Christ." The first is that the "body of the flesh" is the old nature. Thus, the NIV translates these words as "the sinful nature." Taking the text in this way, the "circumcision of Christ" is not the circumcision Christ himself underwent (whether as a baby or metaphorically at his crucifixion) but is the circumcision that Christ provides for believers, that is, spiritual cleansing and regeneration (thus, the NIV translates this as "the circumcision done by Christ"). The second interpretation takes the removal of the "body of flesh" to be a violent metaphor for death and so takes the "circumcision of Christ" to be his crucifixion, with which believers are identified.[26] This is Kline's view. Before proceeding further, however, it is important to note that even this latter interpretation provides little (if any) support for Kline's larger thesis that circumcision is maledictory and a consecration to death. Even if Paul uses the "removal of the body of the flesh" in this way here, he is merely using circumcision as a metaphor for death. He is not necessarily projecting back upon the entire Jewish institution of circumcision an ideology of circumcision as consecration-to-death.

---

[25] Ibid., 46.

[26] Advocates for this view include G. R. Beasley-Murray, *Baptism in the New Testament* (London: Macmillan, 1962), 152–53 and C. F. D. Moule, *The Epistle of Paul the Apostle to the Colossians and to Philemon* (Cambridge: University Press, 1962), 95–96. See especially the discussion of 2:11 in P. T. O'Brien, *Colossians, Philemon*, WBC (Dallas: Word, 1982), 114–21, which also advocates this view. M. Barth and H. Blanke, *Colossians*, trans. A. B. Beck, AB (New York: Doubleday, 1994), 317–19, are rather non-committal.

Having said that, however, there are good reasons for rejecting the idea that circumcision in v. 11 refers to the death of Christ. First, the interpretation involves a complicated reading of the verse that inserts ideas not really present. It requires that circumcision first be a violent physical act, the crucifixion of Jesus, and second, that it constitutes the believer's spiritual identification with that crucifixion. In the text, however, the only explicit object of circumcision is the believer ("you were circumcised"). There is no clear indication that Jesus is here portrayed as circumcised, the words "the circumcision of Christ" being ambiguous. The circumcision of v. 11, moreover, is not a physical act ("done without hands"). Christ's crucifixion was certainly done with hands. One could argue that the circumcision of believers was without hands, while the "circumcision of Christ" (his crucifixion) was done with hands, but that requires reading something into the text. In short, the "circumcision = crucifixion with Christ" interpretation requires that we read the verse in a convoluted fashion and see more than is actually there. By contrast, v. 12 speaks explicitly of our participation via baptism in Christ's experience of death and resurrection.

Second, our burial and resurrection with Christ in v. 12 are said to be "with him." But words such as "with him" are absent from v. 11, suggesting that Paul does not mean for us to think that we were circumcised with Christ. This distinction also gives us reason to believe that the circumcision metaphor and the baptism metaphor do not refer to one and the same thing, even if both are part of the larger event of personal salvation.

Third, circumcision is a poor metaphor for Christian identification with Christ's Good Friday to Easter experience in that there is no representation of resurrection. Immersion-baptism, by contrast, is an excellent metaphor for death and resurrection (v. 12). One may object that the metaphor of v. 11 only speaks of the death of Christ, but we may wonder whether Paul would create a metaphor that describes our death with Christ which cannot also illustrate our resurrection with him.

Fourth, circumcision is in fact not a metaphor for death at all. It is never used that way in the Bible. Elsewhere, not least in Paul, it is a positive thing: the removal of impurity and a mark of righteousness (Rom 2:25–29; 4:11; Phil 3:2–5). In the conflict between Paul and the Judaizers, circumcision became the focus of the conflict over whether Gentile believers should be subject to all the laws of Judaism, but even in Galatians there is no suggestion that circumcision is "maledictory" or represents death. The Israelites of the OT and the Jews of the NT no more regarded circumcision as a metaphor for death than we regard the removal of a wart as a metaphor for death. It was the excision of a foul thing. It would be strange indeed for Paul to create a metaphorical meaning for circumcision that is contrary to everything we see in the Bible, including Paul's own use of the term.

In Col 2:11, Paul exclusively has a spiritual circumcision in view, the removal of the old nature or "flesh" from those who turn to Christ. This applies to us but not to Christ. In the same manner, the "circumcision of Christ" is that which is provided in Christ for us. In short, the circumcision of v. 11 is exclusively done to and for us. This has two implications. First, the circumcision in Col 2:11 is not a consecration to death, a ritual ordeal text, or a malediction. As in the OT passages, circumcision here is positive, the removal of that which is loathsome. It is the circumcision of the heart (Deut 10:16; Jer 4:4) and may be identified with regeneration. Second, the connection between v. 11 and v. 12 is that of regeneration in Christ presented on the one hand as the removal of our old nature (the "body of flesh") as represented by circumcision, and on the other hand as vicarious participation with Christ in his death and resurrection as represented by baptism. Kline's interpretation of circumcision is impossible.

Baptism

The heart of Kline's work is the assertion that baptism corresponds to circumcision as the oath-sign of allegiance to our suzerain. In addition, he introduces the concept of the "water ordeal" to explain baptism and further make the point that the ritual is maledictory and speaks of judgment.

John's Baptism

For Kline, John's baptism was a sign of eschatological judgment. In particular, it was the sign of Yahweh's covenant lawsuit against Israel. John, like other prophets, was sent to denounce Israel's covenant violations. Kline argues that since Malachi spoke of a coming of "Elijah" (John) as a precursor of "the great and terrible day of the Lord," John's mission was to warn Israel before the Lord came in judgment (Malachi 4). He then observes that

> the baptismal waters of John have been understood as symbolic of a washing away of the uncleanness of sin. But the possibility must be probed whether this water rite did not dramatize more plainly and pointedly the dominant theme in John's proclamation…, namely, the impending judicial ordeal which would discriminate and separate between the chaff and the wheat, rendering a verdict of acceptance but also of rejection.[27]

In support of this interpretation Kline appeals to both ancient Near Eastern and biblical analogies. From the ancient Near East, he draws the parallel of the water ordeal as attested in the Sumerian law code of Ur-Nammu as well as in the more famous Old Babylonian code of Hammurabi. In the water ordeal, an accused person is cast into the river so that he might be either both convicted and punished by drowning or be acquitted by surviving. Citing the ancient texts, Kline observes that the rule is: "'If the River shows that man to be innocent and he comes forth safe,' he shall dispossess his false accuser and the latter shall be put to death. But, 'if the River overpowers him, his accuser shall take possession of his estate.'"[28]

Kline claims that the passages of Noah through the flood and of Israel through the Red Sea reflect the water-ordeal judgment. The psalmist's cries for deliverance from the floodwaters in Ps 69:2,15 also reflect this idea. Kline also sees the image of the ordeal judgment in John's words, "He will baptize you with the Holy Spirit and with fire" (Matt 3:11). He appeals for support to a Qumranic text (1QH 3:28ff) that speaks of an eschatological river of fire, and to similar imagery in Persian eschatology. He argues, "we must re-

---

[27] Kline, *By Oath Consigned*, 54.
[28] Ibid., 55.

member that fire was along with water a traditional ancient ordeal element."[29] Finally, John's baptism of Jesus indicates that the main function of the baptism is as a water ordeal: "As covenant Servant, Jesus submitted in symbol to the judgment of the God of the covenant in the waters of baptism. The event appropriately concluded with a divine verdict, the verdict of justification expressed by the heavenly voice."[30] Jesus underwent the water ordeal but emerged vindicated.

Therefore, Kline asserts, "the whole record of John's ministry points to the understanding of his water rite as an ordeal sign rather than as a mere ceremonial bath of purification."[31] This was, furthermore, a restatement of the maledictory oath of circumcision: "John thus proclaimed again to the seed of Abraham the meaning of their circumcision. Circumcision was no guarantee of inviolable privilege. It was a sign of the divine ordeal.... John's baptism was in effect a re-circumcising."[32]

Jesus' Baptizing Ministry

Kline contends that Jesus' baptizing ministry was an extension of John's, as the outward sign of God's covenant lawsuit against Israel. Furthermore, he argues that Jesus abruptly halted the baptizing work of his disciples when John was imprisoned, since that was the decisive event confirming the Jews' rejection of God.[33] We should note, however, that the NT indicates neither if nor when Jesus told his disciples to stop baptizing.

Christian Baptism

With the crucifixion and resurrection of Jesus, Kline asserts, baptism changed in one particular way: it no longer represented God's lawsuit against Israel since Israel's fate was now sealed. Instead, the gospel and the baptizing ministry of the church went out to the

---

[29] Ibid., 58.
[30] Ibid., 59.
[31] Ibid., 56.
[32] Ibid., 62.
[33] Ibid., 63–4.

Gentiles. Baptism still conveyed the same essential meaning, however: a water ordeal, a judgment of God, and a maledictory self-imprecatory oath.

Kline's primary text here is 1 Pet 3:20–21, where Peter compares
Noah's flood to baptism, allowing Kline to assert that for Peter baptism is a "sign of judicial ordeal."[34] When one recognizes that the
"flood waters were the ordeal instrument by which God justified
Noah," then one can understand that baptism is essentially forensic
and also an oath-sign, as Peter affirms by calling baptism a "pledge
to God of a good conscience."[35] Kline sees something similar in 1
Cor 10:1–6, where the Israelites were "baptized" into the cloud and
the sea and yet died in the desert because of their sin, another example of the "judicial ordeal," in which Israel initially passes through
and later falls on account of covenant violations.[36]

Baptism and the New Covenant

Christian baptism, Kline asserts, exhibits the meaning of the new
covenant. He argues that a fundamental problem here is that expositors so emphasize the discontinuity between the old and the new
that they fail to see the continuity.

> The newness of the New Covenant does not consist in a reduction of
> the Covenant of Redemption to the principle of election and guaranteed
> blessing. Its law character is seen in this too that it continues to be a cov-
> enant with dual sanctions. In this connection, account must be taken of
> Jeremiah's classic prophecy of the New Covenant (Jer. 31:31 ff.). Since
> exegesis has often erred by way of an oversimplified stress on the difference
> or newness of the divine work promised in this passage, it is important to
> mark the continuity that is evident even here between the New and the Old
> Covenants. For all its difference, the New Covenant of Jeremiah 31 is still
> patterned after the Sinaitic Covenant.[37]

The continuity of the covenants is this: as in the old covenant, believers in the new covenant are in a suzerain-vassal relationship with
God and take upon themselves the obligation of obedience. Christ

---

[34] Ibid., 65.
[35] Ibid., 66.
[36] Ibid., 67–68.
[37] Ibid., 74–75.

is, after all, not merely savior but also judge, and we Christians, too, face the two alternatives that our suzerain offers: blessings for obedience and curses for disobedience.[38] Thus, baptism is the "oath-sign" of allegiance to Christ, and the great commission is primarily about bringing people into submission to Christ's dominion.[39] Kline asserts, "Christian baptism is a sign of the eschatological ordeal in which the Lord of the covenant brings his servants to account."[40] Even if one is speaking only of the elect, he asserts, the salvation portrayed in baptism only comes about because of Christ's death. There is therefore "a thoroughgoing correspondence between the meaning of baptism and that of circumcision. Both are confessional oath-signs of consecration to the Lord of the covenant, and both signify his ultimate redemptive judgment with its potential of both condemnation and justification."[41] This remains true even though there is a "shift of emphasis" from malediction to benediction in the new covenant.

Evaluation of Kline's Understanding of New Testament Baptism

Kline's analysis of Christian baptism has little to commend it. His interpretation of the text is often misleading, he uses analogies that do not apply, and he fails to address more relevant analogies.

First, baptism cannot be taken to be a "water ordeal," and the material relating to this rite from Ur-Nammu and Hammurabi has no bearing on Christian baptism. The purpose of a water ordeal is to determine one's guilt or innocence. Neither John's baptism nor any subsequent Christian baptism has this purpose, nor does any biblical text suggest any such thing. People come to be baptized because they know that they are guilty, not to determine guilt or innocence. Thus, John's baptism was a "baptism of repentance for the forgiveness of sins" (Mark 1:4) and subsequent Christian evangelism urged people to be baptized and wash away their sins (Acts

---

[38] Ibid., 77–78.
[39] Ibid., 79–80.
[40] Ibid., 79.
[41] Ibid., 81.

22:16). Although no one doubts that John's ministry primarily involved warning people of a judgment to come, this does not mean that baptism is an ordeal or a self-imprecatory vow. Rather, it is a means of escape from judgment. In baptism, one acknowledges guilt and the need for forgiveness (that is, one repents). The alleged parallels from Qumran or Persian texts have no real bearing on the meaning of baptism. Even the biblical texts Kline cites (Noah's flood, Psalm 69) are of limited value in illuminating the meaning of what John was doing.

The one place one might make a case for baptism being an ordeal ritual is in the baptism of Jesus, since Jesus hears a word of approval from the Father upon emerging from the water. One might argue that John's baptism was a judicial ordeal and Jesus was the only person who came through vindicated rather than condemned. If that is the case, however, why was John perplexed that Jesus came to be baptized (Matt 3:14)? On the traditional reading of the event, in which baptism represents the repentance of the candidate, Jesus' desire for baptism is surprising since he (unlike the Pharisees) truly had no need of repentance. The common explanation is that Jesus was baptized in order to identify fully with sinful humanity (and also to recapitulate in his own person the experience of Israel passing through the Red Sea). In Kline's interpretation, however, it is John's confusion, not Jesus' baptism, that must be explained. If baptism is an ordeal meant to determine guilt or innocence, there is no reason that Jesus should not be baptized. Since the text states that Jesus' desire for baptism is surprising, the traditional interpretation of John's baptism as a call for repentance makes more sense than Kline's novel idea that it was a water ordeal.

Second, although Kline acknowledges that a washing away of sin is part of baptism, he treats this as secondary ("a mere ceremonial bath of purification"[42]). Instead, he looks to the water ordeal from late 3rd or early 2nd millennium Mesopotamia as the primary analogy for baptism, seemingly ignoring the contemporary cultural setting of John's baptism. We do not need to look so far afield. A standard feature of Palestinian Judaism in Jesus' day was the *mikveh* (plu-

---

[42] Ibid., 56.

ral: *mikvaoth*), a cistern used for a ritual bath. *Mikvaoth* are found throughout the territory of ancient Judea and Galilee, and Jews going into the Jerusalem temple passed through a great *mikveh*. Every practicing Jew, male and female, would have known the *mikvaoth* and probably would have used them many times. In appearance, a typical *mikveh* is quite similar to a modern church baptistry (of the sort used for immersion). The *mikveh* was expressly for cleansing, not for a water ordeal or oath-sign. In light of the intense focus on cleanness and uncleanness in Judaism (and in the OT), it is odd to give prominence to Sumerian and Akkadian water ordeals in explaining baptism.

Third, while Kline devotes a great deal of attention to his claim that baptism is a water ordeal, he offers little evidence that it is a self-imprecatory oath-sign (except for 1 Pet 3:21, discussed below). Circumcision, in Kline's view, is an oath-sign meant to call down curses upon oneself for failure to keep the terms of the covenant. But an oath-sign and a water ordeal are entirely different things. The former involves the suzerain-vassal treaty and brings the vassal into judgment for violations of the covenant; the latter is a test meant to see whether a person is guilty of a charge or not. Even if one were to accept fully Kline's claims that circumcision is an oath-sign and baptism a water ordeal, the case for relating the two would still have to be made.

Fourth, Kline's primary NT text, 1 Pet 3:20–21, does not sustain his case. The flood was not a "water ordeal" for Noah, a test to determine whether he was righteous. It was a judgment on the world. Since the ark was in water, Peter calls it a "baptism" in order to illustrate that Christians, too, are saved from the wrath of God as they pass through the waters (but with no hint that the water is a test of their righteousness). And Peter tells us baptism represents a cleansing from sin, not a "water ordeal" (1 Pet 3:21).[43]

A famous *crux* in the interpretation of v. 21 is the phrase normally translated either "the pledge of a good conscience toward God" (NIV, HCSB) or "an appeal to God for a good conscience"

---

[43] See also the remarks in E. J. Kilmartin, "Review of Meredith G. Kline, *By Oath Consigned: A Reinterpretation of the Covenant Signs of Circumcision and Baptism*," *CBQ* 31 (1969): 266–67.

(NRSV). The former might suggest that the individual is promising, at baptism, that henceforth he will keep his conscience clean, while the latter would suggest that the individual is appealing to God for a clean conscience (i.e., seeking forgiveness). Kline takes the former view, and takes the phrase to be "a solemn vow of consecration given in answer to the introductory question put to the candidate before baptism."[44] That is, he claims that the text shows baptism to be an "oath-sign."

The matter of whether the Greek word in question, *eperōtēma*, means "pledge" or "request" is complex, with evidence cited for both sides.[45] Regarding the words "good conscience," however, it may well be that neither of the above alternative interpretations is correct. Michaels has observed that the position of the words "good conscience" at the head of this difficult line (in Greek) suggests that it is not the *object* of the pledge/request (as though one were pledging to keep or were requesting a good conscience) but that it means "with a good conscience" (i.e., sincerely and without hypocrisy).[46] The words would thus mean that baptism is an "*earnest and sincere* pledge/request to God." It is rather strange, after all, either to pledge or to request a "good conscience." Conscience is self-directed and somewhat untrustworthy; it may be good or bad regardless of whether the individual is righteous or guilty. If one were either *pledging obedience* to God or *appealing for forgiveness* from God, one would expect to see either "obedience" or "forgiveness" or similar words in the verse rather than "good conscience." But as a statement that the believer comes to baptism in good faith, that is,

[44] Kline, *By Oath Consigned*, 67.

[45] In general, etymological evidence favors "request" while usage in certain papyri favors "pledge." For discussions, see J. H. Elliott, *1 Peter: A New Translation with Introduction and Commentary*, AB (New York: Doubleday, 2000), 679–81; T. R. Schreiner, *1, 2 Peter, Jude*, NAC (Nashville, TN.: Broadman & Holman, 2003), 195–97; L. Goppelt, *A Commentary on 1 Peter*, ed. F. Hahn, trans. J. E. Alsup (Grand Rapids: Eerdmans, 1993), 268–71; J. N. D. Kelly, *The Epistles of Peter and of Jude* (1969; reprint, Peabody, MA: Hendrickson, 1999), 163, as well as lexical discussion of *eperōtēma* in TDNT 2:688–9 and in NIDNTT 2:880–1.

[46] See the full discussion on 3:21 in J. R. Michaels, *1 Peter*, WBC (Dallas: Word, 1988), 213–22. P. H. Davids, *1 Peter*, NICNT (Grand Rapids: Eerdmans, 1994), 145, appears to come to similar conclusions. P. J. Achtemeier, *First Peter*, Hermeneia (Minneapolis: Fortress, 1996), 266–72, speaks against Michaels' view, but his own conclusion that the phrase "of a good conscience" is a subjective genitive is not really far removed from Michaels' view.

without conscious awareness of hypocrisy, the words "good conscience" are appropriate.

The precise meaning of *eperōtēma* is still unresolved. It may be that the word had the same ambiguity for Peter and his readers that it has for modern interpreters. The idea that *eperōtēma* implies an appeal cannot be dismissed, since Peter speaks of baptism as a washing away of sins, which is surely something the candidate is seeking. On the other hand, no one need deny that baptism is also a pledge of oneself to God and to the church, as is indicated in the renunciation of the devil in ancient rites of baptism. For example, the 1662 *Book of Common Prayer*, in its rite for the baptism of those in "riper years," includes the following:

> Question: Dost thou renounce the devil and all his works, the vain pomp and glory of the world, with all covetous desires of the same, and the carnal desires of the flesh, so that thou wilt not follow, nor be led by them?
> Answer: I renounce them all.
> Question: Dost thou believe in God the Father Almighty, Maker of heaven and earth? And in Jesus Christ his only-begotten Son our Lord? And that he was conceived by the Holy Ghost; born of the Virgin Mary...?
> Answer: All this I stedfastly believe.[47]

Even allowing that baptism includes such a "pledge toward God with a good conscience," it is another matter whether baptism is a suzerain-vassal covenant wherein the candidate calls down on his head all the curses of Deuteronomy 28. The real issue here goes beyond the interpretation of 1 Pet 3:21 and gets to the very meaning of the new covenant and to the question of to what extent it is a continuation of the old. This is discussed below.

Other NT texts cited by Kline likewise do not support the idea of a judicial ordeal. For example, 1 Cor 10:1–6, where Paul says that the Israelites passed through the sea and were baptized into Moses, does not mean that they endured a "judicial ordeal" in the Red Sea. As Peter does with Noah's flood, Paul here simply calls the crossing of the Red Sea a "baptism" to make an analogy to Christian baptism and so warn the Corinthians not to be complacent in their status before God. Although Paul warns of judgment, neither the crossing

---

[47] The 1662 Book of Common Prayer is available at http://www.eskimo.com/~lhowell/bcp1662/index.html.

of the Red Sea nor Christian baptism is itself to be construed as a judgment or ordeal for God's people; they are means of salvation. At the same time, Paul distinguishes the Israelite baptism "into Moses" from Christian baptism "into Christ." This analogy should not be pressed to mean that the Israelites were baptized into identification with Moses or into his leadership.[48] Rather, this language probably indicates a contrast between the old covenant of Sinai and the new covenant in Christ. This should make us all the more wary of using the Red Sea experience as a key to interpreting the covenant that is behind Christian baptism.

A full treatment of the new covenant and its relation to the old is far more than this chapter can address, but we will critique Kline's approach in light of some basic principles. Kline stresses the continuity between the covenants, pointing out the "law character" that remains in the new. In order to correct the misperception that the old covenant is "law" and the new is "grace," he seeks to show that the new covenant believer enters a suzerain-vassal covenant with God and calls down curses on himself (should he disobey) via the maledictory aspects of the oath-sign that is baptism.

But how should the continuity and the discontinuity between the two covenants be properly understood? Kline appears to argue the new covenant is little more than a re-issue of the old with some modification due to a change of circumstances (the Messiah has come, the Jews have been condemned and rejected in the "covenant lawsuit," and the gospel has gone to the Gentiles). But its fundamental character as a suzerainty treaty with curses and blessings is still intact. This analysis is entirely inadequate.

The new covenant is different in *kind*, not in *degree*, because the old covenant failed (Jer 31:32). The new covenant is often described as internal, on the heart, rather than external, written on law tables. This is true, but it comes about because the new covenant is much more than that: it is eschatological. Every member of the new covenant knows God (Jer 31:34). The present age, of course, is the age of the eschatological "now" and "not yet."

---

[48] See A. C. Thiselton, *The First Epistle to the Corinthians*, NIGTC (Grand Rapids: Eerdmans, 2000), 724–25.

The new covenant has come, but the new earth is not yet, and the church is still besieged within and without. There are complex issues here involving how the church at the present time can be an eschatological community composed entirely of the elect, and yet there are still those who are unbelievers within the church.[49] Even so, the new covenant is not a suzerainty treaty with the curses hanging like a sword of Damocles over an unbelieving covenant community. The true community of the new covenant is made up entirely of those who are redeemed; they all "know the Lord." Baptism is the mark that one has by faith come to God seeking membership in the eschatological community of the elect. Ideally, it is administered only to those with saving faith. If the ideal is not always in evidence in the present time, this does not change the eschatological orientation of the covenant itself. It is precisely for this reason that Kline's understanding of baptism as something for the unbeliever, bringing him under obligation to the covenant but being no indication that he knows God, is wrong. The Israelites living under the old covenant of Sinai were not an eschatological community and their membership in the covenant was a matter of national identity and not of personal faith. Deuteronomy *is* a suzerainty treaty; the new covenant *is not*.

Administration of Circumcision and Baptism

What are the ramifications of Kline's understanding of circumcision and baptism for the practice of the church? To answer this question, Kline returns again to the ancient Near Eastern suzerain-vassal treaties and their OT parallels. He cites in particular the treaty of Esarhaddon of Assyria with Ramataia, city-ruler of Urakazabanu, and another treaty between the Hittite Mursilis and Duppi-Tessub of Amurru. His main point is that "the servant king who was bound by the treaty was bound not alone but together with his subjects and

---

[49] Baptists believe that baptism should be reserved only for those who profess faith in Christ. The church, then, should comprise only regenerate members. When it becomes clear that a member—by his or her persistence in sin, without repentance—is not a Christian, the church should excommunicate that member. Thus the church in the period of the "not yet" shall attempt to match the eschatological community of God's elect, all the while knowing that the Lord alone ultimately knows those who are his.

his descendants."[50] Warnings from these treaties and from the OT indicate that disobedience brought curses not only on the principal vassal but also on all his descendants.[51] The ancient covenant thus incorporated households or communities under the vassals and not merely the vassals themselves. The personal commitment or willingness of the subordinate members of these communities was not an issue; all that mattered was that they were under the authority of a vassal, who was also under a higher suzerain.

By the end of his book, however, Kline has entrapped himself in his own arguments. What he *tries* to conclude is that baptism, like circumcision, is a maledictory oath-sign whereby the individual submits to the sovereign rule of God and calls down curses on himself for disobedience. In entering a suzerain-vassal relationship, the vassal comes not just as an individual but brings all those under his authority with him, as all of Abram's house was circumcised with him (Genesis 17). Thus, the Christian is obligated to have his children baptized and so bring them under God's covenantal authority even though they may as yet have no personal faith. As baptism does not confer blessing or promise salvation to the baptized infant, but rather places him under divine dominion, there is no need to explain what blessing it confers or represents.[52] Once they have so entered the covenant, the Christian father will do all in his power to bring his children to saving faith and so enable them to avoid the curses of covenant disobedience.

This chapter has already argued that none of Kline's distinctive ideas on circumcision and baptism is correct and that his understanding of the new covenant is seriously flawed. Kline says that baptism is best understood as an oath-sign of a suzerainty treaty, and I believe that he is wrong. If, however, we assume for the sake of argument that Kline's understanding of baptism is correct, the ramifications are profoundly troubling. Therefore, Kline attempts in the last pages of the book to save the reader from the conclusions of

[50] Kline, *By Oath Consigned*, 86.

[51] Ibid., 86–89. He cites, e.g., a treaty between the Hittite Tudhaliyas IV and Ulmi-Teshub to the effect that, should the vassal be disobedient, all of his descendants would be rooted out of the land, and compares texts such as Deut 28:18.

[52] See Kline, *By Oath Consigned*, 90.

his own study. For Kline there are two problematic outcomes, one fairly minor and one quite grave.

The minor problem is that his study suggests that baptism ought to be by immersion, a conclusion Kline wishes to avoid. Apart from the fact that, as he affirms, *baptizō* means to dip or immerse,[53] immersion is by far the best way to indicate death, a water ordeal, and self-imprecation. It is difficult to imagine how sprinkling water on the head could be construed as a life-threatening water ordeal. Kline responds that there is no need to consider immersion essential for Christian baptism, since other "baptisms" mentioned in the NT do not actually involve the immersion of the covenant people (e.g., Noah in the ark; Israel in the Red Sea).[54] Kline's error is in taking OT events that are retrospectively and metaphorically called "baptism" and enlisting them as guides to the ritual mode of actual baptism.

The second, more grave, problem is this: Kline has rightly observed that in Genesis 17 Abraham had all the males of his household, including adult slaves, circumcised. In addition, ancient suzerain-vassal treaties placed all the vassal's subordinates under the authority of the suzerain. If baptism is an oath-rite of a suzerainty treaty and is the NT counterpart to circumcision, then a Christian man should require that all his children be baptized—along with his wife, his servants and anyone else who is legitimately under his authority. *A suzerainty treaty applies not only to the vassal but to all who are under the vassal's legitimate authority.* The vassal's subordinates do not have the option of choosing not to submit to the vassal's suzerain. *Interpreting baptism under the rubric of a suzerainty treaty means that a Christian must require all persons under his authority to be baptized.*

This implies that the Constantinian vision of Christianity, in which the people are to become Christian because the emperor is Christian, is found to be valid after all. Baptism is simply the mark of subservience to Christendom and to the rule of God that it represents, and that mark can be imposed by a higher authority on another person apart from the willingness or faith of the subordi-

[53] Ibid., 69.
[54] Ibid., 83.

nate himself. There is more: if this is what baptism means, can one not extend the domain of God by extending the political domain of Christendom? This certainly has analogy in the suzerainty treaties that the Assyrians and Hittites imposed on their conquered vassals. Evangelism by the sword may, after all, be legitimate. Once a people bows to the suzerainty of a Christian conqueror, should not the conqueror require all those people to undergo baptism?

Kline sees all this, knows that it is wrong, and does all in his power to bring his suzerain-vassal analogy to a screeching halt, insisting that it applies only to the children of a believer and not to his wife, his servants or employees, or to the subjects of a Christian ruler. His arguments, however, do not ring true.

His case for excluding wives and slaves from enforced baptism is essentially this: in the NT we have examples of men who have unbelieving wives and slaves (1 Cor 7:12; Phlm 9–10). Therefore, wives and slaves are excluded from the general requirement that a man's subordinates be baptized, presumably on the grounds that they are adults. This analysis assumes that there was some rule in NT times that Christians were to baptize their children, but no such rule exists in the text itself. Furthermore, this argument ignores Kline's own analogies and the realities of Greco-Roman culture. As mentioned above, the circumcision rite of Genesis 17 specifically included all of Abraham's male slaves. If the main issues in the oath-rite are the vassal's authority over his subordinates and the extension of the suzerain's dominion, the fact that the subordinates are adults and no kin of the principal vassal is irrelevant. Either baptism follows the rules for this pattern, or it does not. Furthermore, the Greco-Roman household, the *oikos*, included not only the children of the citizen but his wife and slaves as well.

Citing Acts 16:31, Kline comments that mentioning the household along with the central authority of the house suggests a missions strategy of enlarging the covenant community by "the accretion of household authority units."[55] But his thinking here is incoherent. Acts 16:31 says that Paul and Silas told the Philippian jailer, "Believe on the Lord Jesus, and you will be saved, you and

[55] Ibid., 97.

your household" (NRSV). This may be taken to mean one of the following: (1) if you believe, your individual faith will be sufficient to save all members of your household, regardless of their faith; (2) if you as head of the house believe, you may use your influence to bring other members of your household to faith and salvation; (3) the message, "believe on the Lord Jesus and you will be saved" also applies to members of your household, so that if they believe, they will be saved, too. Option one is not credible, and option three is certainly valid. In the Roman culture of *pater familias, Pater familias* is a Latin term meaning "father of the family," which represents the absolute authority the male head of the household had over his wife, children, and slaves in the Roman empire. Many ancient readers would read the text in the sense of option two. In the Greco-Roman world, as in any traditional culture, the conversion of the head of a household would often naturally lead to the conversion of other members. This does not mean that the faith of subordinate members of the household could be coerced, and obviously there were cases where subordinates did not believe. But members of an ancient household would often follow the lead of the head of that household as a matter of course.

But in Kline's interpretation, if he consistently followed his presentation of the issue, "you and your household" (v. 31b) would have to mean, "If you believe and are saved, you will be expected to compel your household—here meaning only your small children—to be baptized in order to bring them under covenant authority in the hope that one day they will have saving faith, too." Apart from the fact that such an interpretation is outlandish, no Roman would hear the word "household" and think that only his small children were meant.

Kline himself explicitly denies any sort of Constantinian Christianity: "And to introduce the sword or other cultural sanctions into the new covenant's pattern of human authority in connection with its minor, household focus of authority would be alien to the distinctive spirit of the Covenant and its mission in the present age. The authority of the parent over the child involves no difficulty on this score since it is a spiritual-moral suasion. If the enforcement of parental authority has its corporal aspect, even that is not civil or judicial."[56] In response, it is difficult to see how the use of the sword would be alien to the "distinctive spirit" of the new covenant since Kline has taken great pains to show its continuity with the old covenant as well as with the spirit if not the letter of the suzerainty treaty. Furthermore, a father's baptism of his infant children has nothing to do with "spiritual-moral suasion"; it is simply a matter of authority. The infant has not been persuaded of anything and is in fact not even aware of what is happening to it. Finally, Kline's attempt to separate family authority from "civil and judicial" authority is entirely alien to the ancient world. *Pater familias*, the authority structure of the Roman family, was a matter of law and was judicially enforced. If baptism is a matter of the exercise of authority it cannot be restricted to small children. But if baptism cannot be compelled upon subordinates, Kline's whole argument collapses.

In the NT, baptism represents at least three and possibly four things. First, it signifies cleansing from sin and is thus "unto repentance." Obviously the threat of judgment is behind the need for baptism, but the baptism itself is (symbolically) the means of *escape* from judgment. Those who are baptized acknowledge their guilt and seek to have it washed away. Second, baptism is a ritual dying and rising again, symbolizing the believer's participation in the death and resurrection of Christ. This is the point of Col 2:12, discussed above. Third, it is a "sincere pledge/request to God" because in baptism one comes to God in genuine faith, seeking forgiveness, and desiring to walk in the light. Fourth, it may represent the effusion of the Holy Spirit upon the believer after the patterns of the descent of the Spirit at Jesus' baptism and the reception of the Spirit by Cornelius' household just prior to their baptism (Acts 10:44–48). In no place is baptism a water ordeal or a suzerain-vassal rite, and there is no validity in compelling anyone, infant or otherwise, to be baptized.

---

[56] Ibid., 101.

BAPTISM IN THE STONE-CAMPBELL RESTORATION MOVEMENT

A. B. Caneday[*]

Introduction: Restoring Baptism's Prominence

"There is one body and one Spirit just as also you were called with one hope of your calling. There is one Lord, one faith, one baptism, one God and Father of all, who is over all and through all and in all " (Eph 4:4–6).[1] Today, this unity of which the apostle Paul wrote in the first century seems illusory. From the single root of the apostolic faith many branches have emerged. Among these branches the singular aspect that most visibly distinguishes the varieties of multiple ecclesiastical traditions and theological systems seems to be baptism. It is lamentable that the body of Christ is fissured, particularly over this issue.

Yet, from Paul's questions to the Corinthians, it seems that baptism was partially a source of division even among the earliest Christians, at least in Corinth. Paul asks, "Has Christ been divided? Was Paul crucified on your behalf? Were you baptized into the name of Paul?" (1 Cor 1:13). His expression of gratitude that he personally baptized few of the Corinthians confirms that Paul recognizes that some in Corinth are inclined to attribute to baptism a significance that Christ did not give it (1:14–15). To correct their sacerdotal-born factionalism, Paul subordinates baptizing to preaching the gospel (1:17) and makes clear that sacerdotal power resides neither in baptism itself nor in the hands of the baptizer.

Nevertheless, Paul regards baptism as significant and not a bare symbol, for in his letter to Christians in Galatia he declares, "For as many of you as were baptized into Christ you have clothed yourselves with Christ" (Gal 3:27). He seems to equate all who have

---

[*] Ardel B. Caneday received his Ph.D. from Trinity Evangelical Divinity School, and is Professor of New Testament Studies and Biblical Theology at Northwestern College in St. Paul, Minnesota.

[1] Unless otherwise indicated, Scripture quotations are the author's translation.

put on Christ with all who are baptized into Christ, as though the two were fused as one. To be baptized into Christ by submission to the symbolic washing called for by the gospel is to be clothed with Christ Jesus. This seems remarkable since this statement appears at the pinnacle of Paul's argument against Jewish intruders who have attempted to seduce Christians in Galatia to subject themselves to circumcision of the flesh so that they might become Abraham's children (2:16–3:29, esp. 3:6–7,29). While Paul warns the Galatians that submission to the ritual act of circumcision would be to sever oneself from Christ (5:2–6), he identifies Christian baptism as the ritual act that marks one as clothed with Christ, and if one belongs to Christ, that one is Abraham's child (Gal 3:29). Those who are baptized into Christ, not those who are circumcised in the flesh, are Abraham's children. For him to argue in this manner—appealing to Gentiles not to submit to the rite of circumcision of the flesh but at the same time appealing to their reception of the rite of baptism into Christ—demonstrates that Paul's contention against the Judaizers is not simply or primarily over the effectiveness of circumcision.

In his letter to the Christians in Rome, Paul more expressly links receiving Christ's saving effects with Christian baptism when he says, "Or do you not realize that as many as were baptized into Christ Jesus were baptized into his death? We, therefore, were buried with him through baptism into this death with the purpose that just as Christ was raised from the dead through the glory of the Father, in the same manner we also might walk in newness of life" (Rom 6:3–4). As Paul formulates the matter, to be "baptized into Christ Jesus" is to be "baptized into his death." Thus, "baptism into Christ Jesus" is the *means* through (*dia*) which the believer is "buried with him."[2] This, Paul makes clear when he says, "Thus, we were buried with him *through* this baptism into death" (*sunetaphēmen autō dia tou baptismatos eis ton thanaton*). So, it seems that for Paul those baptized into Christ Jesus share in the redeeming effects of Christ's death.

Given the apostle Paul's appeal to "as many as were baptized," it is understandable, then, that as Christians cite the NT as their

[2] See D. J. Moo, *The Epistle to the Romans*, NICNT (Grand Rapids: Eerdmans, 1996), 361.

source of authority for Christian doctrine, they also disagree concerning how to express baptism's role in relation to salvation. Among Christian denominations, disagreements over baptism persist around four issues: to baptize or not to baptize, how to baptize (immersion, pouring, or sprinkling), whom to baptize (infants or confessors), and the effects of baptizing (*ex opere operato* ["by the work worked"; baptism actually confers grace], remission of sins, or mere symbolism).

How should Christians go about restoring baptism to its rightful prominence within the church and to an appropriate "baptismal consciousness"?[3] The history of one tradition within the American Protestant stream is punctuated with controversy over this question; the Restoration movement of the Second Great Awakening birthed a movement that has eventuated in the rise of the "churches of Christ," the Christian Church, and the Christian Church (Disciples of Christ). From their earliest days these churches have been suspected of heterodoxy. Such suspicions regarding Restorationism's most prominent founder, Alexander Campbell, were not without some warrant, as contemporary scholars of the movement (including its adherents, who seek rapprochement with evangelicals), acknowledge.[4] From its beginning, controversy has dogged the movement both from without and from within.[5] There have been internal disagreements over theological formulations concerning baptism and external accusations of embracing and teaching "baptismal regeneration."[6]

---

[3] On laments concerning "low baptismal consciousness" see D. F. Wright, "Recovering Baptism for a New Age of Mission," in *Doing Theology for the People of God*, ed. D. Lewis and A. McGrath (Downers Grove: InterVarsity, 1996), 51–66; S. J. Wellum, "The Means of Grace: Baptism," in *The Compromised Church*, ed. J. H. Armstrong (Wheaton: Crossway, 1998), 149–70.

[4] See the essays in W. R. Baker, ed., *Evangelicalism and the Stone-Campbell Movement* (Downers Grove: InterVarsity, 2002).

[5] The pejorative designation, "Stone-Campbell Movement," has been adopted by many (but not all) within the movement as an apt description, as indicated in book titles (see notes 4 and 6) and the Stone-Campbell Journal. This suggests that many of the movement's current leaders have come to terms with problems and defects in their theological roots with insightful self-criticism in place of apologetic defensiveness. Their literature confirms this observation.

[6] For a careful discussion of internal disagreements concerning formulations of baptism, see J. Cottrell, "The Role of Faith in Conversion," in *Evangelicalism and the Stone-Campbell Movement*, 71–90. For reflection upon other internal turmoil, including fractures, see R. T. Hughes, "Reclaiming a Heritage," *ResQ* 37: (1995): 129–38.

Alexander Campbell and his father Thomas, Scottish Presbyterian immigrants from Ireland, saw themselves as church "reformers" in early nineteenth-century America. They became prominent among several teachers who pled for religious denominations to follow the Bible alone, without any human additions whether in the form of creeds or formulas of faith. Thomas Campbell summarized his noble but overly optimistic reforming maxim as the premise for unification of Christians: "Where the Scriptures speak, we speak; where the Scriptures are silent, we are silent."[7] Their efforts to restore primitive Christianity from sectarian divisions among churches did not escape sectarianism itself, evident not only from the earliest days of the movement but also throughout its history.[8] The rift between Restorationist churches and evangelicals occurred early, when Baptists with whom Alexander and Thomas had associated withdrew fellowship from the "Reformers."[9] It is fitting, therefore, that a Baptist publication concerning baptism should consider the teachings of Alexander Campbell. It is especially fitting now that many of Campbell's heirs regularly fellowship with Baptists within the Evangelical Theological Society.

Historical-Theological Considerations of Restorationism on Baptism

Alexander Campbell was born into a Scottish family near Ballymena, County Antrim, Ireland September 12, 1788. His father, Thomas Campbell, was a Presbyterian minister of the Old Light, Anti-Burgher, Seceder Presbyterian Church.[10] Divisions and wrangling

[7] R. Richardson, *Memoirs of Alexander Campbell* (2 vols.; Philadelphia: J. B. Lippincott & Co., 1868–70; repr., Indianapolis: Religious Book Service, n.d.) 1:235–38.

[8] See, for example, D. A. Foster, P. M. Blowers, and D. N. Williams, "Baptism," *The Encyclopedia of the Stone-Campbell Movement*, ed. D. A. Foster, P. M. Blowers, A. L. Dunnavant, and D. N. Williams (Grand Rapids: Eerdmans, 2004), 57–67.

[9] R. G. Torbert, *A History of the Baptists*, 3d ed. (Valley Forge, PA: Judson, 1962), 274. Torbert states, "In the eventual separation of the 'Reform' element from the Baptist ranks, the latter were the aggressors. It was they who initiated action to exclude the followers of Campbell. When the excluded body was the larger, the Baptists handled it by withdrawing fellowship from them, as in the case of the North District Association in Kentucky in 1829. The first association to take formal action against the Reformers was the Redstone of Pennsylvania in 1825–26."

[10] The Seceder Presbyterian Church was born when the Church of Scotland attempted to enforce church law that prohibited congregations the right to select their own pastors. The Se-

in the church troubled Thomas Campbell, so that in 1804 he held meetings in an endeavor, without success, to reunify Presbyterians. Church conflict and other factors converged to break his health. In 1807, upon his physician's advice, leaving his academy in Ahorey under the direction of Alexander, his eighteen year old son, Thomas took a voyage to America, with plans that his family would soon follow him. From the Synod of North America he received an appointment to the Chartiers Presbytery in southwestern Pennsylvania, a region settled by Scots-Irish immigrants.[11] Within a year of accepting appointments in Allegheny, Beaver, Indiana, and Washington Counties, Thomas Campbell discovered that the divisiveness that characterized the Seceder church in the old country marked the church in America also. He found himself charged by the Presbytery with expressing beliefs discordant with the Westminster Confession of Faith. These charges, though doubtless arising from his preaching of Christian tolerance and union, also seem to have arisen from the ministerial jealousy of his accusers.[12] His appeal to the Synod of North America brought reversal of suspension but not reprieve. Spied upon and harassed, on September 13, 1808, Campbell finally renounced submission to the Chartiers Presbytery and the Synod of North America.[13] Not until April 18, 1810 was he permanently sus-

ceders were determined that congregations should have the right to select their own preachers, seceding in 1747.

[11] See the discussion of the Scots-Irish settlement of southwestern Pennsylvania in T. Sowell, *Black Rednecks and White Liberals* (San Francisco: Encounter Books, 2005), 4f.

[12] Elder James Foster, who immigrated at the same time as Campbell, describes Thomas Campbell in a personal letter: "A contemporary, he commenced his labors in this country under the direction of the Chartiers presbytery. They viewed him with a jealous eye, being superior to them both as a scholar and a preacher. In the course of some time, they brought a charge against him before the presbytery for not preaching the gospel. He defended himself against this charge but they would not acquit him. He appealed to the Synod and they acquitted him from the charge" (cited by F. D. Kershner, *The Christian Union Overture: An Interpretation of the Declaration and Address of Thomas Campbell* [St. Louis: Bethany, 1923], 17).

[13] Alexander Campbell included within his *Memoirs of Elder Thomas Campbell* the full text that his father had submitted to the Presbytery of Chartiers, of which, the following is noteworthy: "It is with sincere reluctance, and, at the same time, with all due respect and esteem for the brethren of this reverend Synod who have presided in the trial of my case, that I find myself in duty bound to refuse submission to their decision as *unjust* and *partial*, and also *finally to decline the authority*, while they continue thus to overlook the grievous and *flagrant mal-administration of the Presbytery of Chartiers*. And I hereby do decline all ministerial connection with, or subjection to, the Associate Synod of North America, on account of the aforesaid corruptions and grievances; and

pended by the synod. Departure from the Presbyterians neither reduced nor terminated Campbell's ministerial work. During the summer of 1809 Campbell and a group of friends and neighbors with
whom he had been meeting regularly to observe the Lord's Table
formed the Christian Association of Washington. They drafted a
document, "The Declaration and Address," a call for Christian unity,
that reflected a response to the ecclesiastic bickering that Campbell
encountered in America.[14] The signing members specifically stated
that the association was not a church.[15] This association never grew
larger than the friends who followed Campbell out of the Seceder
Presbyterian Church.

On January 1, 1808, Thomas Campbell sent word for his family to join him in America. They began to make preparations and
finally boarded the *Hibernia* at Londonderry on October 1, 1808,
but a storm damaged the ship and delayed their journey. The family settled in Glasgow, Scotland where Alexander entered the university, studying Greek, French, logic, philosophy, ethics, natural
history, and theology, and teaching Latin, grammar, and arithme-
tic. At the University of Glasgow, where Thomas Reid had replaced
Adam Smith and taught as recently as 1781, Alexander's thinking
was shaped by Reid's philosophical thought of the Scottish School
of Common Sense as well as by John Locke and Francis Bacon.[16]

do henceforth hold myself altogether unaffected by their decisions. And, that I may be properly
understood, I will distinctly state that, while especial reference is had to the corruptions of the
Presbytery of Chartiers, which constitute only a part of this Synod, *the corruptions of that Presbytery
now become also the corruptions of the whole Synod; because when laid open to this Synod, and pro-
tested against, the Synod pass them over without due inquiry, and without animadversion.*"

[14] See J. Smith, "The Declaration and Address," *ResQ* 5:3 (1961): 113–18. The first sentence
of the "Declaration and Address" states, "From the series of events which have taken place in
the churches for many years past, especially in this Western country, as well as from what we
know in general of the present state of things in the Christian world, we are persuaded that it is
high time for us not only to think, but also to act, for ourselves; to see with our own eyes, and
to take all our measures directly and immediately from the Divine standard; to this alone we feel
ourselves Divinely bound to be conformed, as by this alone, we must be judged."

[15] The "Declaration and Address" specifically says, "That this Society by no means considers itself a Church, nor does at all assume to itself the powers peculiar to such a society; nor do
the members, as such, consider themselves as standing connected in that relation; nor as at all
associated for the peculiar purposes of Church association; but merely as voluntary advocates
for Church reformation."

[16] See L. Garrett, *The Stone-Campbell Movement* (Joplin, MO: College Press, 1981), 24–60;
R. Tristano, *The Origins of the Restoration Movement: An Intellectual History* (Atlanta: Glenmary

While in Glasgow he also participated in the reform movement led by Robert and James Haldane. Finally departing Scotland on August 3, 1809, Campbell and his family arrived in New York two months later and reached western Pennsylvania soon after.

Initially twenty-one year old Alexander deferred to his father in the newly established Christian Association, at least in public. When Alexander arrived in Pennsylvania, the *Declaration and Address* was at press. He tells of reading the proof sheets and of commenting to his father that, if he truly adhered to the affirmations of the document, he would have to revoke baptizing infants.

> I read to him the third proposition . . . "That in order (to church union and communion) nothing ought to be inculcated upon Christians as articles of faith nor required of them as terms of communion but what is expressly taught and enjoined upon them in the Word of God. Nor ought anything to be admitted as of divine obligation in their church constitution and management but what is expressly enjoined by the authority of our Lord Jesus Christ and his apostles upon the NT church; either in express terms, or by approved precedent."
> On reading this, I asked him in what passage or portion of the inspired oracles could we find a precept or an express precedent for the baptism or sprinkling of infants in the name of the Father, the Son and the Holy Spirit? His response in substance was "It was merely inferential."[17]

Alexander envisioned deeper church reform than his father, as was to become evident after the Christian Association's intended reform movement stalled. In the spring of 1810, as the Christian Association continued to take the form of a church, Thomas Campbell applied to the Synod of Pittsburgh for acceptance by the Presbyterian Church (not Seceder). On October 2, 1810, the Synod deliberated and, two days later, issued a dense statement of rejection, viewing Campbell's remonstration for unity as doctrinally simplistic, even naïve, and hence divisive. From the Christian Association emerged the Brush Run Church on May 4, 1811.[18] The church ordained Alexander Campbell as the minister of the congregationally governed body.

Research Center, 1988), 14–30. See also the discussion by R. C. Kurka, "The Role of the Holy Spirit in Conversion: Why Restorationists Appear to Be out of the Evangelical Mainstream," *Evangelicalism and the Stone-Campbell Movement*, 144ff.

[17] Campbell, *Memoirs of Thomas Campbell*, 23 (cited by Kershner, *The Christian Union Overture*, 35–37).

[18] The Synod minutes state, "After hearing Mr. Campbell at length, and his answers to vari-

When Margaret, Alexander's wife, gave birth to their first child one day after their first anniversary on March 13, 1812, he faced a dilemma. The question about infant baptism was no longer simply academic. After a thorough study of Scripture, he concluded that his daughter did not need to be baptized, but that he did, and by immersion. In June he persuaded Matthias Luce, a Baptist minister, to immerse him without obligating him to submit to any Baptist confession or creed. Alexander and his wife, his parents, and his sister were baptized. Two others from the Brush Run Church also submitted to baptism.[19]

One may get a biased understanding of Alexander Campbell's, and thus Restorationism's, view of baptism if he fails to ponder the ideas and forces that prompted Campbell's intense wrestling with the doctrine of baptism. His turmoil brought him not only to reject paedobaptism and to receive rebaptism by immersion but more so to insist that he be baptized without being required to submit to any confession or creed except one, that "Jesus is the Son of God." Campbell insisted upon this because he had come to reject the approach of administering baptism and admitting into church membership that had come to dominate the frontier church. The practice was to require candidates for baptism in Baptist churches and for membership in paedobaptist churches to offer a "narrative of conversion" to account for their gradual experience of God's work of regenerating grace. These narratives usually included accounts of progression from sorrow for sin to receiving God's peace of forgiveness. They also recounted the individual's use of means, such as prayer, Bible readings, and sermons that brought about assurance of sins forgiven.[20]

ous questions proposed to him, the Synod unanimously resolved, that however specious the plan of the Christian Association and however seducing its professions, as experience of the effects of similar projects in other parts has evinced their baleful tendency and destructive operations on the whole interests of religion by promoting divisions instead of union, by degrading the ministerial character, by providing free admission to any errors in doctrine, and to any corruptions in discipline, whilst a nominal approbation of the Scriptures as the only standard of truth may be professed, the Synod are constrained to disapprove the plan and its native effects" (cited by Kershner, *The Christian Union Overture*, 35–37).

[19] Foster, Blowers, and Williams, "Baptism," *The Encyclopedia of the Stone-Campbell Movement*, 58.

[20] See P. Caldwell, *The Puritan Conversion Narrative: The Beginnings of American Expres-*

When Alexander was still in Ireland at sixteen, he took up deep study, particularly of Scripture's accounts concerning the Holy Spirit. He also read Richard Baxter's *Call to the Unconverted*, John Owen's works on the Holy Spirit and *Christologia, The Person and Glory of Christ* and *The Death of Death in the Death of Christ*.[21] In keeping with the doctrine he had learned in the Presbyterian tradition, Campbell earnestly looked "for a divine interposition of a peculiar character at a certain crisis."[22] He said, "I desired to feel a special interest, and for this I prayed."[23] Earlier he had recounted,

I well remember what pains and conflicts I endured under a fearful apprehension that my convictions and my sorrows for sin were not deep enough. I even envied Newton of his long agony. I envied Bunyan of his despair. I could have wished, and did wish, that the Spirit of God would bring me down to the very verge of suffering the pains of the damned, that I might be raised to share the joys of the genuine converts. I feared that I had not sufficiently found the depravity of my heart, and had not yet proved that I was utterly without strength. Sometimes I thought that I felt as sensibly, as the ground under my feet, that I had gone just as far as human nature could go without supernatural aid, and that one step more would place me safe among the regenerated of the Lord; and yet Heaven refused its aid. This, too, I concealed from all the living. I found no comfort in all the declarations of the gospel, because I wanted one thing to enable me to appropriate them to myself. Lacking this, I could only envy the happy favorites of heaven who enjoyed it, and all my refuge was in a faint hope that I one day might receive that aid which would place my feet upon the rock.[24]

For Alexander, then, the Presbyterian tradition that first guided but then inhibited his religious experience was profoundly negative.

sion, Cambridge Studies in American Literature and Culture (Cambridge: Cambridge University Press, 1983), 45f, 163ff.; J. C. Brauer, "Conversion: From Puritanism to Revivalism," *JR* 58 (1978), 27–43. See also B. T. Leonard, "Getting Saved in America: Conversion Event in a Pluralistic Culture," *RevExp* 82 (1985): 111–27. For examples of "conversion narratives," see H. T. Kerr and J. M. Mulder, eds., *Conversions: The Christian Experience* (Grand Rapids: Eerdmans, 1983). J. M. Hicks's article, "'God's Sensible Pledge': The Witness of the Spirit in the Early Baptismal Theology of Alexander Campbell," *Stone-Campbell Journal* 1 (1998): 5–26, is particularly helpful for resources as well as for content.

[21] Alexander Campbell, "Reply to Robert B. Semple," *The Millennial Harbinger* 1 (March, 1830): 137. Campbell misstates Owen's title as *Death of Deaths in the Death of Christ*. Hicks, "God's Sensible Pledge," 5–26, has been an invaluable resource for this portion of the essay.

[22] Alexander Campbell, "Reply to the Above," *The Christian Baptist* 4 (June, 1827): 228.

[23] Alexander Campbell, "Letter II to Bishop Semple," *The Millennial Harbinger* 1 (April, 1830): 179.

[24] Alexander Campbell, "Conscience.—No. II," *The Christian Baptist* 3 (1826): 218.

As he assessed the matter, they were contrary to what he found in Scripture. Worse still was the blending of that tradition with the religious enthusiasm of revivalism that was sweeping the American frontier. This enthusiasm was attached to various "new measures," particularly the "mourner's bench," and the expectation of pre-scribed "religious experiences" that formed "conversion narratives" widely required for candidacy for baptism and church membership.[25] Thus, Alexander reacted not only against what he called his own "bad education" in the Presbyterian tradition but also against the "enthusiasm" of subjective "conversion experiences" characteristic of the Second Great Awakening's revivalism.[26] With some validity, he contended that "throughout Christendom every man's religious experience corresponds with his religious education."[27] In another place he noted,

> Here this system [of finding the depths of one's depravity] ends, and enthusiasm begins. The first Christians derived their joys from an assurance that the gospel was true. Metaphysical Christians derive theirs not from the truth of the gospel, but because they have been regenerated, or discover something in themselves that entitles them to thank God that they are not as the publican. The ancients cheered themselves and one another by conversing on the certainty of the good things reported by the apostles—the moderns, by telling one another what "the Lord has done for their souls in particular." Their agonies were the opposition made by the world, the flesh, and the devil, to their obeying the truth. Our agonies are a deep and solemn concern for our own conversion. Their doubts were first, whether the gospel were true, and, after they were assured of this, whether they might persevere through all trials in obeying the truth. Ours, whether our conversion is genuine. More evidence of the truth removed their first doubts, and the promises of the gospel, with the examples around them, overcame the last. A better opinion of ourselves removes ours. In a word, the philanthropy of

[25] See Alexander Campbell, "The Times.—No. IV," *The Millennial Harbinger* 2 (1831): 211–15.

[26] Campbell, "The Times.—No. IV," 211–15. Here Campbell argues, "Another, under the same system, receives no comfort because he has not found the infallible signs in himself of being a true believer. He despairs—he is tormented. He concludes that he is one of the reprobates. He is about to kill himself. What about? Not because there is no Saviour, no forgiveness, no mercy. Not because the gospel is not true; but because it is true, and because he cannot find in himself the true signs of genuine conversion. Thousands have been ruined—have been shipwrecked here. This the bible never taught. This case never occurred under the apostles' teaching. It is the genuine offspring of the theological schools. It is the experience of a bad education."

[27] Campbell, "The Times.—No. IV," 211–15.

God was the fountain of all their joys—an assurance that we are safe is the source of ours.[28]

Reacting against his religious education, Alexander eventually became convinced that in Scripture assurance of the remission of sins is found alone in believing God's promise of forgiveness and that his promise is *received through immersion* and through no other means.

Alexander Campbell played a prominent role during the Second Great Awakening, calling Christians to reform by abandoning creeds, confessions, and human instructions and to return to the "primitive" teachings of the apostles. Yet, even many of Campbell's ecclesial heirs acknowledge his theological excesses and over-reactions to the abuses of his times.[29] Although he occasionally indicates awareness that ideas and events of his era influenced him as much as others,[30] he often exhibits presumptuous confidence in his ability to be objective and to rise above influences that ensnared the minds and beliefs of others and made them slaves of human traditions.[31]

[28] Alexander Campbell, "Conscience.—No. II," *The Christian Baptist* 3 (1826): 218.

[29] For example, see Kurka, "Why Restorationists appear to be out of the Mainstream," 140–48. Other contributors to Evangelicalism and the Stone-Campbell Movement also offer cautious criticisms of Campbell's theological views.

[30] For example, see Alexander Campbell, "Letter II to Bishop Semple," *The Millennial Harbinger* 1 (1830): 178. Campbell says, "Brother Semple, you and I were not taught first by Paul, and therefore we will have to wrestle with ourselves for some time before we can rise from among the pots, and think and feel like them who were taught by the Apostles. Some vessels long retain the flavor of the first liquor which filled them. Our minds resemble them a little. Neither you nor I, methinks, will ever understand and feel the whole result of the christian institution upon our minds as though we had never been indoctrinated into the systems of Calvin, Gill, and Fuller. I have been at war with myself, more than with any man living, for many years, to eradicate from my mind every plant which Paul did not plant, nor Peter water. In this I consider myself as having only partially succeeded. Care is to be taken here, as well as elsewhere, that, in rooting out the tares, the wheat is not also rooted out."

[31] See, e.g., the exchange of letters between Spencer Clack and Alexander Campbell, *The Millennial Harbinger* 1 (1830): 265–72. See also a subsequent exchange of letters between the two: "Spencer Clack to the Editor of the Harbinger," and "Reply to Brother Clack," *The Millennial Harbinger* 1 (1830): 289–92; 292–96. Spencer Clack argues that while Alexander Campbell decries creeds and confessions he has written his beliefs and opinions voluminously and that those who follow his views look to his writings as creeds and confessions. "I now ask you, since according to your creed, the gospel facts alone are considered the bond of union, among christians in the millennial day, why do you distract the churches by a publication of your opinions? Why wage a war against the disciples of Christ, because they reject your mere opinions, your favorite inventions, your human, unsafe, unauthorized contrivances. The churches have their creeds—you, your opinions" ("Spencer Clack," 290). Campbell fails to recognize that his writings have creedal significance to his followers in his artful dodging of the question: "But,

Several of Campbell's personal characteristics coalesced to give birth to his provocative theology of baptism with its attendant doctrines of the Spirit and of human capabilities, all of which properly raised questions and caused debate. These characteristics included his Presbyterian rearing, his native intellect, his skill in rhetoric and debate, his reactions to the enthusiasm and new measures of revivalism, his sensitive and defensive responses to criticism, his readiness to engage any who dared oppose his views, and his failure to recognize that his call for unity, though noble sounding, in fact provoked hostilities and schisms. Campbell's reformation of the church was as influenced by the ideas current in his time as were the views and beliefs of any of those he opposed, though he often seemed blind to this fact.[32]

Alexander Campbell's teachings concerning baptism did not at first incite controversy. Having joined the Redstone Baptist Association in 1815, he skillfully championed the Baptists' belief in believers' baptism in debates with Presbyterian ministers John Walker and William L. MacCalla.[33] His beliefs concerning the purpose of baptism, however, noticeably shifted during the 1820s.[34] When he debated John Walker in 1820, his view was in essential agreement with Baptists. The following year he read a tract on baptism that closely associated baptism with remission of sins.[35] When he engaged MacCalla in debate in Washington, Kentucky, he linked baptism

---

brother Clack, your calling immersion for the remission of sins, or any other apostolic institution Campbellism, or an opinion of mine, is like telling me that the divine mission of Moses, or that the sonship of the Lord Jesus, or the resurrection of the dead, are but *opinions* of mine" ("Reply to Brother Clack," 293).

[32] For a careful critical assessment of Alexander Campbell's epistemology, theological assumptions, and his understanding of the Holy Spirit's role in conversion, see Kurka, "Why Restorationists appear to be out of the Mainstream," 138–58.

[33] Foster, Blowers, and Williams, "Baptism," *Encyclopedia of the Stone-Campbell Movement*, 58.

[34] Ibid.

[35] See W. Baxter, *Life of Walter Scott with Sketches of His Fellow-Laborers, William Hayden, Adamson Bentley, John Henry, and Others* (reprint, Nashville: Gospel Advocate Co., n.d.), 47–51. For a full discussion of the significance of the tract by Henry Errett, a Scottish Baptist from New York City, see J. M. Hicks, "The Recovery of the Ancient Gospel: Alexander Campbell and the Design of Baptism," in *Baptism and the Remission of Sins*, ed. D. W. Fletcher (Joplin, MO: College Press, 1990), 111–70.

and remission of sins much more closely.[36] He argued, "The blood of Christ, then, *really* cleanses us who believe from all sin. . . . The water of baptism, then, *formally* washes away our sins. Paul's sins were *really pardoned* when he believed, yet he had no solemn pledge of the fact, no *formal* acquittal."[37] "I do earnestly contend that God, through the blood of Christ, forgives our sins through immersion—through the very act and in the very instant."[38] He contended that forgiveness of sins and salvation come only by the death of Christ Jesus through belief in him, so that one receives "actual" forgiveness of sins apart from baptism, but "formal" remission of sins in the act of baptism.[39] Before the close of the decade, Campbell's view of baptism merged actual and formal forgiveness.[40]

It was not only the seeming closeness of Campbell's views to the Roman Catholic view of baptism as actually conferring grace (*ex opere operato*) that incited opposition.[41] His nearly Pelagian doctrines of human nature and faith, and his doctrines of the Holy Spirit and of the Trinity are all dubious, as Robert Semple, a Baptist minister, uncovered.[42] Campbell's initial reply to Semple's queries exhibits a certain malapert patronization:

[36] R. Durst, "'To Answer or Not to Answer': A Case Study on the Emergence of the Stone-Campbell Movement Amongst the Baptist Churches of Kentucky in the 1820s," *Journal for Baptist Theology and Ministry*, 3 (2005): 84.

[37] Durst, "'To Answer or Not to Answer'," 84. The citation is from *A Public Debate on Christian Baptism between the Rev. W. L. MacCalla, a Presbyterian Teacher and Alexander Campbell* (1842; repr., Kansas City: Old Paths Book Club, n.d.), 116–18.

[38] Alexander Campbell, "The Ancient Gospel—No. VII. Christian Immersion," *The Christian Baptist* 5 (July 7, 1828): 277.

[39] Durst, "'To Answer or Not to Answer'," 84.

[40] Church of Christ scholars—Foster, Blowers, and Williams—agree with the Baptist Durst's observations concerning Campbell's shifting view on baptism during the 1820s ("Baptism," *Encyclopedia of the Stone-Campbell Movement*, 58).

[41] The Council of Trent states concerning baptism: "If any one shall say that these sacraments of the new law cannot confer grace by their own power [*ex opere operato*], but that faith alone in the divine promise suffices to obtain grace, let him be accursed" (Concil. Trid. sess. vii. can. viii).

[42] Semple made seven inquiries that Alexander Campbell published and answered briefly (*The Millennial Harbinger* 1 [1830]: 350–51).

"First: What is your view of the natural *state of man*? Do you believe him to be, according to your interpretation of the scriptures, in a state of total depravity?

Secondly: Do you consider *faith* as the simple act of the mind acknowledging the mere facts of the gospel, irrespective of any divine agency exerted upon the faculties previously?

Think you, Paul would, were he now on earth, propose such questions to me, either to detect my unsoundness in the faith, or to furnish topics for debate? . . . Why not, then, propose to me some *christian* topic from the Christian scriptures? If my soundness, or unsoundness in the faith, be worth an inquiry, why propose to me the questions of the schools?"[43]

Thirdly: In your new translation, you have substituted the term *reformation* instead of *repentance* as it is in the old. Please to define reformation according to your views.

Fourthly: I understand you to assert that *immersion* or *baptism* is the act of regeneration, and the medium of forgiveness of sins; and that the scripture does not authorize us to assent or believe that any are regenerated or forgiven until immersed. In other words, that the blood of Christ is never applied, but through the medium of baptism. Is this a correct statement of your view upon this point?

Fifthly: You speak of the Holy Spirit after baptism. Do you mean by the Holy Spirit what is commonly called the Holy Ghost? or do you mean a holy temper of mind effected by the mere words by obedience to its requirements?

Sixthly: In some of your last numbers, you speak of the *Trinity* in a way which has excited some suspicion of a leaning towards *Unitarianism*. Is there any ground for such suspicion? For truth's sake, for your own sake, be explicit upon this head.

Seventhly: What are your views of the, *future punishment of wicked men*? Is it eternally, and without end? There are some other points of minor importance on which we are widely at variance. To these we may finally attend. If the above be investigated in a proper spirit, I shall hope for good results."

Kurka acknowledges that Campbell's doctrine of human nature is dangerously close to Pelagianism ("Why Restorationists appear to be out of the Mainstream," 146–47).

[43] Alexander Campbell, *The Millennial Harbinger* 1 (1830): 354. Concerning Semple's question about the total depravity of humans, Campbell responds: "But the question about total depravity is an abstract and speculative questions. It is a proper theme of speculative debate. He that affirms that all men are *totally* depraved, makes all men alike depraved, and as depraved as Satan; for Satan is no more than *totally* depraved. If, moreover, every child born be *totally* depraved, there is no possibility of any person becoming worse than another, nor worse at any period of his life than he was when he first saw the Sun. Are you prepared for this? If all infants are totally depraved, how can men become worse and worse, as Paul affirms some do?" (*The Millennial Harbinger* 1, 355). Despite his tutelage in the Westminster Confession, Campbell shows remarkable misunderstanding of the doctrine of total depravity. Campbell also gives indications of being a Glasite and a Sandemanian in his views of faith. See Kurka, "Why Restorationists appear to be out of the Mainstream," 144.

Of faith, the pertinent portion of his reply is: "Whether a man shall believe any thing is always dependent on the testimony, and on his hearing or attending to it. The power of producing faith is in the testimony. The power of producing hearing is in the sound. The power of producing sight is in the object. A man cannot hear an audible sound, nor see a visible object, nor believe a credible testimony, if he do not attend to them. I sometimes hear not the clock strike once in a day, and often do not see the most visible objects; because my mind is absorbed in thought upon other objects. So many do not believe the gospel, although it is perfectly credible, and as much in their power to believe it, as it is in one who has ears, to hear a bell toll, or a trumpet sound at a proper distance, because they have their minds engrossed and preoccupied with other objects." (*The Millennial Harbinger* 1, 355.)

Concerning the Holy Spirit and Trinity, Campbell's responses are insufficient and have led Christian Church scholar Robert Kurka to say that Campbell's view entails "an obvious depersonalization of the Holy Spirit, resulting in an 'unintentional' binitarianism. While Campbell

Campbell seems not to have realized that such responses placed his beliefs beyond examination, while he critically scrutinized others' beliefs and exhibited an intense dislike of the ordained ministry.[44] His Scottish education, keen intellect, and rhetorical and debating skills gave him advantage over his less educated opponents on the frontier. Also, his acquisition of a printing press enabled prodigious publication of his own writings that made him a nationally known figure of considerable influence.[45]

Despite his early alliance with the Redstone Baptist Association in 1815, his developing views on baptism began to alienate him from the Association. When they began to move toward expelling Campbell in September 1823, he and thirty other members of the Brush Run church received permission to establish a church in Wellsburg, Virginia (now West Virginia). The following year, the church secured membership in the Mahoning Baptist Association, in the Western Reserve of Ohio.[46] Despite Campbell's departure from the Brush Run church, in 1824 the Redstone Baptist Association resolved "that this Association have no fellowship with the Brush Run church."[47]

himself refused to equate the Spirit with the biblical text . . . he nonetheless made too many statements that appeared to yield a contradictory conclusion" ("Why Restorationists appear to be out of the Mainstream," 147–48).

[44] Campbell seemed to welcome opportunities to publish comments from others that would aid and abet his cause. Such is the published report of the "Journal of a Traveler," *The Millennial Harbinger* 1 (1830): 341–47. Francis, the traveler, reports that he had encountered a Presbyterian minister, Mr. Lane, who complained, "Campbell is doing a world of mischief to the Baptist denomination, and he regretted it very much." Francis asked, "How?" The Presbyterian replied: "By creating and fomenting divisions." Francis reports, "From a little further conversation, I ascertained that he had never read the writings of A. C. and was altogether ignorant of what he most vehemently opposed. *But this is perfectly in character for a clergyman!*"

[45] On Campbell's skillfulness and efficiency as a printer, see Gary Holloway, "Alexander Campbell as a Publisher," *ResQ* 37 (1995): 28–35.

[46] J. M. Hicks, "The Role of Faith in Conversion: Balancing Faith, Christian Experience, and Baptism," in *Evangelicalism and the Stone-Campbell Movement*, ed. W. R. Baker (Downers Grove: InterVarsity, 2002), 94, states, "Campbell had 'checkmated his opponents in the [Redstone] Association,' and while he was present at the Redstone meeting of 1823, he was not a messenger of the Brush Run church because he was no longer a member there." He had removed himself from the oversight of the Redstone Association in part to avoid being put out of the association and find himself embarrassed. On October 15–22, that autumn, Campbell was scheduled soon to debate W. L. MacCalla, a Presbyterian. "The debate assumed that both parties were representatives in good standing with their denominations" (Hicks, "The Role of Faith in Conversion," 94).

[47] Minutes of the Redstone Baptist Association, September 3–5, 1824, 3. Cited by Hicks, "Balancing Faith, Christian Experience, and Baptism," 95.

In 1829, about six years after Alexander Campbell had joined the Mahoning Baptist Association in Ohio and gained many followers, four churches withdrew from the association to join with the Beaver Baptist Association of Pennsylvania. Together they drafted a document to identify the errors preached by Alexander Campbell and received by the churches in the Mahoning association,[48] particularly the beliefs that there is no promise of salvation without baptism and that baptism procures the remission of sins and the Holy Spirit.[49] In 1830, other Baptist associations followed the lead of the Beaver association as they reproduced the set of anathemas against the self-styled "Reformers." When Baptist associations in Kentucky excluded the Reformers from their fellowships, more than 9,000 members who sympathized with them also left.[50]

Throughout the next decade Campbell had to refine his teaching on baptism as he faced significant questions. Three issues were prominent: (1) whether the validity of baptism depended on the subjects' understanding that they received remission of sins through baptism; (2) whether baptism is a work one does to procure pardon; and (3) whether it is possible to be a Christian but not be baptized.

Concerning the first question, Campbell contended that any person who has been baptized on a simple confession of faith in Jesus Christ truly receives remission of sins. Only those who at the time of their baptism do not believe that Jesus is God's Son, the Messiah, should submit to another immersion.[51] Against objections that his

[48] Hicks identifies the four churches: Youngstown, Palmyra, Achor, and Salem, and he notes the record of the *Minutes of the Beaver Baptist Association*, August 20–22, 1829: "We deeply deplore their state, and feel constrained to warn our brethren in other parts against them: believing that they have departed from the faith and order of the Gospel Church" ("Balancing Faith, Christian Experience, and Baptism," 95).

[49] Hicks, "Balancing Faith, Christian Experience, and Baptism," 95. Hicks indicates that Campbell and his followers were charged with holding eight errors: 1. No promise of salvation apart from baptism. 2. Without examining baptisands concerning any matter, baptism should be administered to everyone who claims to believe that Jesus Christ is God's Son. 3. Prior to baptism the Holy Spirit does not act directly upon one's mind. 4. Baptism procures the remission of sins and the gift of the Holy Spirit. 5. Scripture alone is the evidence of one's interest in Christ. 6. God's power to elect unto salvation is rooted in obedience. 7. Churches need no creed but the Scriptures. 8. All baptized individuals are authorized to administer baptism to others (95–96).

[50] Torbert, A History of the Baptists, 275.

[51] Alexander Campbell, "Re-immersion and Brother Thomas," *Millennial Harbinger* 7 (February, 1836): 56–64; Alexander Campbell, "Reply to Susan," *Millennial Harbinger* 6 (September,

beliefs rendered baptism a work done to procure God's pardon for sins, Campbell insisted that it is God's work, not a human work. One's sins are not remitted by having faith in baptism but by faith in Jesus Christ.[52]

Campbell's response to the third issue caused commotion. John Thomas, a physician who had emigrated from Britain to Virginia and had become an influential leader in the Restoration movement, held views that caused Campbell to clarify his views on the status of believers who (for various reasons, such as ignorance) never receive baptism.[53] Thomas championed the belief that anyone who received baptism without also receiving clear knowledge of the remission of sins needed to be baptized again. A woman who embraced Thomas's teaching wrote Alexander Campbell to express surprise that he had published an article that Christians are found in all Protestant denominations. She inquired, "How does one become a Christian? Does the name of Christ or Christian belong to any but those who

1835): 419. Concerning the three controversial questions Campbell faced during the decade of the 1830s, see the discussion in D. A. Foster, "Churches of Christ and Baptism: An Historical and Theological Overview," *ResQ* 43:2 (2001): 79–94.

[52] See these discussions: Alexander Campbell, "Reformation—No. 3. A Personal Concern," *Millennial Harbinger* 6 (February 1835): 83–84; Alexander Campbell, "Dialogue on Re-immersion," *Millennial Harbinger* 3 (March, 1832): 123; J. M. Hicks, "Alexander Campbell on Christians among the Sects," in Fletcher, *Baptism and the Remission of Sins*, 176–85; and J. Allen, *Rebaptism: What One Must Know to Be Born Again* (West Monroe, LA: Howard, 1991), 75–89. In his later book, *Christian Baptism, with its Antecedents and Consequents* (Bethany, VA: n. p., 1851), Campbell reiterates his early response to allegations that he has made baptism a work: "We do not . . . place baptism among good works. Good works have our brethren, and neither God nor ourselves, for their object. They directly and immediately terminate upon man; while, in their reflex influence, they glorify God, and beatify ourselves. In baptism, we are in spirit, as well as in person, buried with the Lord, 'wherein also we are raised with him.' Dead men neither bury themselves nor raise themselves to life again. In baptism, we are passive in every thing but in giving our consent. We are buried and we are raised by another. Hence, in no view of baptism can it be called a good work. The influence which baptism may have upon our spiritual relations is, therefore, not because of any merit in the act as our own; not as a procuring cause, but merely as an instrumental and concurring cause, by which we 'put on Christ,' and are united to him formally as well as in heart, entering into covenant with him, and uniting ourselves to him in his death, burial, and resurrection. Hence, said the apostle, 'As many of you as have been baptized into Christ have been baptized into his death'—'have put on Christ'" (*Christian Baptism, with its Antecedents and Consequents*, 255–56).

[53] John Thomas left the Restoration movement, c. 1848, to found his own called the Christadelphians, a small religious movement that rejects belief in the Trinity, views Jesus as less than God, and rejects eternal punishment of the wicked.

believe the gospel, repent, and are buried by baptism into the death of Christ?" Campbell answered,

> But who is a Christian? I answer, Every one that believes in his heart that Jesus of Nazareth is the Messiah, the son of God; repents of his sins, and obeys him in all things according to his measure of knowledge of his will. . . . [I]t is possible for Christians to be imperfect in some respects without an absolute forfeiture of the Christian state and character.
>
> I cannot make any one duty the standard of Christian state or character, not even immersion into the name of the Father, of the son, and of the Holy Spirit, and in my heart regard all that have been sprinkled in infancy without their own knowledge and consent, as aliens from Christ and the well-grounded hope of heaven.
>
> There is no occasion, then, for making immersion, on a profession of the faith, absolutely essential to a Christian—though it may be greatly essential to his sanctification and comfort. My right hand and my right eye are greatly essential to my usefulness and happiness, but not to my life; and as I could not be a perfect man without them, so I cannot be a perfect Christian without a right understanding and a cordial reception of immersion in its true and scriptural meaning and design. But he who thence infers that none are Christians but the immersed, as greatly errs as he who affirms that none are alive but those of full and clear vision.[54]

Campbell's response satisfied few of his readers. His opponents regarded his view as still too restrictive. Some of his fellow ministers believed that Campbell's response was too expansive, nullifying their preaching of baptism for remission of sins. To their complaints, he responded that his comments were not about individuals who reject Christ's ordinances, for such people are not Christians. Instead, he clarified that he was speaking of people "who through a simple mistake, involving no perversity of mind misapprehended the outward baptism."[55] Though he would receive these individuals as Christians, he would not receive into the communion of the church any who were not immersed into Jesus Christ.[56]

Controversy over baptism within Stone-Campbell churches has erupted periodically. For almost two decades at the turn of

---

[54] Alexander Campbell, "Any Christians among Protestant Parties," *Millennial Harbinger* n.s. 1 (September, 1837): 411–14.

[55] Alexander Campbell, "Christians among the Sects," *Millennial Harbinger* n.s. 1 (November, 1837): 506–508.

[56] Alexander Campbell, "Reply on Union, Communion, and the Name Christian," *Millennial Harbinger* 2 (September, 1831): 392–93.

the twentieth century, controversy raged over the issue that Alexander Campbell addressed in the John Thomas affair. David Lipscomb, editor of *Gospel Advocate*, and Austin McGary, editor of *Firm Foundation*, were the principal voices in the dispute. The Disciples of Christ followed Lipscomb's moderate position, and the Churches of Christ heeded McGary's "rigorist" position. Leaders of the Churches of Christ feared the theological liberalism they associated with many among the Disciples of Christ. Schism resulted in what eventually became the threefold division that exists today. The conservative Churches of Christ and the rather liberal Christian Church (Disciples of Christ) stand at opposite ends with the Church of Christ (sometimes called Christian Church) holding the centrist position. More recently, the International Church of Christ (ICOC) stirred conflict, viewing its members as the only true Christians and insisting on rebaptism for everyone who joins its fellowship, even those baptized in a Church of Christ "for remission of sins." The ICOC has made its presence known by aggressively proselytizing students on Christian college campuses and among evangelicals at large.[57]

If one reads Alexander Campbell's writings fairly, considering their historical contexts, one quickly recognizes that he had a keen mind, was skilled in rhetoric and debate, had an extraordinary command of the English language, was a knowledgeable exegete of the Greek NT, and was well-read in classical and theological literature. He also labored, however, under disadvantages, some from his own flaws and others beyond his control. Campbell's strengths at times worked against him. What seemed lucid to him he often failed to articulate adequately for those of lesser capabilities. He excoriated others for believing and spreading rumors concerning his beliefs. Yet, both *The Christian Baptist* and *The Millennial Harbinger*, journals that he edited and published, regularly participated in spreading rumors and character assassination. Campbell's pejorative sobriquets and harsh condemnations of opponents, using unfavorable biblical

---

[57] For a helpful summary of the issue of baptism in the Stone-Campbell tradition since its earliest times, see Foster, Blowers, and Williams, "Baptism," *Encyclopedia of the Stone-Campbell Movement*, 61–67.

designations for them (e.g., Pharisees, Sadducees, Philistines, etc.) and favorable ones for himself (e.g., inhabitants of Zion), indicate that he regarded many Christian ministers who opposed him as opposed to God, to Jesus Christ, to the gospel, and to truth, and thus, not Christians at all. When reading his works one can hardly fail to feel the sharp sting of his witty sarcasm and the blunt blow of his impatient dismissals.

Alexander Campbell's commitment to exposing and correcting errors, especially theological ones, inclined him toward over-reaction and austerity. Perhaps his manner and tone prompted opponents to fail to understand him and thus to retaliate with their own overstatements and overcorrections. These factors render Campbell's writings difficult, especially if one is already biased against his views. Yet, if one perseveres in reading his works with care, one discovers that Campbell, particularly on baptism, has been unfairly treated to this day. Regrettably, he alienated opponents and set a pattern for subsequent generations, both for followers and for opponents. Some of his followers took Campbell's beliefs on baptism to extremes, inciting sustained alienation from without and prolonged strain within that resulted in schisms. American Evangelicalism's exclusion of Christians and of churches from the Stone-Campbell tradition has injured both traditions.[58] With this in view, the rapprochement of many within the Stone-Campbell tradition and of evangelicals, particularly within the Evangelical Theological Society, is worthy of commendation. May Christian unity abound by the Spirit and in the bond of peace.

Biblical-Theological Considerations of Restorationism on Baptism

In 1835 Alexander Campbell gathered many of his writings and compiled them as a book, *The Christian System*, which saw a second

---

[58] R. Balmer makes a provocative case that American Evangelicalism is the poorer for failing to embrace a crucial principle that has characterized the Stone-Campbell tradition, namely, "that institutions, be they ecclesiastical or educational, are remarkably poor guarantors of piety. Institutions inevitably serve themselves and eventually suborn themselves to the pressures of building programs and mortgages, parking lots and pension funds" ("Willful Naïveté: American Evangelicalism and the Stone-Campbell Tradition," *Stone-Campbell Journal* 7 (2004): 222.

edition four years later.[59] Campbell devoted more than a third of the book to an exposition of his beliefs concerning baptism and remission of sins. In 1851 he published *Christian Baptism* which reiterated much of his earlier book but with its own format.[60] Because *Christian Baptism* provides Campbell's mature presentation of his beliefs, it is fitting that it should serve as a primary resource for consideration of his beliefs and the beliefs of those who look to him as a patriarch in the Restoration tradition.

"The baptism of repentance for the remission of sins"— Mark 1:4.

Mark's Gospel begins by telling of John the Baptizer who "came proclaiming the baptism of repentance for the forgiveness of sins" (*baptisma metanoias eis aphesin hamartiōn*). Alexander Campbell contends, "The form of the expression is exceedingly familiar and intelligible; and, were it not for an imaginary incongruity between the *means* and the *end*, or the *thing* done and the alleged *purpose* or *result*, no one could, for a moment, doubt that the design of baptism was '*for* the remission of sins'"[61] Few would question his conclusion that the preposition *eis* is legitimately and better translated "for" rather than "unto" or "into."[62] Yet, some may wince when Campbell says,

> While, then, baptism is ordained for remission of sins, and for no other specific purpose, it is not as a procuring cause, as a meritorious or efficient cause, but as an instrumental cause, in which faith and repentance are developed and made fruitful and effectual in the changing of our state and spiritual relations to the Divine Persons whose names are put upon us in the very act.[63]

Only those who persist at waging war against "Campbellism" or nervously seek to guard against "baptismal regeneration" (both conceptually tending to separate baptism from its genitive modifier, *metanoias,* "repentance") will flinch at reading this comment on

---

[59] Alexander Campbell, *The Christian System* (1835; reprint, Joplin, MO.: College Press, 1989).

[60] Campbell, *Christian Baptism, with its Antecedents and Consequents.*

[61] Emphasis added. Campbell, *Christian Baptism,* 249.

[62] Ibid., 249 n 1.

[63] Ibid., 256.

Mark 1:4: "Baptism in such a state of moral reform accomplished, in Mark's words, 'the forgiveness of sins.'"[64]

In his commentary on Mark's Gospel, David Garland, a Baptist, disassociates repentance from baptism and seeks to divert readers from the resulting theological error by saying, "One need not interpret 1:4 to mean that baptism effects the forgiveness of sins. One can translate it, 'a baptism of repentance on the basis of the forgiveness of sins.' The divine action of forgiveness of sins would precede any human action."[65] Because his comments disconnect the genitive qualifier, "repentance," from baptism, the noun it modifies, Garland feels constrained to add his own qualifier to guard Mark's statement from error by assigning the preposition *eis* ("into, unto") an unusual sense, "on the basis of," as some of Alexander Campbell's opponents do. Garland creates his own theological difficulty, however, because he does not retain "baptism of repentance" (*baptisma metanoias*) as an indissoluble unit in which the genitive ("repentance") is the essential qualifier. Mark does not report that John proclaims "*baptism for forgiveness of sins,*" as though the bare act of *baptism* or *washing* effects forgiveness of sins. His proclamation is "the *baptism of repentance* for the forgiveness of sins." In fact, Mark's careful wording qualifying what kind of baptism effects forgiveness of sins actually makes it clear that without repentance, baptism effectuates nothing. In other words, the act of immersion is empty and purposeless unless it is received with repentance. Forgiveness of sins is the effect *only* when the sacred rite is received with repentance. Mark's report

---

[64] J. R. Edwards, *The Gospel according to Mark*, PNTC (Grand Rapid: Eerdmans, 2002), 31. See the discussion by R. T. France, *The Gospel of Mark*, NIGTC (Grand Rapids: Eerdmans, 2002), 67. It is curious that Edwards, a commentator on Mark's Gospel who owes much to the tradition that finds roots in Alexander Campbell's teaching, offers no comment on "baptism of repentance for the forgiveness of sins." See A. Black, *Mark*, The College Press NIV Commentary (Joplin, MO: College Press, 1995), 42–43.

[65] D. Garland, *Mark*, NIVAC (Grand Rapids: Zondervan, 1996), 45 n 10. Against Garland's viewing baptism as "human action," Edwards argues, "The key to understanding John's baptism is that it is *proclaimed*, which means that it is an action of God as opposed to a mere human action" (*Mark*, 31). See E. Lohmeyer, *Das Evangelium des Markus*, KEK, (Göttingen: Vandehoeck & Rupprecht, 1953), 13–15; and J. Marcus, *The Way of the Lord*, (Louisville: Westminster/John Knox, 1992), 18–31, who make the case that the object of the verb *kērussō* is an action of God.

of John's preaching makes it clear that "for John baptism without repentance was futile; repentance without baptism inconceivable."[66]

To understand Mark's words to mean that John proclaimed "the baptism of repentance resulting in the forgiveness of sins" should cause no alarm for evangelicals unless we confuse biblically distinct *causations* concerning salvation, something Campbell seeks to avoid. He clarifies,

> When a man's salvation, for example, is sometimes ascribed to faith, to repentance, to baptism, to the grace of God, to the blood of Christ, to his own efforts, we are desirous to know why a man's salvation should be assigned to so many causes. To prevent confusion, or to relieve the mind from a perplexed, indistinct, and imperfect conception of the influences of numerous and various causes, affecting the existence of any thing, either as respects itself or our conceptions of it, we have given to the word *cause* a very comprehensive meaning, and have been obliged to select names to express the various applications of the word. Thus, we have a *moving* or *original* cause, an *efficient* or *meritorious* cause, an *instrumental* cause, a *concurrent* cause, a *final* cause. . . . Every theory of redemption and salvation, with more or less clearness of perception and precision of expression, admits the necessity of such distinctions as these.[67]

"Whoever believes and is baptized will be saved"— Mark 16:16.

Some Christians are elated when they learn that this passage may not have been original to Mark's Gospel. Yet, for others the passage is a test of Christian orthodoxy that apart from baptism no one can be saved. Alexander Campbell appealed to Mark 16:16 to support his belief that Christian baptism is a single act that embodies the gospel, for all ages giving shape to "the great facts of man's redemption as developed and consummated in the death, burial, and resurrection of the Lord Jesus Christ."[68] Though Campbell was reasonably informed concerning biblical criticism, he offered no comment on the textual questions concerning Mark 16:9–20.[69] Today, NT schol-

---

[66] R. Guelich, *Mark 1–8:26*, WBC (Dallas: Word, 1989), 19.

[67] Campbell, *Christian Baptism*, 254.

[68] Ibid., 257.

[69] See T. H. Olbricht, "Alexander Campbell in the Context of American Biblical Studies, 1810–1876," *ResQ* 33:1 (1995): 13–28.

ars regard this passage as almost surely a later addition by a scribe zealous to provide a suitable ending to the Gospel. The presence of v. 16—"The one who believes and is baptized shall be saved, but the one who does not believe will be condemned"—is no sufficient basis for rejecting the authenticity of the twelve verses. Even if the passage were authentic, v. 16 does not warrant the exploitation that some make of this passage as if baptism itself has effectual power to save. One need conclude nothing more than that the author of the verse means that belief and baptism are integrated just as Jesus calls for baptism as integral to the making of disciples (Matt 28:19).

"Unless one is born of water and the Spirit"— John 3:5.

Jesus told Nicodemus, "Unless someone is born from above, one cannot see the kingdom of God" (John 3:3; *anōthen* [*from above* or *again*], a possible play on words). But Nicodemus, taking Jesus' words too literally, misunderstood. So Jesus explained, "Truly, truly, I say to you, unless someone is born of water and the Spirit, one cannot enter into the kingdom of God" (3:5). From the earliest centuries of the church by far the majority of exegetes have regularly regarded this mention of water (*ex hudatos*; "from water") to speak of Christian baptism. Even the Baptist NT scholar, George Beasley-Murray comments, "At a time when the employment of water for cleansing in view of the last day had taken the specific form of baptism, it is difficult to take seriously any other reference than baptism in the words *ex hudatos*."[70] Tom Alexander, a Restoration scholar, accepts this understanding of the passage without question. Acceptance of Beasley-Murray's understanding of the passage does not obligate one to ascribe to baptism an efficacious power to cause the spiritual birth, whether depicted as "new birth" or "birth from above." Neither Alexander nor Beasley-Murray ascribes such power to water baptism. Nevertheless, it is doubtful that John 3:5 refers to baptism at all. Responding to Alexander, Craig Blomberg correctly observes that Beasley-Murray's assertion does not substitute

---

[70] Beasley-Murray, *Baptism*, 228.

for argument.[71] As Blomberg shows, D. A. Carson's commentary on John's Gospel provides convincing argumentation missing in most other discussions of the passage to demonstrate that "born of water and the spirit" is a hendiadys referring to the singular action of spiritual cleansing that Ezekiel prophesied (36:25).[72]

"Repent and be baptized for the forgiveness of your sins"— Acts 2:38.

In theological discussions and disputes over baptism between evangelicals and Campbell's ecclesial heirs, this passage seems to have attracted the most discussion. It is true that some in the Stone-Campbell tradition have overstated their case from Acts 2:38. It is also true, however, that evangelical critiques have too often been characterized by strong bias, exaggeration, and misrepresentation.

Often those who adopt the most strident posture against a particular view are individuals who once held the view. One minister who now opposes the belief he formerly preached represents his repudiated view in its least cautious, rather than its most careful, articulation.[73]

> Is the demand for baptism (i.e., immersion in water) a part of the Gospel? Should every evangelistic sermon and every Gospel tract, in order to be biblical, include a demand for baptism? Should the unbeliever hear in clear and forceful terms that unless he is baptized he cannot be saved, cannot receive eternal life, cannot have the forgiveness of sins? There are many who believe that baptism is essential for salvation and is of the essence of the Gospel. Many of these same people point to Acts 2:38 . . . to support their belief.[74]

Yet Jesus instructed his apostles to make disciples by both baptizing them in the threefold Name and teaching them to keep all his com-

[71] C. L. Blomberg, "An Evangelical Response to Alexander and Kurka," *Evangelicalism and the Stone-Campbell Movement*, ed. W. R. Baker (Downers Grove: InterVarsity, 2002), 153.

[72] D. A. Carson, *The Gospel according to John*, PNTC (Grand Rapids: Eerdmans, 1991), 191–196. See L. L. Belleville, "'Born of the Water and the Spirit': John 3:5," *TJ* 2 N.S. (1981): 125–41.

[73] L. T. Tanton, "The Gospel and Water Baptism: A Study of Acts 2:38," *Journal of the Grace Evangelical Society* 3:1 (1990): 27–52. This is noteworthy because Tanton lands the same accusation against B. L. Ross (*Campbellism—Its History and Heresies* [Pasadena, TX.: Pilgrim Publications, 1976]; and *Acts 2:38 and Baptismal Regeneration* [Pasadena, TX.: Pilgrim Publications, 1976]).

[74] Tanton, "The Gospel and Water Baptism," 27.

mands. Does not Jesus link baptism with making disciples rather than with joining a local church?

Thus, when Peter proclaimed the gospel to the Jews at Pentecost and was asked, "Men, brothers, what shall we do?" his response, in keeping with Jesus' commission, was "Repent and let each of you be baptized on the name of Jesus Christ, for the forgiveness of your sins, and you shall receive the gift of the Holy Spirit" (Acts 2:38). Evangelicals seeking to preserve salvation by grace through faith have been uncomfortable with the close association of baptism with repentance and forgiveness. Many have looked to Julius R. Mantey's theologically controlled explanation of "unto the forgiveness of sins" (*eis aphesin tōn hamartiōn*) as authoritative.[75] He admits that the expression may mean "*for* the purpose of the remission of sins," but prefers to adopt what he calls an "unusual meaning," "*because* of the remission of sins."[76] This understanding of the preposition *eis* ("into, unto") is lexically doubtful. Murray Harris rightly views the causal sense as "unlikely."[77]

Because the causal sense is doubtful and the view is tendentious, others accept the regular sense of the preposition *eis* ("unto, into") as indicating purpose, "for the forgiveness of sins." But they attempt to escape the apparent difficulty by taking the phrase as directly connected only to the verb "repent" (*metanoēsate*) and merely in loose association with the verb "be baptized" (*baptisthētō*). The resulting translation is "Repent (and be baptized each of you on the name of Jesus Christ) for the forgiveness of sins."[78] Wayne House

---

[75] H. E. Dana and J. R. Mantey, *A Manual Grammar of the Greek New Testament*, 40th printing (Toronto: Macmillan, 1927), 104.

[76] Dana and Mantey, *A Manual Grammar*, 104. Dana and Mantey cite J. R. Mantey, "Unusual Meanings for Prepositions in the Greek New Testament," *Expositor* (June, 1923) to make their case. See J. R. Mantey, "The Causal Use of Eis in the New Testament," *JBL* 70 (1952): 45–58; and "On Causal *Eis* Again," *JBL* 70 (1952): 309–11. Others challenged Mantey's "unusual meaning" for the use of *eis* in Acts 2:38, such as R. Marcus, "On Causal *Eis*," *JBL* 70 (1952): 129–30; and "The Elusive Causal *Eis*," *JBL* 71 (1953): 44. Despite the weakness of Mantey's case, others have followed his lead, such as, W. A. Criswell, *Acts* (Grand Rapids: Zondervan, 1978), 96. See N. Turner, *A Grammar of New Testament Greek* (Edinburgh: T. & T. Clark, 1963), 3:266. Turner says, "Some contexts would certainly suit a causal sense . . . Ac 2:38 *be baptized eis aphesi tōn hamartiōn on the basis of* (but *with a view to* is sufficient, if your theology is satisfied)."

[77] M. J. Harris, "Appendix," in *NIDNTT* (Grand Rapids: Zondervan, 1978), 3:1187.

[78] See N. B. Stonehouse, "Repentance, Baptism and The Gift of the Holy Spirit," *WTJ* 13 (1950): 1–15, esp. p. 15; F. Stagg, *The Book of Acts* (Nashville: Broadman, 1955), 63; and B. Ross, *Acts 2:38 and Baptismal Regeneration*, 45–49.

has recently argued for "the disjunctive nature of 'you repent for the forgiveness of your sins, and let each of one of you be baptized in the name of Jesus,'"[79] contending that "this is a perfectly legitimate understanding of the grammar and would not make baptism a requirement to receive forgiveness of sins."[80] Although reading the verse in this disjunctive manner may be "legitimate," it is clumsy and strained, and therefore doubtful.[81]

Each of these interpretations looks like an attempt to avoid the obvious sense of the verse.[82] The issue is not merely a case of theological bias. The variety of interpretations derives not simply from attempts to skirt a theological dilemma but also from confusion. Failure to give reasonable and close attention to what Alexander Campbell and his heirs actually said concerning the passage has led needlessly to a proliferation of novel attempts to avoid accepting the text's association of repentance and baptism. A. T. Robertson summarizes the situation well when he says that "the interpreter, not the grammarian" must decide the sense of the words "unto forgiveness" (*eis aphesin*) in Acts 2:38.[83]

Peter's double imperative presents the call of the gospel, requiring all to "repent and be baptized . . . for the forgiveness of your sins." The fact that there is a shift of persons, from second person plural ("you repent," *metanoēsate*) to third person singular ("let each one be baptized," *baptisthētō*) hardly warrants restricting connection of the phrase "for the forgiveness of your sins" (*eis aph-*

---

[79] H. W. House, "An Evangelical Response to Baird and Weatherly," *Evangelicalism and the Stone-Campbell Movement*, 189.

[80] House, "An Evangelical Response," 189.

[81] See the taxonomy of views in D. B. Wallace, *Greek Grammar Beyond the Basics: An Exegetical Syntax of the New Testament* (Grand Rapids: Zondervan, 1996), 370–71. His list mischaracterizes the view of Campbell and his heirs this way: "*The baptism referred to here is physical only, and eis has the meaning of for or unto*" (p. 370; emphasis original). They would respond that baptism is never rightly conceived of as "physical only." For if baptism were "physical only," it would not be Christian baptism.

[82] Tanton comments on two interpretations that deserve nothing more than passing mention: (1) the Ultra-Dispensationalist view that regards baptism as passé for the church; and (2) his view that he calls the Transitional view, holding that baptism for Palestinian Jews received forgiveness of sins and the gift of the Spirit through baptism ("The Gospel and Water Baptism: A Study of Acts 2:38," 45–52).

[83] A. T. Robertson, *A Grammar of the Greek New Testament in the Light of Historical Research*, 4th ed. (Nashville: Broadman, 1934), 389, 592, 595.

esin tōn hamartiōn humōn) to "repent" and not to "let each one be baptized."[84] Actually, the grammatical switch in person and number may intensify the bond between the two imperatives so that they should be read as joined—"*repent* and *let each one be baptized.*" Together they bring about what is expressed in the purpose statement, "for the forgiveness of your sins." The resulting translation, then, is: "Repent and let each of you be baptized on the name of Jesus Christ for the forgiveness of your sins and you will receive the gift of the Holy Spirit."

Rejections of this exegetical understanding derive from confusion of the *instrumental cause* and the *efficient cause* of salvation. Expressed another way, the array of interpretations of Acts 2:38 originate from merging the *means* of salvation with its *ground*.[85] The importance of distinguishing the two can hardly be overstated. When we read or hear Acts 2:38, it is easy to confuse the *efficient* and *instrumental* causes of salvation. Out of zeal to enforce Christian baptism, some have mistakenly exalted repentance and baptism to the place of effectual cause. This error of "baptismal regeneration," vesting baptism with effectual cleansing power, invariably diminishes grace. Yet others, excessively fervent to preserve *sola fide*, have committed the opposite error of "creedal (or popularly "decisional") regeneration," assigning to faith the effectual saving power that belongs only to God's grace. Some who advocate creedal regeneration isolate faith from repentance and deny both repentance and baptism any function in our salvation lest they deny *sola fide* and *sola gratia*.[86] Others for the same reason suppress the proper function of baptism as a means of God's grace and abstract baptism from repentance as separable rather than merely distinguishable. Because they confound *grace* and the *means* of grace, they suppose that to speak of repentance and baptism as *means by which God administers*

---

[84] See the interpretation by L. B. McIntyre, Jr., "Baptism and Forgiveness in Acts 2:38," *BSac* 153 (1996): 53–62.

[85] See the discussion of these distinctions in T. R. Schreiner and A. B. Caneday, *The Race Set Before Us: A Biblical Theology of Perseverance and Assurance* (Downers Grove: InterVarsity, 2001), 38–45, 211–12.

[86] This is the basic thesis Tanton argues in "The Gospel and Water Baptism: A Study of Acts 2:38," 27–52. This is the premise of The Grace Evangelical Society that published Tanton's essay.

his grace is tantamount to denying God's redemptive accomplishment in Christ Jesus as the sole *ground of God's gracious, saving act*.[87] Indeed, if one conceptually isolates baptism from repentance, then baptism loses its integral defining connection. The result is that baptism becomes an empty form, ancillary and optional to repentance. For Peter, however, repentance and baptism, though distinguishable, are inseparable—one without the other is unthinkable, especially for the apostles and early Christians.[88]

Against the trend of conceiving of conversion in terms of elements abstracted from one another in these post-Augustinian times, without theological embarrassment the apostles preached, as expressed in Acts 2:38, that baptism and repentance are indivisible elements of conversion to Christ.[89] Baptism is an indispensable aspect of conversion along with at least four other elements: repentance, faith, confession, and regeneration.[90] Robert Stein summarizes well the view of baptism the apostles required of those who heard them preach.

> No one came to the conversion experience with questions as to whether baptism was necessary for becoming a Christian because the apostolic preaching stated that they must be baptized. Thus the rejection of baptism was a rejection of the divine program for conversion! To reject baptism was to reject the gospel message preached by Peter, Paul, and the other apostles who spoke of the need of baptism. Divine provision was made for those who, like the thief on the cross, could not be baptized, but to refuse the community's baptism was the same as a rejection of the Christ whom the community preached. It involved a clear unwillingness to obey the gospel preached by the apostles.[91]

[87] For an example of one who understands the necessity of these distinctions and articulates a careful and accurate understanding of baptism as a means of God's grace, see Wellum, "The Means of Grace: Baptism," 149–70.

[88] See D. A. Carson who says that we "can scarcely conceive of a disciple who is not baptized or is not instructed" ("Matthew," in *EBC*, ed. Frank E. Gaebelein [Grand Rapids: Zondervan, 1984], 8:597). See also G. R. Beasley-Murray who affirms the same point in his discussion of Paul's letter to the Romans (6:4) in "Baptism," in *DPL* (Downers Grove: InterVarsity, 1993), 60.

[89] Wright, "Recovering Baptism for a New Age of Mission," 57. Wright, who is a paedobaptist, says, "Now the baptismal experience of the church of the early Fathers was largely of believer's baptism, or perhaps better conversion baptism. Historical study is steadily consolidating the conclusion that infant baptism did not really come into its own, as the common practice, until after Augustine, perhaps in the sixth century."

[90] See R. H. Stein, "Baptism and Becoming a Christian in the New Testament," *SBJT* 2 (1998): 10ff. See D. Gaertner, *Acts*, College Press NIV Commentary (Joplin, MO: College Press, 1993), 80–81.

[91] Stein, "Baptism and Becoming a Christian in the New Testament," 15.

Thus, willful rejection of baptism after receiving instruction concerning the significance of baptism is unconscionable for anyone who claims to follow Jesus Christ, for it is defiant repudiation of his authority in the gospel. Also, anyone who regards baptism abstracted from repentance as effectual to save lacks faith in the only one who can save.[92]

"Baptism now saves you."—1 Peter 3:21.

It is fitting to follow consideration of Peter's preaching in Acts, which called for repentance and baptism for the forgiveness of sins, with his own written comments on baptism and cleansing. First Peter 3:18–22 appears to be an excursus within a larger discussion of suffering. The difficulties presented by its grammar and train of thought are well known. The excursus concerns the "days of Noah" and the ark "in which a few, that is, eight souls, were saved through water" (3:20). Then Peter writes in v. 21,

> which water, namely baptism, also now saves you, the antitype. This water entails not the removal of filth from flesh, but an appeal to God out of a good conscience through the raising of Jesus Christ.

Though the syntax is complex, the basic sense is not difficult: Noah's family of eight was saved through water, so also Christians are saved through the water of baptism. Nevertheless, difficult grammatical questions remain. What is the antecedent of the neuter relative pronoun "which" (*ho*)? Is it "water" (*hudatos*)? Is it the whole preceding clause—"in which [ark] a few, that is, eight souls, were saved through water"? How should we understand "antitype" (*antitupon*)? Is it an adjective or a noun? How does "baptism" (*baptisma*) relate to the rest of the sentence? What does Peter mean by "pledge" or "promise" (*eperōtēma*)?

Peter sets up the relationship between the figure and its prefigurement in several ways. First, he emphasizes the typology by structuring vv. 20–21 with "formerly [*pote*, "then"] . . . in the days of Noah" in v. 20 contrasted with "now" (*nun*) in v. 21. Peter draws out the

---

[92] See F. F. Bruce, *The Book of Acts*, NICNT, (Grand Rapids: Eerdmans, 1975), 77. He states, "It would, of course, be a mistake to link the words 'unto the remission of sins' with the command 'be baptized' to the exclusion of the prior command 'Repent ye.'"

analogical relationship between Noah's family and Christians by linking "through water" with "baptism" and then by linking the two verbs, "they were saved" (*diesōthēsan*) and "baptism saves" (*sōzei baptisma*).[93]

The negation, "not the removal of filth from flesh" (*sarx* seems to refer to "flesh" as "body" here), is doubly instructive. On the one hand, Peter makes no allowance for anyone to suppose that water when used for baptism has magical powers to effect salvation (*ex opere operato*). On the other hand, by mentioning the ordinary use of water for cleansing filth from one's flesh, he makes it clear that he conceives of baptism as a sacred cleansing ritual that is an integral aspect of the reception of salvation, namely Christian conversion.[94] For Peter, baptismal waters *figure* salvation in Christ as the flood waters that buoyed up the ark *figured* deliverance—and simultaneously *prefigured* the saving work of Christ. So, with his qualifiers in place, Peter puts the *figure*, baptism (understood as cleansing), in the place of *the thing figured*, the "good conscience" that makes a pledge unto God.[95] That is to say, Peter employs the figure for the thing figured when he says, "baptism now saves you."

The final phrase of v. 21, "through the resurrection of Jesus Christ," links to the verb "save." Thus, in this one verse Peter speaks of both the instrumental and efficient causes of salvation: "now baptism saves you . . . through the resurrection of Jesus Christ."

[93] See R. T. France, "Exegesis in Practice: Two Samples," in *New Testament Interpretation*, ed. I. H. Marshall (Grand Rapids: Eerdmans, 1977), 273. I concur with France's translation, taking *antitupon* as a substantive rather than as an adjective. See E. G. Selwyn, *The First Epistle of St. Peter*, 2d ed. (1947; reprint, Grand Rapids: Baker, 1981), 204, 298–99. Contrast J. R. Michaels, *1 Peter*, WBC (Dallas: Word, 1988), 214.

[94] Since Peter gives "putting off" (*apothesis*) an unusual association with washing, is it conceivable that his use of "not the putting off the filth of flesh" (*ou sarkos apothesis rupou*) is a kind of paronomasia, a play on the shedding of the foreskin through circumcision? If, as some have argued, the phrase refers to circumcision, it seems to bear the double sense of removal of filth through bathing and of circumcision as removal of the unclean foreskin. For the clause as referring to circumcision, see J. N. D. Kelly, *A Commentary on the Epistles of Peter and Jude* (London: Black, 1977; Grand Rapids: Baker, 1981), 161–62.

[95] See R. L. Nickelson, "First Peter 3:21, Daniel 4:14[17], and the Ordo Salutis," *Stone-Campbell Journal* 3 (2000): 229–41. He concludes his essay with a discussion of different views of the *ordo salutis* (order of salvation). This systematic-theological discussion is unlikely to foster rapprochement between evangelicals and those within the Stone-Campbell tradition, which must be based on biblical-theological discussions.

Anyone who is tempted to suppress Peter's assured declaration that baptism's water "now saves you" and in its place elevate his attached mention of the effectual cause, needs to recall that this "language concerning the effect of baptism is by no means unparalleled in the New Testament; any view of baptism which finds it a rather embarrassing ceremonial extra, irrelevant to Christian salvation, is not doing justice to New Testament teaching."[96]

"Be baptized and wash away your sins"— Acts 26:16.

The connection between baptism and forgiveness of sins in Acts 2:38 is implicitly present in Paul's comments before the Sanhedrin. As the apostle recites his conversion to Christ and his call to apostleship, he tells how Ananias instructed him in Damascus that God had chosen him to be a witness for Christ Jesus and then said, "And now what do you await? Rise up, submit to baptism and wash away your sins, calling upon his name" (Acts 22:16). These words, "wash away your sins," unmistakably connect baptism and forgiveness of sins through the imagery of *cleansing*, or *washing*. Paul's words tie together the symbol (baptism, washing) and the thing symbolized (washing away of sins). Yet, we would be wrong to conclude that he endorses the idea that bathing the body is effectual to purge one of sins.

Paul shows no concern for modern sensibilities stemming from abstractions with which we work in systematic theology as he recounts his conversion as a unified event, despite its various aspects (including baptism). Paul was in Damascus for three days, blind and fasting (Acts 9:9). The fact that the NT portrays Paul's conversion with multiple but inseparable components in discernible sequence should caution us against allowing questions concerning unusual situations to govern our doctrine of conversion. Would Paul have been saved if he had died before he received baptism three days later? Such a theoretical question distracts us from biblical teaching that resists conforming to contemporary categories devised by the

---

[96] France, "Exegesis in Practice: Two Samples," 274.

impatient enquirer. To yield to it is unwise, unnecessary, and injurious to Christian teaching on conversion because it aims at isolating baptism from conversion on the basis of a theoretical exception. The question unnecessarily raises a *theoretical* exception when the NT provides an *actual* exception with the thief on the cross. To yield to the theoretical question does injury to the clarity of the NT pattern concerning conversion. While the NT accounts for the salvation of the thief on the cross, whose conversion was compressed in its aspects and who did not receive baptism, it shows a discernible pattern of conversion. This pattern should regulate our doctrinal formulation of the relationship of conversion and baptism for those converted before they approach impending death, and yet the Bible also accounts for those rare exceptions. Stein rightly argues that "to establish an understanding of the normal conversion pattern based on extremely rare or unusual experiences is to emphasize the abnormal. In general a person could not be converted to Christianity in the New Testament apart from baptism."[97]

"You were washed"—
1 Corinthians 6:11; Titus 3:5; Ephesians 5:26.

Elsewhere, when Paul reasons with Christians from the symbol, their baptism, to the reality of God's gracious salvation, he says, "You were baptized" (*ebaptisthēmen*, (Rom 6:3 and Gal 3:27). In 1 Cor 6:11 he uses the verb "you were washed" (*apelousasthe*). Paul's affirmation, beginning with "but" (*alla*), sharply contrasts with his catalog of those who "will not inherit God's kingdom" (6:9–10): "And this is what some of you were. But you were washed, but you were sanctified, but you were justified in the name of the Lord Jesus Christ and in the Spirit of our God." The order of verbs hardly depends on a systematic theological order of salvation (*ordo salutis*) but upon contextual placement.[98] For Paul, conversion is a whole,

---

[97] Stein, "Baptism and Becoming a Christian in the New Testament," 15.

[98] "Each of the verbs is thus chosen for contextual, not dogmatic, reasons; and their sequence is theologically irrelevant" (G. D. Fee, *The First Epistle to the Corinthians*, NICNT [Grand Rapids: Eerdmans, 1987], 246). Contrast F. W. Grosheide who attempts to redeem Paul's order in view of dogmatic theology: "The Corinthians are washed: the primary reference appears to be to baptism after conversion. Back of that baptism lies objective grace. Ye were sanctified: sancti-

consisting of washing, sanctification, and justification.[99] Paul, who received Ananias' admonition, "Be baptized and wash away your sins," appeals to the Corinthian believers to recall their conversion, signaled by baptism, as the time of their being washed of these contaminants that prevent inheriting God's kingdom. Stein rightly contends that the verb "you were washed" is not merely a metaphor disconnected from baptism, because Paul attaches the baptismal formula, "in the name of the Lord Jesus Christ" (Acts 10:48; 1 Cor 1:13–15), tightly associating baptism and conversion.[100] Dunn, on the other hand, seems overly concerned to drain baptismal water from Paul's imagery of washing:

> But in fact Paul is not talking about baptism at all—he speaks rather of the great spiritual transformation of conversion which turned the Corinthians' lives inside out and made immoral and impure men into saints, cleansed and justified by the authority and power of God. We may not assume that when Christians in the NT are recalled to the beginning of their Christian lives the reference is therefore to their baptism.[101]

Since, as Stein demonstrates, the NT writers regard Christian conversion as occurring with baptism, "there is no difficulty in seeing

fication is mentioned first in this context which deals with the sanctity of life. Ye are sanctified and are therefore saints. . . . Back of sanctification lies justification: ye were justified by an act of God and so you are righteous. The fact that they desired to be baptized rests upon the fact of their being justified by God" (*Commentary on the First Epistle to the Corinthians*, NICNT [Grand Rapids: Eerdmans, 1953], 140).

[99] "The order of the verbs . . . has no theological significance. Paul does not conceive of Christians being placed on a divine assembly line and having each of these things done to them in a certain order. For Paul, they are all of a piece" (D. Garland, *1 Corinthians*, BECNT [Grand Rapids: Baker, 2003], 216). See Schreiner and Caneday, *The Race Set Before Us*, 72

[100] Stein, "Baptism and Becoming a Christian in the New Testament," 12. See Beasley-Murray, *Baptism*, 162–67.

[101] J. D. G. Dunn, *Baptism in the Holy Spirit* (London: SCM; Philadelphia: Westminster, 1970), 120–21. See Fee, *First Epistle to the Corinthians*, 247. Fee cautiously concedes that Paul's verb may bear "an indirect allusion to baptism; but it is to say that Paul is not here concerned with the Christian initiatory rite, but with the spiritual transformation made possible through Christ and effected by the Spirit. The three metaphors emphasize the aspects of Christian conversion found in the theological terms 'regeneration, sanctification, and justification'; and for Paul these are the work of the Spirit in the believer's life, not the result of baptism." Caution to isolate these as metaphors is understandable, but it is born out of separation of symbol and thing symbolized. Such mental or conceptual separation of baptism from the thing signified by baptism has been an important source for misunderstanding of those who follow Alexander Campbell's formulations concerning baptism. See A. Thiselton, *The First Epistle to the Corinthians*, NICGTC (Grand Rapids: Eerdmans, 2000), 453–54.

justification intimately associated with baptism."[102] That Paul says "you were washed" instead of "you were baptized," accents the *actual washing* symbolized by the *symbolic washing* of baptism as Paul's principal concern.[103] Baptism does not wash away sin's filth but "is the occasion when the Spirit creatively works in the individual."[104] Garland explains, "That is why this verb appears first, since it marks the beginning of the Christian life, when one is transferred from the sphere of darkness into the power field of the Spirit."[105]

In 1 Cor 6:11 Paul uses the compound verb *apolouō* (*wash*) to call the Corinthians, at least allusively, to remember the spiritual washing they received when they submitted to the call of the gospel in baptism. Twice Paul uses the noun *loutron* ("washing") with similar allusive appeal to baptism as the symbolic reference to spiritual washing. In Eph 5:26 he speaks of Christ who loved the church and sacrificed himself for her, "in order that he might make her holy, cleansing her by the washing with the water in the word." Even if "washing with the water in the word" alludes to the bridal bath imagery of Ezek 16:8–14, the ecclesiological context still suggests an allusion to baptism also.[106] Likewise, in Tit 3:5 Paul says that God saved us "through the washing of regeneration and the renewal by the Holy Spirit." "The washing of regeneration" certainly is metaphorical for spiritual cleansing and not expressly a synonym for baptism. Yet, almost surely the imagery of washing alludes to

[102] Stein, "Baptism and Becoming a Christian in the New Testament," 12.

[103] See C. K. Barrett, *The First Epistle to the Corinthians*, HNTC (New York: Harper & Row, 1968), 141.

[104] G. R. Beasley-Murray, "Baptism," *NIDNTT* (Grand Rapids: Zondervan, 1986), 1:153.

[105] Garland, *1 Corinthians*, 216. See R. B. Hays, *First Corinthians*, Interpretation (Louisville: John Knox, 1997), 100.

[106] See Schreiner and Caneday, *The Race Set Before Us*, 76. On the likely allusion to the marital bath, see P. T. O'Brien, *The Letter to the Ephesians,* PNTC (Grand Rapids: Eerdmans, 1999), 422–23. That Ezek 16:8–14 influences Paul's imagery is likely. This need not rule out an allusion to baptism. On the notion that use of Ezekiel's bridal bath imagery excludes any allusion to Christian baptism, see K. Snodgrass, *Ephesians*, NIVAC (Grand Rapids: Zondervan, 1996), 298. Snodgrass also asserts, "Nowhere else in the New Testament is the church baptized." That Paul's imagery likely draws upon the bridal bath *and* alludes to baptism, see A. T. Lincoln, *Ephesians*, WBC (Dallas: Word, 1990), 375. For a full discussion of the passage, see M. Barth, *Ephesians 4–6* (Garden City, NY: Doubleday, 1986), 691–99. Barth is reticent, but he acknowledges that "practically all interpreters in the East and West, in ancient, medieval, Reformation, and modern times, agree in explaining 5:26 as a reference to baptism" (p. 692).

baptism as the symbolic rite that signifies spiritual cleansing from sin (see Acts 22:16; Eph 5:26; 1 Cor 6:11).[107]

"As many as were baptized into Christ Jesus"— Romans 6:3 & Galatians 3:27.

This essay began with reflection on the apostle Paul's appeals to both the Galatians and the Romans with reference to their baptism into Christ Jesus as the basis of his exhortation. In the case of the Roman Christians he reasons, "Or do you not realize that as many as were baptized into Christ Jesus were baptized into his death? We, therefore, were buried with him through baptism into this death with the purpose that just as Christ was raised from the dead through the glory of the Father, in the same manner we also might walk in newness of life" (Rom 6:3–4). For Paul, "baptism into Christ Jesus" (reflecting the baptismal formula Jesus authorized; *eis*, "into, unto," Matt 28:19) is so integral to being a Christian that to speak of those baptized into Christ is to speak of believers. Not all NT scholars agree. James Dunn, for example, argues that Paul draws upon the baptismal rite but does not depict baptism itself. Instead, Paul uses his expression strictly in a metaphorical sense, as a "figurative way of describing the act of God which puts a man 'in Christ.'"[108] Jack Cottrell rightly complains, "It is fairly common for expositors to claim that the baptism to which Paul refers in Romans 6 is a

---

[107] See G. D. Fee, *1 and 2 Timothy, Titus*, NIBC (Peabody, MA: Hendrickson, 1984), 205. On Tit 3:5, Calvin says, "I have no doubt that he alludes, at least, to baptism and even I will not object to have this passage expounded as relating to baptism; not that salvation is contained in the outward symbol of water, but because baptism seals to us the salvation obtained by Christ... . Now the apostles are wont to draw an argument from the Sacraments, to prove that which is there exhibited under a figure, because it ought to be held by believers as a settled principle, that God does not sport with us by unmeaning figures, but inwardly accomplishes by his power what he exhibits by the outward sign; and therefore, baptism is fitly and truly said to be 'the washing of regeneration.' The efficacy and use of the sacraments will be properly understood by him who shall connect the sign and the thing signified, in such a manner as not to make the sign unmeaning and inefficacious, and who nevertheless shall not, for the sake of adorning the sign, take away from the Holy Spirit what belongs to him" (*Commentaries on the Epistle to Titus in Calvin's Commentaries*, trans. William Pringle [reprint, Grand Rapids: Baker, 1979], 21:332–33). See P. Fairbairn, *Pastoral Epistles* (Edinburgh: T&T Clark, 1874), 293–95.

[108] Dunn, *Baptism in the Holy Spirit*, 112; see 140f. See J. D. G. Dunn, *Romans 1–8*, WBC 38a (Dallas: Word, 1988), 311. See a similar view held by D. M. Lloyd-Jones, *Romans: The New Man—Exposition of Chapter 6* (Grand Rapids: Zondervan, 1973), 33ff.

'spiritual' or 'dry' baptism only, as distinct from water baptism."[109] Douglas Moo correctly notes that Paul's ordinary use of "to baptize" (*baptizein*) refers to water baptism.[110] And it is reasonable for John Stott to assert that in the NT "baptism means water baptism unless in the context it is stated to the contrary."[111]

More pertinent here is the meaning of *eis Christon Iēsoun* in 6:3 and *dia tou baptismatos eis ton thanaton* in 6:4. On these questions, Beasley-Murray's work on baptism has done much to call for serious exegesis and to allow the text to have its full force.[112] He argues *eis Christon Iēsoun* is to be understood as being united with Christ, and other scholars agree.[113]

Contemporary evangelical biblical scholars are more willing to acknowledge the full and evident force of the prepositions in Rom 6:3–4 (*eis*, "into, unto," v. 3; *dia*, "through," v. 4) and less reticent than earlier scholars whose exegesis was too much guided by the desire to avoid perceived dangers of "baptismal regeneration" as in the Stone-Campbell tradition. Historical advantage has thawed much of the earlier suspicion that isolated the two groups, so that recent commentators on crucial biblical passages find themselves in guarded harmony with their more cautious and articulate counterparts in the Christian Church and Churches of Christ tradition. For example, evangelicals tend to agree with Cottrell's restrained comments on Rom 6:3:

> This union with Christ is not effected by the ritual itself, either by the water or by the act. It is accomplished by the grace and power of the living God alone. That it happens in the act of baptism is simply a matter of God's free and sovereign choice; he has appropriately designed this event as the oc-

[109] J. Cottrell, *Romans*, College Press NIV Commentary (Joplin, MO: College Press, 1996), 1:383.

[110] Moo, *Romans*, 359.

[111] J. Stott, *Romans: God's Good News for the World* (Downers Grove: InterVarsity, 1994), 173. T. R. Schreiner seems to overstate a case against Stott's comment when he asserts that "any attempt to distinguish between Spirit baptism and water baptism in the Pauline writings goes beyond what Paul himself wrote" (*Romans*, BECNT [Grand Rapids: Baker, 1998], 307). Given the evidence from Paul's writings, it seems one can and should *distinguish* between baptism with water (Rom 6:3) and baptism with the Spirit (1 Cor 12:13), even if one cannot *separate* them.

[112] G. R. Beasley-Murray, *Baptism in the New Testament* (Grand Rapids: Eerdmans, 1962).

[113] Beasley-Murray, *Baptism in the New Testament*, 129–29. See Schreiner, *Romans*, 307; Moo, *Romans*, 360; Cottrell, *Romans*, 1:383.

casion for the beginning of this saving union with the Redeemer. It is not wrong to say that the external ritual of water baptism *symbolizes* or has a metaphorical connection with this saving union. What is wrong is to separate the symbol from the reality as if the temporal connection between them is irrelevant.[114]

The expressions in Rom 6:3–4 invite Christians who view conversion and baptism as separate to acknowledge that Paul regarded them as inseparable though distinguishable as sign and thing signified. Baptism is *into* (*eis*) Christ Jesus. Baptism is *into* (*eis*) his death. Baptism into death is the *means* by which (*dia*, "through") we are buried with Christ as Paul says, "Therefore we were buried with him through baptism into death in order that just as Christ was raised from the dead through the Father's glory, we also may walk in newness of life" (Rom 6:4). Cottrell presses the significance of Paul's words, "through baptism," arguing that the apostle envisions no time separation of the symbol, baptism, from the reality accomplished, burial and death with Christ. Paul connects "our baptism and our death to sin together as cause and effect. This does not mean that the water or the physical act as such produces this spiritual effect. Only spiritual working of God himself, which he graciously performs in conjunction with the physical act, can cause us to die to sin and rise again."[115]

By "cause," however, we do not mean "effectual cause" but at most "instrumental cause." Paul's language in Romans 6 clearly does not attribute to water baptism *itself* an effectiveness that he has already denied to circumcision in Romans 2. There he argues that the external rite, circumcision of the flesh, is not efficacious to render anyone a Jew, for the ritual cannot enable one to practice what the Law requires. God regards as uncircumcised all whose flesh is circumcised but not their hearts. By contrast, however, God reckons Gentiles as circumcised who possess neither the Law nor circumcision but who yield the fruit of faith as they keep the righteous requirements of the Law. From the beginning, being a Jew (i.e., being of Abraham's seed) was never merely a matter of wearing the outward sign of circumcision, for an external sign is meaningless apart from possessing

---

[114] Cottrell, *Romans*, 1:383–84.
[115] Ibid., 1:387.

the inward reality to which the sign points, in this case the reality of a heart circumcised by God's Spirit (Rom 2:17–29).

Therefore, it is inconceivable that Paul, who has already mounted this argument concerning the ineffectiveness of the outward act of circumcision, would suggest in the same letter that the outward rite of baptism effects salvation. At the same time, however, it is equally implausible to suppose that Paul's theologically weighty words of Rom 6:3–4 have no reference to the rite of baptism with water, the rite authorized by Christ Jesus for making disciples. Paul assumes that he is appealing to people for whom the thing symbolized and the symbol converged when they submitted to baptism. Thus, he reasons, "Those of us who died to sin, how can we live in it any longer? Or are you ignorant that as many as were baptized into Christ Jesus were baptized into his death? We, therefore, were buried with him through this baptism into death in order that just as Christ was raised from the dead through the Father's glory so also we will walk in newness of life" (Rom 6:2–4).

The above argument is equally significant if we turn to Paul's summary assertion in Gal 3:27. As in Rom 6:3–4, Paul argues his case on the assumption that the ritual of baptism is full of significance and is not just a symbol. At the same time, it would be irrational to ascribe to baptism an efficacy that he rejects for another rite, namely, circumcision. He brings his argument of Gal 3:1–26 to an apex: "For as many of you as were baptized into Christ, [you] have clothed yourselves with Christ" (3:27). For the sake of his appeal, he associates putting on Christ with baptism into Christ, as if merging the sign and the thing signified into one. He reasons that those who have submitted to the symbolic washing called for by the gospel have been clothed with Christ Jesus.

Paul's appeal to baptism may seem foolish at the apex of his argument against Jewish troublemakers who have attempted to seduce Christians in Galatia into submitting to another ritual, the circumcision of the flesh, in order to become Abraham's children (2:16–3:29; esp. 3:6–7,29). At the same time, Paul cautions the Galatians not to submit to circumcision, for to do so is to sever themselves from Christ (5:2–6). He identifies baptism into Christ as the ritual that marks one as clothed with Christ. One who belongs to Christ is Abraham's child (Gal 3:29). So, Paul summarizes, not all who are circumcised in the flesh, but all who are baptized into Christ, are Abraham's children. The apostle's dispute with the Judaizers is not merely or primarily whether the rite of circumcising the flesh is effectual to set one right with God. Rather, Paul principally argues that submission to circumcision in order to become Abraham's seed is tantamount to repudiating Abraham's one true seed, Jesus Christ. Christ took upon himself the Law's curse on behalf of others so that God's blessing of Abraham (justification, 3:7–8) might come to Jews and Gentiles alike (3:13–14), rendering both of them Abraham's seed in Christ (3:26–29). Before the coming of Messiah, Abraham's true seed (3:16), it was fitting for Gentiles who believed God's promise to Abraham to submit to proselyte circumcision, for salvation was of the Jews. Now that the promised Messiah has come, Gentiles who submit to the rite of circumcision join with the cursed, not with those blessed with Abraham, because by turning to the Law they spurn Christ to whom the Law pointed. Thus, they unwittingly look to the Law, rather than to Christ, to be justified (5:2–6).[116]

Conclusion: Baptism as the Means of Grace

When speaking of God's salvation in Jesus Christ, failure to distinguish the *means* from the *ground*, or *instrument* from *basis*, or *intermediary cause* from *efficient cause* wreaks havoc in Christian theology, in the church, and in the lives of individuals within the church. Some Christians, zealous to guard God's grace against any intrusion of works, regularly confuse faith and grace. Despite Paul's distinction of grace as the ground and faith as the means in Eph 2:8–9, they carelessly speak of *faith* as the *basis* of salvation and isolate faith from other biblically sanctioned means. Other Christians fail to account for Peter's startling words—"baptism now saves you"—as they confidently assert that baptism has nothing to do with salvation and that the gospel of Jesus Christ does not require it, except per-

---

[116] Paul's warning, "you are cut off from Christ, as many as are trying to be justified by the Law; you fell from grace" (5:4), likely seems to be his reasonable inference on the premise of his argument throughout Galatians 3 and 4 rather than the express hope of the Judaizers' gospel.

haps as a mere symbol, and that for church membership. Regrettably, confusion of instrumental cause and efficient cause leads some to regard baptism as itself accomplishing regeneration, and others to make baptism optional, with little, if any, meaning.

The apostles make it clear that God saves whom and when he chooses, and that baptism is a sign of, but not the effectual cause of, regeneration. Yet, to embrace this truth and simultaneously isolate baptism from Christian conversion, whether in time or in theological expression, is an over-reaction to those embracing "baptismal regeneration." Worse, it divorces a symbol and reality that the NT holds together without embarrassment. The church and individual Christians suffer the consequences. This overly-zealous isolation of the symbol of baptism has degraded the distinguishing value and function of the symbol for individual believers and for the church.

Ironically, since the Second Great Awakening, this same zeal has permitted "new measures" of various kinds, such as the "mourners' bench," the "invitation system," or a recited "sinner's prayer" to displace baptism as the rite of conversion, thus shirking and even marginalizing Christ's command to the church. Zeal to avoid "baptismal regeneration," which many perceived to be the necessary consequence of Alexander Campbell's teaching, actually spawned another error, "decisional regeneration." This was an error rooted in revivalism that is now a traditional element in American evangelicalism. If the former error is to relegate regenerating efficacy to the *rite of baptism itself*, the latter error assigns the same efficacy to the *human decision* to act upon whichever measures preachers may use.[117] The Enlightenment's high estimation of the power of human choice took root in the frontier American church. Regrettably, evangelical churches yielded to confluent streams of revivalism and Enlightenment influences. Though Alexander Campbell unwittingly yielded to the Enlightenment's overconfidence in human reason, he rightly opposed the introduction of "new measures" that began to impoverish churches by the acceptance of conversions that did not yield transformed people. Understandably, Campbell's "reformist"

---

[117] For an account of this, see J. E. Smith, "The Theology of Charles Finney: A System of Self-Reformation," *TrinJ* 13 NS (1992): 61–93.

manner, tone, and zeal frequently repelled his contemporaries, so that even some who followed him for some time eventually parted ways with him and his followers. Thus, two traditions—evangelicalism and the Stone-Campbell movement—developed side by side in America, occasionally sparring over baptism, but mostly ignoring each other as each group turned inward to tend to internal disputes.

It is commendable that rapprochement has been taking place between the Stone-Campbell movement and evangelicalism, particularly among scholars, if theological correctives come to both sides. Stone-Campbell exegetes and theologians have been reevaluating and refining their formulations concerning baptism. Conversation with those of the Stone-Campbell tradition should prompt evangelicals to restore a higher "baptismal consciousness" and to represent more carefully the baptismal beliefs of Alexander Campbell and his heirs (true as it is that some have justly received criticism for propounding baptismal regeneration).[118]

This is not to suggest that we pursue a unity that suppresses the significance of baptism.[119] Because baptism is commanded by the Lord Jesus, it is a matter of the first order in Christian practice. Though agreement on form of administration of baptism will be hard to achieve among churches of diverse traditions, all Christians ought to pursue a "single theology of baptism," as David Wright contends, for the apostle's words make it clear that there is but "one baptism" (Eph 4:4–6). Paul's words ring with clarity and force beckoning us to a persistent endeavor to recognize and to retrieve our unity and then "to maintain the unity of the Spirit in the bond of peace" (4:3).

As with all theological squabbles, disputes over baptism have tended to push opposing views toward extremes. One isolates baptism from repentance, disconnecting baptism from the making of disciples and associating baptism at most with church membership.

[118] See Wright, "Recovering Baptism for a New Age of Mission," 51–66; Wellum, "The Means of Grace: Baptism," 149–70.

[119] See D. F. Wright, "Scripture and Evangelical Diversity with Special Reference to the Baptismal Divide," in *A Pathway into the Holy Scripture*, ed. P. E. Satterthwaite and D. F. Wright (Grand Rapids: Eerdmans, 1994), 257–75, and Wright, "Recovering Baptism for a New Age of Mission," 51–66.

Such an approach deprecates baptism's significance and urgency as authorized by Christ (Matt 28:19–20). Some even neglect baptism altogether as they ascribe to human decision an efficacy to bring regeneration ("decisional regeneration"). Another view isolates baptism from the multifaceted call of the gospel that ascribes to baptism a power that it does not have in itself since it is a sign or symbol and not the reality of cleansing itself. Undoubtedly, both sides mean well, but the consequences of the two errors persist longer than the theological squabbles that spawn them.

This essay has focused on the theological formulations of the clearest, most careful, and most articulate representatives within the Stone-Campbell tradition. Many readers may dispute its assessment of the Stone-Campbell tradition concerning baptism. It must be admitted that at the popular level many preachers and members of Christian Churches, the Churches of Christ, and the Disciples of Christ describe baptism as effectual.

From the beginning of the Restoration movement, Alexander Campbell was careful to articulate his beliefs concerning baptism, making it clear that he did not hold that baptism itself regenerates. At least some who associated with and have followed him, however, have lacked the same clarity, prompting allegations that the movement's leaders taught that baptism itself regenerates. That two large and well-known churches in the Stone-Campbell tradition take considerable measures to denounce "baptismal regeneration" is evidence that the tradition continues to suffer under the weight of being accused of advocating such a belief.[120]

[120] Two large and well-known churches in the Stone-Campbell tradition—Oak Hills Church of San Antonio, Texas and Southeast Christian Church of Louisville, Kentucky—expressly guard against treating baptism as efficacious. For detailed consideration of Oak Hills Church's teaching position on baptism, see Hicks, "Balancing Faith, Christian Experience and Baptism," 118–24. Southeast Christian Church poses questions and offers answers (http://www.southeast-christian.org/newmembers_questionsanswered.cfm?doc_id=640). The church's web page asks, "Why should we be baptized?" and answers:

"A person should be baptized to follow the example of Christ (Mat. 3:13–17), to obey Christ's command (Mat. 28:18), to accept forgiveness of sins (Acts 2:38; 22:16), to receive the Holy Spirit (Acts 2:38), to express trust in Christ (Acts 8:12–13), and to testify to God's work in his or her life (Rom. 6:1–8; Gal. 3:27). Baptism also serves to cleanse a guilty conscience (1 Pet. 3:21). The Holy Spirit prompts individuals to recognize their sin and guilt. The only method by which the human soul can be wiped clean of sin is through the blood of Jesus Christ (Heb.

These allegations are not pure fabrications. This essay has shown, however, that it is both historical and theological malpractice for Baptists and others to impute to Alexander Campbell the flaws of his theological heirs. The overwhelming and popular assumption among American evangelicals is that the official dogma of churches in the Stone-Campbell tradition is that baptism regenerates. Perusal of pamphlets and books as well as a search of internet resources readily demonstrates this. The slapdash manner with which many evangelicals judge the entire Restoration movement concerning baptism is regrettable. Diverse as Baptists are, it would be unreasonable, irresponsible, and unkind for anyone to judge all Southern Baptists, for example, as holding the views of Landmark Baptists, of Reformed Baptists, of American Baptists, or of any other variety of Baptists. Diversity exists even among Southern Baptists. Diversity also exists among the heirs of the Stone-Campbell Restoration tradition. Therefore, Christian charity should govern evangelicals, especially ministers and theologians, as we assess the Stone-Campbell tradition concerning baptism by engaging the most biblically and theologically informed leaders in that tradition. Anyone in that tradition who advocates the notion that baptism itself is effectual to save actually diverges from Alexander Campbell's teachings as preserved in his writings.

9:27–10:7). This 'washing away' of sin is most clearly symbolized in the act of baptism (Acts 22:16; 1 Pet. 3:21) ...

   "*The act of baptism cannot save an individual. We are saved only through accepting Christ's sacrifice on the cross.* Baptism demonstrates the believer's acceptance of Christ and is the point of time when the believer receives assurance of his or her faith. Those who were never baptized by immersion but were sprinkled for baptism as infants rest in God's merciful hands. We hope that Jesus will say to any person who has truly submitted to him but was not taught about immersion, 'Your faith has saved you.' Yet someone who understands Christ's command to be baptized and refuses to obey should not consider himself to have submitted to Christ" (emphasis original).

BAPTISM IN THE CONTEXT OF THE LOCAL CHURCH

Mark E. Dever[*]

Introduction: How Baptism Functions in the Life of a Local Congregation

B aptism is the discarded jewel of Christian churches today—even of Baptist churches. Confusion, ignorance, prejudice, and a misplaced and distorting cultural conservatism all beset most churches today in their practice of baptism. The Southern Baptist Convention's own study has suggested that only 40 percent of baptisms in cooperating churches are "first time" baptisms of converts. The majority of reported baptisms are either re-dedications or transfers of membership from other churches.[1] Even if the theology of baptism held by baptistic Christians is correct, our practice seems far from correct.[2] Although larger issues of the gospel, conversion, and evangelism are also involved in our current malpractice of baptism, the understanding of baptism represented in this book, if carefully considered, should go far to helping us recapture more biblical practices.

The meaning and mode of baptism have already been written about admirably. We have been instructed about the NT background of the ordinance and its practice in the first century. We have seen something of its use in the early church and among the early Anabaptists. Arguments for paedobaptism have been summarized and rejected. It now falls to us, before we finish this volume,

---

[*] Mark E. Dever received his Ph.D. from Cambridge University, serves as the Senior Pastor of the Capitol Hill Baptist Church in Washington D.C., and is Director of www.9marks.org.

[1] P. B. Jones, et al., "A Study of Adults Baptized in Southern Baptist Churches, 1993" *Research Report*, January 1995 (Atlanta: Home Mission Board, SBC).

[2] A. R. Cross well summarizes various aspects of baptismal practice in the UK in chapter 10 of his *Baptism and the Baptists* (Carlisle: Paternoster, 2000). I know of no similar survey of the contemporary American scene. J. Tyler has written a careful evaluation of practices from a more theologically liberal Baptist perspective (*Baptism: We've Got It Right . . . and Wrong* [Macon, GA: Smith & Helwys, 2003]). Tyler's examination recounts many common current practices among some Baptist churches in the American south.

to consider constructively the implications of all this for a local church's practice of baptism.

If baptism is so clearly described in the pages of the NT, what should it look like in the life of a local congregation today? Andrew Fuller wrote in 1802 that the proper practice of baptism promotes "piety in individuals, and purity in the church."[3] Baptism itself is a summary of our faith. Baptism is a confession of sin and a picture of repentance. Baptism is a profession of faith in Christ. It reminds us of Christ's humiliation and death as he identified with sinners and of his resurrection from the dead. Baptism presents a preview of the bodily resurrection, and it portrays the radical nature of conversion. When rightly practiced, it distinguishes believers from unbelievers, the church from the world. It is, to cite Fuller again, "The boundary of visible Christianity."[4] Therefore, it should protect the church from nominalism. Baptizing only those who profess to be converted—and give evidence of it—is a foundational matter for a congregation that would be healthy, sound, and growing. The regenerate nature of each member of the church is protected and displayed by the practice of believer's baptism.[5] All these benefits of the right practice of baptism call out to Christians today to think carefully about how theology should be applied to practice at this point.

Many questions present themselves about our practice. Who should baptize? How should the baptism be done? Who should be baptized? When and in what context should they be baptized? These and other questions are to be considered in this chapter.

Who Baptizes?

Many think it should be the minister who baptizes. Sometimes this conclusion comes from a wrong clericalism, with a Roman Catholic-like assumption of the status given to someone who is ordained. Others think it simply does not matter who does the baptizing. Some have felt that it should be those who lead them to the

---

[3] A. Fuller, "Practical Uses of Christian Baptism," *Complete Works of Andrew Fuller* (1848; repr., Harrisonburg, VA: Sprinkle, 1988), 3:339.

[4] Fuller, "Practical Uses of Christian Baptism," *Works*, 3:342.

[5] See J. Hammett, *Biblical Foundations for Baptist Churches: A Contemporary Ecclesiology* (Grand Rapids: Kregel, 2005), especially chapters 4 and 5.

Lord, others that it could be any pastor on staff. Some have felt that an elder should do it. One well-known Baptist—John Smyth—even baptized himself! Who should do the baptizing today?

None of these answers given above are required by the biblical testimony. Neither by explicit instruction nor by example does the Bible teach that a particular administrator is essential for a true, valid baptism. Neither Jesus nor Paul baptized as a central part of their own ministry (see John 4:2; 1 Cor 1:14). Having said that, it is normally prudent to have someone perform the baptism who well represents the congregation as a whole. The senior pastor, the preaching minister, or some other elder recognized by the congregation would most obviously seem to act on behalf of the congregation as a whole and then ultimately on behalf of the Lord in their baptizing.[6]

How Is Baptism to Be Done?

While baptism is not necessary for salvation, water is certainly necessary for baptism! Though baptism has been performed by pouring or sprinkling,[7] there is little doubt of the appropriateness of immersion. Whether done backward or forward, once or three times, immersion is widely acknowledged as the apostolic practice and the practice that most fully conveys what baptism is to display—our participation by faith in the death, burial, and resurrection of Christ.

The physical location of the baptism has actually been a matter of controversy in the past. While baptisms were certainly done in outdoor spaces (like the Jordan River), there have been some questions about exactly which spaces could be used. The *Didache* directed the early Christians to baptize in running water; or if not in running water, then in a standing pool; and if not there, then simply to pour

---

[6] See J. L. Dagg, *A Treatise on Church Order* (1858; repr., Harrisonburg, VA: Gano, 1990), 257.

[7] E.g., *Didache* (chap. 7); see M. J. Erickson, *Christian Theology* (Grand Rapids: Baker, 1985), 1104–5; and G. R. Beasley-Murray, "Baptists and the Baptism of Other Churches," in *The Truth That Makes Men Free: Official Report of the Eleventh Congress, Baptist World Alliance, Miami Beach, Florida, U.S.A. June 25–30, 1965*, ed. J. Nordenhaug (Nashville: Broadman, 1966), 262, 270.

water (presumably if no more water were at hand; *Did. 7:1–3*). By the time buildings were dedicated to Christian use in the fourth century, large baptistries were being constructed in those churches (evidence both for immersion and for the immersion of adults as the normal form of these early baptisms). Among American Baptists, however, indoor baptistries only came into common use in the early nineteenth century, and they created something of a stir. Some denied that such innovations should be accepted because they were not according to the biblical practice. But by the late nineteenth century, in no small part due to the growth of urban congregations, such baptistries became the norm.

What words should be used in the actual baptism itself? In Matt 28:19 Jesus instructs the disciples to baptize "in the name of the Father and of the Son and of the Holy Spirit."[8] In Acts 2:38, Peter instructs inquirers to be baptized "in the name of Jesus Christ." And in Acts 10:48, Luke summarizes Peter's instructions to the believers in Cornelius's house to be "baptized in the name of Jesus Christ." What are we to make of this discrepancy? Calvin reasoned from this difference that the efficacy of the baptism does not depend on the exact words used. Christ did not intend to give "a fixed formula, but the recalling of the faithful to Christ, in whom alone we obtain all that baptism prefigures to us."[9] Certainly no use of the phrase "in the name of Jesus" should ever be allowed if it indicates a denial of the Trinitarian nature of God. But, assuming orthodoxy of intent, the exact wording is not clearly fixed in Scripture. That said, the inclusive dominical form from Matthew 28 seems preferable because of its fullness of expression, recalling to our minds the work of all three persons of the Godhead in our salvation.

Who Is to Be Baptized?

This entire volume has argued that baptism is only for those who are known to be disciples of Jesus Christ. This is taught in Matthew

[8] Unless otherwise noted, the NIV is the translation cited in this chapter.

[9] J. Calvin, *Calvin's New Testament Commentaries*, ed. D. W. Torrance and T. F. Torrance. Vol. 6: *The Acts of the Apostles 1–13*, trans. J. W. Fraser and W. J. G. McDonald (1965; repr., Grand Rapids: Eerdmans, 1989), 81.

28, exemplified in the book of Acts and assumed in Romans 6. Infants, therefore, cannot be baptized. Rather, the subject of baptism should be someone who, as far as the local church has good reason to believe, desires to follow Christ and be baptized and who lives consistently with an earnest confession of sin and repentance and a faith in Christ's life, death, and resurrection for him.[10]

Some baptistic churches have begun the practice of having infant dedications, special services or components of a public service in which the infant is prayed for, along with the parents, sometimes accompanied by vows which the parents take in front of the congregation. While we as Christians should give ourselves to teaching the gospel to our children and praying for them privately and publicly, the Bible nowhere commands such a public act of dedication. Furthermore, such ceremonies, if regularly practiced could be taken to mean more than they do (e.g., to be biblical ordinances, to be required by the congregation, to be making statements about the spiritual state of the children, to make up for a "lack" of infant baptism). Adding a regular component to the life of a congregation, and a component which would be so widely misunderstood, is at least imprudent and may even prove to be dangerous.

How the candidate's spiritual state is to be determined will vary somewhat due to circumstances. The candidate's desire is itself necessary but not sufficient evidence. Regular attendance at meetings of the church is still more evidence. Certainly the church should observe the person's life to help ensure that he is not self-deceived. "Time will tell" is the point of many of Christ's parables (e.g., the parable of the sower [Mark 4:3–9, 13–20]; the house on the rock [Matt 7:24–27]; the two sons [Matt 21:28–32]). Professions can be real and accurate, even when conversions are sudden and dramatic. In fact, if public professions of faith are truly representative of conversion, the Christian will, of course, have been converted even before he makes his first public profession of it. Yet it takes time to manifest whether public professions of conversion are real. False

---

[10] Under exceptional circumstances baptisms may be conducted by individuals (e.g., Acts 8:38), but normally a local church would be the visible community into which the individual is baptized.

professions are made most often by those who are sincere but wrong in their claim to follow Christ. Time—whether a few weeks or a few months—will allow the pastors and others in a congregation to watch and have their initial conclusions confirmed by the continuing discipleship of the one desiring baptism.[11]

Finally, an interview by the pastor, other elder-type figures, or other wise and reliable members is a helpful way to get to know the person better. In such an interview, the person conducting it can sort out simple facts (name, address, job, age) and ask more careful questions (about marital status, current and previous church relations). The pastor can examine the prospective member's understanding of the gospel and the church. Their willingness to sign the statement of faith and the church covenant and to participate in the life of this congregation can be tested. And the interviewer can hear the friend's life history, especially his testimony of conversion and following Christ. At the end of such a thirty-to-sixty minute interview, the pastor could summarize membership duties and can remind those interviewed of the membership process. Concluding such a time with prayer is a helpful way for the congregation visibly to begin exercising a shepherding ministry in the person's life.

Under some circumstances, baptisms could be done more quickly with less time for examination. For instance, a clear, apparently sincere conversion of someone who is about to move to an area with little or no Christian presence may lead a pastor to decide to baptize someone who is not moving to membership in his local church. Other extenuating circumstances which might lead a pastor to decide to proceed with baptizing someone outside the normal course of joining the church could include the case of someone who is apparently converted and seriously ill, someone whose conversion is made more obviously real by the clear and costly repentance that was entailed in it, or perhaps conversions among those coming from anti-Christian families or social circles (as we see in the examples in the book of Acts). Prayer and consultation among leaders of a congregation should help to give wisdom in such situations.

---

[11] More will be said below as to why the pattern in Acts of baptizing immediately after conversion need not be the normative practice today.

Who should make this determination about the readiness of a candidate to be baptized? Certainly the pastor of the church has a particular responsibility as the minister of God's Word. Ministers with large congregations—e.g., from Richard Baxter and C. H. Spurgeon in the past to John MacArthur Jr. and John Piper today—may well have other pastors and elders who exercise this important ministry of guarding and defining the local church. After an opportunity for questions and discussion among the elders, the elders as a whole should be able to affirm the conclusion of the interviewing pastor. The candidate's request for membership, along with the elders' affirmation, should be brought before the entire congregation because the congregation as a whole then becomes part of the covenanted community of that believer (Eph 4:25; cp. the extended discussions in Romans 12 and 1 Corinthians 12). Not even all these stages can prevent the occasional baptism of someone who proves to be unregenerate. Hypocrisy cannot finally be prevented, but it can be discouraged.

Once it is determined that someone is to be baptized, he should be prepared. In the church, teaching is the responsibility of the elders. It is the responsibility of these undershepherds, then, to instruct those who are to be baptized (see Heb 13:17; 1 Pet 5:1–4; Matt 28:19–20; 2 Pet 3:18). Baptismal candidates should normally be regular in their attendance and participation at church. Furthermore, some kind of membership classes are appropriate requirements for candidates; matters that would cause hesitation in joining a local church may indicate larger problems or questions best addressed before baptism.

At a preparation meeting prior to the candidate's baptism, the candidate could be given a list of biblical passages about baptism and encouraged to study them. Appropriate materials on baptism and the Christian life could also be given to him.

When Is Baptism to Be Done?

While the question of who should be baptized is most nearly related to the nature of baptism, the question of the context for performing baptism is also important. Should Philip's baptism of the Ethiopian eunuch in the wilderness (recorded in Acts 8) be taken as normative, or should the congregation be the normal witnesses of baptisms? Practically, in congregational celebrations of baptism, when should the baptisms occur? What should be part of those services, and why?

Baptisms are normally to be conducted in the assembly which the person will be joining. While no biblical passage explicitly teaches this, the common circumstances of life conspire to ensure that most people will be baptized where they live. Moreover, the situation of multiple yet differing churches in one town did not exist during the NT period. Most examples of baptism in Acts involve the initial establishment of a church (e.g., in Jerusalem, Philippi, Ephesus) and therefore do not directly instruct us on every question concerning the practice of baptism in the continuing and settled life of a congregation.

Philip's baptism of the Ethiopian in Acts 8 was done in private in the sense that the baptism itself was done outside of the presence of others from that church. The situation was exceptional—even for missionaries. The Ethiopian was on his way home. God himself had supernaturally brought Philip there at that moment. The man was reading from Isaiah about the Messiah, and his heart was prepared. God's evident activity alone would undoubtedly have been sufficient to encourage Philip to recognize the reality of this conversion. Certainly there would have been no churches back in Ethiopia to baptize him.

The congregation is responsible for affirming initially that the individual to be baptized is a repentant sinner, is orthodox in his understanding of God's grace through Christ, is not trusting in anything else, is living in such a way as to indicate that he is more committed to Christ than to immorality, and is not divisive. Should any of these not be the case, then the congregation should move to exclude the professing Christian from membership (as in 1 Cor 5). In the same way the person desiring baptism should be forbidden it until repentance for sin is evidenced. That which would exclude from membership in the assembly one who is already baptized would surely prohibit the baptism of one initially seeking it.

If such responsibility rests with the congregation, then it is particularly appropriate for the baptism itself to take place in the presence of the gathered congregation as a whole. The one baptized has been united to Christ by faith; he is also being united to the congregation by covenant and fellowship in the gospel. As Paul says in Ephesians 4, it is in the congregation that we are being knit together into maturity (Eph 4:16). Or, as he says in 1 Corinthians 12, we are parts of one another (1 Cor 12:27). It is most appropriate, then, for the baptism to be done in the congregation.

Given that the congregation is the most appropriate context for the celebration of baptisms, should baptisms occur at a special meeting or in a normal service? Whether the service is considered the normal gathering of a congregation or not, it is best not to isolate the administration of either baptism or the Lord's Supper from the preaching of God's Word. Baptism and the Lord's Supper are best understood when they are part of a service in which Christ and his promises are proclaimed through the preaching of the word. Furthermore, simply having a service built around baptism or the Lord's Supper could suggest that salvation comes through the religious actions themselves—an error that we are disposed to and that is damning.

Given that the normal service—or at least a service containing the preaching of God's Word—is the best context for baptisms, when in the service should the baptisms occur? They could, of course, be at any time in the service. It is most common today to have them at the beginning of the service. In some churches the pastor appears in the baptistry, the candidates will be introduced and baptized, and then the regular service proceeds. While this is a dramatic way to begin a service and allows those being baptized to participate in the rest of the service, it can sometimes feel as if the baptism is being trivialized—placed with the welcome and announcements.

Perhaps a better place for baptisms is at the end of a service. After the word has been clearly preached and Christ held out in the gospel, then the baptisms occur as the last part of the time together, exemplifying the imperative in every sermon—whole-hearted commitment to Jesus Christ. The visual representation of Christ's resurrection and the promise of new life and resurrection for believers powerfully drives home other impressions made during the service. Placing baptisms in such a climactic location seems to say, "This is a picture of what we've been talking about!" And this encourages the congregation to join in the celebration of God's work in the person's life.

Hearing from those about to be baptized makes the event more meaningful to the congregation. Formal questions from the pastor can elicit Christian testimony from each candidate. "Do you make profession of repentance toward God and of faith in our Lord Jesus Christ?" "I do." "Do you promise, depending on God's grace, to follow him forever in the fellowship of his church?" "I do."

Also, a more personal testimony from those about to be baptized both solidifies their own understanding of their baptism and informs the congregation. While such testimonies should not be required, surely in them Christ is exalted, the gospel explained and exemplified, Christian obedience demonstrated, and faith portrayed. Particularly in situations where the baptismal candidate is clearly "switching loyalties," his testimony can be powerful. New believers explaining their conversion from paganism, Hinduism, Unitarianism, or Islam, for example, show the reality of the gospel proclaimed. Such testimonies encourage evangelism. The congregation is brought into the life story of at least one former non-Christian and is aided in celebrating and welcoming the new believer into the Christian family.

The testimonies can be limited in time (for obvious reasons). The pastor or staff may work with the baptismal candidate in order to help shape an edifying and appropriate testimony. Long and detailed accounts of sin are not good. It is not the right setting to get into the details of denominational distinctives (like infant baptism). The gospel should be the focus. It should be clearly expressed and the believer's faith in Christ clearly professed. Even his description of himself before his conversion may help the watching members to realize witnessing opportunities they have at work or with neighbors, and to take advantage of those opportunities for the gospel. Surely

God is glorified when a life story is told in terms of God's work of conviction and regeneration.

Such times of celebrating baptism become highlights in a congregation's life, so that common memories are treasured. Tales of a quiet and consistent, or a dramatic and monumental, change in an individual excite interest and encourage faith. The children of the church are instructed, the young believers encouraged, the older believers provided evidence that God is calling to himself those who will continue on after them. And in all of this, the whole body "joined and held together by every supporting ligament, grows and builds itself up in love, as each part does its work" (Eph 4:16). The church's growth becomes visible. Through such public baptismal testimonies, non-Christians who attend hear the gospel, the church is built up, Christians are encouraged and unified, and, in all this, God is glorified.

Remaining Questions

Should the Unbaptized Come to the Lord's Supper?

Paul's letter to the Romans seems to assume that the Christians in this church he had never visited were all baptized. And he seemed to assume that all those baptized were Christian believers. When he wrote, then, to the Corinthians about their abuse of the Lord's Supper, his assumption was certainly that all those coming to the table had been baptized. Those who were persevering in sin (like the man in 1 Cor 5) were to be denied the Lord's Table, and thereby effectively had the truthfulness of their conversion and subsequent baptism questioned. The practice of corrective church discipline, and especially of exclusion or excommunication, is part of meaningful church membership. Baptism and the Lord's Supper are normally the formal acts of being admitted to and continuing in the fellowship of the church. Without a correct understanding of baptism, membership and church discipline are more difficult to practice. Conversely, without a careful practice of church membership and discipline, both baptism and the Lord's Supper can be cheapened.[12]

[12] For more consideration of the practice of membership in Baptist churches, see my book-

Without discipline, the ordinances even biblically observed can become nothing more than what the Puritan minister Richard Sibbes called "a seal to a blank"[13]—a ceremonial sign of something that does not really exist, a check written on a bankrupt account.

Normally there would be no reason that someone who is baptized should not come to the Lord's table. Nor should there be a reason why the Lord's table should be denied to anyone who is baptized (apart from unrepentant sin). Both ordinances or signs indicate participation in the forgiveness of Christ and his power in giving believers new life. That which would disbar from one ordinance (e.g., sin, unbelief) would seem to disbar from the other. Furthermore, since Paul calls believers to self-examination before coming to the table (1 Cor 11:27–29), failing to obey Christ's call to be baptized calls into question the claim of being Christ's follower (since Christ commanded baptism in Matt 28:19–20). Even if the disobedience is unintentional (as in the case of an evangelical infant baptism), it is still sin and cannot be countenanced by the church.

Generally Baptists, along with other Christians—have understood the Bible as teaching that baptism should precede participation in the Lord's Supper.[14] For example, the New Hampshire Confession of Faith, article XIV, "Of Baptism and the Lord's Supper," reads:

> We believe that Christian Baptism is the immersion in water of a believer, into the name of the Father, and Son, and Holy Ghost; to show forth in a solemn and beautiful emblem, our faith in the crucified, buried, and risen Saviour, with its effect, in our death to sin and resurrection to a new life; that it is pre-requisite to the privileges of a church relation; and to the Lord's Supper, in which the members of the church by the sacred use of bread and wine, are to commemorate together the dying love of Christ; preceded always by solemn self-examination.[15]

let, *A Display of God's Glory: Basics of Church Structure: Deacons, Elders, Congregationalism and Membership* (Washington, DC: Center for Church Reform, 2001); also Hammett, *Biblical Foundations for Baptist Churches.*

[13] R. Sibbes, "The Providence of God," in *Works of Richard Sibbes*, ed. A. B. Grosart (1862–64; repr., Carlisle, PA: Banner of Truth, 1977), 5:43.

[14] An example of a Baptist who would not take this position is Wayne Grudem. See his *Systematic Theology* (Grand Rapids: Zondervan, 1994), 996–97.

[15] W. L. Lumpkin, *Baptist Confessions of Faith*, rev. ed. (Valley Forge, PA: Judson, 1969), 366.

That baptism is a prerequisite for coming regularly to the Lord's table seems to be supported both from Scripture and from Baptist history.[16]

Should the Unbaptized
Be Admitted to Church Membership?

As noted above, the NT seems to assume that Christians were baptized. Therefore it is no stretch of the imagination to conclude that members of churches were baptized. For the more modern question, "Was baptism required for church membership?" the answer would seem to be yes. That is, we know of no one who was claiming to be converted and yet who refused baptism. Therefore, the NT believer's relation to the local church was as one who both called himself a Christian and who had been baptized. Refusing to be baptized would then call into question the claim to be living in obedience to Jesus Christ. While a local congregation will want to inquire into areas other than baptism to determine the fitness of a candidate for membership, it should not neglect this basic and simple matter of Christian obedience. After all, to disagree on the subjects and meaning of baptism may well be to disagree on the fundamental shape and purpose of the church and on who is to constitute it.

The command to be baptized is clearly taught in Scripture, is simple to obey, and is significant for the boundaries of the church. To require it for membership is to do no more than Scripture does of Christians. Even if a Christian has understood that he has obeyed this command through having been baptized as an infant, his misunderstanding does not excuse his sin. To require baptism for membership is not to lay a command too difficult to be obeyed. And to require baptism for membership is to continue to define the church as the congregation

---

[16] Questions of visitors coming occasionally to the table may be separated from the question of Christians regularly coming as members under the care and guidance of that particular congregation. Such occasional communion may be considered as similar to occasional pulpit fellowship, or other kinds of Christian cooperation between congregations that may not agree on secondary matters but that would agree on the primary issue of the gospel. On the issue of pulpit fellowship with those who have not been baptized as believers, see Dagg, *Church Order*, 286–298. Dagg concluded that it was not inconsistent for a Baptist congregation to allow someone to preach to it and yet for the congregation to deny that same paedobaptist minister membership in their Baptist congregation.

of believers, as opposed to a mixed congregation of believers and others (e.g., children, grandchildren, spouses, and dependents). When a noncongregational style of government is adopted, the acceptance of the unbaptized into membership may seem initially without effect. But a subtle indifference to doctrine may be communicated. Furthermore, the bulk of members may come to hold the allowed exception, and the teaching ministry of the church on this—and other—points may begin to stray. Such a tendency would not be unprecedented in the history of once great evangelical churches.

Should Baptisms from Other Churches Be Accepted?

Sometimes Christians of different denominations share more common ground about baptism than the well-known differences may suggest.[17] Defining what constitutes baptism leads to defining

---

[17] Statements Regarding Baptism on Which We Agree—Mark Dever (SBC), David Coffin (PCA). (Unpublished summary of a public conversation held at the Capitol Hill Baptist Church in the Summer of 2001.)

1. No one disagrees with professor baptism (except Quakers).
2. This is a subject of great import.
3. There are clear commands for and examples of professors' baptism in the New Testament.
4. This fact is not evidentially determinate of the question (i.e., it does not preclude infant baptism).
5. God's Word alone should settle the matter (but we do not mind using history as confirmation of a biblical pattern).
6. There are no commands for or clear examples of infant baptism in the New Testament
   DC: Uncertain about the word "examples." What do you make of household baptism (Philippian jailer, Lydia, etc.)? These examples are problems only for baptistic Christians
   MD: there is no reason the first reading of the text should not refer to baptism of believers. For example, the word was preached to the Philippian jailer's whole household.
7. Baptism was appointed by Christ to be of permanent value in the Christian church.
8. Baptism is a rite of initiation; the Lord's Supper is a rite of continuance.
9. There is no articulation of a Reformed understanding of infant baptism before Zwingli.
   DC: Someone in 250 A.D. would not have thought baptism to be salvific.
   MD: *Didache* suggests that believer's baptism was assumed in the early church.
10. Infant baptism is widely practiced by the late second century AD.
    MD: By this point in time, church fathers assume baptismal regeneration
    DC: Their words only mimic biblical language.
    MD: Guidelines for believer's baptism exist in second century AD
    DC: This is perfectly understandable in a missionary enterprise.
11. There are some who are baptized who are not in fact saved.
12. There are some who are not baptized who are in fact saved.
13. There is a regular temptation of the visible church to trust in the outward rather than the inward.

what baptisms a local congregation may accept as true baptisms. So, for example, a baptism of an infant is in no sense the baptism commanded in Scripture. But what about a believer who was baptized upon his profession of repentance and faith, but in a non-Baptist church? Is the administrator or congregation essential to the ordinance? Or are some matters normal but nonessential? Could there be a baptism that is true, but irregular? If so, what would such irregularities be?

Baptists have split into many camps on such questions. Sometimes they have even withdrawn fellowship from one another over their differing conclusions. Other times they have simply allowed for such variances due to congregational autonomy, knowing that each congregation will give account to God. The nineteenth-century Landmarkists represented one end of the spectrum. They understood that only true churches could perform valid baptisms, and they tightly defined what constituted a true church. On the other hand, many Baptists historically have accepted baptisms from other gospel-preaching churches if the people being baptized were believers. So, for example, the Philadelphia Baptist Association meeting in 1765 received a query from Smith's Creek church, "Whether it be proper to receive a person into communion [i.e., membership] who had been baptized by immersion by a minister of the church of England, if no other objection could be made?" The Association answered "Yea, if he had been baptized on a profession of faith and repentance."[18] Questions about which baptisms to accept are unavoidable. Most decisions, however, will be fairly straightforward once a few biblical principles are agreed on.

14. God can create faith in a child before that faith is evident.
15. The texts urging "believe and be baptized" or referring to "household" baptisms do not of themselves constitute conclusive evidence for either side.
16. The covenant made with Abraham is an administration of the covenant of grace. Nothing in this particular administration violates the general covenant.
17. Children of believers enjoy particular privileges and have special obligations.
   MD: Do not treat your children as if you presume they are elect
   DC: Tell them that they are disciples in the school of Christ. By virtue of Christ's command to the contrary, they will in some way be lacking if they have not been baptized.
[18] A. D. Gillette, ed., *Minutes of the Philadelphia Baptist Association 1707–1807* (1851; repr., Springfield, MO: Particular Baptist Press, 2002), 95.

Should Those Not Coming into Membership
Be Baptized?

One question of prudence concerns whether to separate baptism from the normal process of joining a congregation. That is, should the pastor baptize a person who has come to him claiming repentance and faith but who is not, for whatever reason, desiring or even willing to join his church? Nothing in Scripture would either prohibit or demand this baptism by a particular minister, and arguments can be made on either side. On the one hand, the candidate's profession of faith and desire for baptism are good and are to be encouraged. If his life seems to confirm his faith, one could be even more encouraged to baptize him. On the other hand, his testimony would be strengthened if the candidate understood the practical demands of following Jesus in a particular Bible-believing church and professed himself willing to meet those demands. What is indicated by his unwillingness? While there may be exceptions, churches should normally delay baptism until the person becomes willing to commit himself to membership.[19]

Should Baptism Ever Be Delayed?

The question of knowing when to baptize an individual can become more complicated when it is understood that neither infant baptism nor baptismal regeneration are biblical ideas. With an understanding of the baptism of believers, the paramount question becomes, "Is this person a publicly demonstrable believer?" Some have answered that those professing Christ should simply be received upon reaching an age of accountability (whatever the particular age may be, i.e., whether 8 or 14, etc.). Others, recognizing a difference between simple regeneration and the responsibilities a public disciple and church member have, advocate setting an "age of responsibility"—most often 12 or 18—which would then function as

---

[19] Churches should discern a person's reason for being unwilling to covenant with their congregation upon his public profession of faith. There may be legitimate, practical reasons for not joining the church (e.g., about to move to an unchurched area); on the other hand, there may be a misunderstanding of what it means to follow Christ which misunderstanding is brought to light by the additional inquiries required to join a local church.

a minimal baptismal age in that congregation. Whatever the appropriate age for baptism is, the average age of actual baptisms among Baptists has definitely been declining during the last century.

Often at such an age, special classes have been offered, and young people have been encouraged to confess publicly their faith and their sin (often at the same service in which they are baptized). Some Christians have tried to hold "baptismal candidates" until certain days—e.g., a day on which the church would celebrate the Lord's Supper, or have a members' meeting, or perhaps Easter, following an ancient tradition.

No delay is present in baptism accounts in Acts, but in Acts there would have been little question of the state of those people (as in the cases of Pentecost in Acts 2, the Ethiopian eunuch in Acts 8, and Cornelius's household in Acts 10). If we are to baptize only believers—and we are—then pastors must question why baptismal ages have been falling. Could there be certain pressures pastors are facing to do this? Certainly the Bible gives us no command for immediacy or for delay, but the nature of baptism clearly shows that it is to be only for those who profess saving faith. Therefore, if delay is necessary to ascertain genuine saving faith in the person, then delay would seem to be the path of prudence.

One special case of delay has been the delay of children claiming regeneration. Here all the cautions mentioned earlier should be borne in mind. But are there no more questions to be considered in the case of baptizing minors?[20] Some will conclude that there are not and that to encourage delay in such cases is to disobey Scripture. Others, however, are less certain of that. Spurgeon is a good example of someone who both preached and practiced the importance of leading children to conversion[21] and yet who waited to baptize his own sons—evidently Christians for years—until they were eigh-

---

[20] Advocates of infant baptism also have unresolved questions about the involvement of children in the life of the congregation. See, for example, D. F. Wright, "Children, Covenant and the Church," *Themelios* 29 (Spring 2004): 26–39.

[21] See, for example, his sermon "To Sabbath-School Teachers and Other Soul-Winners," *The Metropolitan Tabernacle Pulpit: Containing Sermons Preached and Revised by C. H. Spurgeon* (Pasadena, TX: Pilgrim, 1969–80), 19:577–588.

teen.[22] This practice of delaying for maturity—similar to other delays commanded in Scripture (e.g., marriage, responsibility in OT Israel, service in the army in the OT)—is common around the world today[23] and was formerly common in the United States.[24] Baptisms of children eight or nine years of age, or even younger, were either unheard of or very rare. Tony Hemphill has concluded that between

[22] See W. Y. Fullerton, *Thomas Spurgeon: A Biography* (London: Hodder & Stoughton, 1919), 43–45.

[23] E.g., A. Cross notes that Southern Baptists tend to approve of baptizing younger persons than do Baptists in England (*Baptism and the Baptists* [Carlisle, UK: Paternoster, 2000], 393, n 23). For this "age of responsibility" position on baptismal age, see T. Griffith, *The Case for Believer's Baptism* (Eastbourne, UK: Kingsway, 1990), 51–55. For a brief treatment of the challenge this shifting presents to Southern Baptists today, see T. Hemphill, "The Practice of Infantile Baptism in Southern Baptist Churches and Subsequent Impact on Regenerate Church Membership," *Faith & Mission*, Vol. 18, No. 3 (Summer 2001): 74–87. See also J. Withers, "Social Forces Affecting the Age at Which Children are Baptized in Southern Baptist Churches" (Ph. D. diss., The Southern Baptist Theological Seminary, 1996).

[24] John Gill was brought up in a Baptist home and was baptized at age 19, in 1716 (just 3 weeks shy of his 20th birthday).
Samuel Medley was brought up in a Baptist home and was baptized at age 22, in December 1760.
Richard Furman was brought up in a non-Christian home and was baptized at age 17, in 1772.
John Dagg was baptized in Middleburg, Virginia at age 18 in the spring of 1812.
J. Newton Brown was baptized in Hudson, New York at age 14 in 1817.
J. M. Pendleton was baptized near Pembroke, Kentucky, at age 18 in 1829.
P. H. Mell was brought up in a strong Christian home and was baptized at age 18, in 1832 (according to his biography by his son).
J. R. Graves was brought up in a strong Christian home and was baptized at age 15 in 1835 (according to Hailey's biography).
Sylvanus Dryden Phelps (author of the hymn "Something for Thee") was brought up in a Christian home and was baptized at age 22, in 1838 (according to William Cathcart's *Baptist Encyclopedia*). [Pastored 1st Baptist, New Haven, CT 1846–1874]
John A. Broadus was brought up in a strong Christian home and was baptized at age 16 in 1843 (according to A. T. Robertson, *Life and Letters of John Albert Broadus*).
Charles Fenton James was baptized in 1864 at age 20 in the trenches near Petersburg, VA, while he was a Confederate soldier. (George B. Taylor, *Virginia Baptist Ministers*, 38)
C. H. Spurgeon baptized his two sons when they were 18. (Arnold Dallimore, *Spurgeon: A New Biography* [Carlisle, PA: Banner of Truth, 1985], 141).
John R. Sampey was brought up in a Christian home and was baptized at age 13 in 1877 (according to his *Memoirs*, 7). [worked on his dad's farm]
E. Y. Mullins was brought up in the home of a Baptist minister in Texas and was baptized at age 20 in 1880. Bear in mind that adult responsibilities to contribute to household income came earlier in the eighteenth and nineteenth centuries. So, for example, the above all had jobs by the time they were baptized.
H. Wheeler Robinson was brought up by a Christian mother in Northampton, England and was baptized at age 16 in 1888.
Frank Stagg was baptized at 11 in 1922 in southwest Louisiana.
Dale Moody was baptized at 12 in 1927 in Grapevine, Texas.

1977 and 1997 there was a 250 percent increase in the number of baptisms in Southern Baptist churches of children under the age of six.[25] Why is this happening? Many reasons have been suggested. In 1996, John Withers submitted a doctoral dissertation at The Southern Baptist Theological Seminary in which he noted this trend and suggested that it occurred in the twentieth century largely due to social pressures on the pastor.[26]

Whatever the reason for the change in practice, Christians today should be careful about participating in a well-intended but ill-fated baptism that seems to have tragically resulted in the confirmation of millions of people in conversions that have evidently proved to be false. So-called Christians are deceived, churches are diminished in their power, and the witness of the gospel is confused and weakened.

In the 1840s, J. L. Reynolds (1812–1877) published some stern words on the danger of growing nominalism in churches:

> The recognition of unconverted persons, as members of a Christian Church, is an evil of no ordinary magnitude. It throws down the wall of partition which Christ himself has erected and obliterates the distinction between the Church and the world. A society composed of believers, and sustained and extended by spiritual instrumentalities, has the promise of the Redeemer pledged for its perpetuation. Such a community is indestructible. . . . It becomes the disciples of the Saviour to guard well the door of admission into their fraternity. Upon their fidelity, in this respect, depend its efficiency, prosperity, and safety. An accession of nominal Christians may enlarge its numbers, but cannot augment its real strength. A Church that welcomes to the privileges of Christ's house, the unconverted, under the specious pretext of increasing the number of his followers, in reality betrays the citadel to his foes. They may glory in the multitudes that flock to their expanded gates, and exult in their brightening prospects; but the joy and the triumph will be alike transient. They have mistaken a device of the enemy for the work of God. They hailed, as they thought, an angel of light; they have received Satan. I admire and love the many sincere and zealous Christians that are found in such Churches; but I fear that this Trojan horse will finally prove their ruin.[27]

[25] Hemphill, "The Practice of Infantile Baptism," 77.

[26] Withers, "Social Forces Affecting the Age at Which Children are Baptized in Southern Baptist Churches."

[27] J. L. Reynolds, *Church Polity or the Kingdom of Christ (1849)*, in *Polity*, ed. M. E. Dever (Washington, DC: Center for Church Reform, 2001), 327.

While Reynolds' concerns were elicited by advocates of infant baptism, the falling of the average age of baptism has seemed to have some similar, clearly negative consequences, including the increase of "second baptisms," nominalism, and the declension of adult conversions in Baptist churches.[28]

[28] Our own congregation in Washington teaches the following on the baptism of children:

"We, the elders of the Capitol Hill Baptist Church, after prayerful searching of the Scriptures and discussion conclude that, while Scripture is quite clear that believers only are to be baptized, the age at which a believer is to be baptized is not directly addressed in Scripture. We do not understand the simple imperative command to be baptized to settle the issue, nor do we understand the imperative to be baptized to forbid raising questions about the appropriateness of a baptismal candidate's maturity. We do understand that the consideration of an appropriate age for a believer to be baptized is a matter not of simple obedience on an issue clearly settled by Scripture, but rather is a matter of Christian wisdom and prudence on an issue not directly addressed by Scripture. Though the baptisms in the New Testament seem largely to have occurred soon after the initial conversion, all of the individuals we can read of are both adults and coming from a non-Christian context. Both of these factors would tend to lend credibility to a conversion. The credibility of the conversion is the prime consideration, with the effect upon the individual candidate and the church community being legitimate secondary concerns.

"We believe that the normal age of baptism should be when the credibility of one's conversion becomes naturally evident to the church community. This would normally be when the child has matured, and is beginning to live more self-consciously as an individual, making their own choices, having left the God-given, intended child-like dependence on their parents for the God-given, intended mature wisdom which marks one who has felt the tug of the world, the flesh and the devil, but has decided, despite these allurements, to follow Christ. While it is difficult to set a certain number of years which are required for baptism, it is appropriate to consider the candidate's maturity. The kind of maturity that we feel it is wise to expect is the maturity which would allow that son or daughter to deal directly with the church as a whole, and not, fundamentally, to be under their parents' authority. As they assume adult responsibilities (sometime in late high school with driving, employment, non-Christian friends, voting, legality of marriage), then part of this, we would think, would be to declare publicly their allegiance to Christ by baptism.

"With the consent and encouragement of Christian parents who are members, we will carefully consider requests for baptism before a child has left the home, but would urge the parents to caution at this point. Of course children can be converted. We pray that none of our children ever know any lengthy period of conscious rebellion against God. The question raised by baptism is the ability of others to be fairly confident of that conversion. The malleable nature of children (which changeableness God especially intends for the time when they are living as dependents in the home, being trained in all the basics of life and faith) is a gift from God and is to be used to bring them to maturity. It should also give us caution in assuming the permanence of desires, dreams, affections and decisions of children. Nevertheless, should the young person desire to pursue baptism and membership in the normal course set out by the church, we will examine them on a case-by-case basis, with the involvement of the parents.

"In the event of young persons from non-Christian families coming to the church for an extended period of time, professing faith and giving evidence of the reality thereof, requests for baptism and membership would be considered without the involvement of the parents. While all the previous comments on the nature of immaturity still pertain, the fact that such a young

Parents should not presume to be certain of their children's faith but should pray for them and teach them. There are good reasons to delay the baptism of children. It tests the reality of their profession and reduces nominalism and false conversions. It emphasizes the importance of baptism and clarifies that it is faith, not baptism, that saves. It allows time for the child to be better taught, to evidence humility while waiting, to mature, and to better remember, cherish and use the experience of his baptism. True conversion manifests itself over time. Children are childlike and trusting for a reason. To ask a pastor to try to separate out the tightly knit strands of affection for parents and for God, and to discern which is primary in a child

person would be doing so despite indifference, or even opposition from their parents would or could be evidence for the reality of their conversion.

"Nothing in this statement should be construed as casting doubt about the legitimacy of the baptism of any among us, regardless of how young they were when they were baptized. Because they have continued in the faith into their adult years we assume the legitimacy of their initial profession made at baptism. The question we are concerned with here is looking forward, not backward. To put it another way, we are raising the question about how many people have been baptized at this church in the past as younger people and children who went on to give no evidence of ever having been savingly converted, and what damage was done to them, and to the witness of the gospel through the church's premature baptism of them. It is our judgment that while there is some danger of discouragement on the part of those children who do give some good evidence of being converted and yet are not baptized and welcomed into communicant membership in the church, through good teaching in the home, and through the loving inclusion of the families in the church as we currently do, that danger is small. There is, however, we believe, a greater danger of deception on the part of many who could be wrongly baptized at an age in which people are more liable to make decisions which are sincere, but ill-founded and too often short-lived.

"Two other notes in conclusion. First, we realize that this issue is an issue of great emotion for some, and we in no way are trying to lead anyone to disobey their conscience on this matter; we simply are trying to inform and educate our consciences from the Scriptural necessity of a credible profession of faith for baptism. Second, while it is not generally known among American evangelicals today, the practice of baptizing pre-teenage children is of recent development (largely early 20th century) and of limited geography (largely limited to the United States, and places where American evangelicals have exercised great influence). Baptists in the past were known for waiting to baptize until the believers were adults. Baptistic Christians around the world are still much more cautious than modern American Christians, often waiting in Europe, Africa and Asia to baptize until children are grown and are in their 20's."

For a recent, careful statement opposing this position among Baptists, see Ted Christman, *Forbid Them Not* (n.p.; n.d.). Christman, pastor of Heritage Baptist Church in Owensboro, Kentucky, self-published this booklet in 2004. A pastoral treatment in between these two positions is found in D. Gundersen, *Your Child's Profession of Faith* (Amityville, NY: Calvary Press, 1994). I have preached a sermon on "At What Age Should Believers be Baptized?" It can be found at www.capitolhillbaptist.org.

is to ask more than may be best for the child. Time allows the child's faith to mature and evidence itself consistently.

Proponents of both sides of the debate about baptizing children intend to obey Scripture and to see churches flourish. They read the same Scriptures and teach—largely, if not entirely—the same on baptism's significance and role. Neither side inflates its value; neither side ignores it. In surveying Christians and congregations, perhaps one of the most telling differences between the two sides is whether they think the greater danger is the unwitting discouragement of young believers or aiding the deception of false believers. Those who tend to put greater weight on not discouraging young believers tend to be in favor of baptizing at younger ages, while those who are more concerned about not helping the unconverted deceive themselves tend to be in favor of more maturity being required for baptism.

Proponents of both sides of this Baptist debate agree with evangelical paedobaptist friends in affirming the possibility of the salvation of people at the earliest ages of responsible action and repentant faith. Quite apart from deciding the question of an "age of accountability," Baptist Christians can desire and work for the spiritual health of the children of their congregation who are unbaptized but who attend regularly. Children being included in prayer, helping their parents in church service, having a youth Bible study or other age-specific groups can all be encouraged with no inconsistency. A refusal to baptize is not intended as a statement asserting that the child is not regenerate but simply as a reluctance publicly to affirm that which has not yet been maturely evidenced. Parents can hold a baptistic position and still love and spiritually care for their children. The children of believing parents do not need baptism to be taught the Ten Commandments, the Lord's Prayer, and the gospel in all its fullness.[29]

---

[29] In our congregation in Washington, D.C., we print an updated membership directory every week or two. This directory has many uses, one of which is as a prayer guide for the members. We have a separate section in it in which we list all the children of the church. We encourage members to use this for a reminder to pray as regularly for these children as for the adult members of the church.

Teaching Resources on Baptism

One duty that is paramount for us as Christians, and particularly as parents and leaders, is to teach. In Deut 6:6–7 the Lord commanded the Israelites, "These commandments that I give you today are to be upon your hearts. Impress them on your children. Talk about them when you sit at home and when you walk along the road, when you lie down and when you get up." How are we to teach? By example and by word in family conversations and devotionals. By regular attendance at church. By ensuring that there is careful teaching of the Bible there. By providing good literature in the church to educate and inform church members.

Churches should educate their members about the meaning and significance of the ordinances, and there are many resources for this task. Much good literature on baptism is produced by local congregations to reflect their own practices. Examples of this can be found on many Web sites. Good books should be made available to church members. Some good books to use in this task are Larry Dyer, *Baptism: The Believer's First Obedience* (Kregel, 2000), and Brian Russell, *Baptism: Sign and Seal of the Covenant of Grace* (Grace Publications, UK, 2001). On thinking through matters about children and baptism, see Dennis Gundersen's *Your Child's Profession of Faith* (Calvary Press, 1994). Other good books for pastors and church leaders to have available for reading and for purchase, particularly on the debate about infant baptism (in addition to this one), are Paul Jewett's classic work, *Infant Baptism and the Covenant of Grace* (Eerdmans, 1978) and Fred Malone's excellent book, *The Baptism of Disciples Alone: A Covenantal Argument for Credobaptism Versus Paedobaptism* (Founders' Press, 2003). More general but related books are Don Whitney's *Spiritual Disciplines within the Church* (Moody Press, 1996), and finally my *Nine Marks of a Healthy Church* (Crossway, 2004).

Summary

As a public act, baptism can be of great significance. Muslims, Hindus, and Buddhists who have come to Christian faith have often been unmolested by family and friends as long as they hold their faith privately and do not bring shame on the family. But when their decision is made public in baptism, great suffering sometimes has followed. In most of colonial New England, even among Christians, baptistic conclusions were illegal. The first president of Harvard College, Henry Dunster (1609–1659), after heroically and self-sacrificially establishing and leading the college for its first thirteen years, came to baptistic conclusions. Because of this, Dunster was made to resign his position, was publicly admonished, and was forced to move away from the college. It may be that we are once again coming into a time of more open antagonism to biblical faith publicly displayed. If so, we may join our brothers and sisters around the world and in our own history in realizing the importance of our conclusions about following Christ.

And yet in all this baptism is not the point. The great nineteenth-century English Baptist pastor, Andrew Fuller, said that "the sign, when rightly used, leads to the thing signified."[30] That is surely the desire of all true Christians with baptism—that it would lead us to Christ, who for us and for our salvation came, was crucified, buried, and raised again for our justification. This is signified in baptism. This is the point. It is our job to hold up the picture that Christ left us in order to draw our minds to this reality. We do this in obedience to his personal command and so bring him the honor that is his due.

---

[30] Fuller, "Practical Uses of Christian Baptism," *Works,* 3:341.

Author Index

Subject Index

Scripture Index